# Sophisticated Sabotage: The Intellectual Games Used to Subvert Responsible Regulation

## Thomas O. McGarity
## Sidney Shapiro
## and
## David Bollier

D1210939

published by the
ENVIRONMENTAL LAW INSTITUTE
Washington, D.C.

# Table of Contents

# About the Authors

**Thomas O. McGarity** holds the W. James Kronzer Chair in Trial and Appellate Advocacy at the University of Texas, Austin. A former Articles Editor of the *Texas Law Review*, Professor McGarity is a leading scholar in the fields of both administrative law and environmental law. He also teaches torts. He has written three influential books: WORKERS AT RISK (Praeger 1993) (coauthor), THE LAW OF ENVIRONMENTAL PROTECTION (West 2d ed. 1991) (coauthor), and REINVENTING RATIONALITY: THE ROLE OF REGULATORY ANALYSIS IN THE FEDERAL BUREAUCRACY (Cambridge 1991). His recent articles include *The Expanded Debate Over the Future of the Regulatory State* (University of Chicago Law Review 1996). He is currently serving (with Peter Strauss of Columbia University) as Co-Reporter for Rulemaking on the American Bar Association's restatement project of the Administrative Procedure Act and related statutes.

**Sidney Shapiro** holds a University Distinguished Chair in Law at Wake Forest University. Professor Shapiro is nationally recognized for his work in administrative law and regulatory law and policy. He is the author of leading law school texts in both fields and has written numerous articles concerning both subjects. His most recent book is RISK REGULATION AT RISK: RESTORING A PRAGMATIC APPROACH (Stanford Press) (coauthored). He has served as a consultant to the Occupational Safety and Health Administration, the Administrative Conference of the United States, and the Office of Technology Assessment, U.S. Congress, and has testified before Congress on regulatory and administrative law issues. He has served as the Secretary of the Administrative Law Section of the American Bar Association and as the Chair of the Administrative Law Section of the American Association of Law Schools.

**David Bollier** is an independent strategist, journalist, and consultant with a varied public interest portfolio. He has been an advisor to television writer/producer Norman Lear since 1984, and he is a Senior Fellow at the Norman Lear Center at the USC Annenberg Center for Communication, where he heads the Creativity, Commerce, and Culture project. Bollier is also active with Public Knowledge, a public interest advocacy organization that represents the public's stake in copyright, digital technology, and Internet issues. He co-founded Public Knowledge with Gigi Sohn, its President, and the Center for the Public Domain. Much of Bollier's recent work has been focused on developing a new analysis and language for reclaiming "the American commons," a critique set forth in his book SILENT THEFT: THE PRIVATE PLUNDER OF OUR COMMON WEALTH (Routledge) and in a number of essays and reports. He is the author of six books, and lives in Amherst, Massachusetts.

# Foreword

O ver the past three decades, our nation has enacted a system of federal laws and regulations to protect public health, the environment, consumers, and worker safety. These laws were developed despite significant resistance from industrial polluters and other regulated entities. Although the foundation of our system of environment, health, and safety laws is now firmly established, the battle over the extent, specifics, and implementation of federal regulation has not abated.

As a member of Congress since 1974, my career has spanned much of this struggle. I have fought to uphold the rights of individuals to clean air, clean water, health care, safe workplaces, safe products, and public lands and resources. The fundamental issues have remained unchanged over the years, but the framing and language of the debate has shifted.

Today, these fights often involve claims that we should make a decision about regulation using specific analytical tools, such as "sound science," "risk assessment," and "cost-benefit analysis." These claims are appealing in the abstract. Who could argue against relying on valid scientific data? Why wouldn't we want to look at both the costs and benefits of a possible regulation?

In my experience, however, these analytical tools are often abused and they have not, in fact, led us to the best regulatory outcomes. One problem is that they are inconsistently applied. The proponents of cost-benefit analysis are vociferous when they think the analysis will provide a reason for not regulating, but they become suddenly silent whenever it is demonstrated that the benefits of regulating would outweigh the costs. Legislation to protect kids from tobacco or to protect the public from exposure to secondhand smoke would have enormous health benefits and very low costs, yet the advocates of cost-benefit analysis do not endorse these commonsense measures.

There are many other problems. Opponents of health and environmental regulations often call for application of these analytical tools to slow down the regulatory process. Their goal is delay, not informed decisionmaking. Advocates for "sound science" often oppose regulation in the absence of scientific certainty. Yet such certainty is rarely achievable until after the damage is already done. These tools are also subject to manipulation. As detailed in this book, the supposedly hard numbers produced by a risk assessment or cost-benefit analysis are actually highly dependent on numerous underlying assumptions and inputs. This provides professional analysts tremendous discretion to skew the outcomes, while making it difficult for the public to have a meaningful voice in the debate.

Moreover, cost-benefit analyses are consistently wrong. In virtually every regulatory fight I have been in, the opponents of regulation have vastly overstated the costs and minimized the benefits. When Congress was debating the Clean Air Act of 1990, industry advocates testified that if Congress phased out ozone-depleting chlorofluorocarbons (CFCs) it would cause severe economic and social disruption, including shutdowns of supermarket refrigerators and air conditioners in offices and hospitals. Six years later, production of CFCs ended and our hospitals and supermarkets were still operating normally.

*Sophisticated Sabotage* compellingly details these and other flaws in how these analytical methods are used. But this book also makes a more fundamental argument about the nature of the methods themselves and their implications for public interest regulation. The authors point out that the development and use of analytical approaches such as risk assessment and cost-benefit analysis have been heavily funded and promoted by opponents of government regulation. The result, they argue, is a set of analytical tools that are not neutral, and that are not sufficiently accurate to be used as the determining factors in a decision on regulation. By surveying a broad body of scholarly work on these issues, the authors show that the increasingly heavy reliance on these analytical tools is not universally accepted, and is, in fact, strongly criticized by many observers.

A key message of *Sophisticated Sabotage* is that the analytical tools we use and our underlying assumptions affect the outcome of government regulatory decisions. Accordingly, the authors argue, it is critical to understand the implications of how we choose to frame the debate over government regulation.

A simple example is how difficult or impossible it is to express some values in dollar terms. These are generally the values supporting regulation, such as protecting biodiversity or avoiding pain and suffering. If quantified cost-benefit analysis is the only method used to make a decision about regulation, some things that people care about are simply not taken into account.

Regulatory decisions also depend on the starting assumptions. Americans commonly assume that if a person (or entity) harms someone else, that person is responsible for minimizing the harm or compensating the person harmed. As *Sophisticated Sabotage* points out, however, we are increasingly using a different set of assumptions when debating regulation. Cost-benefit analysis assumes that the goal of government is to identify an efficient level of harm, such as an efficient level of health damage from air pollution. If it would cost an entity more to reduce the harm than such harm reduction is "worth," as calculated by the analysts, cost-benefit proponents would allow the harm to continue without compensation. Both approaches frame the issues and allow us to make choices, but the regulations we adopt may not be the same.

I believe that government regulation should express society's values and meet the public's goals. To achieve this, debates over regulations to protect public health and the environment must be conducted honestly and transparently. *Sophisticated Sabotage* will make an enormous contribution to these debates.

—Representative Henry A. Waxman
June 14, 2004

# Preface

The idea for this book was born during a gathering of scholars and public interest activists assembled by Joan Claybrook of Public Citizen in January 2001. Although the public interest community had been largely successful in preventing the radical regulatory reformers of the "Gingrich Revolution" from dismantling the existing structure of federal health, safety, and environmental protections, there were only a few substantive gains during the second half of the Clinton Administration. With President George W. Bush in office, proponents of strong governmental protections against corporate malfeasance now faced the grim prospect of at least four years without a friend (or at least a person who recognized the value of federal regulation) in the White House.

Reflecting on this situation, the activists were concerned that, having won many of the regulatory reform battles of the late 1990s, they were in danger of losing the larger war. They understood that the public interest movement had virtually conceded to the other side an important aspect of the battle to protect people and the environment—the process of crafting the intellectual tools for distinguishing good regulation from bad regulation. Housed in industry-created and -supported think tanks, like the American Enterprise Institute and the Heritage Foundation, and in industry-financed academic centers, like the Mercatus Center and the Weidenbaum Center for the Study of American Business, unsympathetic observers of the regulatory process were pouring out mountains of simplistic, but easily accessible analyses of "regulatory failures," and those books, pamphlets, and articles were playing a powerful role in the regulatory reform battles.

The meeting was called to explore what could be done to correct what appeared to be a dearth of scholarly effort to contest these studies and reports. The problem, however, was different. There was an extensive literature challenging antiregulatory claims written by some of the nation's leading scholars. People were largely unaware of this literature, however, because, unlike the business community, the public interest movement did not have millions of dollars to spend to publicize and popularize their arguments. What was lacking was a vehicle to make this literature better known and more accessible.

Two of the academics attending that meeting, Sid Shapiro and Tom McGarity, promised on the spot to assemble an anthology of scholarly work on three topics that had been much debated during the regulatory reform battles of the 104th Congress—risk assessment, cost-effectiveness analysis, and cost-benefit-based regulatory decisionmaking. This book is the result of that ambitious promise. With the generous support of the Deer Creek Foundation, which also supported the original gathering, Shapiro and McGarity pressed Randy Rabinowitz and Ruth Ruttenberg into service to help in locating, selecting, and (in Ruttenberg's case) drafting articles for inclusion in the anthology.

Having assembled and excerpted a collection of strong assessments and critiques of these darlings of regulatory reformers' toolbox, they realized that much of the material still remained inaccessible to people who had not actively participated in the regulatory reform debates. Again with the support of the Deer Creek Foundation, Shapiro and McGarity drafted David Bollier to mold the individual articles into coherent chapters and to weave the chapters into a coherent book.

The authors are grateful to Frank Clemente, the Director of Public Citizen's Congress Watch, for his sound advice and guidance throughout the project. And, of course, we are grateful to the authors and publishers of the many articles excerpted in the following pages for their permission to bring their ideas to the attention of the readers of this book.

We anticipate that this book will be the first of many to be produced by a new organization of scholars that also grew out of the January 2001 meeting—the Center for Progressive Regulation (CPR). Founded in May 2002, CPR is a §501(c)(3) nonprofit research and educational organization of university-affiliated academics with expertise in the legal, economic, and scientific issues related to regulation of health, safety, and the environment. CPR supports regulatory action designed to protect the life and health of human beings and to preserve our environment.

# Introduction

In the 1960s and early 1970s, when a series of environmental, workplace, and consumer disasters came to public attention, there was little question that Congress and the American people regarded them as outrageous tragedies. The public was shocked to learn that Lake Erie and several other bodies of water were considered ecologically "dead." In workplaces, dangerous chemicals were making thousands of people sterile. Chronic noise was rendering workers deaf. Poorly designed factory equipment was severing fingers and limbs. General Motors was castigated by U.S. senators for spending only $1 million of its $1.7 billion in 1964 profits for external automobile accident research—even as millions of Americans were being injured and killed by dangerous automotive designs and manufacturing defects.

Since the 1970s, regulation has succeeded in mitigating many of the previous types of hazards. Aggregate emissions of six principal pollutants regulated under the Clean Air Act (CAA) have been cut by 48% even as economic activity has increased 164%.[1] Between 1982 and 2002, there was a 93% reduction in lead emissions, which can cause brain damage and mental retardation in children.[2] The level of ozone-depleting chemicals in the lower atmosphere has declined by between 14 and 22% over the last 20 years,[3] a trend that will help protect humans and plant life from harmful radiation. Scientific evidence also indicates that the rate of ozone depletion in the upper atmosphere is slowing.[4]

Regulation under the Clean Water Act prevents the release of 700 billion pounds of water pollutants each year, including toxic pollutants known to cause or to contribute to cancer, liver and kidney damage, and problems in mental and motor development in children.[5] In 2001, deaths from motor vehicle crashes hit a new historical low of 1.52 persons killed per 100 million vehicle miles traveled.[6] In America's workplaces, too, fewer people were injured or killed on the job.[7]

This remarkable progress does not mean that the challenge of protecting people and the environment from preventable harms is nearly finished. The U.S. Environmental Protection Agency (EPA) estimates that 146 million people live in areas that are not in compliance with health-based CAA standards and are therefore exposed to harmful levels of air pollution.[8] Thousands of power plants and large industrial facilities still emit high levels of sulfur dioxides, which can cause permanent lung damage, and high levels of mercury, which can cause brain and kidney damage and birth defects.[9] In New Jersey alone, air pollution from trucks and automobiles is related each year to the premature deaths of 2,300 to 4,500 residents, 7,800 to 15,000 respiratory and heart-related hospital admissions, 170,000 asthma attacks in kids and 600,000 missed school days because of pollution-related illnesses.[10] The increasing effects of global warming threaten cataclysmic climate changes for millions of persons.[11] Although 31 countries have banned asbestos on the ground that there is no safe

1

level of exposure, the United States imports about 30 million pounds of asbestos each year.[12] One result is that mechanics who install replacement brakes are routinely exposed to asbestos in their jobs and have received no protection from the Occupational Safety and Health Administration (OSHA).[13] EPA estimates that 40% of our streams, 45% of our lakes, and one-half of our estuaries are not clean enough or healthy enough to support fishing, swimming, water supply, and protection of fish and wildlife.[14] The National Highway Traffic Safety Administration (NHTSA) reports that over 42,000 people died in vehicle traffic accidents in 2001 and another 3 million were injured.[15] The U.S. Department of Labor reports that nearly 6,000 workers lost their lives in workplace accidents in 2001,[16] and there were 5.2 million work-related injuries and illnesses.[17]

Despite these and many other significant risks, the Bush Administration is actively involved in dozens of initiatives to reduce existing protection of people and the environment. It has proposed to exempt indefinitely power plants and other large facilities that currently do not have to comply with the CAA,[18] a move that will cause an estimated 20,000 premature deaths, 400,000 asthma attacks, and 12, 000 cases of chronic bronchitis.[19] President George W. Bush has repudiated the 1997 Kyoto Protocol, an agreement between the United States and other industrialized nations to address the causes of global warming, and the Administration has not yet proposed any plan for addressing this issue.[20] The NHTSA rejected a regulation developed under the Clinton Administration that would have required car manufacturers to install monitors that would notify drivers if their tires were dangerously low in favor of a system that would, by the agency's own data, prevent only about one-half as many deaths and injuries.[21] EPA adopted a watered-down version of a regulation proposed in the Clinton Administration to reduce the extent to which our streams and rivers are polluted by the 220 billion gallons of liquefied manure produced each year by large factory farms.[22] The U.S. Department of Energy withdrew efficiency standards established by the Clinton Administration for air conditioners and heat pumps with the intention of proposing weaker regulations.[23] After Congress rejected a Clinton Administration proposal to regulate ergonomic injuries among workers even though such injuries result in 70 million physician office visits each year and result in between $45 and $54 million dollars annually in compensation costs, lost wages, and lost productivity,[24] OSHA announced that it will rely on the voluntary compliance by employers.[25]

Most of the actions cited here were taken by agencies at the behest of the Office of Management and Budget (OMB), the executive branch overseer of the regulatory process. OMB has also pressured EPA to exempt firms that emit hazardous air pollutants from compliance with the CAA[26]; weaken rules that would prevent runoff from construction sites that contaminates our water supplies; weaken water pollution rules for power plants that would protect trillions of fish; and reduce the pollution caused by snowmobile emissions.[27]

In addition to weakening existing regulatory standards, the Bush Administration lags far behind previous administrations in proposing and issuing new regulatory protections. The government keeps track of the number of "significant regulations"—generally the most important regulations adopted by the government. In President William J. Clinton's first two years, EPA finalized 23 new rules; in the first years of the first President Bush's Administration, EPA finalized 14 new rules. In the current President Bush's first two years, EPA completed only two significant regulations.[28] The Department of Health and Human Services did not finish a single significant regulation in the current Bush Administration's first two years. The U.S. Department of the Interior produced only two significant regulations. OSHA managed to get out one regulation, but it involved deregulation.[29]

The government has also been delinquent in enforcing the regulations that are currently on the books. Under the Bush Administration, EPA has devoted less staff to inspection and enforcement than at any time since the Agency was established.[30] Not surprisingly, EPA is catching and punishing fewer polluters than the two previous administrations.[31] Since January 2001, the average number of violation notices issued each month by EPA has dropped 58% over the average number issued by the Clinton Administration.[32]

Despite these trends, the president's 2003 budget sought to eliminate the positions of over 200 enforcement personnel.[33] OSHA typically inspects fewer than 1% of all workplaces annually, but the Bush Administration has conducted even fewer inspections than the Clinton Administration.[34] The president's 2003 budget proposed to cut OSHA by $9 million, thereby eliminating 64 full-time enforcement positions.[35]

Most of these actions have gone unnoticed by the news media and the general public. While these egregious, preventable harms are no less threatening than the ones that first sparked public outrage and government reform in the 1970s, public perception has shifted dramatically. We now *see* these harms in different terms.

Over the past generation, some regulated entities have succeeded in inventing and popularizing a new, revisionist language about regulation. This language is ostensibly about improving the quality of regulatory decisionmaking. In truth, its chief goal is to discredit and stymie federal regulation while defending the economic interests and power of corporate investors and management. The language deliberately shifts the political terms of debate away from the morally charged terrain of human tragedy and corporate blame, substituting in its stead an impersonal, "objective" lexicon of economic and statistical analysis.

Novelist Milan Kundera once warned that "the struggle of man against power is the struggle of memory against forgetting." Which facts and interpretations shall we choose to remember—and which shall we forget, substituting in their place a more congenial, sanitized story? This is the unstated, but absolutely critical question of health, safety, and environmental regulation today. Shall we remember the terrible diseases, injuries, and fatalities that unsupervised entities tend to inflict on workers, consumers, the public, and nature? Or shall we instead see such tragedies through the lens of economic abstractions and learn to forget some harsh truths?

The new lexicon is all about forgetting. It essentially says that the hazards facing consumers, workers, and the environment are not really so bad. Government regulation long ago solved the important health, safety, and environmental problems. The real problem now is government regulation itself. Regulation, we are told, poses a fundamental threat to our "freedom to choose." It represents a left-wing attack on the "free market" by a "new class" of journalists, academics, and public interest advocates based on "junk science."

Regulation was originally the story of *expanding* people's freedoms, of course. By helping to prevent life-threatening illnesses and hazards, Americans could enjoy freedom from cancer-causing consumer products, defective tires, unsafe factory equipment, pesticide-tainted drinking water, among many other unnecessary hazards.

In certain hands of the regulated entities and the stable of academics they fund, however, the story of regulation has been twisted into a story about a relentless and irrational economic attack on efficiency. Regulation is portrayed as a subversive, prosperity-destroying crusade against the free market and as a paternalistic intrusion on our personal freedoms.

In this new discourse, questions of responsibility for harm strangely disappear. The demonstrated concerns of the public are dismissed as misguided. The legislative policies endorsed by Congress fade into the background. According to the new language, such concerns are subjective, anecdotal, and fuzzy-minded. Who can measure a *social value?* Surely something as consequential as regulation, goes the new story, should not be based on the pathetically misinformed opinions of the American people or the self-serving political agendas of bureaucrats. If it is to be responsible, regulation ought to be wholly "rational" and "objective." It ought to be based on hard statistics and economic analyses. This means that recognized experts in risk assessment and cost-benefit analysis—not mere citizens, legislators, or bureaucrats—should determine whether and how to regulate.

The shift in the predominant language used for understanding regulation represents a remarkable political coup. It represents the triumph of a bland, numbers-driven vocabulary that is well-suited for concealing the rogue effects of unfettered markets.

The rise of this framework is no accident, of course. It is a case of sophisticated sabotage. Over the past generation, dozens of major corporations and right-wing foundations have spent millions of dollars to develop a respectable oeuvre of antiregulatory research. The engine of this "sponsored scholarship" is a well-funded apparatus of Washington think tanks, university centers, endowed professorships, and research projects. Prominent Washington players include the Heritage Foundation, the American Enterprise Institute, the Cato Institute, and the Competitive Enterprise Institute, but there are university centers such as the Harvard Center for Risk Analysis and the Center for the Study of American Business at Washington University in St. Louis.

While the literature turned out by the think tanks and centers purports to be disinterested, the conclusions are seldom disappointing to its financial backers: automakers, steel companies, some pharmaceutical and chemical companies, and activist-minded conservative foundations.[36] Notwithstanding its academic trappings, the literature produced by these various entities has little to do with improving health, safety, and environmental protections for Americans.

The point of *Sophisticated Sabotage* is to reveal the profound intellectual deficiencies of this literature. It is to expose and explain the disingenuous assumptions, suspicious numbers and fallacious inferences of quantitative risk assessment, cost-benefit analysis, and other analytic tools. This book seeks to showcase the many problematic intellectual concepts that some regulated entities and their intellectual allies have invented and refined. In order to argue against regulation, many analysts, for example, rely on such dubious techniques as "revealed preferences" (What would you *pay* to be safe from a given hazard?) and "quality-adjusted life-years" saved, or QALY (What dollar sum shall we put on an improved quality of life at any given stage of that life?).

While some of these tools, properly employed, have an appropriate place in regulation, most of them have serious conceptual flaws or rely upon very slippery empirical data. Analytic models that may be theoretically sound turn out to be impossible to implement properly. No matter. Cynical politicians and recalcitrant industries find it immensely valuable to use the questionable numbers prepared by shoddy analytic models to rally political opposition to regulation.

Sophisticated sabotage is the only appropriate term for these complicated academic methodologies because at bottom, they are intellectual games supported by opponents of government regulation to stymie responsible regulation. These foundations and businesses seek to rewrite the actual history of the laissez-faire market and smother its output of human tragedy with bland, benign abstractions. The new language is an attempt to redefine the meaning of regulation so that the chief concern is no longer the moral grievances and physical harm of victims, but the economic priorities of industry. As Jay Michaelson writes in one excerpt below, the economistic framework reverses the burden of proof; it "coerces individuals to give up their right to live because another private actor wishes to make a profit."

The end-goal of sophisticated sabotage is to make the new language for discussing regulation so utterly pervasive, uncontestable, and "normal" that its terms become the primary reference points of debate. Alternative ways of coming to regulatory judgments become nearly impossible to imagine. Making "sound science" and laissez-faire economics the normative discourse for regulation has the intended effect of inducing a sort of social amnesia. Ensnared in economic categories, we forget about the injustices and tragedies that animated regulation in the first place. What matters now, in the regulatory Newspeak, is how *industry* is being hurt.

### Monkey-Wrenching the Regulatory Process

The anatomy of forgetting is complex. It is not easy to change the "attention frame" for understanding regulation. Serious hazards and catastrophes cannot simply be swept under the rug. The presence of mad cows, dead bodies, and diseased people must somehow be explained. Involvement in such tragedies must be justified—or it will be indicted.

Over the past generation, certain regulated industries and right-wing foundations have developed some shrewd and highly effective strategies: don the guise of "sound science" and insist that hard numbers be the basis for any new regulation. Speak as if the real issue in regulatory disputes is economics, not the public health. Depict advocates of regulation as irrational sensationalists who traffic in "junk science." Denigrate the knowledge and participation of the public, and celebrate the expertise of economists and credentialed academics.

Responsible regulation necessarily requires a lot of technical expertise and analysis. This provides a crucial opening for the sophisticated saboteur intent on intellectual mischief. For example, by generating a large amount of quantitative data and analysis—material that is impenetrable to the layperson and too boring for the mainstream press to investigate—the sophisticated saboteur can "monkey-wrench" the regulatory process by requiring gratuitous mandatory studies. The predictable result: new procedures, research, and court challenges that delay government action for years, saving the relevant industry millions of dollars.

The saboteur has a larger ambition, however: to commandeer regulatory debate and change the normative metrics for decisionmaking. This is especially strategic. Rather than having to fight one regulatory proposal after another, opponents can secure a more enduring polemical advantage (and favorable political outcomes) by changing the accepted categories for carrying on regulatory discussion. That is exactly what has happened over the past generation.

*Sophisticated Sabotage* probes the mendacious mindset of this fairly obscure but highly influential antiregulatory literature. It seeks to identify and deconstruct the many flawed analytic models that have been developed and regulatory agencies used. It shows how these models privilege the economic freedoms of industry while de-legitimizing regulatory policies based upon moral equity, social policy, and noneconomic criteria. By relentless promotion of this new discourse, the statutory intent of Congress has been marginalized and new, business-friendly decisionmaking norms have been installed in its place. The political objectives of the new norms are ingeniously camouflaged by the trappings of scholarly objectivity. The literature purports to be "beyond politics" and controversy, its interpretations wholly neutral. Political partisans find this immensely useful because they can then wave the "objective scholarship" of their intellectual confederates in front of the press and the public.

What neither the press, the public, nor even many members of Congress may realize is that there is, in fact, a robust scholarly literature that vigorously challenges the sponsored scholarship of regulated industries. This book draws upon the large body of dissenting literature to explain the intellectual deceptions and political motivations of the many antiregulatory sub-disciplines. While the complexities of cost-benefit analysis, quantitative risk assessment, and other analytic tools can be technical and arcane, they can be decisive in determining regulatory outcomes. It is therefore important to understand precisely how these tools are conceptually flawed or misused in practice. It is important to understand how these intellectual models are not innocent concepts, but serve as political weapons.

## Varieties of Intellectual Error and Deception

Since the 1970s, a veritable menagerie of economistic and quantitative tools has been introduced to the regulatory process. Most serve to delay or derail government action. This book presents a comprehensive survey of these methodologies and evaluation of their usefulness and rigor.

Chapter 1 sketches the origins of the modern environmental, workplace and consumer protection statutes of the late 1960s and 1970s, and it explains how some regulated entities soon began to mobilize a series of fierce regulatory "reform" crusades. At bottom, those entities resented government mandates that forced them to shoulder more of the costs of their "economic externalities"—dangerous products, toxic chemicals, environmental pollution, and so on. They regarded such government "interference" with the "free market" as economically irrational and costly, and they began to agitate for a new layer of regulatory procedures that would cripple swift and effective government action.

Cost-benefit analysis was the first of many new analytic tools introduced to make economic criteria the trump card in the regulatory process. Its embrace by regulators, and especially by OMB, represented a fundamental reorientation of the purpose of regulation. A system meant to address public health risks, environmental threats, and moral inequities was reconceptualized as an economic enterprise that was presumptively harmful to the economy. Instead of sanctioning rapid action to prevent human harm, new procedural barriers were erected to make regulation meet near-impossible standards of quantitative proof.

A companion project of intellectual revisionism—insisting upon "sound science" in the face of regulatory uncertainty—is chronicled in Chapter 2. The goal of "sound science" seems unassailable. Who could object to it? A closer look shows that its proponents in the business community are frequently disingenuous; they have little interest in scientific rigor and complexity, but a great deal of interest in antiregulatory outcomes. How else to explain companies who zealously resist providing health and cost data to regulators while complaining that regulatory decisions are not based on rigorous and complete data? To these regulated industries, sound science really means "our science."

The first problem with "sound science" is the unstated assumption that regulatory agencies are not already conducting rigorous research and analysis. In fact, government agencies generally sponsor and solicit some of the best scientific research available. Leaving aside the question of agency performance, the "sound science" crusade assumes that science *can* determine what levels of protection are "safe." This is simply not true. Scientific knowledge about certain risks—say, the etiology of cancer—is often quite rudimentary and speculative. Furthermore, it is often impossible to amass enough reliable scientific data to make conclusive judgments. Uncertainty is an inescapable part of regulatory policymaking. More fundamentally, science is theoretically unequipped to answer questions of a moral and social nature, such as: "How safe do we want our society to be?" or "Which segments of our citizenry shall be protected from man-made harms?"

## The Quantification Quagmire

The intellectual deceptions of sophisticated saboteurs begin with the uncritical quantification of all costs and benefits, however intangible or elusive. This process is examined in Chapter 3. To perform a cost-benefit analysis—or any other economic analyses—a regulator is required to express all prospective costs and benefits in numbers or dollar terms. By so doing, a rigorous balancing of costs and benefits can be made and sound regulatory choices adopted. That, at least, is the theory.

It sounds simple. But embedded in any quantification and monetization technique—especially as applied to intangibles like the number of cancers caused by exposure to toxic chemicals, the value of a person's life or the value of a species' survival—are profound uncertainties and value judgments. The process of translating moral, social, or ecological values into dollar sums does not mean that value judgments disappear; it simply means that they are misrepresented by numbers and go unacknowledged and undiscussed.

This is precisely the point, say critics. Since the methodologies for cost-benefit analysis (and other models) are highly technical, flexible, and inscrutable, it becomes easy to construct a model that can justify virtually anything. The political or social value judgments that are used in the calculations disappear from view.

EPA, in 2003, estimated that the life of a person over 70 is worth $2.3 million while a younger person's life was worth $3.7 million. The math for these calculations, based on the earning power and expected longevity of Americans, may be impeccable. But why make such differential estimates of the value of a person's life in the first place? Environmentalists argued that the resulting numbers were being used to justify not issuing stronger clean air regulations. After all, the "benefits" of preventing premature death, at $2.3 million per life, simply were not "worth it" when compared to the higher costs that more stringent clean air regulation would impose on industry. The Clinton Administration had once calculated the monetary benefits of the proposed regulations at $77 billion; now, through mathematical legerdemain, the Bush Administration was estimating that the same benefits amounted to a mere $8 billion.[37] Such is the false certitude of "hard numbers."

Once the principle of quantification is accepted, however, the door opens wide to all sorts of mathematical mischief and analytic tricks. The point of these games is to use numbers to convey a false sense of accuracy, which in turn helps paper over enormous uncertainties and justify regulatory inaction.

Chapter 4 examines how this scenario plays out with two widely used methodologies—comparative risk assessment and cost-effectiveness analysis—both of which rely upon "hard numbers" to set regulatory priorities. The rationale for these methodologies is to help regulatory agencies use their limited resources in more efficient, effective ways. In theory, this goal—like "sound science"—seems unassailable.

But how are the calculations actually carried out? And do they take account of the proper factors in assessing risk? In practice, comparative risk assessment and cost-effectiveness analysis stack so many assumptions and rickety data sets on top of each other, like some towering house of cards, that the end results are more useful for ideological purposes than for informed decisionmaking. Fixated on distilling complexity down to numbers, risk comparisons assume that reliable scientific knowledge can be obtained and quantified. Conscientious scientists, by contrast, often prefer to make only provisional guesses hedged with qualifications. Should the carcinogenic risks of a chemical be judged by the appearance of tumors in test animals, alterations in cells, or detectible effects on genetic material? The ultimate risk calculations—and regulatory decisions—often pivot upon such highly debatable judgments.

As Chapter 4 explains, risk assessments not only debase the scientific complexities, they do not even purport to represent inequities that one set of people might suffer (poor people living near toxic waste dumps) at the hands of another party (a chemical company). Risk assessment metrics simply do not recognize social injustices. Nor is the intensity of risk adequately represented. By aggregating the risks facing different populations, for example, risk assessments may declare the risks to two populations identical—even though one risk (a toxic waste site) may devastate entire families and neighborhoods while the "identical" other risk (tainted water used by an entire region) is dispersed among millions of people.

Cost-effectiveness analysis makes analogous slights-of-hand. It attempts to put diverse sorts of risks into a single statistical table so that regulatory agencies can set priorities in more a cost-effective way. If Regulation A is estimated to save one life for $5 million, for example, while Regulation B is estimated to save one life for $1 million, Regulation B is obviously a "better buy" for the agency to focus on. But such "efficiency" calculations falsely assume that if an agency forgoes the "expensive" regulation, the "cheaper" regulation will necessarily be adopted.

The calculation also has the convenient effect of exonerating parties responsible for harming people and the environment. Should a corporation responsible for a nasty hazard be allowed to avoid correcting it, and profit from so doing, simply because there is another hazard out in the world that is theoretically cheaper to ameliorate? This sort of gross injustice is inevitable when economic efficiency becomes the test for whether or not to regulate.

## The Eclipse of Moral Judgments by Economics

The proliferation of economic models that enshrine efficiency as the touchstone for action corrupts the very purpose of health, safety, and environmental regulation. The sophisticated saboteurs have not only insisted that federal regulatory agencies set their priorities by applying economic efficiency criteria (using comparative risk assessments and cost-effectiveness studies), they want federal regulatory policy *in its entirety* to be constrained by efficiency standards. The idea is that regulatory policies should maximize "social welfare"—as measured economically, of course. A regulatory policy is "efficient" if those who gain from it (the "winners") could fully compensate those who lose out from it (the "losers"). The greater the differential, the greater the efficiency.

Thus, if coal miners whose lungs are damaged by coal dust say they would be willing to pay $5 million to have regulatory health protections (their "revealed preference"), but the coal industry could gain $10 million in profits by avoiding such requirements, our society's overall wealth would be increased by $5 million by *not* adopting regulatory protections. This would be "efficient" under the "Kaldor-Hicks" test, named for the two economists who proposed it in 1939.

The morally bankrupt nature of this test becomes clear when one understands that Kaldor-Hicks efficiency doesn't require the winners to actually compensate the losers. The test purports only to measure overall gains in societal wealth, and it is not affected by the distribution of wealth. The actual value of prevention and other social equity concerns are also ignored. Hence under Kaldor-Hicks, a polluter or careless drugmaker is entitled to inflict harm on other persons so long as the costs of reducing that harm are greater than the benefits of reducing the harm. Such perversities are the height of "rationality" in the minds of many analysts and regulated industries (though it is revealing that they rarely apply the same efficiency criteria to the public policies governing street criminals or national security).

What these intellectual games reveal is a commitment to dubious economic models over the fate of actual people. In fact, the efficiency models sanction the idea of "statistical deaths," in which it becomes socially acceptable to inflict hazards on people so long as their identities remain unknown. The awful human and ecological consequences of failing to regulate are thereby sanitized.

The misuse of economics reaches still further levels of absurdity and intellectual dishonesty when it comes to valuing the benefits of regulation. As we see in Chapter 6, once regulators decide that economic factors will govern decisionmaking, they commit themselves to a highly problematic enterprise—assigning monetary values to ecosystems, the quality of life, and people's lives and health.

Once again, the process depends upon a variety of jerry-rigged methodologies based on conjecture, malleable data, and contestable value judgments. How shall we value regional biodiversity, wilderness areas, or unique geological features? Since none of these resources are traded on markets—they generally cannot be "consumed" or replaced—there is no "natural" price for them. Undeterred, economists estimate their value based on restoration and replacement costs and "behavioral use" valuations (the implicit premium that a resource commands because people use it for, say, recreation).

One of the most contorted attempts to squeeze non-economic values into an economic straightjacket is the analytic model known as "contingent valuation." This is an attempt to assign surrogate prices to such intangibles as aesthetic and philosophical appreciation of a resource. People are asked how much the Grand Canyon is worth to them in dollar terms, for example. A related tool is the "willingness-to-pay" standard: How much is a worker willing to pay to avoid a given hazard?

The average of the answers becomes the fanciful "value" of risk avoidance. That workers are not likely to secure such payments from their employer through higher wages is irrelevant. Nor does the model consider that economically vulnerable workers are more likely to accept lower "prices" for endangering their health than affluent people with a higher sense of entitlement and ability to pay. Instead of treating all Americans by an equal standard, the willingness-to-pay standard sanctions and exploits social inequality.

## The Triumph of Theory Over Reality

The bogus methodologies seem to grow like kudzu. Why regulate the risks of carcinogenic chemicals, the analyst blithely muses, when it is so much cheaper to curb the more serious risks of smoking and junk foods? Of course, the analyst then shows no interest in the empirical realities; the money that a chemical company might save by avoiding regulation, for example, is not going to be spent instead on anti-smoking and nutrition education. The company will simply pocket the money, and *no* preventive action will occur.

This example illustrates a recurrent tactic of the sophisticated saboteur: assert theoretically plausible propositions and develop a logical chain of thought—but then avoid exploring how real life may actually defy the theoretical model. Typically, empirical data are unavailable or deficient. Or the importance of moral judgments, social policies and aesthetic concerns is grossly distorted as they are converted into economic sums. The alchemy of converting intangible values into monetary sums provides just the opportunity needed for the saboteurs to interject their own subjective biases, quietly and without public scrutiny. The result: "Authoritative" hard numbers.

To acknowledge this practice—to admit that "soft" values are inevitably a part of the "neutral" models that generate "hard" numbers—is to force a point that many analysts and most regulated industries prefer to avoid: *whose values shall prevail?* Champions of cost-benefit analysis insist that their economic modeling is entirely objective and fair-minded. They refuse to admit that economic valuation is itself a contestable tool for determining the worth of human life and many aspects of nature. This reaches surreal dimensions when economists presume to calculate the costs of global warming—and the benefits of preventing it—in monetary terms.

The mandarin presumptions of cost-benefit modeling that began with early cost-benefit analyses of dams and similar public works projects have greatly metastasized since the 1970s. As we explore in Chapter 7, federal agencies, at the insistence of regulated industries, are required to estimate the industry compliance costs for proposed standards—and the overall costs of federal regulation in general. As with cost-benefit analysis, a seemingly rational, straightforward process is riddled with questionable methodologies.

For starters, some companies have strong incentives to exaggerate the expected costs of compliance. What better way to combat a proposed regulation? But the U.S. General Accounting Office (GAO) in 1996 suggested that companies literally don't know what they are talking about. The GAO found that corporate cost estimates did not accurately correlate actual compliance costs with specific regulations, for example. They also conflated normal business expenses with compliance costs, thereby failing to identify the actual incremental costs of regulatory compliance.

Corporate estimates of compliance costs are often inflated, as well, because they typically do not take into account how regulation often *enhances* a company's economic performance. In two excerpts in Chapter 7, economists Michael Porter and Nicholas Ashford argue that regulatory standards often stimulate new production efficiencies and superior technologies. EPA's automobile emission control standards, for example, helped prod the development of cleaner, more fuel-efficient engines, which proved to be an enormous competitive boon. The phaseout of chlorofluorocarbons, which erode the earth's ozone layer, helped prod chemical companies to pioneer new markets for benign substitutes.

If regulatory decisionmaking based upon flawed estimates of costs and benefits represents the victory of the sophisticated saboteurs, as Chapters 1-7 document, what then are the alternatives? Fortunately, there are a number of approaches that would improve health, safety, and environmental regulation that do not suffer from the defects of narrow cost-benefit-based regulatory decisionmaking. Refusing to assume that the only legitimate role for government is to fix broken markets, many progressive observers of the current regulatory gridlock are identifying and rediscovering alternative decisionmaking frameworks.

The "precautionary approach" to regulation begins with the assumption that "it is better to be safe than sorry," gives credence to reasonable "worst-case" analyses, and adopts a preference for protection in evaluating regulatory alternatives. Many pragmatic observers urge regulators to focus on the source of risk-producing activities and demand that those responsible for those sources do the "best that they can" to protect potential victims. The focus is on identifying and installing pollution reduction and safety-enhancing technologies, rather than on divining just the right level of protection. Although neither of these approaches may be the most "economically efficient" route to protection, it has a much better chance of reducing risks in the real world than burdensome and time-consuming quantitative risk assessments and cost-benefit analyses. Indeed, sometimes the most effective (and, ironically, even the most efficient) way to get from a risky situation to a much safer one is by completely banning risk-producing activities or other "radical technology-forcing" techniques.

For those decisionmakers who want to examine as many aspects of a problem and its potential solutions as possible, "multiple alternative-multiple attribute" analysis is a far preferable alternative to reductionist cost-benefit analysis. Less quantitative approaches, like "open-ended balancing," also provide pragmatic vehicles for examining the pros and cons of alternative regulatory interventions without descending into the quagmire of quantitative cost-benefit analysis.

Concerns for fairness, a concept that is wholly foreign to cost-benefit analysis, motivate many observers to insist that regulatory decisionmakers devote more attention to the distributional impacts of their choices and provide greater protections for otherwise unempowered workers and poor and minority communities.

Similar fairness concerns suggest caution in devolving regulatory decisionmaking authority from the federal government to states and local entities. Although many states and local governments are well-placed to understand and do something about health and environmental risks, their citizens can become victims of a pernicious "race-to-the-bottom" as local economic interests threaten to re-locate if state and local governments are insistent on providing regulatory protections. The solution is a process of "differential oversight" under which states that consistently provide a threshold level of protection are given greater flexibility to administer federal programs.

In addition to its inherent fairness, proponents of the "polluter-pays" principle stress that making employers "internalize" the costs that their activities impose on their workers, their neighbors, and the environment provides a constant incentive to come up with more efficient and more effective ways to ameliorate health and environmental harms.

Finally, many modern cutting-edge scholars are reminding us of the ancient wisdom that we did not inherit the earth from our fathers; we are borrowing it from our children. We do not have an inexhaustible supply of resources available to use as we please; we are the stewards of a very large spaceship that must be maintained for future generations. A new form of economic analysis, called "ecological economics" is rapidly becoming available to guide decisionmakers. This new kind of analysis begins with a firm realization of the reality of resource limits and attempts to inculcate an understanding of the meaning "too much" in today's consumers. This greater regard for the future, for example, would justify applying a negative discount rate to the benefits of regulations that recognizes the enhanced value of today's regulations to tomorrow's citizens.

* * *

The noble mission of health, safety, and environmental regulation has been under siege for many years. It is no secret that the process is far from perfect. Nothing is ever tidy for an enterprise at the cusp of scientific knowledge, the epicenter of political controversy and the frontier of evolving social norms. Yet regulation remains our best vehicle for protecting Americans' freedom from harm. No other venue exists for the open consideration of scientific knowledge and the forging of social consensus for preventing hazards in legally enforceable ways.

While critics of regulation who legitimately seek to improve government regulation often raise valid points about the deficiencies of the regulatory process, the practitioners of sophisticated sabotage are pursuing another agenda altogether. They have little interest in improving regulation; they seek to paralyze it. Their analytic models do not attempt to make regulatory decisions more informed and intelligent; they seek to exploit the uncertainties that will always exist in order to force interminable analysis and secure indefinite delay. Theirs is a singularly callous spirit of inquiry. It is seen in a relentless, narrow focus on economic costs and efficiencies; a lack of interest in moral responsibility and social inequity; and a zeal for airtight theories and logical reasoning but indifference toward aching human tragedy.

The only way to recover the animating spirit of regulation—the imperative to prevent harm, save the environment and restrain those responsible for inflicting damage—is to debunk the cynical intellectual games that some regulated entities play. A cocoon of abstract discourse has grown up around so many regulatory issues that one can easily forget that "statistical deaths" happen to real people.

We must begin to challenge the pernicious analytic models and economic theories that are choking responsible regulation, and begin to invent new ways to appreciate the actual value of regulation. Sophisticated sabotage must give way to a fresh vocabulary that recognizes the humanistic, qualitative purposes of regulation. Any new analytic models or terms of art are likely to be challenged (as regulation already is), but a new discourse of this sort would have the virtue of being empirical, attentive to Americans' moral and social values, and mindful of actual scientific complexities. That can only be an improvement over the deceitful tyranny of shiny numbers that has paralyzed regulation for too long.

# INTRODUCTION

## Introduction Endnotes

1. U.S. Environmental Protection Agency (EPA), *2002 Trends Report: Air Quality Continues to Improve*, at http://www.epa.gov/airtrends/.

2. U.S. EPA, *Trends in Lead Levels and Emissions*, at http://www.epa.gov/airtrends/lead.html.

3. U.S. EPA, *Trends in Ozone Levels, Related Emissions*, at http://www.epa.gov/airtrends/ozone.html.

4. U.S. EPA, *Trends in Stratospheric Ozone Depletion*, at http://www.epa.gov/airtrends/strat.html.

5. U.S. EPA, A STRATEGY FOR NATIONAL CLEAN WATER INDUSTRIAL REGULATIONS, EFFLUENT GUIDELINES, PRETREATMENT STANDARDS, AND NEW SOURCE PERFORMANCE STANDARDS 9 (Draft, Nov. 5, 2002), *available at* http://www.epa.gov/guide/strategy/304mstrategy.pdf.

6. National Highway Traffic Safety Administration, *Traffic Safety Facts 2001: Overview*, at http://www-nrd.nhtsa.dot.gov/pdf/nrd-30/NCSA/TSF2001/2001overview.pdf.

7. THOMAS O. McGARITY & SIDNEY A. SHAPIRO, WORKERS AT RISK: THE FAILED PROMISE OF THE OCCUPATIONAL SAFETY AND HEALTH ADMINISTRATION (1992).

8. U.S. EPA, *Six Principal Pollutants*, at http://www.epa.gov/airtrends/sixpoll.html.

9. *See* David Hawkins, Natural Resources Defense Council, Inc. (NRDC), *Testimony on S. 485, Clean Skies Act of 2003, Presented Before the U.S. Senate Comm. on Environment and Public Works, Subcomm. on Clean Air, Climate Change, and Nuclear Safety* (Apr. 8, 2003), *available at* http://www.nrdc.org/air/pollution/tdh0403.asp#repeals.

10. Terrence Dopp, *Report: Garden State Failing in Air Pollution Standards*, BRIDGETON NEWS, Dec. 9, 2003, *available at* http://www.nj.com/news/bridgeton/local/index.ssf?/base/news-6/107097630719710.xml.

11. *See* NRDC, *Voluntary Greenhouse Gas Reduction Programs Are Not Enough*, at http://www.nrdc.org/globalWarming/avoluntary.asp.

12. Andrew Schneider, *Panel Urges U.S. to Ban Asbestos Imports*, ST. LOUIS POST DISPATCH, May 4, 2003, at A1.

13. Andrew Schneider, *EPA Warning on Asbestos Is Under Attack*, ST. LOUIS POST DISPATCH, Oct. 26, 2003, at A1.

14. U.S. EPA, WATER QUALITY CONDITIONS IN THE UNITED STATES: A PROFILE FROM THE 2000 NATIONAL WATER QUALITY INVENTORY (2002), *available at* http://www.epa.gov/305b/2000report/.

15. *See supra* note 6.

16. BUREAU OF LABOR STATISTICS, CENSUS OF FATAL OCCUPATIONAL INJURIES (2002), *available at* http://data.bls.gov/cgi-bin/surveymost.

17. BUREAU OF LABOR STATISTICS, WORKPLACE INJURIES AND ILLNESSES IN 2001 (2002), *available at* http://www.bls.gov/iif/oshwc/osh/os/osnr0016.pdf.

18. U.S. EPA, Prevention of Significant Deterioration (PSD) and Non-Attainment New Source Review (NSR): Equipment Replacement Provision of the Routine Maintenance, Repair and Replacement Exclusion, 68 Fed. Reg. 61247 (2003).

19. Statement of Angela Ledford, Director, Clear Air Task Force, The Air on Today's Bush Administration Changes to New Source Review (Aug. 27, 2003), *available at*

http://cta.policy.net/proactive/newsroom/release.vtml?id=24900&PROACTIVE_ID=cecfcfccc6cfc6c9c6c5cecfcfcfc5cececdcac8c8c6cecbcdc5cf.

20. Andrew C. Revkin & Jennifer 8. Lee, *Administration Attacked for Leaving Climate Policy to the States*, N.Y. TIMES, Dec. 11, 2003, at A22 (national edition).

21. *See* Public Citizen v. Minetta, 340 F.3d 39 (2d Cir. 2003).

22. U.S. EPA, National Pollutant Discharge Elimination System Permit Regulation and Effluent Limitation Guidelines and Standards for Concentrated Animal Feeding Operations, 68 Fed. Reg. 7176 (2003).

23. U.S. Department of Energy, Energy Conservation Program for Consumer Products; Central Air Conditioners and Heat Pumps Energy Conservation Standards, 67 Fed. Reg. 36368-01 (2002).

24. NATIONAL ACADEMY OF SCIENCES, INSTITUTE OF MEDICINE, MUSCULOSKELETAL DISORDERS AND THE WORKPLACE: LOW BACK AND UPPER EXTREMITIES 1 (2001).

25. *See* U.S. OSHA National News Release, Ergonomics Guidelines Announced for the Nursing Home Industry (Mar. 13, 2003), *available at* http://www.osha.gov/pls/oshaweb/owadisp.show_document?p_table=NEWS_RELEASES&p_id=10129 (announcing voluntary guidelines).

26. OMB Watch, *Industry, OMB Press EPA to Offer Exemptions to Clean Air Act Standards* (Mar. 19, 2003), *available at* http://www.ombwatch.org/article/articleview/1382/.

27. OMB Watch, *Administration Advances Few Health, Safety, and Environmental Protections* (Jan. 15, 2003), *available at* http://www.ombwatch.org/article/articleview/1256/1/110/#finalized.

28. OMB Watch, *Administration Advances Few Health and Safety Protections* (Dec. 15, 2003), *available at* http://www.ombwatch.org/article/articleview/1256/1/110/.

29. *Id.*

30. Rena Steinzor, *Testimony Before the Subcomm. on Fisheries, Wildlife, and Water of the U.S. Senate Regarding Implementation of the Clean Water Act* (Sept. 16, 2003), *available at* http://www.progressiveregulation.org/articles/EPA_Enforcement_Testimony_091603.pdf.

31. Seth Borenstein, *Fewer Polluters Punished Under Bush Administration, Records Show*, PHILA. ENQUIRER, Dec. 8, 2003, *available at* http://www.philly.com/mld/inquirer/news/front/7446525.htm.

32. *Id.*

33. Steinzor, *supra* note 30.

34. OMB Watch, *Ignoring Enron's Lessons, Bush Rollbacks Continue* (Nov. 6, 2002), *available at* http://www.ombwatch.org/article/articleview/1174/#limiting.

35. *Id.*

36. Sally Covington, *How Conservative Philanthropies and Think Tanks Transform U.S. Policy*, COVERT ACTION Q., Winter 1998. The foundations include the Lynde and Harry Bradley Foundation, the Carthage Foundation, the Earhart Foundation, the Charles G. Koch, David H. Koch, and Claude R. Lambe charitable foundations, the Phillip M. McKenna Foundation, the JM Foundation, the John M. Olin Foundation, the Henry Salvatori Foundation, the Sarah Scaife Foundation, and the Smith Richardson Foundation.

37. Katharine Q. Seelye & John Tierney, *EPA Drops Age-Based Cost Studies*, N.Y. TIMES, May 8, 2003, at A26.

# Chapter 1: Civic Values Versus Corporate Science and Economics

The consumer and environmental movements of the late 1960s and early 1970s represent a colossal achievement in civilizing our industrial, market society. Most Americans probably do not remember that the Cuyahoga River once contained so many pollutants that it caught fire. It used to be commonplace for factories to dump highly toxic chemicals into pits behind a factory. Smokestacks used to belch large quantities of unknown chemicals into the sky. The effects of pollution on human health, other species, and ecosystems were not well known. Automobiles lacked either seat belts or airbags. Workers routinely became ill and died from breathing coal dust, cotton dust, and other dangerous fumes or were killed as the result of workplace accidents. For these and many other advances, we can thank the great wave of congressional legislation of a generation ago.

Although the U.S. Congress set many ambitious goals in this legislation, it recognized that it lacked the scientific and analytical resources to write necessary rules for the new regulatory regime. Congress therefore delegated this authority to the newly created regulatory agencies, most notably the U.S. Environmental Protection Agency (EPA), the Occupational Safety and Health Administration, the National Highway Safety Administration, and the Consumer Product Safety Commission. Congress directed the agencies to use an administrative process called "rulemaking"—fair, open procedures based on defensible science and legal mandates—to set acceptable levels of contaminants in workplaces and in the air, surface water, groundwater, soil, and other media. Congress also told the agencies to promulgate standards to require corporations to adopt safety precautions and to take other actions to protect individuals and the environment.

Polluting companies soon began to realize that compliance with the new regulatory requirements would not come cheaply. In fact, even before the first round of health, safety, and environmental statutes had been fully implemented, the trade associations for many regulated industries began to demand relief. Characterizing the new regulatory requirements as "unduly burdensome" and "overly prescriptive," they complained that the new rules were not based upon "sound science." Accordingly, they sought to interpose a new layer of procedure—"quantitative risk assessments"—to guide how the congressional statutes would be implemented.

**The Rise of New Analytic Techniques**

Eager to mitigate or avoid the costs of compliance, industrial polluters—with support from academia and business-oriented think tanks—began to imagine still other analytic techniques and procedures to delay or stymie regulation. In

17

the 1970s, for example, industry began to urge Congress and agencies to issue formal quantitative "cost-benefit analyses" of proposed regulations, a technique that sought to combine quantitative risk assessments with estimates of the costs of compliance.[1] Soon even this was not enough. Industry insisted that *every* major health, safety, and environmental regulation be justified by a full-blown cost-benefit analysis, an affirmative showing that the estimated (quantified) benefits exceeded the estimated (quantified) costs.[2]

Although federal regulatory agencies initially resisted such demands, the president and executive branch, responding to political pressures by regulated industries, eventually required agencies to conduct such analyses. A series of executive orders issued by President Gerald Ford (1974-1976) required agencies to prepare regulatory impact analyses (RIAs) for major rules, which detailed estimates of their costs and benefits.[3] As RIAs gradually became part of the agencies' standard operating procedures, business groups and their allies began to press for more thorough analyses using even "sounder" science. The stated goal was to prevent the promulgation of new regulations until there was uncontestable evidence that the benefits outweighed the costs.

The business sector's drive to stymie health, safety, and environmental regulation reached a fever pitch during the contentious 104th Congress of 1995. As part of its so-called Contract With America, a newly elected Republican majority in the U.S. House of Representatives, led by Speaker Newt Gingrich (R-Ga.), made "regulatory relief" a high priority and enacted the Omnibus Regulatory Reform legislation. The "relief" did not serve to "cut red tape," as politicians so often demand, but to slather on complicated, time-consuming new layers of bureaucratic procedure. Among other things, the proposed Act required agencies to conduct a formal "peer review" procedure to ensure that the studies underlying regulatory efforts represented "sound science"; to develop a set of detailed and prescriptive requirements for formalized quantitative risk assessment, comparative risk assessment and cost-benefit analysis; and to adopt an across-the-board cost-benefit decision criterion for new regulations.

The net effect of this new layer of bureaucratic process—if not the actual, thinly veiled goal—would be to make it more difficult for regulators to abate health, safety, and environmental hazards. Proponents of the new analytic techniques and regulatory procedures insisted they were not advancing any political agenda, however. They merely wanted to improve the scientific rigor and economic prudence of federal regulation. Moreover, they claimed that within academia, there was no ongoing controversy about the value of the analytic techniques and their use in major rulemaking initiatives, but a clear "consensus in favor of them."[4]

This so-called consensus is far from clear. To date, Congress has rejected most attempts to incorporate formal peer review, risk assessment, and cost-benefit decision criteria into the major health and environmental statutes. No political consensus has crystallized to enact such sweeping changes. In academic circles, too, debate about the value of the analytic techniques and regulatory procedures remains very much alive and well.

18

In the meantime, federal agencies generally can and do employ quantitative risk assessment, comparative risk assessment, and cost-benefit analysis as part of their rule-writing efforts. These business-friendly practices grew more widespread during the Clinton Administration's efforts to "reinvent" the federal government. With the arrival of the second Bush Administration in 2001, these attempts to achieve "regulatory reform" (which critics dubbed regulatory "deform") were intensified and given new vigor.

The goal of bringing rigorous scientific and economic analysis to bear in regulatory decisionmaking is a worthy one, of course. When used properly, risk assessment and cost-benefit analysis can establish regulatory priorities and help clarify the best way to regulate. But quite frequently, calls for increased use of cost-benefit analysis and comparative risk assessment are simply a pretext for impeding effective regulation. The information required by these techniques is often not easily obtained, and therefore expensive and time-consuming to assemble. Moreover, the gold-plated standards of analytic precision that regulatory critics often demand are fraught with broad, slippery assumptions. The precision claimed is, in fact, a specious rigor.

The net effect of the hyper-analysis, as then-EPA Administrator Carol Browner noted during the "regulatory reform" debates of the 104th Congress, is to divert regulators from addressing urgent, genuine threats to human health, safety, and the environment. This, of course, is precisely the outcome that regulated industries generally prefer. If agencies must tackle all potentially higher risks before regulating a given activity, and if it must navigate a highly Byzantine maze of procedures and analyses, it should not be surprising if the regulatory process grinds to a standstill.

It is important, therefore, to understand the limits of scientific and economic analysis. Ultimately, neither can decide the "trans-scientific" issues and extra-market judgments of social ethics that lie at the heart of the rulemaking process. An issue is "trans-scientific" when it can be answered by science as a theoretical matter, but as a practical matter cannot be resolved through scientific methods. Decisions to prevent known environmental harms and human diseases cannot be based on the criteria of an economic or scientific matrix alone.

## The Rationale for Regulation

Contrary to the champions of cost-benefit analysis and comparative risk assessment, regulation is not primarily an economic act. It is a vehicle for asserting common ethical and social values in the face of unacceptable threats to individuals, public health, and the environment.

In the following passages, Profs. Zygmunt J.B. Plater and Lynn E. Blais explain the institutional justification for regulation: a theme that echoes throughout the rest of the book. Absent a system of environmental laws, regulated industries have no particular incentive to limit pollution and every incentive to impose the costs of pollution damage (or "externalities") on others. Indeed, even after environmental laws have been enacted, regulated industries have keen incentives to resist their implementation. The status quo is cheaper and more convenient for them.

Regulatory agencies charged with implementing environmental laws must therefore struggle against the constant resistance of regulated industries. As Professor Plater makes clear, this corporate resistance is not a matter of evil corporations wreaking devastation upon an innocent and unsuspecting world. It is a predictable and inevitable consequence of our market-based economy.[5]

---

* * * Environmental law, reflecting a paradigm shift in how we perceive the world, has emerged over the past three decades as one of the primary realms in which society attempts to insert short and long-term public civic values into practical economic affairs. This role inevitably makes environmental law a political battlefield. * * *

Since 1960, beginning in the United States and continuing onto the international plane, our society has experienced an extraordinary development of scientific knowledge, law, and policy regarding the physical and ecological world in which we live. Our quest for this learning was driven by a recognition of systemic environmental problems and threats that were only incidentally perceived prior to 1960. At its heart, environmental law has come to incorporate a set of principles representing and accounting for civic values that extend far beyond the realm of science and current events. Perhaps only in environmental law has the modern legal system directly incorporated issues of long-term societal survival into its operative norms and doctrinal provisions.

It is no surprise that the Marketplace resists the imposition of public values upon private enterprises. For years in Corporate Law, we have taught that the duty of corporations—which play a dominant role in every free society, and in none more so than ours—is to maximize the interest of their shareholders, not to advance any altruistic broader public good. "Get Government out of the way of the Marketplace" would theoretically be an acceptable societal principle if the Market could and would accomplish the necessary public duties for which government is designed. But it cannot or will not. Establishments do not self-correct when faced with the discovery that their self-interest conflicts with external civic values. The doing of public good (beyond some positive spillover effects of corporate self interest) is systematically consigned to voluntary organizations like churches and scout troops—a thousand points of light confronting a million points of profit?—and, more tangibly, to government.

But market forces are arguably the most dominant and powerful structures in modern society, a position that sets up a serious problem. When governments attempt to impose "artificial" non-market public values upon an industry (or upon private individuals), there is an understandable and inherent instinct to attempt to avoid or resist such imposition and the attendant costs. Multiply the tendency of each economic entity to resist cost internalization by tens of thousands of corporations, and the result is a vast concurrent resistance that permeates and erodes the effort to instill civic values in the governance process.

20

# CHAPTER 1: CIVIC VALUES VERSUS CORPORATE SCIENCE AND ECONOMICS

How do marketplace actors react to regulations and guidelines applying public values that undercut private gain? They react in quite understandable human terms:

- seeking to comply, especially (though not exclusively) when regulations are mandatory and credible enforcement is likely;
- seeking to avoid compliance, on the facts by denying the existence or validity of the problem and trying to avoid proof of violations, or on the law by contesting the authority of agencies, courts, or private citizen plaintiffs, and aggressively litigating every step of the way;
- trying to undercut regulatory effectiveness by advocating cuts in appropriations, particularly appropriations for enforcement;
- trying to modify or repeal the restrictive requirements of statutes and regulations, arguing that "the pendulum has swung too far."

These strategies can run concurrently. In the first decade of environmental law, when enforcement structures were new and uncertain, resistance to enforcement was probably a prevalent mode, along with simultaneous limited gestures toward compliance. Subsequently, as environmental law enforcement has become surer and better known, many corporate enterprises have institutionalized compliance efforts through vigorous inspection, self audits, and organizational redesign. "We have seen the light," say some executives. "Now trust us, and go after someone else." The fact that industries generally move toward compliance, however, does not mean that they also abandon their attempts at avoidance strategies.

The antidote * * * is a process that ensures the consideration of public merits—within environmental law, and within legislative initiatives that attempt to override environmental law. This process requires informed and engaged professionals, an incisive press, and an active citizenry. Environmentalism, in other words, often ends up being another word for democracy.

---

Looking at the regulatory process through an *economic* lens can be helpful, but it is often an attempt at historical revisionism. The impetus for environmental laws enacted during the early 1970s, after all, was not chiefly economic, but social and moral: people were appalled at the pollution and damage being wrought by unregulated industries. As a result, the statutes enacted set certain goals *without regard to the economic consequences.* The laws, for example, did not require explicit cost-benefit balancing.

To the regulated industries and their allies in academia, the regulations that resulted were seen as "absolutist." The industries regarded the legally compelled behaviors as economically irrational. Thus began the concerted drive to require federal agencies—usually through executive orders—to prepare cost-benefit analyses of major regulations, regardless of their statutory mandates. Soon corporate-sponsored academics began to press for even more ambitions reforms employing quantitative risk assessment. By the end of the 20th century, Professor Blais points out, economists had effectively "conquered" environmental regula-

tion. By contriving a diverse array of abstract analytic tools and regulatory procedures, industry-retained economists soon established a new normative matrix for
understanding regulation. This economic perspective fundamentally revised—and denied—the animating justification for regulation in the first place:
the irreducible personal, social, and environmental harm.

This revisionism has been especially pernicious, Professor Blais notes, because the advocates of quantitative risk assessment and cost-benefit analysis
typically fail to acknowledge the considerable practical and theoretical limitations of these techniques.[6] Instead they tacitly belittle important "non-economic" norms as somehow having less credibility. It bears remembering that
members of Congress originally enacted the various regulatory statutes not because of compelling *economic* evidence, but rather because of the unacceptable
"non-economic" factors: squalid rivers, elevated cancer risks, dead and dis-
membered workers, soaring highway death and injury rates, declining wildlife
populations, rampant ecosystem deterioration.

Quantifying the costs and benefits of regulation is wrong, Professor Blais
points out, because it does not correspond to the social judgment reflected in
the statutes as enacted. For example, Congress wanted companies to reduce
pollution *beyond* what might be "cost-justified" by a regulatory agency.
Moreover, quantitative measurement is simply too unreliable. The data and
models used in quantitative cost-benefit analysis are far too riddled with uncertainties to deliver the precise estimates, let alone be decisive tools in justifying regulatory outcomes.

---

### The Statutory Revolution in Environmental Protection

The decade of the 1970s represents a watershed in the law of environmental
protection. The early part of that era witnessed the remarkable passage of extensive environmental protection statutes that departed radically from the efforts of
previous decades. Between 1969 and 1973, the federal government enacted the
National Environmental Policy Act, the Clean Air Act Amendments of 1970, the
Federal Water Pollution Control Act Amendments of 1972, and the Endangered
Species Act of 1973. These statutes mark a dramatic break from the preceding
common law regime in two important respects. First, the statutes and their implementing regulations constitute "one of the most pervasive systems of national
regulation known to American law."[7] Second, they consistently reject the common law paradigm of balancing competing rights and entitlements by reference to
reasonable behavior, substituting in its place a presumption against pollution.

Such dramatic transformations are not often easily explained, and scholars
continue to debate the origin and cause of the environmental protection revolution. Also unresolved are lingering questions about the original scope and purpose of these revolutionary statutes. Much environmental scholarship argues
that the statutes were intended to produce decisive regulatory responses to existing environmental crises, regardless of the costs. Other scholars have different views. * * *

Regardless of which view eventually prevails in the official history of the environmental protection revolution, however, one thing is clear: the environmental revolution was not cost-conscious. The original versions of the major federal environmental statutes embodied strong public statements that the benefits of environmental protection were not to be measured, regulation by regulation, against the costs of achieving those benefits.

*The Post-Revolutionary Battle: The Triumph of the Economic Approach to Environmental Protection*

The noneconomic focus of the environmental movement was short-lived, however. Soon after the major environmental statutes were enacted, regulated entities and legal commentators began to quantify the costs and benefits of the resulting regulations. Critics of the environmental protection revolution were quick to decry the adoption and implementation of policies that appeared to impose costs in excess of the benefits they generated. In particular, legal scholars and economists quickly evaluated and rejected the regulatory scheme's extensive reliance on command-and-control regulation, lamenting the gross inefficiencies of industrywide, technology-based, environmental standard setting.[8]

Environmental policymaking followed suit. In 1981, President Reagan issued an executive order requiring that all executive branch regulatory agencies conduct extensive cost/benefit analyses for major regulatory decisions and, to the extent permitted by statute, promulgate the most cost-effective policy to achieve a particular regulatory objective.[9] This executive mandate survives, in a slightly different form, under the current administration.[10] As a result of these executive orders and several statutes that require cost/benefit analyses in certain circumstances,[11] government agencies routinely engage in cost/benefit analysis and spend a lot of money doing it.

Attempts to apply cost/benefit analysis to environmental policymaking led, almost inexorably, to quantifying risks because most environmental benefits had to be measured by decreases in risk. Eventually, the "science" of quantitative risk assessment gave way to the more "useful" exercise of comparing those risks, and, by the end of the 1990s, comparative risk assessment techniques were exalted by many leading environmental scholars as the means to regulatory coherence.

Three factors account for the rush to quantify. First, the initial costs of environmental protection were high and immediately apparent, especially to the industries that were compelled to comply with technology-forcing regulations. Second, the environmental benefits were more elusive and, in many contexts, did not appear for years or even decades. Finally, as Professor Wendy Wagner has eloquently argued, regulators attempting to implement these grand and imprecise statutory mandates increasingly sought to legitimize their policymaking by cloaking policy decisions in the protective mantle of "hard numbers."[12]

For these reasons, economists have conquered the environmental protection universe twenty years after the deliberately uncost-conscious environmental protection revolution. Although the basic language of the governing statutes remained substantially the same, the scholarly story of pollution control has come, for the most part, to be retold as a fable of market failure. In this story, regulatory responses were deemed justified only to the extent that they consciously addressed and ameliorated relevant market defects.

In the environmental context, economists point to two forms of market failure justifying government intervention: the inability of the competitive market to produce and distribute optimal amounts of public goods and the presence of externalities, which distort the rational decision-making process. Much of the law and economics environmental scholarship of the 1980s and early 1990s was devoted to the proposition that environmental protection statutes were not well designed to address the market failures at which they were aimed.

Unfortunately, in the rush to quantify, economic tools have been wielded in legal and policy battles with little regard to the limitations of the methodology or the importance of non-economic norms. In some important cases, arguments that the high cost of a regulation far outweighed the demonstrated benefit generated by the regulation prevailed, even at the expense of good policy judgment and sound legal reasoning. In the scholarship arena, massive reforms have been proposed on the basis of questionable comparative risk data that was subject to virtually no scholarly scrutiny for more than a decade.

Elevating quantification over other values in environmental policymaking is wrong for two reasons. First, it does not accurately reflect the prevailing political will for environmental protection beyond that which is "cost-justified." Second, as it is currently advocated, quantified economic policymaking relies on the most basic forms of economic analysis and risk assessment, which are fraught with the disadvantages of simplified modeling and inherent uncertainty.

Used judiciously, of course, the economist's tools are indispensable to sound policymaking. In circumstances where there are several alternative regulatory mechanisms by which society can achieve the same level of pollution control, for example, careful analysis of the comparative costs and effectiveness of each option is essential. Only then can the policymaker clearly focus on the normative factors relevant to the choice of one policy over the other. The information obtained from these cost/benefit comparisons is inherently abstract and unavoidably crude, however, and the policymaker must be constantly conscious of the limitations of the data the information generates. This data represents only the very beginning of a long process of policymaking and not the resolution of any issues of importance.

---

Profs. Sidney A. Shapiro and Thomas O. McGarity offer some additional insights into economic approaches to regulation[13]:

---

Economists defend the use of cost-benefit standards in formulating social policy on risk reduction by arguing that, in some cases, it is less expensive for society when employers pay compensation for illnesses rather than spending money to prevent them. This argument, however, ignores the ethical distinction between preventing death and compensating the victim's family after death occurs. * * *

[Economic] critics have difficulty believing that Congress really rejected the use of cost-benefit analysis. Because no rational consumer would pay $25 in a private market for something that is worth only $20, the economist assumes that voters also intend for their representatives to reject policies whose costs exceed their "economic" benefits.

However, the economist fails to understand that public, social decisions provide citizens with an opportunity to give certain things a higher valuation than they would otherwise choose to give them in their private activities or in their capacity as individuals. In public forums, individuals are often willing to vote for outcomes that economic analysis would characterize as inefficient because these outcomes can confirm and serve important non-economic values. As consumers, we may dislike paying more for manufactured products because of the costs of protecting workers, but as citizens we can rationally vote for these types of costly and (by the economist's "willingness to pay" measure) irrational goals. We vote in favor of such costly goals because they permit us to reaffirm our ideal that preventable occupational diseases are not merely inefficient—they are wrong.

* * * Acknowledging that society cannot vest workers with an unqualified right to an absolutely safe workplace, one may rationally assert that workers do have a right to insist that employers "do the best they can" to protect human health. In other words, society might justifiably decide to reduce risky behavior beyond the point indicated by a cost-benefit test. Indeed, society may choose to limit its protection of workers only at the point where the protection would cause industry substantial economic dislocation. * * *

---

## Democratic Values Versus Runaway Markets

The revolutionary environmental statutes of the late 1960s and early 1970s were premised upon a shared conception, that human beings had badly despoiled the planet and that drastic change was required before it was too late to reverse the march toward environmental devastation. Those claims, which still resonate strongly in an age of global warming and declining ecological diversity, meant that serious changes were needed in "business as usual." Through an open process based on scientific evidence and legal mandates, environmental regulation was an attempt to provoke just such change in industrial behavior. When Congress took a look at the deplorable standards of occupational and product safety that resulted in *laissez-faire* markets, it came to a similar conclusion, that federal laws and regulation were needed to prod improvements.

It did not take long for the targets of early regulatory efforts and their allies in academia and think tanks to launch a counter-offensive. Much of it hinged upon discrediting the efficacy of early regulatory efforts. Technology-forcing requirements and ambitious emissions standards were denigrated as "command-and-control" strategies that made unwarranted interventions in the "free market." Instead of allowing regulation to be judged as a social policy, regulated industries insisted that they be assessed by strict economic metrics: is regulation compatible with market efficiency and other economic criteria? Quantitative cost-benefit balancing tests were the first stage of this larger effort.

By establishing market criteria as the normative standard, any government initiatives that might "interfere" with the market would be seen as presumptively illegitimate or unwise. Under this paradigm, government would be allowed to demand changes in industry practices only if there were "market failures"—compelling demonstrations that free markets are not working properly. And any government interventions would have to be the least intrusive governmental measures capable of remedying the problem. In this way, the standard for government regulation would be raised. It would not be enough for the regulator to demonstrate that human health is endangered or the environment is being destroyed. The market paradigm requires that the government must demonstrate that a health risk or environmental destruction is "inefficient." The burden shifts from industry to correct the problem, and instead *government* must show that the benefits of corrective measures outweigh the costs. This new equation conveniently disguises the distributional justice issues, that the costs are borne by the people and environments at risk, not the companies that created the risks in the first place.

The unidimensional economic view of the world simply ignores important civic values that are reflected in the health, safety, and environmental laws. It allows the modern corporation to continue to focus intently upon delivering short-term value to shareholders, and relieves them of the costly burden of grappling with the long-term survival of the planet. Understanding regulation therefore requires that we strip away the veneer of economic discourse, and recover the original meaning and purpose of health, safety, and environmental regulation—to prevent irreversible harm, assert shared social values, and act as a check on systematic market abuses.

Law is an indispensable force in this process. In the face of demonstrated evidence that unfettered markets create undue risks to human health and safety and to the environment, law plays a vital role in taming socially unacceptable corporate behavior. This task continues long after the enactment of corrective legislation; it is the very reason for ongoing regulatory oversight. After all, corporations have every incentive, and the power, to attempt to avoid corrective action and its costs. The story of federal regulation, then, is the ongoing struggle to abate industrial hazards in a fair, practical, systematic way, long after the social memory of the original crises may have faded.

**Suggestions for Further Reading**

Other sources of information on the origins of modern environmental law and the reaction to the early implementation of the modern environmental statutes include the following:

Alfred C. Aman Jr., *Administrative Law in a Global Era: Progress, Deregulatory Change and the Rise of the Administrative Presidency*,

73 CORNELL L. REV. 1101 (1988).

*Prof. Alfred Aman places the regulatory reform movement of the Reagan presidency in broad historical context and demonstrates how one of the consequences has been an arrogation of power in the executive branch.*

THOMAS O. MCGARITY, REINVENTING RATIONALITY (1991).

*A comprehensive examination of the role of regulatory impact analysis in regulatory decisionmaking in the early years of the Reagan Administration. Drawing heavily upon case studies of regulatory impact analysis in practice, Professor McGarity suggests that agencies have employed four models for incorporating regulatory analysis and argues that it is not at all clear that the benefits of cost-benefit analysis so employed outweigh the costs.*

Robert L. Rabin, *Federal Regulation in Historical Perspective*, 38 STAN. L. REV. 1189 (1986).

*This broad-brush description of federal regulation across more than a century provides an excellent historical introduction to the current debates over the proper role for federal health, safety, and environmental regulation in modern society.*

There are several critical analyses of the risk assessment and cost-benefit requirements of the "regulatory reform" legislation considered during the 104th Congress that met in the wake of the "Contract With America." Some of the best of those commentaries are:

John S. Applegate, *The Role of Risk Assessment in Environmental Decision-Making*, 63 U. CIN. L. REV. 1643 (1995).

*Professor Applegate examines several common elements in the risk assessment bills that the Republican regulatory reformers introduced in the 104th Congress. He suggests that the real goal of the reforms was to change the fundamental regulatory principles underlying modern environmental regulation and concludes that "risk assessment is a poor way, and ultimately a dishonest way, to effect" such changes.*

William W. Buzbee, *Regulatory Reform or Statutory Muddle: The "Legislative Mirage" of Single Statute Regulatory Reform*, 5 N.Y.U. ENVTL. L.J. 298, 313-24 (1996).

*After describing the omnibus regulatory reform bills of the 104th Congress, Prof. William Buzbee argues that a one-size-fits-all approach to changing all federal environmental regulation by mandating a single cost-benefit decision criterion is inappropriate.*

Victor B. Flatt, *Environmental "Contraction" for America? (Or How I Stopped Worrying and Learned to Love the EPA)*, 29 LOY. L.A. L. REV. 585 (1996).

*Prof. Victor Flatt describes in detail many of the regulatory reform bills that were intended to implement the Republican House members' "Contract With America." He argues that the bills "would freeze all health and environmental protection, effectively repeal 25 years of health protection through a 'risk assessment' bill and allow industry to hold up environmental safeguards through endless lawsuits."*

Robert L. Glicksman & Stephen B. Chapman, *Regulatory Reform and (Breach of) the Contract With America: Improving Environmental Policy or Destroying Environmental Protection?*, 5 KAN. J.L. & PUB. POL'Y 9 (1996).

*This comprehensive analysis of the progress of the most important regulatory reform bills through the 104th Congress concludes that the real intent of those bills was to provide regulatory relief for regulated industries.*

# CHAPTER 1: CIVIC VALUES VERSUS CORPORATE SCIENCE AND ECONOMICS

## Chapter 1 Endnotes

1. *See* W. Kip Viscusi, *Regulating the Regulators*, 63 U. CHI. L. REV. 1423, 1429-30 (1996).

2. *See id.* at 1436 (arguing that "no regulatory policy should be pursued unless the benefits exceed the costs").

3. For a description of the early efforts during the Reagan Administration to implement the regulatory impact assessment requirements of the executive orders, see THOMAS O. McGARITY, REINVENTING RATIONALITY (1991).

4. *See* Cass R. Sunstein, *Legislative Foreword: Congress, Constitutional Moments, and the Cost-Benefit State*, 48 STAN. L. REV. 247, 257-67 (1996).

5. Professor Plater teaches environmental law at Boston College School of Law. The full article from which the excerpts are drawn, *Environmental Law As a Mirror of the Future: Civic Values Confronting Market Force Dynamics in a Time of Counter-Revolution*, appears at 23 B.C. ENVTL. AFF. L. REV. 733, 737-41 (1996).

6. Professor Blais teaches environmental law at the University of Texas School of Law. The full article from which the excerpts are drawn, *Beyond Cost Benefit: The Maturation of Economic Analysis of the Law and Its Consequences for Environmental Policymaking*, appears at 2000 U. ILL. L. REV. 237, 238-40.

7. E. Donald Elliott et al., *Toward a Theory of Statutory Evolution: The Federalization of Environmental Law*, 1 J.L. ECON. & ORG. 313, 317 (1985).

8. *See, e.g.*, Bruce A. Ackerman & Richard B. Stewart, *Reforming Environmental Law*, 37 STAN. L. REV. 1333, 1334-35 (1985); Richard H. Pildes & Cass R. Sunstein, *Reinventing the Regulatory State*, 62 U. CHI. L. REV. 1, 96 (1995); Richard B. Stewart, *United States Environmental Regulation: A Failing Paradigm*, 15 J.L. & COM. 585, 587 (1996); Cass R. Sunstein, *Administrative Substance*, 1991 DUKE L.J. 607, 625-31.

9. *See* Executive Order No. 12291 (1981), 3 C.F.R. 127 (1981), *reprinted in* 5 U.S.C. 601 app. at 431-34 (1982).

10. *See* Executive Order No. 12866 (1993), 3 C.F.R. 638, 638-49 (1993), *reprinted in* 5 U.S.C. 601 (1995).

11. For example, the Unfunded Mandates Reform Act of 1995 requires agencies to undertake a "qualitative and quantitative assessment of the anticipated costs and benefits of the Federal mandate" before promulgating a rule or regulation that may result in a nonfederal entity spending more than $100 million per year. *See* 2 U.S.C. §1532(a) (1994).

12. *See, e.g.*, Wendy E. Wagner, *The Science Charade in Toxic Risk Regulation*, 95 COLUM. L. REV. 1613, 1651 (1995).

13. Professor Shapiro teaches administrative and regulatory law at the University of Kansas School of Law. Professor McGarity teaches environmental law at the University of Texas School of Law. The full article from which this excerpt is drawn, *Not So Paradoxical: The Rationale for Technology-Based Regulation*, appears at 1991 DUKE L. REV. 729, 739-44.

# Chapter 2: The Myth of "Junk Science"

**P**erhaps the most frequent criticism of many health, safety, and environmental regulations is that they are based on "junk science." When the U.S. Environmental Protection Agency (EPA) bans the use of chemicals like the fumigant Alar because of the harmful residues it left on fruit, and when juries hand down large awards to victims exposed to substances like the chemical dioxin or the drug DES, the affected industries frequently complain that the action is being taken without the support of sound scientific evidence.[1] The implication—and sometimes, the bald accusation—is that political ideology or bureaucratic caprice is trumping known scientific facts.

Over the past generation, a hardy corps of industry-associated academics and think-tank polemicists have arisen to actively promote this viewpoint. It can be seen in academic books such as John D. Graham's *In Search of Safety* and Robert Hahn's *Costs and Lives Saved*, and in popular counterparts such as Peter Huber's *Galileo's Revenge* and Philip Howard's *The Death of Common Sense*. The echo-chamber effect reaches its peak effect when the *Wall Street Journal's* editorial pages and sympathetic journalists such as John Stossel of ABC-TV's *20/20* news-magazine ridicule supposed instances of "junk science" in regulatory decisionmaking.

Many of the criticisms of junk science *sound* reasonable. John Graham, for years the head of the Harvard Center for Risk Analysis and now the head of Office of Management and Budget's (OMB's) Office of Information and Regulatory Affairs, has said that it is "important that the government's risk-assessment determinations be based on sound scientific principles and procedures." Congress should therefore "require that any official risk determination issued by a federal agency, regardless of whether or not it has been used to justify a final regulatory action, be based on an objective, weight-of-the-evidence evaluation that is peer reviewed by a group of independent scientists."[2]

Prof. Cass Sunstein of the University of Chicago School of Law repeats a canard that citizen fears and press sensationalism frequently triumph over hard science. "When citizens are misinformed," writes Sunstein, "government should not base regulatory decisions on their judgments. Instead, government should act on the basis of scientific realities. Public judgments should dictate regulatory policy only when they are undergirded by sound science, as opposed to sensationalist anecdotes or scare tactics."[3]

But is "junk science" really the issue here? Or is the invocation of science a red herring—a convenient mantle of "objectivity" for opinions that are based on particular social or economic interests? This chapter debunks the attractive myth that health, safety, and environmental regulation can be based solely on the "hard facts" of science. We challenge the seductive notion that *there are sufficient supplies of neutral, hard scientific evidence* available and that sound regulatory judgments can be based on that information.

The truth is that regulation is necessarily an inexact art. Science cannot expunge all or even most of the uncertainty that plagues regulatory decision-making. While it is important for regulatory agencies to marshal the most rigorous possible empirical evidence and scientific analysis, any regulatory decision ultimately reflects certain ethical judgments, social priorities and, yes, political values. It is tempting to believe that science can banish such messy, contentious issues from regulatory decisionmaking, but it cannot. This chapter explores some key reasons why uncertainty persists in regulation and why science is so often enlisted—unrealistically—to address this uncertainty.

A good place to start is with the inherent limits of scientific knowledge itself. There are certain things—such as the etiology of cancer or the actual behavior of airborne pollutants—that scientists *simply do not know enough about.* In some cases, the scientific theories do not exist and no consensus interpretation of the problem has developed. In other cases, it is difficult or prohibitively expensive to gather all the data that may be theoretically possible to collect. These issues are discussed in the section "Scientific Uncertainty: An Inescapable Aspect of Regulation."

For example, it takes millions of dollars to put a single pesticide through the battery of tests necessary to determine its toxicity to laboratory animals and the environment. For ethical reasons, human testing is ordinarily out of the question, but when it is not, it is very expensive. Epidemiological studies of humans who have already been exposed to chemicals (frequently workers) are also expensive and notoriously difficult to undertake.

Once completed, studies are always subject to criticism because they can never avoid all possible "confounding factors" that render the statistical analysis suspect. For 50 years, the tobacco industry successfully defended cigarettes from claims that they caused lung cancer by challenging each and every one of the dozens of epidemiological studies that suggested that cigarettes were indeed cancer-causing products. Defending cell phones from claims that radiation from them causes brain cancer based upon a single epidemiological study is trivial by comparison.[4]

The bottom line is that agencies must often resolve "trans-scientific" questions that could be answered by science as a theoretical matter, but as a practical matter are not scientifically determinable. When faced with such quandaries—inadequate scientific data and an inability to gather a higher threshold of evidence—agencies have no choice but to use appropriate regulatory policies to make decisions.

Another key reason for uncertainty—one that regulatory critics rarely mention—is industry resistance to generating or providing useful data. Regulated companies are far better-situated to acquire solid information about a given hazard. But they have serious disincentives to provide that data because it could end up triggering regulation or liability lawsuits. Government, for its part, often cannot afford to pay for in-depth scientific analyses of the risks of modern products and technologies. The disincentives for companies to acquire rigorous data to help prevent harm are explored in the section: "Why Companies Choose Ignorance."

Much of the uncertainty in the regulatory process occurs because of the misuse of science. Rather than admit that regulatory decisions necessarily reflect social values (as articulated in the congressional statute), many observers try to make science decide more than it can legitimately decide. They pretend that science can properly dictate regulatory outcomes. Any "wrong" outcome must therefore be based on shoddy science, goes the thinking, and any "right" outcome must be based on "sound science." In either case, such regulatory observers are expressing a social policy judgment—but disguising it behind the veneer of scientific objectivity.

These are "science charades," says Prof. Wendy Wagner in an excerpt reprinted below. They are a way for regulatory agencies (and outside partisans) to avoid taking responsibility for politically contestable policy choices. Framing a regulatory decision as a scientific matter encourages people to regard any unsatisfactory outcome as scientifically deficient; critics complain that the decision could only have been based on incomplete data or "junk science." But disagreements about regulation are, in many instances, not really about the quality of scientific evidence or interpretation. They are about clashing political values and social policy goals.

Proponents of "sound science," it turns out, often are quite happy with the most minimal scientific evidence. When the question is whether EPA—after years of scientific study and review—has adequately supported its national ambient air quality standard for fine particulate, sound-science champions will call for more study. Yet when EPA approves a potentially allergenic genetically engineered pesticidal plant—based solely on industry assurances that it is "substantially equivalent" to natural plants—they are satisfied that the science is adequate. "Sound science" advocacy has shown itself to be highly disingenuous, revealing that its real concern is not science, but which policies will guide the decisionmaking outcomes. These themes are explored in the section "Scientific Charades as an Evasion of Responsibility."

When political and social issues are miscast as scientific matters, another pathology ensues. Only "experts" are considered reliable enough to make the "right" judgments. This dynamic has given rise to professional risk assessors criticizing the public for their "inaccurate" perceptions of actual risks. "So you think that dioxin is a serious problem?" the academic "expert" may ask with a patronizing smile. "Gotcha!" he replies—smoking causes far more deaths and disease. The clear implication is that we should ignore "lesser" risks until the larger ones are abated—even though a "lesser" risk might be more easily controlled and controlled less expensively by a corporation than by individual consumers. By inflating the truth-claims of science, the professional risk assessors set themselves up as a priesthood that "knows better" than the woefully misguided, uninformed American people.

In another section below, "The Seductions of Expertise in Risk Assessment," two excerpts explain the problems with "expertise-ism." Even experts who know a great deal about formal risk assessment models may not be knowledgeable about a particular type of risk—say, the pathways through which humans are exposed to toxic substances in the environment. But more to the point, the views of experts are colored by their own life experiences. They are not necessarily more credible or valuable than the perspectives of citizens or victims, whose actual experiences, let us recall, are nearly always the impetus for congressional action in the first place.

Regulatory agencies live in a nether zone between science, which prefers to defer judgment until sufficient evidence and testing have been completed, and government policymaking, which has an affirmative responsibility to take action against known dangers as rapidly as possible. No federal agency can ever fully resolve all of the scientific issues facing it, yet it still must decide what protections should be required. Regulatory policy is the tool used by agencies to bridge the inevitable factual gaps and take into account the social values embedded in congressional law.

For too long, risk assessment proponents in academia and the agencies have pretended that regulation is an exercise in scientific expertise—no more, no less. But the real question posed by risk assessment is whose policy judgments shall be enacted—those of Congress or those of purported "experts" making "scientific" judgments? If the democratic process means anything, we should prefer the difficult complexities of the former to the specious certitude of the latter.

## Scientific Uncertainty: An Inescapable Aspect of Regulation

In 1983, a committee appointed by the National Research Council (NRC) of the National Academy of Sciences (NAS) concluded that scientific uncertainty is the "dominant analytic difficulty" in the risk assessment process. The committee's seminal report on risk assessment, often referred to as the "Red Book," declared:

> Risk assessment draws extensively on science, and a strong scientific basis has developed for linking exposure to chemicals to chronic health effects. However, data may be incomplete, and there is often great uncertainty in estimates of the types, probability, and magnitude of health effects associated with a chemical agent, of the economic effects of a proposed regulatory action, and of the extent of current and possible future human exposures.

> These problems have no immediate solutions, given the many gaps in our understanding of the causal mechanisms of carcinogenesis and other health effects and in our ability to ascertain the nature or extent of the effects associated with specific exposures. Because our knowledge is limited, conclusive direct evidence of a threat to human health is rare.[5]

A decade later, in 1994, another NAS/NRC committee concluded that "those gaps in our knowledge remain, and yield only with difficulty to new scientific findings."[6] The report identified 16 separate generic sources of uncertainty that plague a typical risk assessment exercise.[7] These included uncertainties in:

- hazard identification (e.g., different study qualities; different study results; extrapolation of available evidence to target human populations);
- dose-response assessment (e.g., the definition of "positive responses" in a given study; the model selected for low-dose risk extrapolation);

- exposure assessment (e.g., exposure-route identification; population stability over time; characterization of the contamination-scenario); and
- risk characterization (uncertainties in the above components of hazard identification, dose-response assessment, and exposure assessment).

The report also criticized the "'false sense of certainty,' which is *caused* by a refusal to acknowledge and (attempt to) quantify the uncertainty in risk predictions."[8]

*Taking Action Despite Imperfect Knowledge: The Case of Ethylene Oxide (EtO)*

How does a regulatory agency grapple with inevitable gaps in its scientific knowledge while still moving forward to protect the public health? Perhaps the best way to gain a practical understanding of this challenge is to examine a representative case study. We have selected the case of EtO, a highly carcinogenic toxic substance used as a sterilizing agent, fumigant, pesticide, and chemical additive.

The science and the Occupational Safety and Health Administration (OSHA) rulemaking that eventually lowered the exposure level for EtO were both highly complicated. But the court's opinion upholding OSHA's regulation—written by Judge Carl C. McGowan, a highly regarded judge near the end of his career—is a lucid explanation for how regulatory agencies can responsibly assess and regulate the risks posed by toxic substances despite (inevitable) limits in scientific knowledge.

Judge McGowan's opinion in *Public Citizen Health Research Group v. Tyson*[9] starts by invoking the statutory mandate for OSHA—that the agency "assure . . . every working man and woman in the Nation safe and healthful working conditions." After reviewing the legal history of the case, the opinion considers the scientific evidence, its limitations and the risk assessment process. Finally, the opinion illuminates the sometimes-intrusive institutional role that the OMB, which has come to be the executive branch instrument for requiring agencies to prepare formal risk assessments and cost-benefit analyses for major rules.

EtO was originally developed as a poison gas in World War I, but it soon found applications in a number of consumer products—automobile antifreeze, textiles, films, bottles, and detergents. Judge McGowan described how EtO posed hazards to certain workers:

> The bulk of EtO usage occurs in manufacturing, and a small fraction is consumed in the sterilization of hospital instruments. EtO is a highly reactive gas. Thus, in manufacturing processes employing EtO, tightly closed and highly automated systems are used. Nevertheless, workers can be exposed to the chemical during both shipping and equipment maintenance. While hospital sterilization accounts for only a small portion of the nation's EtO usage, it is far more hazardous to workers. Workers must enter areas where EtO is, or has been, present. For example, instruments are typically placed in a sterilization chamber which is then flooded with EtO. These sterilization chambers must be purged of

35

the gas before workers can enter. The process is imperfect, and workers risk exposure to the chemical.[10]

When OSHA first began operations as a regulatory agency, it adopted existing exposure limits for EtO of 50 parts per million (ppm) averaged over an eight-hour period (a time-weighted average (TWA)). The standard had been developed by the American Conference of Governmental Industrial Hygienists (ACGIH). At this level, it was estimated that 40 to 500 people out of every 1,000 exposed would die of cancer.

In 1981, ACGIH lowered its recommended permissible exposure level (PEL) to 10 ppm. It also designated EtO as a suspected carcinogen and proposed an even lower PEL of 5 ppm. The industrial hygienists based their reconsideration on a two-year study of rats exposed to EtO. In June of 1982, ACGIH recommended a PEL of 1 ppm, to take effect in 1984.

Citing the scientific evidence and the ACGIH recommendation, Public Citizen and the American Federation of State, County, and Municipal Employees union that represents hospital workers, filed a petition with OSHA in 1981 requesting that the exposure limit be reduced from 50 ppm to 1 ppm over an eight-hour period. OSHA initially denied the petition, but after some legal prodding by Public Citizen, OSHA agreed that it would complete the rulemaking by June 15, 1984.

On June 14, OSHA had a final rule in hand, one that provided for a 1 ppm exposure limit and a 10 ppm short-term exposure limit (STEL) for a 15-minute TWA. OSHA did not publish that final rule.

Judge McGowan explained the legal circumstances that led to the court challenge:

> Pursuant to Executive Order No. 12,291, OSHA transmitted its final rule to the Office of Management and Budget (OMB) for review. Executive Order 12,291 provides that to the extent permissible by law, regulations of agencies within the executive branch must comply with certain substantive requirements. The Order requires agencies to consider cost/benefit analysis, cost effectiveness, maximization of benefit to society, condition of the regulated industries, and conditions of the national economy. Moreover, the Order requires agencies to prepare a "Regulatory Impact Analysis," a document evaluating the proposed regulations in light of the above substantive requirements. This analysis must be sent to OMB. Finally, agencies must defer final action until they have responded to OMB's view. In this case, OMB questioned several aspects of OSHA's final rule, especially the benefits that the EtO rule would provide to society and its cost-effectiveness. These objections applied to both the PEL and the STEL. OMB objected to the STEL in particular as unsupported by any reasonable risk assessment or inference from the available scientific evidence.

> Notwithstanding OMB's objections, OSHA published as a final rule the long-term limits embodied in the PEL. The final rule requires employers to ensure that their employees are not exposed to an airborne concentration of EtO in excess of 1 ppm as an eight-hour TWA. * * *

> While OSHA did not heed OMB's objections with regard to the PEL, it did reserve judgment on the STEL. Rather than issue the STEL as part of the final EtO standard, OSHA reopened the record for comments on the desirability of a

STEL. Commentary was once again divided, and on January 2, 1985, OSHA issued its final rule declining to impose a STEL. This action contrasted with OSHA's earlier decision, prior to receiving OMB's comments, to issue a 10 ppm STEL.

Petitioner Public Citizen launches a two-pronged attack on OSHA's decision not to issue the STEL. First, Public Citizen claims that the decision not to issue a STEL is unsupported on the record. The Ethylene Oxide Industry Council (EOIC) appears as amicus to support OSHA's decision not to issue a STEL. Second, Public Citizen argues that OMB's role in these proceedings was unlawful. In the latter argument, Public Citizen is joined by several members of the House of Representatives as amici.

The Association of Ethylene Oxide Users (AEOU) also petitions this court for review, arguing that OSHA's decision to issue the PEL is unsupported on the record.[11]

## OSHA's Risk Assessment of EtO

To listen to the critics of "junk science," one might conclude that regulatory agencies live in some *Alice in Wonderland* world, issuing arbitrary edicts based on nonsense. Judge McGowan's review of OSHA's risk assessment, however, shows how painstaking and conscientious the scientific evaluations generally are.[12] While somewhat technical, the following passage from the court opinion is instructive for what it reveals about the rigor of agency risk assessments:

---

\* \* \* \*

A. Evidence of Carcinogenicity
 OSHA concluded that there is a relationship between exposure to EtO and a significant increase in the risk of death from cancer. The agency based its finding on two types of evidence: epidemiological studies and experimental studies.

1. Epidemiological Evidence.
 OSHA relied on a study by Morgan and two studies by Hogstedt for evidence of "a possible association between occupational exposure to ethylene oxide and death from leukemia."

 Morgan studied the mortality levels of workers employed at an EtO chemical plant over the course of twenty-two years. Measurements taken at the plant in 1977 showed no detectable EtO levels in most of the production areas. Measurements elsewhere at the plant showed levels well below 50 ppm. The mortality rate among the workers was less than expected from such a population sample and no incidence of leukemia was reported. The study did find, however, a significant increase in pancreatic cancer and Hodgkin's disease.

 Hogstedt I revealed three cases of leukemia occurring between 1972 and 1977 among 230 workers at a Swedish factory where EtO was employed to sterilize hospital equipment. Only 0.2 deaths were expected in such a population during that time span. In 1977, the EtO level in the area where two of the employees who died had worked was estimated at 10-30 ppm.

Hogstedt II examined 243 workers who had worked at a Swedish EtO production facility for at least one year. The workers were tracked for 16 years, and the study revealed a significant excess mortality rate among employees who worked full-time in EtO production areas. The authors found no excess mortality among part-time or intermittently exposed workers.

OSHA admitted that each of these studies was flawed in some way. AEOU [the Association of Ethylene Oxide Users, an industry group] renews here its arguments against the probative value of these studies, urging us to fault the agency for relying on them at all. OSHA, however, did not blindly rely on these studies; the agency recognized and accounted for the methodological weaknesses inherent in the studies.

The agency heard conflicting testimony on the Morgan study, including a statement from Morgan himself that the study failed to support a causal link between EtO and leukemia and thus should be considered as negative evidence on EtO's carcinogenic properties. The study clearly demonstrates, however, a link between EtO and pancreatic cancer and Hodgkin's disease. As some commenters suggested, the study underestimated the cancer risk, the study was inconclusive rather than negative on leukemia risk, and the study was "a strong piece of evidence indicating that even in very small cohorts, with exposures well below the current OSHA standard, excess cancer risk . . . was detected."

Commenters criticized Hogstedt I because of the small sample size, and the fact that the subject workers were exposed to methyl formate along with EtO. OSHA, however, noted that it had no evidence that methyl formate was carcinogenic. Hogstedt II faced similar criticism: workers were exposed to multiple chemical combinations along with EtO. Despite these criticisms, only two commenters concluded that the evidence did not establish an increased risk of cancer. Even one of those commenters stated that the studies "may not provide as much reassurance [that EtO is not a carcinogen] as some would like." In contrast, NIOSH [the National Institute for Occupational Safety and Health] concluded that the Hogstedt studies provide evidence of a possible relationship between EtO exposure and leukemia.

We cannot accept AEOU's [American Ethylene Oxide Users'] proposition that these studies are rendered totally valueless by their methodological flaws. While each study does suffer from defects, OSHA did not rely on the epidemiological studies as conclusive evidence of the carcinogenic nature of EtO. Rather, OSHA found "that the epidemiological evidence, although not by itself conclusive, is supportive of EtO's potential carcinogenic . . . effects." Moreover, OSHA did not reach this position in the face of unified, contrary scientific thought. Indeed, the record demonstrates that OSHA's acceptance of these studies for some, but not conclusive, evidence of EtO's potential carcinogenic effects was supported by a substantial portion of the scientists who attended the rulemaking hearings.

These epidemiological studies, while of some value by themselves, take on added significance when viewed in light of the experimental evidence in the record.

2. Experimental Evidence.

OSHA relied on two studies examining the effects of EtO exposure on animals for further evidence of the chemical's carcinogenicity: the Bushy Run rat study and the NIOSH rat and monkey study.

In the Bushy Run study, researchers at the Bushy Run Research Center in Pittsburgh exposed rats to EtO at concentrations of 100, 33, and 10 ppm for 6 hours per day, 5 days per week. This study produced a number of significant results, indicating that ETO exposure was related to development of various types of cancers. Many commenters objected to four particular aspects of the Bushy Run study.

First, the rats suffered a viral infection during the course of the study. Some commenters suggested that the infection could have adversely affected the immune systems of the rats, thus invalidating the results. OSHA concluded, however, based on testimony of the director of the study and an expert pathologist from the National Cancer Institute, that the outbreak had no substantial effect on the outcome of the study.

Second, other commenters suggested that the type of leukemia produced in the Bushy Run rats had no counterpart in other strains of rats, in mice, or in humans. OSHA specifically rejected this assertion, relying on expert testimony that recent studies had described similar leukemia in humans.

Third, EOIC [Ethylene Oxide Industry Council] suggested that the only types of tumors appearing in the test rats were types that occur in rats spontaneously. This fact indicated that ETO might promote tumor growth, rather than initiate it. OSHA heard expert testimony that tumor-promoters can simultaneously be tumor-initiators, and thus carcinogenic, as well. The same expert stated that tumor-promoters might be as dangerous in ultimately causing cancer as chemicals that are not categorized as promoters.

Finally, OSHA rejected an argument that the statistical analyses performed on the Bushy Run data were misleading. OSHA confirmed the Bushy Run researchers' statistical methodology and specifically reanalyzed the evidence under a "worst case" theory, concluding that the results were essentially accurate. Thus, OSHA found that the Bushy Run study demonstrates that exposure to EtO significantly increases mortality and the incidence of tumors among rats.

The second experimental study was a two-year study of rats and monkeys conducted by NIOSH. These animals were exposed to EtO at concentrations of 50 and 100 ppm. During the study, however, the rats contracted an infection that killed a large portion of the group. Once the infection had dispersed, researchers resumed the study.

The NIOSH study revealed an increased incidence of leukemia in rats exposed to 50 ppm EtO, but not in rats exposed to 100 ppm EtO. The study did reveal a relationship in rats between tumor production and EtO exposure. The results paralleled those of the Bushy Run study. None of the monkeys demonstrated any evidence of leukemia, but there was some evidence of central nervous system damage.

Significantly, "the overwhelming majority of comments on the NIOSH study agreed with OSHA's conclusions that these preliminary results provide additional evidence of EtO's carcinogenicity in experimental animals." Two commenters stated that taken together, the Bushy Run and NIOSH studies produced consistent, disturbing results with regard to tumor production.[13]

### 3. OSHA's Conclusions.

Taking the epidemiological and experimental studies together, OSHA found that EtO causes cancer in laboratory animals and poses a significant cancer risk for humans. While each study individually may not be a model of textbook scientific inquiry, the cumulative evidence is compelling. OSHA takes precisely this view: "Although these studies do not provide definitive evidence of carcinogenicity, they are suggestive of an association between occupational exposure to EtO and cancer (leukemia) mortality."

This court's role is not to review the evidence *de novo* to arrive at our own estimate of the risks; rather, we look for substantial evidence supporting OSHA's finding of EtO carcinogenicity. A reasonable person could draw from this evidence the conclusion that exposure to EtO presents a risk of cancer. Thus, the substantial evidence test is met. Even if a reasonable person could also draw the opposite conclusion, we must uphold the agency's findings.

---

*The Court's Ruling on EtO*

Judge McGowan rejected OSHA's claim that there was insufficient scientific evidence to lower the PEL. Citing the U.S. Supreme Court's ruling requiring automatic crash protection in motor vehicles,[14] the court wrote that in cases such as these, it is not infrequent that the available data do not settle a regulatory issue, and the agency must then exercise its judgment in moving from facts and probabilities on the record to a policy conclusion.

> OSHA faces just such a problem in regulating EtO exposure. The scientific evidence in the instant case is incomplete but what evidence we have paints a striking portrait of serious danger to workers exposed to the chemical. When the evidence can be reasonably interpreted as supporting the need for regulation, we must affirm the agency's conclusion, despite the fact that the same evidence is susceptible of another interpretation. Our expertise does not lie in technical matters.[15]

The court, however, rejected OSHA's rationale for refusing to promulgate an STEL. While the court acknowledged its deference to an agency's expertise in most cases, it held that OSHA had not "exercised its expertise" regarding the issue of whether a STEL was necessary to protect workers. The court found that OSHA had made an assumption regarding the behavior of employers—that they would reduce short-term exposures in order to meet their mandate to reduce long-term exposures—for which there was no evidence in the rulemaking record, and it remanded the issue back to the agency for further consideration of this point.

## Why Companies "Choose Ignorance"

What levels of risk in consumer products and technologies are socially accept-able? Advocates of "regulatory reform" typically argue that the marketplace is the best judge. Citing free-market economic theory, they argue that the laws of supply and demand should determine which products are too risky and which have benefits that outweigh the risks.[16] If that choice is made by some paternal-istic "federal nanny," it will trample upon people's freedom of choice and intro-duce wasteful "inefficiencies" to the market.

So goes the theory. In real life, however, the theoretical assumptions of the free market do not necessarily prevail. Consumer choice has a moral legitimacy and functional power only if consumers are fully informed. But that is fre-quently not the case in matters of health, safety, and environmental risk. Indeed, in this context, the marketplace in practice tends to produce *uninformed* con-sumers. Most manufacturers and retailers find this an attractive situation.

This section explores the perplexing reality that manufacturers have keen in-centives to *choose ignorance.* There are practical economic and competitive rea-sons why the manufacturer of a chemical or other technology prefers to remain ignorant of the actual risks it is dispersing via the marketplace. It might jeopar-dize sales and profits. Naturally, every company wishes to project a safe and san-guine perspective of its product and has very little incentive to call attention to its product's risks. No shareholder or potential investor is eager to hear about a prod-uct's downside potential, and the buying public may well shun a product if it ap-pears to be unsafe or ecologically harmful. Not surprisingly, corporations are not eager to spend money to generate troublesome information.

A company might reasonably worry that any risk-related information it gen-erates could provoke new regulatory controls or an outright recall of a product already on the market. Of course, there is always a risk that a product that causes harm will give rise to lawsuits in the future. But as Professor Wagner points out in excerpts below, that potential is easily ignorable at the time a manufacturer is deciding whether to put a product on the market in the first place.[17]

Professor Wagner suggests that companies who manufacture potentially dangerous products have strong incentives to "choose ignorance" instead of spending resources to ascertain the actual health, safety, and environmental risks of their products. She points out that common-law rules do not encourage companies to test their products because in toxic tort litigation, the burden of proving causation is on the plaintiff. Companies are also disinclined to sponsor probing product safety studies lest the results prove useful in a regulatory con-text. This is especially true because even a minimal testing project can yield considerable information at very little expense.

It should not be surprising that regulatory agencies seeking to develop new protective regulations often find that there is only scarce or irregular scientific information available. Even though the industries responsible for the risks could clarify the scientific uncertainties, often at small cost, they have few in-centives to do so. University scientists sometimes investigate health, safety, and environmental risks, but their work may or may not satisfy regulatory risk assessments. In many instances, corporate funding skews the research agendas of a given scientific field, rewarding research that might produce marketable outcomes and ignoring research that might trigger regulatory attention.

In certain areas, Congress has enacted statutes, like the Federal Insecticide, Fungicide, and Rodenticide Act and the Federal Food, Drug, and Cosmetics Act, to empower agencies to require private companies to test their products. But these powers are either limited—applying to only particular products, for example—or are fiercely resisted by industry. The Toxic Substances Control Act empowers EPA to order testing of chemical substances, but companies fight such testing requirements, forcing EPA to justify them in lengthy rule-making exercises.

It should therefore come as no surprise that very few chemical substances that have found their way into the environment and workplaces have been adequately tested to determine their health, safety, and environmental risks. This dearth of data has obvious implications for the larger risk assessment enterprise.

---

There is a widely held perception that scientific research on the long-term safety of products is produced spontaneously and in abundance, irrespective of the law. Some commentators even appear to believe that, to the extent the law matters, it encourages safety research. For the vast majority of potentially toxic products, however, these perceptions are wrong. No toxicity research is available for over 80 percent of the chemicals in commerce, and the common-law rules are, in part, responsible for this dearth of information.

Indeed, rather than promoting safety testing for latent harms, the current common-law liability rules act to penalize it. Before a complaint can be filed against a manufacturer for latent harms, the common law requires victims to produce scientific research that demonstrates a cause-and-effect relationship between the manufacturer's product and the plaintiff's injuries. Unfortunately, it is the manufacturers that are better able, but disinclined, to produce this research due to pervasive failures in both the market and government regulatory programs. Manufacturers can thus minimize their liability through their research programs. A manufacturer that conducts no research can generally avoid liability because plaintiffs and government research programs are unlikely to conduct scientific research on their own. Voluntary safety research, on the other hand, might reveal a long-term risk associated with a product, a revelation that could provide vital evidence for aggressive plaintiffs' attorneys and ultimately increase, rather than reduce, the manufacturer's exposure to lawsuits and potentially catastrophic liability. The failure of the common-law courts to provide manufacturers with reliable immunity after the manufacturer has conducted an exemplary safety testing program exacerbates the self-incriminatory effect of voluntary safety research.

Given this common-law treatment of safety research, it would be surprising if manufacturers ever conducted voluntary research on the long-term hazards of their products. * * * If manufacturers face virtually no penalty for remaining ignorant about the latent health risks of potentially toxic products, but risk crushing liability if they learn of long-term hazards, it is only rational for manufacturers to choose ignorance. Studies documenting the paucity of testing available for most products confirm that manufacturers are making this rational choice.

Although the "trans-scientific" limitations of science are significant, science can provide considerable information about the long-term risks a chemical poses to human health. Over a decade ago, the NRC recognized the need to conduct cost-effective toxicity tests. As a result, it identified a battery of thirty-three laboratory tests that scientists can use to reach some general conclusions regarding the potential of a chemical to cause cancer, neurological and reproductive hazards, and birth defects.[18] Such tests generally provide, within several orders of magnitude, a rough idea of the human health risks posed by a product. For substances in commerce that are likely to have more limited paths for exposure to humans, the NRC recognized that as few as eleven of the thirty-three recommended toxicity tests could be sufficient for a health assessment, while an initial basic screening of the health risks posed by a substance could be accomplished with one or two tests.

To determine which scientific uncertainties regarding a chemical's toxicity are "preventable," safety testing can be split into a very basic or "minimal" level of research and a much higher or "comprehensive" level of research. Minimal safety research generally consists of one or more short-term laboratory tests designed to determine if a product is likely to constitute a serious hazard. The second level of testing, or the comprehensive level of research, consists of a series of studies sufficient to resolve most remaining, scientifically answerable questions regarding the extent of the hazard. These studies constitute a full assessment. Depending on the concentration of the product and routes of exposure, this second level of testing might require a substantial investment of resources and time.

An examination of the research conducted on the long-term safety of chemicals reveals that considerable preventable scientific uncertainty exists, even at the minimal level of testing. In its comprehensive 1984 study, which still remains largely up-to-date, the NRC found that for approximately 80% of the estimated 48,523 unregulated chemicals in commerce, no toxicity information existed. For the remaining chemicals in commerce, scientific uncertainty was also prevalent—a full health assessment could not be completed for any of these chemicals. In addition, the NRC found that the quality of testing was inadequate for over 30% of the studies that had been conducted.

Market forces, internal management practices, and regulatory shortcomings combine to create an environment where preventable scientific uncertainty is prevalent. From a market perspective, comprehensive testing programs are not only costly and time-consuming, but they do little to improve the marketability of a product. Consumers appear to assume that most products are safe, regardless of the presence or absence of costly research programs. The long delay from exposure to injury, the relatively low probability of harm, and the unlikelihood that customers will be able to link latent adverse effects with the manufacturer, provide further assurance that the market will not discriminate between a tested and an untested product. In contrast, if a manufacturer does invest in testing, and in doing so discovers that some risk of latent harm exists, marketing the product typically will be much more difficult.

Governmental efforts to correct the underproduction of safety information only partially offset a manufacturer's tendency to remain ignorant regarding the latent effects of products. Several federal regulatory programs do require safety testing prior to, and in rare cases after, registration of the product, but these testing requirements have been severely criticized for their less than perfect implementation.[19] Even giving these testing requirements the benefit of the doubt, the vast majority of products remain largely unaffected—testing is simply not required for most chemicals.

In fact, in some circumstances existing regulatory programs may create additional incentives for manufacturers to remain ignorant rather than invest in developing information on the long-term safety of their products. If a manufacturer voluntarily reports research demonstrating that its product might not be safe, it is likely to be rewarded only with a demand by a regulatory agency either to conduct additional testing or to undergo lengthy regulatory proceedings regarding possible market restrictions on its product. In contrast, a manufacturer who reports no knowledge of adverse effects of its product—precisely because it has avoided investigating possible harms—is likely to be successful in dodging regulatory oversight. The low proportion of chemical products that are accompanied by long-term safety research suggests that, at the very least, disclosure requirements do not encourage toxicity research for a large percentage of potentially toxic products.

Public testing programs, which are often created as part of a regulatory program, also fail to fill the information void. Although government testing provides vital information, resource constraints often limit testing to only a small number of chemicals annually, leaving the vast majority of products unstudied. As of 1987, the government had conducted animal carcinogenicity bioassays on only 308 substances out of 594 that were nominated by various agencies for testing,[20] but since that time a gradually shrinking budget has led the government to test even fewer chemicals.[21]

---

### Scientific Charades as an Evasion of Responsibility

If good science is based upon a humility about making judgments—an eagerness to wait for better data and more conclusive studies—the regulatory process operates under a very different set of imperatives. When there is a chemical or technological hazard endangering the public, regulators have legal and moral obligations to take action. It is not a realistic option to commission additional studies, wait for a scientific consensus and make an airtight case.

Necessarily, policy must play a large role in interpreting the best scientific data available. Regulators must draw reasonable inferences from the data and use mathematical models to extrapolate from laboratory data to real-world hazards. The NAS Red Book observed that "both scientific judgments and policy choices may be involved in selecting from among possible inferential bridges, and we have used the term *risk assessment policy* to differentiate those judgments and choices from the broader social and economic policy issues that are inherent in risk management decisions."[22]

This section explores this tension between science and regulation, and explains why policy must inevitably drive most risk assessments. In the first of two excerpts, Prof. Howard Latin challenges the notion that risk assessment is merely a matter of applying scientific expertise to the available facts. First, he points out, the "facts" are frequently not ascertainable because no one has commissioned the studies needed to divine the facts. Some studies could not be practicably designed even if someone were willing to pay for them.

Second, scientific expertise is inadequate because there is much that science simply does not know. Scientists have a poor understanding of the basic science underlying toxicity assessment, for example, and so cannot truly resolve many of the uncertainties that pervade regulatory decisionmaking. Inescapably, "social consequences" and "political values" must play a large role in any risk assessment, even before the agency applies the risk assessment in the larger decisionmaking process. It is important to keep in mind that the real goal of the risk assessment exercise is not "scientific truth" (because that cannot be determined) so much as sound regulatory decisions.

But many people simply do not want to acknowledge that social policy plays an influential, legitimate role in regulatory judgments. They prefer to hide the policies that drive the decisionmaking process behind the veneer of scientific objectivity—a practice that Professor Wagner called a "science charade." By pretending that science can lead to unassailable regulatory decisions, federal agencies often seek to avoid responsibility for the policies that they actually use in risk assessments. By adopting a scientific perspective, it may *seem* that policy values have been purged from the risk assessment process. In fact, they may simply be incorporated in a tacit, *sub rosa* fashion, without public scrutiny or discussion. That is why pleas by regulated industries and their academic allies for "sound science" are frequently disingenuous. What they really seek are business-friendly outcomes, not better quality science. The rigor of the science can already be addressed by companies themselves, but the real goal is not high quality science, but a "favorable" regulatory judgment. These issues are discussed by Professor Latin in the excerpt that follows[23]:

---

Regulation of toxic substances is an extremely complex, uncertain, and controversial enterprise. The regulatory process is customarily divided into two discrete functions: risk assessment ostensibly is a scientific activity that develops estimates of health hazards at varying exposure levels, while risk management is a political activity that balances competing interests and values to determine whether identified toxic risks should be considered unacceptable or tolerable. This sharp distinction between the scientific and social policy dimensions of toxics regulation is embodied in EPA's guidelines for estimating carcinogenic hazards, which provide that risk assessments must "use the most scientifically appropriate interpretation" and should "be carried out independently from considerations of the consequences of regulatory action." The requirement for adoption of the "most scientifically appropriate interpretation" reflects EPA's current priority on attaining "good science" in risk-assessment proceedings. In other words, EPA and other federal agencies now stress the need for scientifically credible risk assessments and presume that their analyses should be grounded exclusively on the best available scientific theories and data even if the resulting predictions do not achieve the degree of reliability ordinarily required for valid scientific conclusions.

This Article challenges the conventional view that scientific perspectives should dominate the risk-assessment process. To paraphrase Talleyrand, risk assessment is too important and too uncertain to be left exclusively to the risk-assessors. I contend instead that social policy considerations must play as prominent a role in the choice of risk estimates as in the ultimate determination of which predicted risks should be deemed unacceptable.

Three interconnected themes, which are developed throughout the ensuing discussion, support the Article's central thesis that explicit social policy choices should influence agency selections of risk-assessment principles and specific risk estimates:

Inadequate scientific knowledge and inadequate data usually prevent derivation of risk estimates based on reliable science. Toxic risk assessment suffers from fundamental uncertainties about causal mechanisms for cancer and other hazards, extrapolative relationships between high-dose and low-dose responses and between animal test data and human risks, latent effects and latency periods, special sensitivities in exposed subpopulations, synergistic or co-carcinogenic effects of various substances, past and present exposure levels, dispersion patterns for contaminants, and virtually every other area of required knowledge. These uncertainties generally preclude reliable assessments of relevant effects, and there is no scientific consensus on how they should be resolved. For example, conflicting risk estimates submitted in Food and Drug Administration (FDA) proceedings on saccharine varied by more than a millionfold; and predictions of the hazards posed by TCE, a drinking-water contaminant, varied by many millions. One discussion of TCE regulation noted that the "estimates provide a range of uncertainty equivalent to not knowing whether one has enough money to buy a cup of coffee or pay off the national debt."[24]

Under current regulatory practices, Agency scientists produce risk assessments that seldom approach the level of reliability normally expected of scientific findings; indeed, many estimates are little more than educated guesses. Yet, the choice among competing estimates—a prediction of only a minuscule hazard or one million times greater—can determine whether toxic exposures are characterized as "acceptable" or "unacceptable" irrespective of any values in the risk-management process. Absent a scientific consensus on which risk-assessment principles should be applied, I contend that an agency's choice among competing risk estimates should not be exclusively a result of provisional scientific judgments. If substantial uncertainty exists about the extent of toxic hazards and the possible benefits from risk reduction, social consequences and political values must play an integral role in determining which speculative risk estimates are adopted.

There is an inherent tension between the disciplinary norms of good science and good regulation. Unlike in pure scientific research, where the proper response to uncertainty is reservation of judgment pending the development of adequate data and testable hypotheses, the risk-assessment process cannot be suspended without significant social consequences. A finding that a vital issue is currently indeterminate would be entirely consistent with the practice of good science, but "no decision" on a possible toxic hazard inescapably is a decision that promotes interests which benefit from the regulatory status quo. Risk assessment is not driven by the pursuit of knowledge for its own sake, the explicit goal of science, but by the need to decide whether potentially severe health hazards should be allowed to continue or whether high control costs should be imposed with potentially severe economic consequences. Thus, scientists in regulatory proceedings are expected to produce "answers" in a timely manner even if their predictions are highly speculative. Any reluctance to relax the standards of proof and certainty generally required of valid science may introduce a bias in favor of regulatory inaction.

Science aims at the dispassionate pursuit of truth. In contrast, scientists in risk-assessment proceedings frequently represent industries, labor unions, consumers, environmentalists, or agency bureaucracies with great interests at stake. These affiliations may often explicitly or unintentionally color interpretations of available evidence. Scientists seldom base conclusions on data and experiments that cannot be reproduced, but information in regulatory hearings is routinely submitted by affected parties and frequently cannot be replicated or effectively challenged by other participants. Scientists tend to design research studies in light of which data are available and which experiments may be feasible, whereas the critical questions in risk-assessment proceedings are usually determined by statutory or judicial requirements that need not be responsive to the state of scientific knowledge. Budgetary and time limitations often influence the scientific research agenda, but no good scientist would feel that definitive answers must be produced irrespective of resource constraints. The opposite predisposition may be appropriate for good regulators. These comments are not intended to call into question the competence or ethics of all scientists who participate in risk assessments. Rather, the point is that the risk-assessment process is fundamentally shaped by the requirements, constraints, and adversarial climate of regulation, not by the disciplinary norms of science.

The illusion that risk assessment is a purely scientific activity reduces the visibility and political accountability of policy judgments that often guide regulatory decisions on toxic hazards. A comparison of conflicting risk-assessment principles adopted by agencies under different administrations shows that regulators frequently do consider policy criteria when they select specific risk estimates. Federal agencies have recently employed controversial risk-assessment assumptions to justify inaction on some hazardous substances. Regulators have also attempted to make determinations based on "good science" without considering the implications of this approach for decisionmaking costs, regulatory de-lays, and opportunities for obstructive or strategic behavior by affected parties. Risk assessors often respond to scientific uncertainties by adopting conservative safety-oriented positions on some important issues while they use best-current-scientific-guess, middle-of-the-range, methodological-convenience, or least-cost treatments on other material issues. EPA and other agencies have never explained the scientific or policy rationales underlying these inconsistent treat-ments of uncertainty, and risk managers may not recognize that substantial in-consistency exists. In light of these diverse risk-assessment practices, I contend that regulatory policy judgments as well as scientific judgments must be applied coherently, explained forthrightly, and tested actively through public debate. * * * It is important to stress that thousands of lives and billions of dollars in regu-latory costs may depend on an agency's choice of controversial risk-assess-ment principles.

There has been any number of discussions in the legal and public policy litera-ture about mechanisms intended to improve the efficiency of environmental regu-lation through reliance on cost-benefit, risk-utility, or cost-effectiveness analyses. These strategies are fundamentally dependent on the quality of regulatory risk assessments, and yet most commentators treat the risk-assessment process as a "black box" and assume that agencies must always produce the best available scientific predictions regardless of the imperfect state of the art. Regulators can-not avoid determining the social and legal consequences of scientific uncertainty, but there is no assurance that they will do so in a systematic manner responsive to legislative objectives. Not only have agencies generally failed to explain the im-plicit policies that shape their risk-assessment practices, but it also appears that regulators often have not recognized the social ramifications of their own treat-ments. Moreover, current risk-assessment practices are less consistent and less reliable than agency scientists typically concede.

Because predictions of toxic effects generally cannot be grounded on reliable scientific judgments, social policy criteria must play an influential role in the choice among competing risk estimates. Once we recognize that toxic sub-stances regulation requires a panoply of policy determinations to supplement provisional scientific judgments, it is essential that risk-assessment agencies ex-plicitly consider the social ramifications of scientific uncertainty, strive for analyti-cal coherence in their treatments of currently indeterminate issues, and clearly explain the principles, practices, and values underlying particular estimates of toxic hazards.

---

The scientific charade that many regulatory agencies conduct is explored further in the excerpt below by Professor Wagner.[25]

---

Science has been the thorn in the side of environmental policy-makers since the dawn of environmental law. Sound environmental policy cannot be developed without some scientific basis; yet attempts to incorporate science into environmental regulations have met with failure. Reduced public participation, excessive regulatory delays, and the incomplete and inaccurate incorporation of science have plagued science-based environmental regulation for nearly three decades.

Despite growing pressure for an improved science-based regulatory system, however, surprisingly little effort has been dedicated to determining why past science-based regulatory strategies have failed. This Article squarely confronts this question by positing that these past failures are at least partly attributable to a pervasive "science charade," where agencies exaggerate the contributions made by science in setting toxic standards in order to avoid accountability for the underlying policy decisions. Although camouflaging controversial policy decisions as science assists the agency in evading various political, legal, and institutional forces, doing so ultimately delays and distorts the standard-setting mission, leaving in its wake a dysfunctional regulatory program.

First, and despite appearances to the contrary, contemporary science is incapable of completely resolving the level at which a chemical will pose some specified, quantitative risk to humans. In assessing the health risks of formaldehyde, for example, scientific experimentation can establish the effects of high doses of formaldehyde on the total number of nasal tumors in laboratory mice, but quantification of the effects of low doses on humans currently lies beyond the reach of science.

Nuclear physicist Alvin Weinberg first identified these gaps in knowledge as "trans-science"—"questions which can be asked of science and yet which cannot be answered by science."[26] In contrast to the uncertainty that is characteristic of all of science, in which "the answer" is accompanied by some level of unpreventable statistical noise or uncertainty, trans-scientific questions are uncertain because scientists cannot even perform the experiments to test the hypotheses. This can be due to a variety of technological, informational, and ethical constraints on experimentation. For example, ethical mores prohibit direct testing on humans, leaving investigators to extrapolate the effects of a toxic substance on humans from studies conducted on animals. Even when some segment of the human population has been exposed to a toxic substance, isolating that substance's impact may be statistically impossible because of the many other factors that adversely affect human health.

Since trans-scientific issues arise from a variety of practical and theoretical limitations on scientific experimentation, the ability of science to quantify adverse health effects of low levels of toxins can be quite limited. To reach a final quantitative standard, policy considerations must fill in the gaps that science cannot inform. This combination of science and policy necessary to the resolution of issues concerning toxics regulation has led to the classification of these issues as "science-policy" problems.

A second problem arising in the attempt to quantify health risks is that those insights which science is able to provide are fragmented and occur sporadically throughout the larger investigation. The search for a "safe" concentration of a chemical, which poses only minimal risks to human health, immediately breaks down into a sequence of smaller sub-questions that often alternate between questions that can be resolved with science and others that cannot.

Even for those questions that cannot be resolved by science, however, science plays a small but important role in defining the scientifically plausible "default options" available at each trans-scientific juncture. For example, although the ultimate selection of an extrapolatory model that predicts the effects of a substance at low doses based on high dose data must be based on policy factors, the types of curves which are possible originate in scientific theory. As a result, the contributions of science and policy, although generally separable, are mixed in complicated ways.

In a perfect world, scientists and policy specialists would strive to separate trans-scientific issues from issues that can be resolved with scientific experimentation. Policy choices would be made at each trans-scientific juncture, the basis for each choice would be explained, and the public would find the agency's policy decisions clear and accessible.

Not surprisingly, in the real world a completely different picture emerges. Agency scientists and bureaucrats engage in a "science charade" by failing first to identify the major interstices left by science in the standard-setting process and second to reveal the policy choices they made to fill each trans-scientific gap. Toxics standards promulgated under science-based mandates are covered—from the preamble to the regulatory impact analysis—with scientific explanations, judgments, and citations. Major policy decisions that undergird a quantitative toxic risk standard are at best acknowledged as "agency judgments" or "health policies," terms that receive no elaboration in the often hundreds of pages of agency explanations given for a proposed or final toxic standard and appear in a context that gives readers the impression they are based on science. Although this science charade appears to pervade virtually every toxics rule promulgated since the late 1970s, whether the agency engaged in the charade deliberately or inadvertently appears to vary from standard to standard.

* * * Although some of the reasons agencies disguise policy choices as science seem self-evident, an in-depth analysis of the incentives that motivate an agency and its employees is necessary for a full understanding of the scope and importance of the charade in contemporary toxic risk regulation. Far from uncovering incompetence or carelessness, such an analysis reveals that the agencies are responding to multiple political, legal, and institutional incentives to cloak policy judgments in the garb of science. In fact, no rational agency or administrative official acting in her own self-interest would expose the underlying policy choices when faced with the numerous benefits of engaging in the science charade and the high price to be paid for proceeding any other way. * * *

* * * The tendency of the charade to distance the public, and in some cases even elected or appointed policymakers, from major decisions affecting not only public health but also economic well-being is, in and of itself, a matter of considerable concern. The ramifications of the science charade extend well beyond intrusion into the democratic process, however: the science charade impairs the es-

sential progress and prioritization of standard-setting by miring it in unresolvable scientific complexities. The quality of the science supporting the regulations is also impaired because the agency escapes not only review by the public, but scientific review due to its failure to divulge those questions it considered scientifically uncertain and the sources and range of error it considered in resolving them. In addition, because gaps in scientific knowledge are not highlighted, incentives for scientific research decline, and the public's confidence in science erodes as scientific answers appear illusive and subject to debate.

## The Seductions of Expertise in Risk Assessment

Who is the most appropriate judge of whether a chemical or technological harm should be abated? According to our Constitution, a representative Congress responding to the people is the proper mechanism for determining when government action is needed to control harms to the public. This, in fact, is what led to the enactment of the major health, safety, and environmental statutes—a technological harm became a palpable crisis; a social consensus emerged that a constellation of related problems should be addressed; and Congress responded, issuing appropriate instructions to regulatory agencies.

In recent decades, however, the very critics who rail against unelected bureaucrats making ridiculous health and safety rules want to assign such decisions to another corps of unelected experts—professional risk assessors. They are quick to point out that such assessments must be made according to the most exacting, rigorous metrics, chiefly quantitative, economic and technical. And while the results of such evaluations may indeed be illuminating, they typically do not reflect congressional intent as set forth in federal statutes. Professional risk assessors are frankly contemptuous of democratic verdicts on health, safety, and environmental risks.

"Communities are technically incompetent and therefore in a poor position to make efficient allocations of scarce resources for public health and environmental protection," write John Graham and March Sadowitz.[27] U.S. Supreme Court Justice Stephen Breyer, in his well-known book *Breaking the Vicious Circle*, concludes that the risk perceptions of ordinary folks are often fatuously misinformed: "Study after study shows that the public's evaluation of risk problems differs radically from any consensus of experts in the field."[28]

Once a regulatory controversy is framed as a scientific matter, as explained above, it is a natural corollary that the best judges of what should be done are experts. With the help of corporate backers, a number of academic centers and think tanks have nominated themselves to offer their expertise as professional risk assessors.

Their conclusion? That public perceptions of environmental risks are grossly inaccurate. The argument goes something like this: individual citizens generally lack the time and/or the inclination to inform themselves about the nature and magnitude of health and environmental risks. As a result, they make bad decisions concerning risk in their daily lives, avoiding pesticide-laced apples that pose minimal risk while failing to buckle their automobile seat belts. How can such people be trusted to set national regulatory policies that affect major sectors of the economy?[29] The implicit (and sometimes explicit) solution is for public policymakers to rely much more heavily on professional risk assessors. Only highly trained academics with sufficient expertise in measuring and evaluating risk can make wise and efficient decisions about appropriate government intervention.

Risk assessment advocates are so confident of their superior insight that they do not trust even regulatory agencies to get risk assessments right. John Graham, while at the Harvard Center for Risk Analysis of the Harvard School of Public Health, declared it "questionable whether outstanding research into the scientific foundations of risk analysis can be accomplished within mission-oriented regulatory agencies such as EPA or FDA."[30] Prof. Frank Cross of the University of Texas has warned that reliance on public perceptions of risk invites powerful elites to attempt to manipulate risk perception.[31]

Unwilling to trust either Congress or the regulatory agencies to set intelligent priorities for managing health, safety, and environmental risks, Justice Breyer advocates the creation of an entity patterned on the French Conseil d'Etat, composed of experts in risk assessment to sit in judgment over risk assessments prepared by the regulatory agencies.[32]

The following two articles dispute the suggestion that decisionmaking should be turned over to the experts. Both authors implicitly suggest that the claims of the "experts" frequently reflect the healthy egos of those making such claims. Prof. Eileen Gauna, a long-time student of the environmental justice movement, focuses upon the implications of "expertise-ism" on poor and less well-educated people of color. She notes that even the supposedly objective views of the experts are colored by their own life experiences.

Experts may know a lot about formal risk assessment models, but they may lack expertise in the area that is most relevant to many risk assessments—the pathways through which humans are exposed to toxic substances in the environment. They may also be ignorant of the actual circumstances that give rise to a harm. In a very real sense, the residents of pollution-plagued low-income neighborhoods are experts in environmental injustice, and any scientific or statistical abstractions that seek to represent their situation are likely to omit its moral and social dimensions. Professor Gauna concludes that expertise-ism is at best highly undemocratic, and at worst it produces a regulatory system that unfairly discriminates against the least economically and politically powerful groups in our society.[33]

---

Reliance solely upon formal expertise is unwise. Agency officials cannot be perfect and cannot escape their own interests. They sometimes opt for the path of least resistance in order to avoid pressure and conflict, or pursue a course that allows them to obtain rewards or recognition. Additionally, budget constraints impose limitations upon the full potential of agency expertise. Even the hypothetical selfless, perfectly competent agency official cannot escape the limitations of formal expertise. After all, even the most technical issues involve value judgments and therefore raise political questions beyond the ken of agency expertise. Moreover, a pure expertise model presumes an objectivity that is increasingly subject to question.

From an environmental justice perspective, the ideal of expertise proves particularly problematic when agency expertise is substituted for the participation of powerless and excluded groups. A possible consequence of promoting expertise as paramount is that the agency will proceed without thinking about the environmental justice implications. Or, to the extent that environmental justice is considered, it might be too easy to conclude that an agency expert knows what is best for poor, uneducated people of color. This attitude is reflected in the statement of a former president of NAS who argued that "most members of the public usually don't know enough about any given complicated technical matter to make meaningful informal judgments," and thus science-policy decisions should be left to the "knowledgeable wise men [of science]."[34]

An environmental justice issue that illustrates this risk is the development of water quality standards under the Clean Water Act. Water quality standards are formulated in reference to various uses, such as fishable, swimmable water bodies. Under the act, water bodies are not expected to remain pollution-free, and fish in the water bodies are not expected to be free of pollutants. Rather, the act attempts to keep pollutants below levels that are harmful to people who eat the fish caught from the water body.

Developing the criteria for the water quality standards therefore requires an assumption regarding how much fish people generally eat. One assumption used in the development of standards is that persons potentially consume 6.5 grams per day of fish caught in the same water body over a 70-year period. This assumption was based in part upon surveys of licensed fishers that indicated that the average individual consumed 6.5 grams of estuarine fish per day and 14.3 grams of all types of fish per day. Upon closer examination, it appears that the standards were developed with reference to an occasional fish eater with a varied diet (the licensed angler), a hypothetical person with experiences probably similar to those of the experts who designed the development of the standards.

But what of the experience of residents of rural African-American communities along a 100-mile stretch of Mississippi River where over 125 oil and chemical giants discharge pollutants daily, an area that health and environmental specialists refer to as "Cancer Alley"? These and other poverty-stricken residents rely upon fishing, and thus a diet heavily dependent upon local fish, for subsistence. And what of the experience of certain ethnic minorities, who tend to consume more fish or different fish prepared in ways not contemplated by the experts? The EPA workgroup found that "ethnic minorities are more likely to eat fish with the skin, may be less likely to trim the fat, and are more likely to eat the whole fish."[35] Pollutant-containing, bottom-dwelling fish are consumed more by non-white, low-income populations, and clams and hepatopancreas of crabs are disproportionately consumed by Asians. These patterns of consumption matter because fish with a high-fat content bioaccumulate some pollutants to a higher degree, causing higher exposure to the pollutants in populations that prefer fish with a high-fat content. These behavioral realities defy the assumptions which were central to the development of the standards.

The point is neither to malign experts nor to disparage an agency attempting in some fashion to respond to environmental inequities, but to recognize that everyone, including the expert, is influenced by her own experiences. If experiences of outsiders remain peripheral to the experts' vision, the expert-generated standards might be inadequate to protect excluded groups, regardless of the good intentions of regulators.

Experts have recently come under academic scrutiny, resulting in a variety of related criticisms. These include a "professional myopia," an inability to go beyond their area of expertise to other disciplines as well as to social context; a tendency to focus inquiry upon areas where data is already available while avoiding unstudied but more troubling areas; an inclination to incorporate values differently than would be considered appropriate by the general public; and an approach of reducing multiple, complex risks to a series of independent incomplete risks. These charges have contributed to the ongoing debate over the appropriate role of lay perceptions of risk in environmental regulation.

Not surprisingly, environmental justice activists are critical of expertise as it is understood in the traditional sense. They firmly insist that community residents are experts in their own right and should be consulted and respected as such. The recognition of the community resident as expert is a rejection of traditional reliance solely upon formal expertise. Environmental regulation cannot proceed while blind to social realities, and social realities cannot be explored adequately without the assistance of those whose lives are most impacted by environmental risk. In a very real sense, residents from impacted communities are experts in the reality of environmental inequity. Indigenous, cultural, and community expertise arises not from formal study but from intimacy with social and physical environments over time and often over generations. These forms of expertise are exogenous to the agency and are as important as formal expertise in law, science, and technology. A decisionmaking structure that precludes meaningful participation by community groups cannot hope to achieve systematically equitable environmental protection.

More importantly, reconstruction of the term "expert" to include alternative forms of knowledge destabilizes the position of privilege that formally educated participants enjoy in the environmental policy arena. This reconstruction is necessary when considering that the experts' privileged position unintentionally helped create a status quo of unfair distribution of environmental risk and benefit. The reconstructed term is also consistent with the principles of environmental justice which denounce hierarchies that promote inequity and with the over-arching project for social, economic, and environmental justice.

A second excerpt about "expertise-ism" comes from Prof. Catherine A. O'Neill, a sensitive observer of Native American cultures.[36] She questions the claims of risk assessment experts to know more about some aspects of health and environmental risk than the people who are exposed to those risks on a day-to-day basis. She carries forward Professor Gauna's suggestion that the victims of pollution may be the most qualified experts in the risks that polluting activities pose to human health and the environment. For example, Native

Americans practiced ecological science long before modern ecologists began to study ecosystems. Yet the "dominant society" does not afford "Native science" the same respect that it gives to nonNative science, even when Native scientists are in a far better position to study and understand natural phenomena than their nonNative counterparts.

---

The dominant society has often failed to recognize or credit the wealth of ecological knowledge among Native peoples. Historically and today, non-Native society has tended not to count Native understandings of the world as valid bodies of knowledge. Non-Native society has, for the most part, withheld from Native methods of understanding the appellation "science." By the same token, non-Native society has been unlikely to view Native knowledge holders as "scientists." Meanwhile, as Vine Deloria has observed, members of the dominant society have increasingly looked to scientists for reliable, authoritative explanations of the world: "In our dominant society we have been trained to believe that scientists search for, examine, and articulate truths about the natural world."[37] Against this backdrop, to the extent that the dominant society has been reluctant to recognize Native science as "science," it has continued to deny the reliability, validity and authority of Native experiences and understandings of the world. This failure has taken several forms.

*Existence and Contribution of Native Knowledge Not Credited*
The dominant society has often failed to acknowledge the existence of Native sources of knowledge. Sometimes, this apparent vacuum has enabled non-Native individuals to take credit for the products of Native science and technology. Yet Native knowledge is the source of numerous instances of enlarged scientific understanding and enhanced application.[38] Native environmental management techniques have also shaped numerous ecosystems, often in places that get described as "untouched by humans" or as "pristine."[39] * * *

*Validity of Native Knowledge Denied*
The dominant society has often questioned the validity and reliability of Native knowledge. It has viewed Native science and scientists as insufficiently "objective," and their observations as unreliable. * * *

*Native Knowledge Recognized Only Upon "Verification" by the Science of the Dominant Society*
The dominant society has sometimes acknowledged the conclusions of Native science, but only if they have been "verified" by the science and methods of the dominant society. Even here, the acknowledgment may be begrudging or skeptical. Instances of Native knowledge are often viewed as exceptional, surprising, or the result of a lucky guess. Such skepticism on the part of non-Native society is especially likely where the Native knowledge holders are traditional or spiritual leaders, or where knowledge acquisition occurs (or is believed to occur) by methods outside dominant society orthodoxy.

*Recognition of Native Knowledge Conditioned Upon Presentation According to Conventions of the Dominant Society*

The dominant society has sometimes acknowledged the conclusions of Native science, but only if and to the extent that these conclusions have been presented according to the conventions and preferences of the dominant society. Recognition of Native science as "science" may thus be conditioned upon it having been quantified, written, or peer-reviewed, and upon it having observed formal conventions for presenting data in the form of studies or reports. Acknowledgment, however, may be begrudging or skeptical. Moreover, there is often no attempt to ask what might have gotten lost in the translation or even to recognize that translation and loss are issues.

*Native Knowledge Subjected to Greater Scrutiny Than Similar Sources From the Dominant Society*

The dominant society has often subjected the conclusions of Native science to greater scrutiny than the conclusions of the dominant society, even when the sources and methods may be similar. Whereas the dominant society has been willing to rely on its members' years of experience in a field, or familiarity with a given place or subject matter, it has been less willing to rely on experience or familiarity as the basis for Native knowledge. Recollections, inferences, and opinions by "expert" members of the dominant society are likely to be subjected to a less exacting and skeptical scrutiny than recollections, inferences, and opinions by Native knowledge holders.

Even when Native sources of knowledge would appear to fare better than non-Native sources according to the dominant society's own criteria for reliability, Native sources may be ignored or rejected in favor of the competing non-Native sources. With respect to fish consumption data, for example, the possibility for study bias is believed to be minimized when the data is gathered for longer periods of time, when it is gathered throughout the course of a year's seasonal fluctuations in food availability and intake. The fish consumption study on which EPA proposes to base its revised water quality criteria was conducted in three successive years over a three-day period—that is, the study drew its conclusions from nine days' worth of data provided by survey participants.[40] Compare this to EPA's earlier rejection of data presented by the Mattaponi and Pamonkey tribal leaders, which was likely based on daily observation over the course of years.

*Native Scientists Not Consulted as Experts*

The dominant society has often passed over Native scientists in its efforts to consult the "experts." It has, on the one hand, declined to turn to Native knowledge holders even on matters having to do with tribal resources with which Native managers are intimately familiar and where Native peoples have developed an extensive and profound knowledge as a result of having resided in place for millennia. The dominant society has, on the other hand, declined to turn to Native scientists even when these individuals have training and credentials of the sort recognized by the dominant society.

*Occasions for Discrimination Against Native Ecological Science*

When members of the dominant society preface their observations about a particular ecosystem, when they highlight the considerable uncertainties against which restoration plans are fashioned, or especially when they emphasize the need for further study before restoration efforts can confidently go forward, they often invoke some version of the statement that "we" have only just begun to study this ecosystem.

Such statements may remind humans of the need for humility, usefully countering decades of rhetoric in the dominant society extolling man's ability to duplicate and even "improve" upon natural systems. Such statements may emphasize the complexities of ecosystems, usefully counseling attention to the interrelatedness of the various parts of natural systems. However, these sorts of statements may work at the same time to obscure the existence of Native knowledge about the place or natural system in question, or to deny its relevance. By universalizing the inattention of the dominant society, moreover, such statements are not only misleading but offensive to peoples for whom attention and reciprocal relationships are fundamental to their ways of living.

*Affection for Quantitative Methods of Analysis*

Quantitative methods of analysis such as quantitative risk assessment and cost-benefit analysis have enjoyed a spectacular ascendancy in recent years, and are now a staple of federal and state regulatory approaches. These methods exclude or discount information or understandings that are not readily quantified.

*Suspicion of Orality*

Another likely occasion for discrimination stems from the fact that agency regulators, along with the general dominant society, are suspicious of orality. Many agency decisionmakers believe that information in written form is more trustworthy, more reliable, and more likely to be true than information in oral form.

*Preoccupation With "Objectivity"*

* * * [N]on-Native scientists, even those working in applied fields or in the regulatory context where "science" is often difficult to separate from "policy," tend to pride themselves on their "objectivity." Objectivity depends on the claim that the scientist's own values and commitments do not affect the observations she makes nor the questions she frames in the first place. Numerous commentators have expressed serious doubt that humans can be such bias-free participants in inquiry. Yet non-Native society continues to attach authority to those conclusions that don the mantle of objectivity. It speaks of "objective truths" on the one hand, and conclusions "marred by subjectivity" on the other. There is no place in this either/or discourse for conceding that a person inevitably brings a host of biases, values, and commitments to her work: to own up to one's values would be tantamount to admitting that one had fudged a conclusion.

* * *

Because of this preoccupation with objectivity, non-Native decisionmakers may discount any results or ways of knowing that do not deny the participation of the person seeking knowledge.

*Presupposition of the Universality of Knowledge*
The dominant society presupposes that knowledge is universal and impersonal, available equally to all who choose to access it. This presupposition often goes unstated among scientists and policymakers in the dominant society, yet determines a host of practices regarding information collection, use, and dissemination. This presupposition may itself introduce occasions for misunderstanding and discrimination.

On Native understandings, knowledge is often local. It is place-based. It often results from "generations of careful observation within an ecosystem of continuous residence."[41] Knowledge is user-based. It often must be practiced in order to be regenerated. On Native understandings, some knowledge may be specialized and personal, properly usable only by the individual, or group, that has come to possess it.

---

## Conclusion: Scientific Illusions and Regulatory Needs

Many of the problems that regulatory agencies encounter in trying to control health, safety, and environmental risks stem from illusions about what science can and cannot do. Science obviously can help us understand many risks better. But it cannot, by itself, answer many of the challenges facing regulators.

There are many reasons for this. Sometimes the definitive scientific study cannot be implemented because of ethical considerations or practical limitations. Those studies that can be conducted are rarely perfect and many are seriously flawed. Indeed, imperfection is the hallmark of epidemiological studies of humans exposure to toxic agents. Although animal studies can be more carefully designed and implemented, they too entail practical difficulties, e.g., infectious diseases that skew results. And inevitably there will be questions about the legitimacy of extrapolating tests results from "mouse-to-man."

To make matters worse, companies have few incentives to gather useful scientific data about the risks they create. If government approval is needed to market a product (drugs, medical devices, pesticides), their incentive is to collect only the minimum amount of data necessary to win that approval. If no approval is needed to market a product, a company has little incentive to test for toxicity since such testing can only lead to government intervention or tort liability.

The state of the science for a given risk is not necessarily the decisive issue for regulators in any case. In the face of known hazards, regulatory decisionmaking cannot wait for a scientific consensus to form about questions "on the frontiers of scientific knowledge." As a practical necessity, public policy must make decisions despite inevitable uncertainties. Numerous cases have shown that calls for "sound science" in the regulatory process are not so much demands for better scientific data (which companies are in the best position to provide) as they are attempts to force the agencies to delay or scuttle any regulatory action.

For their part, agencies are often eager to cloak their policy judgments in the mantle of science because it helps them shirk responsibility for choices that tend to be politically contentious. It is easier to assign responsibility to impersonal scientific facts than to shoulder policymaking responsibility. Nonetheless, the "science charade" has become a common practice among agencies. It has served to disguise accountability for policy choices, delay the regulatory process and divert agencies from their statutory missions.

The evasion of policy responsibility by relying upon "sound science" has reached a new plateau with the rise of self-proclaimed risk assessment experts. While holding themselves forth as disinterested seekers of truth, it is apparent that most risk assessment experts come to the task with their own axes to grind. They are not at all reluctant to fill the factual gaps left by scientific uncertainty with their own (unacknowledged) policy preferences.

Such "expertise-ism" is especially problematic when the beneficiaries of the regulatory programs at issue are poorly educated people of color. It is, in fact, an open question whether residents of "impacted communities" are less qualified than Harvard-trained risk assessors to assess the health, safety, and environmental risks that they encounter. Just as inner-city residents may be highly knowledgeable about environmental injustice, Native peoples frequently have an understanding of their ecological surroundings that may be far more empirical and informed than science.

The cult of expertise is an insidious and pervasive aspect of regulatory debate, however. It has many manifestations. We therefore turn now to the problems of quantification in risk assessment: another strategy by which the moral, social and political impetus for controlling industrial hazards is neutralized. Just look at the numbers, say the quantitative risk assessors, and it will be clear that corrective action is unnecessary.

**Suggestions for Further Reading**

*Scientific Uncertainty: An Inescapable Aspect of Regulation*

Much of the early literature on the use of risk assessment in regulatory decisionmaking highlighted the uncertainties that risk assessors encounter when they attempt to quantify health, safety, and environmental risks. Prominent articles include:

Marcia Gelpe & A. Dan Tarlock, *The Uses of Scientific Information in Environmental Decisionmaking*, 48 S. CAL. L. REV. 371 (1974).
*This article analyzes why the legal system must adjust its standards of scientific evidence in order to justify adequate regulatory protection of the environment.*

James Leape, *Quantitative Risk Assessment in Regulation of Environmental Carcinogens*, 4 HARV. ENVTL. L. REV. 86 (1980).
*James Leape examines the role of risk assessment in regulation in*

*light of the fact that "[i]gnorance about the biology of cancer plagues quantitative risk assessments with huge uncertainties that are impossible to quantify and difficult to comprehend."*

Thomas O. McGarity, *Substantive and Procedural Discretion in Administrative Resolution of Science Policy Questions: Regulating Carcinogens in EPA and OSHA*, 67 GEO. L.J. 729, 737-38 (1979).
  *McGarity points out the "huge uncertainties" that "cloud any attempt to demonstrate that a chemical has carcinogenic effects on humans at typical exposure levels." This article discusses the role of policy in resolving regulatory disputes in light of uncertainty.*

  Two of the very first scientists to raise the spectre of environmental degradation in the 1960s, Paul and Anne Ehrlich, entered the fray again to defend EPA's scientific analyses from critics unconcerned about the plant growth regulator Alar and the "greenhouse gases" in the earth's atmosphere.

PAUL R. EHRLICH & ANNE H. EHRLICH, BETRAYAL OF SCIENCE AND REASON: HOW THE ANTI-ENVIRONMENTAL RHETORIC THREATENS OUR FUTURE (1996).
  *The authors regret that "much of the progress that has been made in defining, understanding, and seeking solutions to the human predicament over the past thirty years is now being undermined by an environmental backlash, fueled by anti-science ideas and arguments ...."*

*Why Companies "Choose Ignorance"*

  Scholars have devoted very little systematic attention to the incentives (or lack thereof) for companies to test their products for health, safety, and environmental risks. In addition to the excerpts in this chapter, see the following treatments of the incentive problem.

Clayton P. Gillette & James E. Krier, *Risk, Courts, and Agencies*, 138 U. PA. L. REV. 1027, 1038 (1990).
  *An economic analysis of the incentives of corporations finds that "producer firms simply won't have good information about risks (often because * * * they are not stimulated to produce it) or, if they do, won't act on it or share it with typically uniformed consumers and employees."*

Mary L. Lyndon, *Information Economics and Chemical Toxicity: Designing Laws to Produce and Use Data*, 87 MICH. L. REV. 1795 (1989).
  *A documentation of why current laws establish "little incentive" to produce and distribute data about the adverse effects of chemicals or even the identity of the chemicals to which persons are routinely exposed.*

*Scientific Charades as an Evasion of Responsibility*

The observation that policy considerations dominate the risk assessment exercise is as old as risk assessment itself. Many of the readings suggested in the previous section of this chapter note that policy must fill the gaps when scientific uncertainties leave risk assessments incomplete. More recent commentaries include the following:

> Nicholas A. Ashford et al., *A Hard Look at Federal Regulation of Formaldehyde: A Departure From Reasoned Decisionmaking*, 7 HARV. ENVTL. L. REV. 297, 313-14 (1983).
> *Detailed case studies lead the authors to warn about the "need to examine scientific determinations carefully, lest social policy decisions be hidden in alleged assessments of technical or scientific facts."*

> Sanford E. Gaines, *Science, Politics, and the Management of Toxic Risks Through Law*, 30 JURIMETRICS J. 271 (1990).
> *An argument that because it is counterproductive and impossible to divorce politics from science, regulatory institutions should be designed to ensure that decisionmakers have unfettered access to political as well as scientific advice.*

> Robert R. Kuehn, *The Environmental Justice Implications of Quantitative Risk Assessment*, 1996 U. ILL. L. REV. 103.
> *An examination of why EPA's risk assessment practices place disproportionate burdens of pollution and environmental hazards on racial minorities and low-income groups. One reason: barriers that prevent them from participating in the risk assessment process.*

> Howard Latin, *Regulatory Failure, Administrative Incentives, and the New Clean Air Act*, 21 ENVTL. L. 1647, 1653-82 (1991).
> *This article describes the considerable policy discretion that EPA has in implementing the Clean Air Act because of the inherent limitations of science. Bureaucratic and political factors are therefore highly influential in how EPA's discretion is exercised, to the detriment of environmental protection.*

*The Seductions of Expertise in Risk Assessment*

There is a large scholarly literature criticizing professional risk assessors for making expansive claims to objectivity and expertise and the effects on policymaking. Some of the more comprehensive critiques are listed below.

> Adam M. Finkel, *A Second Opinion on an Environmental Misdiagnosis: The Risky Prescriptions of Breaking the Vicious Circle*, 3 N.Y.U. ENVTL. L.J. 295, 318 (1994).
> *Adam Finkel, a professional risk assessor, explains why risk analysis cannot determine what are appropriate regulatory policies concerning risk.*

Daniel Fiorino, *Environmental Risk and Democratic Process: A Critical Review*, 14 COLUM. J. ENVTL. L. 501, 532-34 (1989).

*Daniel Fiorino argues that risk assessment practices favor scientific elites over citizen participation in risk policymaking. New procedures are necessary to ensure a democratic regulatory process regarding risk regulation, he writes.*

Robert V. Percival, *Responding to Environmental Risk: A Pluralistic Perspective*, 14 PACE ENVTL. L. REV. 513, 526 (1997).

*Robert Percival writes: "Rather than a high priesthood of quantitative risk assessors, the public may do a better job of assessing some risks and it may respond more quickly than the regulatory system when information about risks becomes available."*

## Chapter 2 Endnotes

1. PETER HUBER, HARD GREEN: SAVING THE ENVIRONMENT FROM THE ENVIRONMEN-TALISTS: A CONSERVATIVE MANEFESTO (2000).

2. John D. Graham, *Legislative Approaches to Achieving More Protection Against Risk at Less Cost*, 1997 U. CHI. LEGAL F. 13, 41-42 (1997).

3. Cass R. Sunstein, *Legislative Foreword: Congress, Constitutional Moments, and the Cost-Benefit State*, 48 STAN. L. REV. 247, 266 (1996).

4. *See* GEORGE CARLO & MARTIN SCHRAM, CELL PHONES: INVISIBLE HAZARDS IN THE WIRELESS AGE (2001).

5. COMMITTEE ON THE INSTITUTIONAL MEANS FOR ASSESSMENT OF RISKS TO PUBLIC HEALTH, NRC, NAS, RISK ASSESSMENT IN THE FEDERAL GOVERNMENT: MAN-AGING THE PROCESS 11 (1983) [hereinafter NRC, MANAGING THE PROCESS].

6. COMMITTEE ON RISK ASSESSMENT OF HAZARDOUS AIR POLLUTANTS, NAS, NRC, SCIENCE AND JUDGMENT IN RISK ASSESSMENT 160 (1994).

7. *Id.* at 163, tbl. 9-1.

8. *Id.* at 161.

9. The full opinion for this ruling, Public Health Research Group v. Tyson, is printed at 796 F.2d 1479 (D.C. Cir. 1986). At the time of this decision, Judge McGowan was a senior circuit judge on the U.S. Court of Appeals for the District of Columbia Circuit, a court that reviews most important health, safety, and environmental regulations promulgated by federal agencies like EPA and OSHA.

10. *Id.* at 1482.

11. *Id.* at 1483-84.

12. *Id.* at 1479.

13. OSHA reviewed at least five other studies, finding further evidence for a relationship between EtO exposure and tumor production. *See* 49 Fed. Reg. 25743 (1984). This additional evidence further supports OSHA's conclusion that EtO exposure poses a risk of cancer.

14. Motor Vehicle Mfrs. Ass'n of the United States v. State Farm Mut. Auto. Ins. Co., 463 U.S. 29, 13 ELR 20672 (1983).

15. 796 F.2d at 1495.

16. *See* CHARLES L. SCHULTZE, THE PUBLIC USE OF PRIVATE INTEREST 16-22 (1977); Stephen Breyer, *Analyzing Regulatory Failure: Mismatches, Less Restrictive Alternatives, and Reform*, 92 HARV. L. REV. 547, 586-604 (1970).

17. Professor Wagner teaches environmental law and torts at the University of Texas School of Law. This excerpt is derived from an article, *Choosing Ignorance in the Manufacture of Toxic Products*, published at 82 CORNELL L. REV. 773, 774-75, 780-90 (1997).

18. *See* STEERING COMM. ON IDENTIFICATION OF TOXIC AND POTENTIALLY TOXIC CHEM-ICALS FOR CONSIDERATION BY THE NATIONAL TOXICOLOGY PROGRAM, NRC, TOXIC-ITY TESTING: STRATEGIES TO DETERMINE NEEDS AND PRIORITIES 60, 151-63 (1984). The NRC also listed basic criteria that should be followed in undertaking the studies, *id.* at 61-62, and preferred protocols for conducting the studies, *id.* at 62-64, 165-68.

19. There is substantial evidence that the regulatory agencies have done a disappointing job overseeing safety testing for many products within their jurisdictions. *See, e.g.,*

U.S. GENERAL ACCOUNTING OFFICE (GAO), LAWN CARE PESTICIDES: RISKS RE-MAIN UNCERTAIN WHILE PROHIBITED SAFETY CLAIMS CONTINUE 12-14, 20 (1990) (criticizing EPA and the Federal Trade Commission for inadequate testing and investigation of the long-term safety of 34 of the most widely used lawn care pesticides); GAO, TOXIC SUBSTANCES: EPA's CHEMICAL TESTING PROGRAM HAS MADE LITTLE PROGRESS 17-21 (1990) (reporting alarming delays in EPA's issuance of test rules requiring manufacturers to generate additional safety data on their products, and noting that as of 1989 the "EPA had received complete test data for only six chemicals and had not finished assessing any of them for possible further action").

20. U.S. OFFICE OF TECHNOLOGY ASSESSMENT, IDENTIFYING AND REGULATING CARCINOGENS 160, 174 (1987).

21. *See, e.g., id.* at 161 (noting that "the number of chemicals selected for testing is consistent with the NTP budget," which was adversely affected by cutbacks in 1986).

22. NRC, MANAGING THE PROCESS, *supra* note 5, at 3.

23. Professor Latin teaches environmental law and international environmental law at Rutgers-Newark School of Law. The article from which this excerpt is taken, *Good Science, Bad Regulation, and Toxic Risk Assessment,* is published at 5 YALE J. ON REG. 89, 89-95, 146-48 (1988).

24. C. Richard Cothern et al., *Estimating Risk to Human Health,* 20 ENVTL. SCI. & TECH. 111, 113-15 (1986).

25. This excerpt is derived from an article published at 95 COLUM. L. REV. 1613 (1995).

26. Alvin M. Weinberg, *Science and Trans-Science,* 10 MINERVA 209, 209 (1972).

27. John D. Graham & March Sadowitz, *Superfund Reform: Reducing Risk Through Community Choice,* 10 ISSUES IN SCI. & TECH. 35 (1994).

28. STEPHEN BREYER, BREAKING THE VICIOUS CIRCLE: TOWARD EFFECTIVE RISK REGULATION 33 (1993). *See also* Robert Hahn, *Achieving Real Regulatory Reform,* 1997 U. CHI. LEGAL F.

29. *See* Frank B. Cross, *Public Role in Risk Control,* 24 ENVTL. L. 888 (1994) (exploring "the divergences in public and scientific interpretations of risk, which lie at the source of much of the disagreement regarding which activities are risky and therefore properly regulated by the government").

30. John D. Graham, *The Risk Not Reduced,* 3 N.Y.U. ENVTL. L.J. 382, 401 (1994).

31. Frank B. Cross, *The Risk of Reliance on Perceived Risk,* 3 RISK–ISSUES IN HEALTH AND SAFETY 59 (1992).

32. BREYER, *supra* note 28, at 72.

33. Professor Gauna teaches environmental and property law at Southwestern University School of Law. The excepts here are taken from *The Environmental Justice Misfit: Public Participation and the Paradigm Paradox,* 17 STAN. ENVTL. L.J. 3 (1998).

34. Philip Handler, *In Science, No Advances Without Risks,* U.S. NEWS & WORLD REP., Sept. 15, 1980, at 60.

35. U.S. EPA, OFFICE OF POLICY, PLANNING, AND EVALUATION, ENVIRONMENTAL EQUITY: REDUCING RISK FOR ALL COMMUNITIES 12-13 (1992).

36. Professor O'Neil teaches environmental law and environmental justice at Seattle University School of Law. The article from which the excerpts are taken, *Restoration Affecting Native Resources: The Place of Native Ecological Science,* appears at 7 ARIZ. L. REV. 343 (2000).

37. Vine Deloria Jr., Red Earth, White Lies: Native Americans and the Myth of Scientific Fact 5 (1997).

38. Jack D. Forbes, *Native Intelligence: Intellectual Property Rights of Indigenous Peoples*, J. for Native & Nat. People, Spring 1997, at 14 (noting contribution of Native science and technology to crops such as maize, potatoes, sweet potatoes, beans, tomatoes, cacao, peanuts, persimmons, bananas, yucca, tapioca, chayote, jicama, and papayas; medicinals such as witchhazel, quinine, golden seal, and American ginseng; and miscellaneous inventions such as applications of rubber, kayaks, and toboggans).

39. *See, e.g.*, Thomas Blackburn & Kat Anderson, *Introduction: Managing the Domesticated Environment, in* Before the Wilderness: Environmental Management by Native Californians 15, 18 (Thomas C. Blackburn & Kat Anderson eds., 1993) (discussing the compelling and unequivocal evidence that has emerged that deliberate Native intervention maintained and regenerated "the extremely rich, diverse, and apparently 'wild' landscape that so impressed Europeans at the time of contact—and which traditionally has been viewed as a 'natural, untrammeled wilderness' ever since"); Dennis Martinez, *First People, Firsthand Knowledge*, Sierra, Nov./Dec. 1996, at 50 ("Modern environmentalists have . . . failed to appreciate the high degree of Indian influence on what they see as a 'pristine' environment.").

40. *See* Draft Water Quality Criteria Methodology Revisions: Human Health, 63 Fed. Reg. 43756 (1998); U.S. Dep't of Agric., Continuing Survey of Food Intake by Individuals 1 (1998).

41. Winona LaDuke, *Traditional Ecological Knowledge and Environmental Futures*, 5 Colo. J. Int'l Envtl. L. & Pol'y 127, 127 (1994).

# Chapter 3: The Quantification Quagmire

The starting point for a cost-benefit analysis of a governmental intervention aimed at protecting public health or the environment is a risk assessment. Broadly speaking, risk assessment is any analytical attempt to grapple
with the risks posed by human conduct, the technologies that humans employ,
or even natural phenomena like earthquakes and diseases. Nothing inherent in
the concept demands that the analysis be quantified or reduced to numbers. On
the other hand, numerical risk assessments can be quite useful in setting priorities about which risk-producing activities to address in what order.

Pressed even farther, quantitative risk assessment can produce estimates of
lives saved or environmental entities protected that, when monetized, can serve
as the basis for one side of a cost-benefit equation that could inform decisionmakers attempting to determine the stringency of a protective intervention. Harvard economist W. Kip Viscusi, for example, believes that "some comparison of
risks and costs is necessary to assess whether the beneficial aspects of the regulatory policy warrant the cost."[1] The critical question is whether quantitative risk
assessment, as currently practiced, can be pressed so far.

This chapter will continue to clarify the boundaries between science and policy in risk assessment. It will also explain why policy necessarily plays an important role in quantitative risk assessment. It will describe the mixed art and
science of quantitative risk assessment and probe some of its limitations. All of
the authors are asking, and to some extent answering, the broad question
whether quantitative risk assessment is "ready for prime time."

## What Is Quantitative Risk Assessment?

A classic exegesis on quantitative risk assessment is the 1983 report prepared
for the National Research Council (NRC) of the National Academy of Sciences
(NAS), frequently referred to as the "Red Book." The Red Book—officially,
*Risk Assessment in the Federal Government: Managing the Process*[2]—was
prepared by a committee of experts chaired by Dr. Reuel A. Stallones of the
University of Texas School of Health. Dr. Stallones was well known at the time
for his research on the carcinogenic effects of smoking.[3] The NRC committee,
representing many constituencies and viewpoints, produced a report that has
been highly influential in the evolution of quantitative risk assessment as a
decisionmaking tool.

What is risk assessment? The Red Book states:

---

We use risk-assessment to mean the characterization of the potential adverse
health effects of human exposures to environmental hazards. Risk assessments

include several elements: description of the potential adverse health effects based on an evaluation of results of epidemiologic, clinical, toxicologic, and environmental research; extrapolation from those results to predict the type and estimate the extent of health effects in humans under given conditions of exposure; judgments as to the number and characteristics of persons exposed at various intensities and durations; and summary judgments on the existence and overall magnitude of the public-health problem. Risk assessment also includes characterization of the uncertainties inherent in the process of inferring risk.

The term risk assessment is often given narrower and broader meanings than we have adopted here. For some observers, the term is synonymous with quantitative risk assessment and emphasizes reliance on numerical results. Our broader definition includes quantification, but also includes qualitative expressions of risk. Quantitative estimates of risk are not always feasible, and they may be eschewed by agencies for policy reasons. Broader uses of the term than ours also embrace analysis of perceived risks, comparisons of risks associated with different regulatory strategies, and occasionally analysis of the economic and social implications of regulatory decisions—functions that we assign to risk management.

The Committee uses the term risk management to describe the process of evaluating alternative regulatory actions and selecting among them. Risk management, which is carried out by regulatory agencies under various legislative mandates, is an agency decision-making process that entails consideration of political, social, economic, and engineering information with risk-related information to develop, analyze, and compare regulatory options and to select the appropriate regulatory response to a potential chronic health hazard. The selection process necessarily requires the use of value judgments on such issues as the acceptability of risk and the reasonableness of the costs of control.

A risk assessment might stop with the first step, hazard identification, if no adverse effect is found or if an agency elects to take regulatory action without further analysis, for reasons of policy or statutory mandate.

Of the four steps [involved in risk assessment], hazard identification is the most easily recognized in the actions of regulatory agencies. It is defined here as the process of determining whether exposure to an agent can cause an increase in the incidence of a health condition (cancer, birth defect, etc.). It involves characterizing the nature and strength of the evidence of causation. Although the question of whether a substance causes cancer or other adverse health effects is theoretically a yes-no question, there are few chemicals on which the human data are definitive. Therefore, the question is often restated in terms of effects in laboratory animals or other test systems, e.g., "Does the agent induce cancer in test animals?" Positive answers to such questions are typically taken as evidence that an agent may pose a cancer risk for any exposed humans. Information from short-term in vitro tests and on structural similarity to known chemical hazards may also be considered.

Dose-response assessment is the process of characterizing the relation between the dose of an agent administered or received and the incidence of an ad-

68

verse health effect in exposed populations and estimating the incidence of the effect as a function of human exposure to the agent. It takes account of intensity of exposure, age pattern of exposure, and possibly other variables that might affect response, such as sex, lifestyle, and other modifying factors. A dose-response assessment usually requires extrapolation from high to low dose and extrapolation from animals to humans. A dose-response assessment should describe and justify the methods of extrapolation used to predict incidence and should characterize the statistical and biologic uncertainties in these methods.

Exposure assessment is the process of measuring or estimating the intensity, frequency, and duration of human exposures to an agent currently present in the environment or of estimating hypothetical exposures that might arise from the release of new chemicals into the environment. In its most complete form, it describes the magnitude, duration, schedule, and route of exposure; the size, nature, and classes of the human populations exposed; and the uncertainties in all estimates. Exposure assessment is often used to identify feasible prospective control options and to predict the effects of available control technologies on exposure.

Risk characterization is the process of estimating the incidence of a health effect under the various conditions of human exposure described in exposure assessment. It is performed by combining the exposure and dose-response assessments. The summary effects of the uncertainties in the preceding steps are described in this step.

---

*Why Is Risk Assessment Necessary?*

The Red Book explained why regulatory agencies developed risk assessment tools: to help carry out the U.S. Congress' desire to protect the public health while dealing with the uncertainties posed by new types of scientific analysis.

---

Through Congress the American public has granted authority to federal administrative agencies to restrict private actions, such as the production and use of chemicals, when this is deemed necessary to protect the health of the public. The 1970s are notable for the large number of new federal regulatory laws that are applicable to the environment, both in the workplace and in the community. These laws reflect a dramatic and relatively rapid shift in public priorities toward the protection of health.

Concurrently with shifts in social priorities, advances in science have contributed to policy problems, for the advances have revealed the extent of the environmental health problem. Some earlier regulatory programs had addressed exposure to toxic chemicals, but they were directed mainly at the risk of poisoning and other acute effects. Much policy-making related to such effects involved routine, short-term, acute animal studies to establish "no-observed-effect" doses and then the straightforward calculation of allowable human exposure based on the application of safety factors to relatively uncomplicated scientific findings. Such an approach reflected little recognition of problems that might be associated with smaller exposures. Cancer, birth defects, and other conditions were seldom seen as preventable by government intervention. Only in the last 15 years has the potential extent of the linkage between such conditions and toxic substances been revealed. The often-cited estimate that a large fraction of all cancers may be attributed to human exposure to toxic agents (including smoking, diet, lifestyle, and occupation) originated fairly recently, and it was not until the 1970s that regulatory agencies focused their attention on cancer and other chronic health risks.

Scientific advances entered the picture in a second way. The technology that has made it possible to detect relations between particular agents and cancer or other chronic effects has evolved rapidly from the days when exposure through skin-painting and subcutaneous injection were relied on in animal tests of carcinogenicity. Increasingly, epidemiologic investigations have either confirmed the findings of animal experiments or provided evidence that linked exposures to particular chemicals to particular chronic health effects. The introduction of reliable testing methods resulted in broader government testing requirements and, steadily, the discovery of more and more suspect chemicals—many of them in common use—that demanded agency attention. The techniques are still developing, and we are still looking for better ways to design and interpret animal bioassay experiments.

The increase in newly suspect chemicals was accompanied by the development of instruments and procedures that permitted the detection of chemicals at lower and lower concentrations. Even if the number of suspect chemicals had not increased dramatically, these sensitive detection methods would have revealed the presence of such chemicals in concentrations that earlier methods would have missed. Combined with all those changes were the development and refinement of analytic methods of estimating the degree of human risk on the basis of data from human studies and animal experiments.

Public policies are not immediately adaptable to rapid changes in social priorities and scientific advances. Many of the fundamental difficulties of regulatory risk assessment result from attempts to bend old laws and policies to fit newly perceived risks. * * *

---

*Dealing With "Pervasive Uncertainty"*

Risk assessment is meant to be a tool that can help regulators isolate and grapple with the many scientific ambiguities about a given hazard. If scientific knowledge can be more clearly isolated, goes the thinking, then the judgments that inform an agency's policy choices can also be better identified and improved. The idea is that risk assessment can help regulators deal more systematically and rationally with the uncertainties they face.

---

The uncertainties inherent in risk assessment can be grouped in two general categories: missing or ambiguous information on a particular substance and gaps in current scientific theory. When scientific uncertainty is encountered in the risk assessment process, inferential bridges are needed to allow the process to continue. The Committee has defined the points in the risk assessment process where such inferences must be made as components. The judgments made by the scientist/risk assessor for each component of risk assessment often entail a choice among several scientifically plausible options; the Committee has designated these inference options.

[There follows a table listing fifty "components" or opportunities for risk assessors to exercise scientific and policy judgment in choosing among "inference options."]

A key premise of the proponents of institutional separation of risk assessment is that removal of risk assessment from the regulatory agencies will result in a clear demarcation of the science and policy aspects of regulatory decision-making. However, policy considerations inevitably affect, and perhaps determine, some of the choices among the inference options. * * *

The dominant analytic difficulty is pervasive uncertainty. Risk assessment draws extensively on science, and a strong scientific basis has developed for linking exposure to chemicals to chronic health effects. However, data may be incomplete, and there is often great uncertainty in estimates of the types, probability, and magnitude of health effects associated with a chemical agent, of the economic effects of a proposed regulatory action, and of the extent of current and possible future human exposures. These problems have no immediate solutions, given the many gaps in our understanding of the causal mechanisms of carcinogenesis and other health effects and in our ability to ascertain the nature or extent of the effects associated with specific exposures. Because our knowledge is limited, conclusive direct evidence of a threat to human health is rare. * * *

Ethical considerations prevent deliberate human experimentation with potentially dangerous chemicals, and the length of the latent period for cancer and some other effects greatly complicates epidemiologic studies of uncontrolled human exposures. Animal models must be used to investigate whether exposure to a chemical is related to the incidence of health effects, and the results must be extrapolated to humans. To make judgments amid such uncertainty, risk assessors must rely on a series of assumptions.

Limited Analytic Resources

The many problem chemicals in an agency's jurisdiction compete for attention of analysts and decision-makers. If an agency is considering new action on many substances at once, its scientific staff is stretched thin. Most agencies do not have the analytic resources to do a thorough risk assessment for priority-setting and must rely on less formal methods to ensure that the highest-risk chemicals are examined first.

Complexity

For most chemical agents that might be subject to regulation, a great variety of factors must be assessed, including potential toxicity, extent of human exposure, effectiveness of technologies to reduce exposure, the nature of possible substitute chemicals, effects on and interests of various population groups, and economic effects of regulatory alternatives. Decision-makers in a regulatory agency may encounter a large amount of highly technical information as they work toward their decisions; many scientific disciplines and technical fields are usually involved. An agency would like to have simple rules and analytic procedures to ensure consistency and competence in its decision-making, but, in the face of scientific uncertainty, such simplicity is difficult to achieve without an inadvertent loss of crucial scientific insight from the decision process.

---

## Why Quantification Dominates Regulatory Decisionmaking

As regulatory agencies turn to the difficult task of carrying out their statutory mandates, a number of problems soon became evident. What level of scientific evidence is needed to justify regulations that will invariably require new industry expenditures? How should an agency go about choosing which hazards to regulate?

Quantitative risk assessment, it was soon discovered, could help address such questions. For one thing, the technique promises to generate objective and accurate knowledge about the actual risks posed, as well as the estimated benefits of regulatory action.[4] Risk assessment is also attractive because its use of quantitative techniques gives decisionmakers information that is coherent and understandable.[5] By isolating technical issues from policy judgments, quantitative risk assessment can also help to make the policy judgments more explicit.[6]

If used widely enough, quantitative risk assessment begins to provide still other advantages, its proponents argue. It can help agencies establish regulatory priorities in a more rational way.[7] And because risk assessment facilitates quantitative comparisons of alternative ways to reduce risk, it can make decisionmaking within and among regulatory programs more consistent.[8]

As the following two passages reveal, these arguments have certainly been persuasive to regulators. Even though no law requires the use of quantitative risk assessment, the technique is now a standard part of most health and environmental decisionmaking. From a theoretical perspective, it is hard to find fault with a procedure that purports to measure the magnitude of health and environmental risks and help compare them. As we will see, the actual ability of risk assessment to make good on these claims is another matter.

Ultimately, the intellectual rigor of the technique may be less important to its backers than its ability to provide a plausible rationale for regulatory choices. As Prof. John S. Applegate explains below, politically besieged agencies are not willing to interpret statutory mandates for a "safe" air quality or workplace as meaning "risk-free." Such interpretations might require draconian, politically unacceptable reductions in a dangerous chemical or manufacturing process. But through artful uses of risk assessment techniques and terms such as "acceptable levels of risk," agencies have found that they can declare air quality and workplaces "safe" without imposing dramatic measures or outright bans. Quantitative risk assessment, in other words, gives agencies a way to implement protective legislation without being excessively protective.

The technique has also proved to be useful in persuading the courts that regulatory decisions are not "arbitrary and capricious" and therefore inconsistent with the law. When agencies are able to invoke "hard numbers" in support of their regulations, courts tend to defer to their judgment. The agencies are, after all, the designated technical experts.

The political conservatism of the 1980s seems to have made quantitative risk assessment much more attractive to regulatory agencies, perhaps because it offered a coherent, seemingly rational justification for less stringent regulation. Another influential force during this period was a major U.S. Supreme Court ruling that challenged the Occupational Safety and Health Administration's (OSHA's) regulatory standard for benzene. In that case, a plurality of the Court agreed with the petroleum industry that the word "safe" in the statute did not mandate a risk-free workplace. Rather, it required OSHA to demonstrate that its standard was necessary to reduce worker exposure to benzene levels that cause a "significant risk" of cancer. OSHA and other agencies interpreted this to mean that they should employ quantitative risk assessment to determine whether or not risks posed by toxic substances were "significant." President Ronald Reagan soon codified this interpretation into administration policy through an executive order that has been amended only slightly in the intervening administrations.

Below, Prof. Robert R. Kuehn[9] describes why quantitative risk assessment became a popular regulatory tool: it served a number of compelling political, judicial, and administrative needs.

---

Although the use of quantitative risk assessment has become pervasive at the EPA, its growth has not been driven by spectacular advances in the science underlying the assessment.[10] Instead, as the history of risk assessment shows, risk assessment's meteoric rise is largely due to the politics of the era and the desires of policy makers. What we today call risk assessment can be traced to the 1930s and the development of dosage versus response displays based on epidemiologic data and animal test results. By 1976, several mathematical models had been developed to estimate the excess lifetime cancer risk for humans based on dose-response curves obtained from animal studies.

Although such models were in use during the Carter administration, agencies such as the EPA generally relied on qualitative analysis to determine a substance's toxicity and did not attempt to produce a quantitative estimate of the risk from exposure. In 1979, the position of the federal government was that quantitative assessments of cancer risks should be used only in establishing rough priorities and for purposes of obtaining very rough estimates of the magnitude of risk.[11] Even during the Reagan administration, the Assistant Secretary for Health of the

Department of Health and Human Services testified before Congress that "we simply do not yet have the appropriate scientific base to use risk assessment with full confidence in regulatory decisions."[12]

But the early 1980s saw a major shift in the use of risk assessment by federal agencies. No environmental law, then or now, expressly authorizes quantitative risk assessment, and surely none requires its use. The Supreme Court's decision in *Industrial Union Department, AFL-CIO v. American Petroleum Institute* (the benzene case),[13] however, raised doubts about the ability of federal agencies to set risk-based standards without some quantification. In that case, the Court threw out an Occupational Safety and Health Administration (OSHA) benzene exposure standard that was based on the agency's generic cancer policy that there is no safe exposure level for carcinogens and, therefore, exposure standards should be set at the lowest technically feasible level. In a plurality decision, four Justices held that to determine if a workplace is safe there must be some showing of the significance of the risk faced by the worker, rather than just the presence of a risk; quantification of the risk would demonstrate "a significant risk of harm and therefore a probability of significant benefits."[14] Although both Justice Powell's concurrence with the plurality opinion and the opinion of the four dissenting Justices noted that agencies are not prevented from taking regulatory action when reasonable quantification cannot be accomplished, agency regulators largely interpreted the case to require reliance on quantitative risk assessment even where the results are of questionable validity.

Shortly thereafter, President Reagan issued an executive order requiring a cost-benefit analysis for all major regulations and providing, to the extent permitted by law, that "regulatory action shall not be undertaken unless the potential benefits" from the regulation outweigh potential costs.[15] Although the order did not explicitly require the use of risk assessment, the technique provides a framework for cost-benefit analysis because it gives numerical values on risk that can be translated into the quantitative benefits of regulation and then compared with other regulatory alternatives.

A final influence on the rise of risk assessment was the appointment of William Ruckelshaus as EPA administrator in 1983. Ruckelshaus took over an agency that had been rocked by scandals that drew into question its scientific credibility. To Ruckelshaus, risk assessment, under the banner of "good science," was a way to restore public confidence in the agency.[16] Perhaps unspoken but equally important, heavy reliance on risk assessment also would slow the pace of regulatory efforts and promote President Reagan's desire for less government regulation, because quantitative risk assessment places intense resource demands on an agency.[17]

Today, the EPA and other federal and state environmental agencies use risk assessment for a variety of regulatory decisions. Perhaps the most common and controversial use of quantitative risk assessment is to decide if actions or chemicals are "safe" or if the risk presented by a chemical or activity is "acceptable" or "significant." For example, the EPA uses quantitative risk assessment to set levels for pesticide residues in food under the Federal Insecticide, Fungicide, and

Rodenticide Act; carcinogenic contaminants in drinking water under the Safe Drinking Water Act; industrial discharges of carcinogens to surface waters under the Clean Water Act; hazardous waste characterizations under the Resource Conservation and Recovery Act; approval of new commercial chemicals under the Toxic Substances Control Act; and hazardous air pollutant emissions after installation of the maximum achievable control technology under the Clean Air Act. The EPA also uses quantitative risk assessment to make site-specific cleanup decisions at Superfund waste sites and for corrective actions at facilities covered by the Resource Conservation and Recovery Act.

------------

While the politics of the 1980s helped promote the rise of quantitative risk assessment, scientific developments also were influential, as Professor Applegate describes here.[18] As the scientific understanding of health risks increased, so did the uncertainties. Paradoxically, Applegate points out, the scientific ambiguities encouraged regulators to search for more definite, rational analytic models for making decisions. Quantitative risk assessment filled the bill:

------------

As understanding of the mechanism of carcinogenesis increased * * * confidence in the idea of a "safe" level of a carcinogen eroded. The dominant supposition (it is not a certainty) that cancer is triggered by one chance "hit" of a molecule of a carcinogen on one receptive target cell suggests that there is theoretically no level of exposure above zero—no "threshold"—below which a carcinogen has no effect. Lacking the ability to identify a safe/unsafe cut-off for regulation, regulators began to speak in terms of "unreasonable risk" to describe a greater-than zero level of risk that would be permitted by regulation. In other words, EPA would not try to eliminate all risk from exposure to a chemical, because that would require eliminating all exposure to the chemical, which would usually require discontinuing its use. Elimination is possible (often desirable), but more expensive than EPA or Congress was willing to impose. Further, in the case of chemicals already in the environment, such as hazardous wastes, elimination of exposure is simply impossible to achieve. Thus, the later environmental statutes that focus primarily on toxic substances use various formulations to impose a greater than-zero, "unreasonable" risk standard.

The problem with the unreasonable risk standard is that it defies precise *ex ante* definition in two respects. First, the idea of risk means potential, not actual harm; therefore, the regulation is based on preventing, not actual illness, but the chance of the illness occurring. As the basis for imposing thousands or millions of dollars of costs on the economy, this is not the firmest of grounds. Second, it is indefinite as to the level of risk that it denotes. Assuming that risk is expressed as the excess lifetime risk of death from cancer caused by the chemical, the term "unreasonable" does not tell us whether a one in ten risk is acceptably low, or whether a one in one hundred thousand is unacceptably high. Nor, indeed, does it tell us how to make that judgment. Generally speaking, however, "unreasonable" is taken to mean that a number of non-health factors may be considered, notably cost and technical feasibility in determining the risk level.

Paradoxically, the indefiniteness of the unreasonable risk formulation resulted, not in a tendency to rely on narrative or qualitative descriptions of the hazard and the residual risk level, but rather in a great deal of pressure to quantify the risk before regulation and the residual risk after controls were imposed.[19] This was the result of several overlapping developments: a general effort to rationalize disparate approaches to toxic substances, a demand for more rigorous justification of regulatory restrictions, and a repeated judicial demand for justification through quantification. The upshot was that courts and regulators, and ultimately Congress, settled on a technique known as quantitative risk assessment to be the primary measure of environmental harm and of remedial efforts. Quantitative risk assessment responded to the uncertainties of the unreasonable risk standard with apparently scientific, objective, and precise numbers reached through a well-defined and rational methodology.[20]

Quantitative risk assessment also responded to a broader interest in regulatory rationality, that is, the desire to make regulatory actions consistent with each other and efficient in objective, quantifiable terms. Rationality is a bulwark against judicial challenge and also against political dissatisfaction with the costs that regulation imposes on the constituents of elected officials. If quantitative risk assessment held out, in Donald Hornstein's words, the "allure of science" for courts reviewing agency action under indefinite legal standards, it also held out the "allure of rationality" and the "allure of synopticism" for EPA's own policy analysis. Quantitative risk assessment provides one of the numerical inputs to cost-benefit analysis, some version of which is the overarching analytical structure of regulatory rationality and the implicit counterweight to human health in making the "unreasonableness" determination. Because risk appears to be a common characteristic of many different environmental programs in different areas, it provides a way to make comparisons across those programs to evaluate the consistency and relative cost-effectiveness of regulatory interventions. Risk was thus attractive to regulators as a powerful tool for internal management as well as external justification.

In roughly this way risk became established as the principal measure of EPA's activities. At that point, risk took on a life of its own, and it came to be perceived as the *raison d'etre* for the agency. By the end of William Ruckelshaus' second stint as Administrator of EPA, risk reduction defined EPA's mission. If risk reduction in the various media for which EPA is responsible (air, water, solid waste, industrial chemicals, etc.) is the goal, then the logic of making risk comparisons across EPA's programs is well nigh irresistible. EPA wanted to know if it was applying the same standards to air, water, and radiation, for example. EPA also wanted to know whether it was targeting the most serious threats and whether its efforts in various programs were equally effective in reducing risk. Given the chronic and substantial gap between EPA's actual resources and the number of environmental threats that EPA might usefully address, these questions are not just interesting, they are essential to responsible management. The acceptance of the basic risk metric, in other words, opened up whole new vistas of useful analysis within and across EPA's many programmatic areas, and it was not long before EPA vigorously pursued these possibilities.

———————

## The Specious Accuracy of "Shiny Numbers"

Once the idea of quantitative risk assessment took root, its use quickly spread because it helped address the scientific uncertainty and political controversy that so often surrounds proposed regulations.

For most of the hazards that regulatory agencies must address, the scientific data are sparse. Consensus about the theoretical assumptions of predictive models is rare. In such circumstances, it is easy to understand the appeal of quantitative risk assessment. It offers the appearance of rational certitude. It gives regulators an intellectual justification to proceed as if the proper public policy were clear. Some regulatory analysts have such confidence in the accuracy of the numbers that they have assembled point estimates in tables comparing risks.[21]

Such problematic extensions of quantitative risk assessment are not abuses of an essentially sound tool. They exemplify the methodological core of quantitative techniques. It is impossible to make quantitative cost-benefit comparisons without fairly precise quantifications of health and environmental risks, and such numbers are absolutely essential for regulatory policies based on cost-benefit decision criterion.

The "hard numbers" of quantitative risk assessment disguise an unsettling truth, however. Risks can vary over several orders of magnitude depending upon the assumptions used. Thus, one set of assumptions can make it seem imperative to take protection action, while another set make it seem unjustified. But rarely are those contestable assumptions given full, probing scrutiny. In this way, the precise quantitative portrayals of risks create a conspiracy of false certitude. Regulators, politicians, the press and the public acquiesce in the fiction that "the experts" of quantitative analysis know more than they do.[22]

In the following passage, Mark E. Shere suggests that precision in quantitative risk assessment is frequently not justified.[23] A practitioner whose clients are primarily regulated companies, Shere finds common ground with many environmentalists in his suspicion of quantitative techniques as applied to environmental risk assessment. In his experience, quantitative risk assessment is "anything but scientific, objective, and credible." Quantitative predictions give the *appearance* of precision without the reality of precise calculations based upon actual data. Subtle refinements of the tools are not likely to cure the problem because the tools are, at their core, no more than "long chains of controversial assumptions."

———————

"Risk assessment" is all the rage these days in environmental regulation. It is already a cornerstone of current administrative practice. The Environmental Protection Agency ("EPA"), in particular, currently uses risk assessment to predict the

77

health threat from contaminants in air, water, and soil; to identify hazardous wastes and toxic industrial chemicals; and to evaluate pesticides.

Despite its disagreement with some of the current legislative proposals, EPA has been a leading proponent of risk assessment. The agency describes risk assessment as a process that generates "scientific information" in a manner that is "credible, objective, realistic, and balanced"—without consideration of "non-scientific factors." Risk assessment, however, is almost always used to produce estimates that defy objective verification. For example, [a one-in-one-million] lifetime chromium cancer risk would be imperceptible among the several thousand people who may live near an industrial site. Because of the small number of people involved and the relatively low level of risk, it is likely that no one would actually develop cancer because of chromium exposure. Even if one or more cancers did occur within the population's lifetime, they would be indistinguishable from the much greater number of cancers from other sources. The risk assessment in the example is thus impossible to verify, raising serious questions about its supposed scientific basis, objectivity, and credibility.

Indeed, closer examination shows that environmental risk assessment as currently practiced is anything but scientific, objective, and credible. A typical risk assessment consists of about fifty separate assumptions and extrapolations, each of which may skew the analysis by a factor of ten or more. Taken together, these assumptions and extrapolations can alter the final numeric estimate of risk by a multiple of billions, and this result, again, is unverifiable. As one scholar suggests, it is as if you had no idea whether your wallet contained enough money to pay for coffee or to pay for the national debt, and no way of finding out.[24] The hard fact is that quantitative risk assessment generates numbers that are meaningless.

The unreliability of risk assessment is an open secret. Commentators have described risk assessment as being "fraught with gaps in knowledge that are filled with guesses and assumptions."[25] Because of these guesses and assumptions, "[w]hile EPA cancer risk estimates appear precise, the final numbers conceal profound scientific uncertainties."[26] Indeed, the "outstanding characteristic" of risk assessment "is chronic and pervasive uncertainty."[27] In this context, the National Academy of Sciences has similarly observed that "[c]onclusions based on a large number of sequential, discretionary choices necessarily entail a large, cumulative uncertainty."[28]

This open secret about risk assessment has not, however, reached the administrative agencies or the courts, which continue to speak in precise terms about the number of lives purportedly "saved" by various regulations. Academic observers and practitioners often make the same mistake, treating risk assessments as if they provide an accurate count of lives at risk. Even when uncertainty is acknowledged, it is almost always treated as a limited, manageable problem that can be resolved through refinements in the risk assessment process. These suggested refinements include improving the consistency of risk assessment methods; building scientific consensus on issues that create uncertainty; using risk assessment only to arrive at "upper bound" estimates of risk; or presuming that protection of public health means resolving all doubts in favor of regulation.

The implicit premise in these and similar proposals is that risk assessment provides a solid core of information that can be reached if only the surrounding uncertainty were stripped away. This premise is incorrect. As currently practiced, risk assessment is no more than the elaborate quantification of long chains of controversial assumptions. The quantification process could be refined endlessly, and it would not make the starting assumptions any more certain or valid. Quantitative risk assessment creates meaningless numbers, and it always will as long as it defies objective verification.

* * * [T]he uncertainties in dose-response assessment are enormous and confirmed in practice. Actual assessments for vinyl chloride, for example, showed more than a millionfold variation.[29] Even this range understates the issue, because these assessments did not take account of alternative scaling factors and differences in interspecies sensitivity. Actual dose-response assessments for saccharin similarly showed uncertainty "greater than 10 million-fold,"[30] as did estimates for trichloroethylene ("TCE")[31] and polychlorinated biphenyls ("PCBs").[32] These enormous ranges are all the more remarkable because vinyl chloride, saccharin, TCE, and PCBs are among the relative handful of chemicals that have received exhaustive regulatory attention.

The problem is not a lack of data, resources, or brilliant minds. The problem is that extremely low risks in people are not subject to direct observation and verification. Without such verification, the uncertainties are inseparable from each stage of the process—selecting the most appropriate study and counting the tumors; constructing a dose response curve; determining a scaling factor; and taking account of (or ignoring) the problems of chemical interactions, species sensitivity, and individual sensitivity. Indeed, the more data, resources, and brilliant minds that are devoted to the problem, the more possibilities that are likely to come to light. Massive uncertainty will remain.

With encouragement from the courts, EPA and other administrative agencies have made quantitative risk assessment an important component of the regulatory system for evaluating and responding to environmental threats. * * * A close analysis of the methods used in risk assessment, however, shows that the process is so laden with uncertainty as to render the quantitative results meaningless. This uncertainty is inherent in the process; it has not been diminished by repeated reforms in the past and it is unlikely to be diminished by the latest set of reforms proposed for the future.

A more promising approach would be to separate the protection of public health (the sole consideration in risk assessment) from other issues in environmental regulation. Under this approach, public health issues relating to pollutants would be evaluated and prioritized by the medical community in the same manner as other health threats. This separation would free EPA to focus on true environmental protection—steadily improving the quality of life and providing a forum for the debate and resolution of issues of environmental ethics. This separation would also free the public from the reign of risk assessment's language of numbers and computer models. This artificial and ultimately meaningless language allows unchecked government authority over risks that cannot be perceived or verified, putting the very concept of limited government in danger. Environmental issues are too important to be shut off from public debate in this manner. Risk assessment is no way to run a government or protect an environment.

---

## The Hidden Value Judgments of "Best Estimates"

Where should value judgments be made in regulatory decisionmaking? When risk assessment becomes the matrix for making judgments, value judgments are no longer made through an open, public process accessible to everyone. They become the quasi-private concern of credentialed experts. Since those experts are likely to disagree, the value questions are not eliminated but simply migrate to a different, more abstracted and inaccessible arena.

What deserves scrutiny—but is now less available to nonexperts to study—are the embedded assumptions of quantitative risk assessment. Some critics argue that agency assessments often over-predict risks as a way to justify burdensome regulatory requirements. They complain that agencies tend to use "conservative" default assumptions that result in the agency's "erring on the side of safety."[33] John Graham, the current head of the Office of Management and Budget's (OMB's) Office of Information and Regulatory Affairs, has urged Congress to restrict the agency practice of using "worst-case" scenarios in assessing health and environmental risks. Instead, he wants to require agencies to use "best-case" or "most likely" default assumptions. To come up with such intermediate risk ranges, Graham would poll knowledgeable scientists and attempt to arrive at a "scientific" consensus on risk assessment default assumptions.[34]

The following authors believe that assigning "best case" default assumptions is likely to be a highly subjective process in itself, and not at all "scientific." The conventional wisdom—exemplified in Justice Stephen Breyer's widely read book *Breaking the Vicious Circle*—is that "worst-case" default assumptions in agency risk assessments are "wildly conservative." In a review of Breyer's book, Adam Finkel disputes this argument, pointing out that all risk assessments involve value judgments and that many risk assessments minimize the actual risks.[35] For example, even though the same chemical exposure can pose a much larger risk to one individual than another (because human physiological sensitivities differ widely), risk assessments typically ignore these very important differences. Exposure estimates for environmental pollutants typically do not consider all sources of exposure, which can synergistically increase the risk to humans. Yet risk assessments frequently do not consider synergistic effects and so understate the actual risks.

---

*The Fallacies of Justice Breyer's* Breaking the Vicious Circle

The engine that drives the vicious circle, according to Breyer, is the predilection of scientists to produce routinely, perhaps deliberately, exaggerated, "conservative" estimates of risk, "using a long series of conservative assumptions [that can lead to] monumental overestimates of health risks."[36] This conservatism completes the vicious circle, he claims, in that scientific exaggeration fuels public concern, which in turn increases the "pressure upon the agency to prove it has erred on the side of safety."[37]

The critics of conservatism in risk assessment have at least one thing right: there is no question that in a number of the many component steps of risk assessment, analysts believe they are being conservative, and that in a smaller subset of those cases, substantial theory and evidence exists to support such a belief. For example, an assumption must be made for the number of hours per day a person is exposed to a pollutant, and the commonly (but not universally) used value of 24 hours/day has to be conservative—it may introduce an overestimation of a factor of two or three if the person in fact leaves the neighborhood to work, shop, etc., during the day.

But merely finding such isolated instances of conservative aspects of risk assessment does not begin to answer the correct and complete scientific question, nor does it consider at all the ethical, regulatory, and pragmatic context in which the science resides. The assertion that current modes of risk assessment routinely produce results that are wildly conservative, and the implicit message that such results are unscientific and undesirable, has been repeated so often in the last several years that it has become somewhat of a mantra—it may have some truth to it, but its currency now derives more from the sheer weight of endless repetition than from whatever inherent merit underlies the position.

There are two fundamental questions scholars such as Breyer should be asking, one empirical and testable, and the other a matter for informed public debate: (1) are the final outputs of risk assessments (as opposed to some hand-picked subset of their component parts) systematically conservative? and (2) even if the results are conservative, would that be an inappropriate science-policy response to uncertainty? These questions are vastly more complicated, value-laden, and easier to answer in part than in totality than Breyer's brief recounting acknowledges.

All Estimates Involve Value Judgments
When uncertainty prevents us from knowing the true value of a quantity we need to estimate, every conceivable kind of estimate we could choose strikes some unique, value-driven balance between the magnitude (that is, the likelihood and severity) of errors following from underestimation of the quantity and errors following from overestimation. Thus, the idea that conservative estimates of risk may be no less legitimate than "best estimates" should be second nature to persons trained in decision theory. This logic may be counter-intuitive, however, for analysts used to working in areas where uncertainties are small and the "right answer" is the only goal of the exercise. Critics of risk assessment often designate as "good science" (as opposed, presumably, to "bad science") any model or interpretation of data that is designed to come as close as possible to the "correct answer." But uncertainty means that we can't know what that correct answer is—all we can do is pick a number we believe will be too low and too high with equal probability (the median), with unequal probability (some other percentile of the distribution), or a number for which the size of the two kinds of errors will cancel out on

average (the mean). It is naïve as well as factually suspect to modify science with the term "good" or "bad" without considering the context in which the science is being applied. Rather, thoughtful critics of risk assessment should be asking whether the science is good or bad for the question being asked. For example, the data, models, inferences, and procedures useful for answering the question "what is the most likely value of risk to the average person in the population?" are simply not the same as the corresponding data and procedures that would be useful for answering a different and equally legitimate question such as "how high might the risk reasonably be to a person who is more highly exposed than most of the rest of the population?"

In addition to loaded words such as "good" and "best," the specter of "bias" is also frequently invoked to criticize conservatism. Bias also has both a technical and a colloquial meaning, however. To be faithful to both meanings, in light of the multiplicity of legitimate estimates given uncertainty, bias must be defined as a procedure or result that causes one to incorrectly estimate the quantity one intends to estimate. Real biases clearly have cropped up in risk assessment over the years, but they have occurred in both directions. An upward bias, for example, might result if an assessor failed to account for the fact that (given a fixed total quantity of some substance) the uncertainties in its volatilization rate and in the total length of time persons could be exposed to the toxin via inhalation must be negatively correlated (the substance cannot both evaporate quickly and present risk for a long period of time). On the other hand, systematic downward biases due to the nonrepresentativeness of populations sampled for exposure parameters have affected a number of past risk assessments. For example, there is a downward bias inherent in using a value of twenty grams per day as a "plausible upper bound" for fish consumption given that this might hold true for a population that gets fish only from supermarkets, but not for one where a significant fraction consists of subsistence or sport fishers.

Myth and Fact in Gauging "Conservatism" in Risk Assessment
Even if our values led us to generate—and perhaps even to regulate according to—central estimates of average risk, advocates of overturning a system they deem overly conservative have two burdens. First, they need to demonstrate that current risk estimates are in fact overly conservative (by any reasonable and consistent numerical criterion they want to use to define what ratio of a regulatory estimate to a "true" estimate constitutes being too conservative). Second, they need to show that science can distinguish exaggerated estimates from best estimates (other than by tautologically defining the latter as anything smaller than the former) and can pinpoint how to change risk assessment methodology to increase accuracy (again, as opposed to simply dividing an existing number by some arbitrary factor and declaring victory). The first showing cannot be made merely by endless repetition, and the public should not simply act on the faith that the revisionists know how to make the scientifically justifiable changes.

Current Versus Alternative Dose-Response Models
Breyer seems to favor the opinion that alternative scientific theories which

82

would result in downward estimates of risk are truths waiting to be recognized. Nowhere is this more apparent than in his discussion of various "threshold theories," which question the current assumption that carcinogenic effects to humans and test animals given relatively high doses of substances are relevant to predicting the effects of those substances at lower doses. * * *

Human Variation in Dose-Response

The issue of human variation in susceptibility to cancer is now beginning to be to be recognized as perhaps the most important source of potential underestimation of cancer risks. A recent National Research Council report referred to this issue as the "missing default," because EPA's current guidelines implicitly assume that all humans are of equal susceptibility as the strain of rodent used to extrapolate from animals to humans.[38] Breyer devotes special attention to the possibility that low doses may be qualitatively different than high doses (or, equivalently, as far as risk management is concerned, that humans may be qualitatively different from rodents), but virtually ignores the countervailing probability that individual humans differ markedly from each other. In his discussion of the uncertainties in risk estimation he refers to "humans" nearly a dozen times. The collective noun neatly obscures the fact that the same exposure to a carcinogen may put one person at a near-negligible risk of (say) 10-6/lifetime, and yet present an intolerable risk of (say) 10-2 to another, merely because the latter individual's physiology less effectively converts the chemical to a non-mutagenic form, or that individual's DNA less readily repairs itself.

Observational Evidence

There are two basic kinds of "reality checks" that can be invoked either to bolster or refute current estimates of the carcinogenic potency of substances: actual animal dose-response experimentation and human epidemiological observations. Breyer mentions one major example of the first kind of investigation. Specifically, Breyer acknowledges the finding of John Bailar and others that the linear dose-response model underpredicts the actual tumor rates observed in experimental animals at lower doses in a substantial minority of cases.[39] He fails, however, to discuss the implications of the second type of investigatory reality check on potency—studies on the comparison of predictions from animal studies with actual observations from human epidemiology. A study conducted by Bruce C. Allen et al., using assumptions similar to those employed by EPA, found a strong agreement between the potencies extrapolated from the animal studies and the measures of potency gleaned from the actual number of excess cancers found in human populations with known exposure.[40] On average, the EPA procedures applied to animal data only overestimated human potency by a factor of approximately seven, a far cry from the allegations of hundreds- or thousands-fold cited by Breyer. More importantly, among the 20 chemicals for which unusual routes of exposure such as injection were not used in the bioassays, there was virtually an exact split between cases where rodent data underpredict and overpredict human risk.

With regard to the estimation of exposure, which along with potency estimation provides the raw materials for risk analysis, other recent studies have revealed that EPA's and other agencies' procedures for estimating exposure are also not nearly as conservative as critics initially alleged. * * *

In summary, science may well find in the future that some of our risk estimates are extremely conservative, in that we are using dose-response models that predict some hazard at levels below biologic thresholds. In the meantime, however, a clear and unbiased reading of the theoretical and evidentiary factors should cast serious doubt on one of the cornerstones of Breyer's book. If there is no vicious circle of over-estimation and fear, then one has to ask whether the policy changes Breyer advocates represent a cure in search of a disease.

---

*Value Judgments*

Value judgments are so influential in quantitative models, according to Professor Kuehn, that "best-case" risk assessments may be no more accurate than "worst-case" estimates. Kuehn suggests that the results of quantitative studies are highly suspect because the risk assessors themselves may carry both conscious and unconscious policy biases into the process.[41]

For example, the people who prepare risk assessments for nuclear power plants tend to be proponents of nuclear power or consultants to the nuclear power industry. When their risk assessments are compared with actual incidents, they seem to have had a blind spot for some sources of risk, such as human error. Risk assessments prepared for toxic waste Superfund sites are usually prepared by consultants to the companies responsible for cleaning up those sites; they naturally have a self-interest in concluding that the risks are low. Because risk assessments are very expensive, they are usually prepared by highly educated technical experts who do not live in the neighborhood imperiled by pollution or dangerous technologies. The residents of such neighborhoods are likely to come to the task with different and perhaps more realistic biases. They may also have a better understanding of the way that risks manifest themselves in the real world.

---

Individuals conducting a risk assessment bring to the analysis personal values and professional training that can act to influence the selection and interpretation of information. The accident at Three Mile Island, for example, revealed the typical overconfidence of experts in their own judgments and predictions. Similarly, Dutch researchers compared the predicted failure probabilities in the Oak Ridge National Laboratories' risk assessment of possible mishaps at nuclear reactors with the actual failure rates experienced some years later. The researchers found that all of the failure values from operating experience were greater than the ninety percent confidence bands predicted in the risk assessment.[42] Thus, the most famous and allegedly best risk assessment ever performed exhibited a sizable overconfidence bias.

A risk assessor's professional judgments and personal opinions affect not only his or her view of how the environment or human body operates, but also influence beliefs about what regulatory approach an agency should take. A study of occupational health scientists found a correlation between the beliefs of a scientist's employer and his or her own scientific beliefs. Scientists employed by industry "chose scientific assumptions that decreased the likelihood that a substance would be deemed a risk to human health and increased the likelihood that a higher level of exposure would be accepted as safe."[43] Another study found that scientists who read a basic set of facts describing a well-known environmental substance and who were given the name of the substance were more likely to rate the substance an environmental or health hazard than scientists who were only told about the substance and not given its name.[44] The researchers concluded that the values and experiences of the scientists influenced their evaluation of the hazards and that "such influences could lead to biased estimates of environmental health risks."[45]

Thus, risk assessors, like all scientists, have values and opinions that enter their work, and the risk assessment process provides many opportunities for these interests to bias the results. The more public an issue or the higher the stakes, as often happens with environmental risk assessments, the more expert judgments are likely to be influenced by preexisting values or training. In addition to these unintentional influences on the judgments of risk assessors, more conscious biases also exist. An assessor may be motivated to conduct the assessment in a way that supports a previous position on a subject. In addition, the opinions of risk assessors, like those of other experts, are often for sale. The results of a risk assessment, therefore, are likely to reflect not just the values and training of the risk assessor, but also the values and result sought by the person hiring the assessor. If "the scientific community is large and heterogeneous, and a Ph.D. can be found to swear to almost any 'expert' proposition,"[46] and if risk assessment procedures provide multiple opportunities for the exercise of judgment, there is no reason naively to believe that risk assessment results do not at times reflect the wants of the person financing the risk assessment.[47] At the very least, parties will tend to hire those risk assessors who have revealed that they will exercise their professional judgment in the manner sought by the party footing the bill. Of course, the parties with the resources to hire scientists to support their positions are rarely minority and low-income communities. This is not to single out risk assessment for these problems of bias. Instead, it is a reflection of the influence of values and training in everyone's judgment, the reality of expert opinions in a milieu of adversarial science, and the imbalance of resources to hire risk assessment expertise.

One purpose of the default assumptions used by the EPA in its risk assessment guidelines is to narrow the opportunities for a risk assessor's values and biases to enter the process. However, the guidelines themselves reflect certain values, if not outright political influence, and representatives of peoples of color or lower incomes generally have not taken part in the development of the guidelines. In addition, the EPA's guidelines are incapable of curbing the considerable influence that the individual risk assessor can have on the risk assessment results. The EPA announced in 1990 that it would no longer allow responsible parties or their contractors to perform risk assessments at Superfund sites. This prohibition came after the EPA found that, even with Superfund risk assessment guidelines in place, the results of risk assessments prepared by responsible parties differed considerably from those prepared by the EPA or the state.[48]

As an example of the variability that can result from an individual risk assessor's assumptions and biases, teams of risk assessors from eleven European countries were asked to calculate the risk from a small ammonia storage plant. The results of the eleven risk assessments for this straightforward facility varied by a factor of 25,000.[49] Similarly, repeated risk estimates prepared for the proposed Brooklyn Navy Yard incinerator suggest that some risk assessments are manipulated to yield a risk estimate close to the acceptable regulatory risk level. The first risk assessment by the permit applicant concluded that the maximum lifetime risk from dioxin would be 0.13 per million, below the 1 per million regulatory guideline. A critique of the risk assessment by a group of concerned scientists found significant errors and calculated that the proper risk was 29 per million, a 200-fold increase. The permit applicant then hired a new consultant to review the original assessment; that consultant calculated a risk of 5.9 per million, forty-five times higher than the original risk assessment value and outside the allowable regulatory range. Unhappy with this higher estimate, the permit applicant hired yet another consultant to prepare a new risk assessment; the new risk estimate was 0.78 per million, again conveniently under the standard. A review by concerned scientists of this new risk assessment, however, lead to a calculated risk of 12 per million, still well over the standard.[50]

Thus, there is reason to doubt the objectivity of risk assessment results and reason to believe that the data and assumptions used in risk assessments may be selected to yield a certain result. A leaked draft of a risk assessment for another incinerator bore the comments of the project's lawyer exhorting the risk assessor to take advantage of the opportunities to generate the lowest possible risk numbers that were defensible. Not surprisingly, the risk estimate in the final assessment was substantially lower than in the earlier draft.[51] Some risk assessments, therefore, are "merely used as a way to defend a decision which has already been made."[52]

---

## Inducing Paralysis Through Analysis

For regulated industries that lose their fights in Congress against new protective statutes, risk assessments often amounts to a "second bite at the apple." They offer a prime opportunity—outside of the glare of publicity and cloaked in obscure technicalities—to prevent regulators from carrying out the law with vigor and dispatch.

It is a classic Washington tactic—paralysis through analysis. The basic strategy is to require mountains of new information before any protective action can proceed. Some of the information may be genuinely valuable, but much of it is not. In any case, the sheer magnitude of the challenge of generating and studying the information, and questioning and litigating the inevitable gaps and omissions in the models, achieve their intended result: delay, delay, and still more delay. With much flourish and fanfare, Congress may enact a new law. Its actual implementation, however, can be quietly crippled in the regulatory labyrinth.

Risk assessment provides a tailor-made opportunity for such sabotage. The process requires a lot of information, analysis and synthesis. Then, since the factual gaps must be filled with policy-based assumptions—which are highly contestable in Congress, the OMB, the courts and the regulatory agency itself—there are still further opportunities for industry to delay government action. To the extent that the agency wants to avoid political controversy and worries that its risk assessments are inevitably open to challenge, it often wallows in indecision.

The following two commentaries describe how stringent quantitative risk assessment requirements can lead to the "ossification" of the regulatory process. Quite often, the risk assessments prevent agencies from deliver the protections that Congress meant to provide when it enacted health, safety, and environmental statutes.

Below, Prof. Thomas McGarity examines how risk assessments are frequently used by the courts, the OMB and the president to short-circuit congressional intent.[53] Presidential orders have for many years required agencies to conduct risk assessments, and the OMB during Republican administrations has enforced these requirements so stringently that agencies have had trouble meeting their statutory obligations. In interpreting statutory words like "safe," courts have imposed quantitative risk assessment requirements on agencies without recognizing the uncertainties and ambiguities that risk assessors encounter in the real world.

---

As the "rulemaking era" dawned in the early 1970s, the courts, commentators, and most federal agencies agreed that informal rulemaking under section 553 of the Administrative Procedure Act (APA) offered an ideal vehicle for making regulatory policy. Professor Kenneth Culp Davis captured the prevailing sentiment only somewhat hyperbolically when he called informal rulemaking "one of the greatest inventions of modern government."[54] Twenty years later, the bloom is off the rose. Although informal rulemaking is still an exceedingly effective tool for eliciting public participation in administrative policymaking, it has not evolved into the flexible and efficient process that its early supporters originally envisioned. During the last fifteen years the rulemaking process has become increasingly rigid and burdensome. An assortment of analytical requirements have been imposed on the simple rulemaking model, and evolving judicial doctrines have obliged agencies to take greater pains to ensure that the technical bases for rules are capable of withstanding judicial scrutiny. Professor E. Donald Elliott, former General Counsel of the Environmental Protection Agency, refers to this troublesome phenomenon as the "ossification" of the rulemaking process,[55] and many observers from across the political spectrum agree with him that it is one of the most serious problems currently facing regulatory agencies.

Judicially Imposed Analytical Requirements

The courts can * * * impose analytical requirements in a * * * direct way by reading into agency statutes analytical obligations not obvious in Congress's words. The Supreme Court deftly accomplished this in the Benzene case when it remanded OSHA's attempt to reduce worker exposure to benzene from ten parts per million to one part per million.[56] Writing for a plurality of only three Justices, Justice Stevens found that the agency had skipped an analytical step when it determined that exposure to carcinogens in the workplace should automatically be reduced to the lowest "feasible" level. According to Justice Stevens, implicit in the word "safe" in OSHA's statute was a requirement that it make a threshold determination that existing exposures of employees to a chemical in the workplace present a "significant risk" of harm. At the same time, the Court suggested that mathematical risk assessment models were available to OSHA for use in making these "significant risk" threshold determinations. The Court thus found the words "significant risk" in a statute that did not use those words in order to require the agency to engage in a particular analytical methodology (risk assessment) the statute did not explicitly require.

Although it is generally a good idea for agencies to analyze carefully the consequences of proposed rules on the public and on regulatees, the discovery of a new requirement for an additional analytical methodology midway through the process of implementing a statutory command can hamstring a regulatory program. The Benzene decision, for example, completely disrupted OSHA's ongoing attempt to promulgate a comprehensive Generic Carcinogen Policy to regulate workplace exposure to carcinogenic substances on a generic basis. The perverse impact of the Benzene decision on individual rulemakings became apparent not many years later when a union petitioned the agency to promulgate an emergency temporary standard (ETS) for formaldehyde. A then-recently prepared risk assessment based upon animal carcinogenesis studies had projected a 1.5-in-10,000 risk of contracting cancer "for the great majority of workers" who were exposed to formaldehyde at levels lower than the 3 ppm standard. OSHA concluded that this risk did not approach the 1-in-1000 risk that the Court in the Benzene case suggested might constitute a significant risk. OSHA further found that "[e]ven the 'minority' of workers exposed to levels near the existing three parts per million exposure limit face 'only a four in 1,000 risk—a level not elevated dramatically above the Court's benchmark for permanent rulemaking.'"[57] OSHA engaged in this exceedingly precise analysis with full knowledge that the estimates provided by existing risk assessment models could vary millionfold, depending upon the model selected. Nevertheless, the perceived need to employ quantitative risk assessment techniques to analyze its decision led OSHA to conclude that no ETS for formaldehyde was required.

Congressionally Imposed Analytical Requirements

Congress has * * * enacted statutes specifying broad analytical requirements for all agency rulemaking. The Regulatory Flexibility Act, for example, requires agencies to prepare regulatory flexibility analyses (RFAs) for all significant rules describing the impact of proposed and final rules on small businesses and exploring less burdensome alternatives.[58] * * * The National Environmental Policy Act (NEPA)[59] requires agencies to prepare an Environmental Impact Statement (EIS) for every proposal for legislation or other major federal action significantly affecting the quality of the human environment. * * *[60]

Presidentially Imposed Analytical Requirements

From the beginning of the rulemaking revolution in the early 1970s, presidents have attempted to maintain some degree of control over this powerful policymaking tool. Drawing on the agencies' experience in complying with NEPA, President Nixon established a "Quality of Life" review of regulations promulgated by activist agencies like EPA and OSHA in which proposed regulations were circulated through the executive branch for comment before being published in the *Federal Register.* This evolved into an analytical requirement in the Ford and Carter Administrations, when agencies were required to prepare Inflation Impact Statements and Regulatory Analyses. The scope of the required analysis increased dramatically during the Reagan Administration with the promulgation of Executive Order 12,291,[61] which require[d] agencies to prepare extensive Regulatory Impact Analyses (RIAs) for all major rules. *[Ed.—President Clinton extended the RIA requirement in Executive Order Executive Order 12866. President Bush has so far left the Clinton Executive Order in place, but the OMB in the Bush Administration has been much more vigorous in demanding quantitative analysis.]*

The net result of all of [various] procedural, analytical, and substantive requirements is a rulemaking process that creeps along, even when under the pressure of statutory deadlines. In the absence of deadlines, the process barely moves at all. Given all of the barriers to writing a rule in the first place, few agencies are anxious to revisit the process in light of changed conditions or new information. Knowing that mistakes or miscalculations in rules will be very difficult to remedy, agencies are also reluctant to write innovative or flexible rules in the first instance. Consequently, an important policymaking tool has become extraordinarily cumbersome.

---

In another excerpt, Prof. Valerie Watnick explores how "regulatory ossification" effectively stymied the EPA's implementation of the Food Quality Protection Act of 1996.[62] She concludes that quantitative risk assessment requirements—combined with the huge uncertainties of assessing the risks that pesticides pose to children—resulted in an almost complete failure to implement the ambitious "kid protection" provisions of the statute. Of perhaps greater concern, Professor Watnick believes that EPA has used quantitative risk assessment to cloak an overall policy of favoring the economic concerns of pesticide producers and agribusiness over the interests of the children that the statute was designed to protect. Such ossification and delay may be precisely what the regulatory "reformers" have in mind.

Yet long delays in promulgating health and safety standards simply means that the intended beneficiaries suffer from dangerous exposures that much longer. The problem is, their political clout is much weaker than industry. The beneficiaries of regulation tend to be diffuse, anonymous and not well informed about the nature of the health risks they face. The regulated industries, by contrast, are keenly aware of their economic interests and generally have the organized political power—lobbyists, political action committees, publicity machines—to advocate those interests.

Politically, therefore, the path of least resistance for an agency is to delay. It is easier for an agency to conclude that more data and more study are necessary before it can prepare a sound quantitative risk assessment. Absent a statutory deadline, the result is that protective action gets put off to another day.

---

In 1996, Congress reaffirmed its commitment to quantitative risk assessment ("QRA") as an important regulatory tool by passing the much publicized Food Quality Protection Act of 1996 (FQPA).[63] At the time of its passage, the FQPA was called "one of the most significant environmental and public health bills passed in 20 years, [which] indeed may distinguish itself in time as the most significant."[64] Consumer groups and politicians hailed the FQPA as a victory because it established a single safety standard for processed and raw foods and contained special safeguards for children. For the first time, the FQPA requires the Environmental Protection Agency (EPA) to consider the special susceptibilities of children to pesticides when setting legal limits on the amount of pesticide residues allowable on food. Additionally, the FQPA requires the EPA to quantitatively assess the risks of individual pesticide residues on all types of food and set tolerances so that the risk to humans is negligible.

The reality of the post-FQPA era is that the EPA is not strictly implementing many of the Act's protections for children.[65] This article considers whether the QRA process plays a part in the EPA's failure to implement the FQPA mandate to protect children, and the larger question of whether QRA is an effective tool for environmental health regulations in general. Major criticisms about the QRA process loom large in the face of Congress' recent willingness to rely on QRA as the basis for FQPA, as well as other environmental legislation. These criticisms include questions about the accuracy of QRA and about whether the executive branch of government can rationally and apolitically apply a scientific framework to regulate environmental toxins.

Additionally, the FQPA and statutes based on QRA, which have their roots in risk management, create no incentives for reducing environmental pollution; instead, these regulations are more likely characterized as "command and control" regulations. These types of regulations attempt to quantify the desired environmental condition or, as here, an acceptable level of risk from environmental toxins, and demand that those creating the risk stay within this level. Regulatory action based on QRA thus attempts to quantify and manage, rather than reduce, risks from environmental pollutants.

The pervasive uncertainty inherent in the risk assessment process dictates that EPA scientists fill in scientific gaps, taking into account external social and economic factors, political considerations, and their own personal value judgments when making risk assessments. For example, at the hazard identification and the dose response stages, a risk assessor using animal studies must make certain fundamental assumptions, including the assumption that humans and animals will react to a toxin in a similar way and that low doses on humans will yield a toxic effect similar to the effect of high doses on animals. When the risk assessor is considering risks to children, the complexity is multiplied. The researcher is forced to consider whether humans would respond to a toxin in the same manner as animals, and whether children will respond in the same manner as the immature animal specimens.

Similarly, when performing the exposure assessment portion of the QRA, the risk assessor must make many other assumptions. To assess the risks of an environmental contaminant found in the air, such as the pesticide methyl bromide, the risk assessor must make assumptions about air dispersion patterns, the quantity of the pesticide that the wind will actually carry, human inhalation rates, and the length of exposure. With regard to pesticides on food, the exposure assessment portion of the QRA requires the assessor to make assumptions about the percent of the crop treated, the amount of pesticide residue that is on the product when received by the consumer, the quantity of the product that is consumed and about how and whether it is actually absorbed by the consumer. At the exposure assessment stage, one author has said that "almost every single number in this area may be modified, with relative impunity, by the risk assessor."[66]

The many assumptions required in the QRA process call into question the reliability of any resulting risk characterization. In this regard, QRA is "almost always used to produce estimates that defy objective verification."[67]

Failure to Implement the Food Quality Protection Act's Safeguards for Children
In at least three respects, the EPA has been remiss in implementing FQPA. First, in accord with the legislative requirements contained in the FQPA, the EPA is required to review the approximately 10,000 existing pesticide tolerances by the year 2006. It was supposed to have reviewed 33 percent of all such tolerances by August 1999, continue to review an additional 33 percent by August 2002, and complete its review by August 2006. Pursuant to an FQPA mandate, the EPA was to review the riskiest tolerances first. * * * Instead, as of August 1999, the agency had mainly revoked tolerances that were no longer in use and reassessed tolerances that pose little or no risk.

Second, in making tolerance decisions, the EPA has not routinely or consistently applied the additional tenfold safety factor [required by the statute] to protect children. As of March 15, 1999, the EPA reported that it had made 120 regulatory decisions under the FQPA, and that it had applied the tenfold additional child safety factor in only fifteen of those 120 decisions. In fifteen of the remaining 105 decisions, it has applied a threefold margin of safety, and in the remaining ninety cases, it has used no safety factor to increase protections for children.[68] The EPA generally continues to use a standard safety factor of hundred-fold without taking into account the special susceptibility of infants and children to pesticides, unless specific research data exists to show that the pesticide is toxic to infants and children.

Third, although the FQPA requires the EPA to assess a pesticide for a broader range of toxic effects than previously required, the EPA has still not required prospective pesticide registrants to test for these effects in adults or children. For example, the "core" or mandatory tests do not effectively require a prospective registrant to test a pesticide for effects on the adult or immature immune system or for effects on a child's developing neurological system.

How the EPA Uses Risk Assessment and Science to Justify Lax Enforcement of the FQPA

The EPA [has] acknowledged * * * that a QRA requires the risk assessor to make many assumptions and that existing science is not able to inform all of the assumptions required to perform QRA with regard to food tolerances. Thus, risk assessors must fill in these assumptions on the basis of external factors—such as social, economic and political considerations—thereby politicizing decisions that are said to be based strictly on "scientific" rational. Therefore, the result of any risk analysis is dependent on the assumptions the risk assessor makes, and the EPA can "back into" a QRA analysis to reach a final standard-setting decision consistent with predetermined agency policy.

Circumstantial evidence showing the EPA's attempts to back into a predetermined policy not to stringently enforce the FQPA exists. Consider, for example, the EPA's decision not to apply the additional tenfold safety factor with regard to the bulk of tolerances it has set since the Act was passed. This track record is strongly indicative of an agency policy not to implement the FQPA more forcefully at the current time.

The "cloaking" of the EPA's policy decisions in science also prevents the lay public from being truly informed about the nature of agency decisions and prevents the public from challenging administrative decisions. At times, the information needed for the public to question an agency decision is extremely complex and difficult to garner because some parts of the decision-making process are mired in difficult policy choices and others are obscured by high-level scientific analysis. The initial information costs are so high that the general public will shy away from challenge.

---

## Conclusion

Quantitative risk assessment is a process through which an expert attempts to estimate in a quantitative fashion the magnitude of the health or safety risk that exposure to a risk producing activity poses to human populations. Animal studies and mathematical models of reality frequently play large roles in quantitative risk assessment. Risk assessment is frequently distinguished from "risk management," which is the process of selecting from among various regulatory options. Risk assessment, for example, may provide an estimate of the magnitude of the health risk posed by an activity, but it cannot provide an answer to the question of how much risk is too much. Policy considerations play a dominant role in risk management, but they also play a role in quantitative risk assessment.

Because health and safety risk assessment frequently operates on the "frontiers of scientific knowledge," risk assessors frequently encounter large uncertainties that make it very difficult to employ quantitative measurement techniques to derive numerical estimations of risk. If agencies had to wait until the scientific community reached consensus on all critical scientific questions that typically arise in quantitative risk assessment, no assessments would ever be completed and no regulatory decisions would ever be possible. Most risk assessors, therefore, do not limit risk assessments to the quantitative expressions, and they attempt to express risk qualitatively, as well. However, for many reasons, some inherent in existing governmental approaches to risk regulation and some more overtly political, decisionmakers feel pressure to emphasize quantitative statements of risk over qualitative assessments, despite the fact that quantitative risk assessments are inevitably driven by policy as well as scientific considerations. The resulting numbers can convey a false sense of accuracy to decisionmakers and the public in general, especially if the risk assessors are not very careful to flag the uncertainties in their estimates in an understandable way.

Applying a precautionary approach to risk assessment, agencies typically employ "conservative" or risk averse "default options" to fill in gaps in the scientific knowledge in preparing quantitative risk assessments. Because this generally results in higher quantitative estimates than less protective default options, regulated industries have recently begun to demand that risk assessments be based upon "sound science," rather than default options or that agencies use quantitative techniques to make "best" estimates instead of "worst-case" estimates. Unfortunately, there is little agreement as to how one would go about identifying the "best-case" scenario that would lead to the "best" estimate. Sometimes, the "worst-case" scenario is the "best-case" scenario. The choice of "best-case" scenario is, in any event, a policy choice. Steering risk assessments toward "best-case" scenarios can lead risk assessors to employ unduly optimistic assumptions driven by policies that are less concerned with reducing risk than with reducing costs borne by the private sector.

Although there are no "scientific" or policy-neutral principles for determining which default options are most appropriate, it is important that risk assessors be open and honest about the policy considerations that determine the default options that they employ. Thus, even though quantitative risk assessment cannot be value-neutral, it can and should be transparent. As importantly, agencies should not allow their reliance on quantitative risk assessment techniques to exclude the public, especially regulatory beneficiaries, from participation in the regulatory process. Public trust is critical to regulation, yet it is hard to trust, let alone understand, decisions cloaked in secrecy and technical jargon by a cadre of risk assessment experts.

Finally, quantitative risk assessment requirements offer agencies a powerful excuse to put off regulatory action while the agency studies the matter further. Even agencies that are strongly inclined to take protective action find themselves frustrated by the need to prepare and support quantitative risk assessments in various review forums. Depending on the administration in power at the time, the insistence of the OMB on perfection in quantitative risk assessment can greatly delay if not stop agency rulemakings. The courts, too, are known to demand nearly impossible standards of perfection in quantitative risks assessments. It is not surprising if it takes years for an agency to take action against a hazard—which may be precisely the intended result.

### Suggestions for Further Reading

*What Is Quantitative Risk Assessment?*

The literature on risk assessment is at this point vast. Some of the more noteworthy works include:

COMMITTEE ON RISK CHARACTERIZATION, NRC, NAS, UNDERSTANDING RISK: INFORMING DECISIONS IN A DEMOCRATIC SOCIETY (1996).
   *NAS report focusing on communicating risk.*

PROTECTING PUBLIC HEALTH AND THE ENVIRONMENT: IMPLEMENTING THE PRECAUTIONARY PRINCIPLE (Carolyn Raffensperger & Joel A. Tickner eds., 1999).
   *Addresses the role of health risk assessment in implementing the precautionary principle.*

KRISTIN S. SHRADER-FRECHETTE, RISK AND RATIONALITY: PHILOSOPHICAL FOUNDATIONS FOR POPULIST REFORMS (1991).
   *Advocates "scientific proceduralism" as a middle ground approach to risk assessment as an alternative to "cultural relativism" and "naive positivism."*

COMMITTEE ON RISK ASSESSMENT OF HAZARDOUS AIR POLLUTANTS, NRC, NAS, SCIENCE AND JUDGMENT IN RISK ASSESSMENT 8 (1994).
   *The NRC of the NAS assembled another panel in the early 1990s to revisit the 1983 report. One goal was to offer recommendations on how EPA should go about addressing the residual risks following EPA's issuance of technology-based standards for hazardous air pollutants. The second committee reaffirmed the earlier committee's work, and it approved of EPA's 1986 attempt to reduce the lessens of that report into a set of risk assessment guidelines:*

   *EPA has acted reasonably in electing to formulate guidelines. EPA should have principles for choosing default options and for judging when and how to depart from them. Without such principles, the purposes of the default options could be undercut. The committee has identified a number of criteria that it believes ought to be taken into account in formulating such principles: protecting the public health, ensuring scientific validity, minimizing serious errors in estimating risks, maximizing incentives for research, creating an orderly and predictable process, and fostering openness and trustworthiness. There might be additional relevant criteria.*

*The choice of such principles goes beyond science and inevitably involves policy choices on how to balance such criteria. After extensive discussion, the committee found that it could not reach consensus on what the principles should be or on whether it was appropriate for this committee to recommend principles. Thus, the committee decided not to do so.*

## Why Quantification Dominates Regulatory Decisionmaking

CARNEGIE COMMISSION ON SCIENCE, TECHNOLOGY, AND GOVERNMENT, RISK AND THE ENVIRONMENT: IMPROVING REGULATORY DECISION MAKING ch. 5 (1993).
*Provides good overview and assessment of risk regulation in the federal government.*

James Leape, *Quantitative Risk Assessment in Regulation of Environmental Carcinogens*, 4 HARV. ENVTL. L. REV. 86 (1980).

The following books provide very critical descriptions of how companies manipulate the risk assessment process.

GEORGE CARLO & MARTIN SCHRAM, CELL PHONES: INVISIBLE HAZARDS IN THE WIRELESS AGE (2001).

DAN FAGIN & MARIANNE LAVELLE, TOXIC DECEPTION: HOW THE CHEMICAL INDUSTRY MANIPULATES SCIENCE, BENDS THE LAW, AND ENDANGERS YOUR HEALTH (1996).

JOHN STAUBER & SHELDON RAMPTON, TRUST US, WE'RE EXPERTS: HOW INDUSTRY MANIPULATES SCIENCE AND GAMBLES WITH YOUR FUTURE (1995).

## The Specious Accuracy of "Shiny Numbers"

Many scholars have commented on the tendency of quantitative risk assessment to convey a false sense of accuracy. A representative sample includes the following.

Donald T. Hornstein, *Reclaiming Environmental Law: A Normative Critique of Comparative Risk Analysis*, 92 COLUM. L. REV. 562, 573 (1992).
*"Critics view [risk assessment] results suspiciously, as artifacts of the chosen methodologies rather than as representations of reality."*

Ellen Silbergeld, *Comments on the Importance of the Technical Characteristics of Hazardous Materials in Considering Environmental Risk*, 11 RISK ANALYSIS 33, 33 (1991).
*Notes that most agency risk assessments ignore many aspects of the potential risks of toxic substances, including neurotoxic and teratogenic effects.*

Howard M. Friedman, *The Oversupply of Regulatory Reform: From Law to Politics in Administrative Rulemaking*, 71 NEB. L. REV. 1169, 1181 (1992).
*Argues that "cost-benefit analysis is likely to create a kind of false precision and lead policymakers to assume that economic efficiency as measured by quantifiable data is all that counts" and the "difficulties in quantifying other humanistic values inevitably leads to such values being ignored."*

*The Hidden Value Judgments of "Best Estimates"*

The following articles and reports suggest that agencies should adopt "conservative" assumptions in risk assessments that are to be used in health, safety, and environmental regulation.

COMMITTEE ON RISK ASSESSMENT OF HAZARDOUS AIR POLLUTANTS, NRC, NAS, SCIENCE AND JUDGMENT REPORT 10 (1994).
*Recommends that EPA "continue to use as one of its risk-characterization metrics, upper-bound potency estimates of the probability of developing cancer due to lifetime exposure."*

William D. Knox, *Regulatory Reform: The Present Viability of Risk Assessment*, 3 WIS. ENVTL. L.J. 49, 57-58 (1996).

Nicholas C. Yost, *Don't Gut Worst-Case Analysis*, 13 ELR 10394 (Dec. 1983).

Whether or not conservative assumptions in risk assessments are warranted from a "scientific" perspective, they may be required by the agency's statute. For scholars making this case, see the following articles.

Christopher J. Daggett et al., *Advancing Environmental Protection Through Risk Assessment*, 14 COLUM. J. ENVTL. L. 315, 320 (1989).

Howard Latin, *Good Science, Bad Regulation, and Toxic Risk Assessment*, 5 YALE J. ON REG. 89, 135 (1988).

Thomas O. McGarity, *Substantive and Procedural Discretion in Administrative Resolution of Science Policy Questions: Regulating Carcinogens in EPA and OSHA*, 67 GEO. L.J. 729, 737-38 (1979).

Talbot Page, *A Generic View of Toxic Chemicals and Similar Risks*, 7 ECOLOGY L.Q. 307 (1992).

*Inducing Paralysis Through Analysis*

Robert R. Kuehn, *The Environmental Justice Implications of Quantitative Risk Assessment*, 1996 U. ILL. L. REV. 103, 145-49.
*Provides "examples of environmental hazards not addressed because of the demands of quantitative risk assessments," including air toxics, water toxics, pesticides, and workplace risks.*

# CHAPTER 3: THE QUANTIFICATION QUAGMIRE

Howard Latin, *Good Science, Bad Regulation, and Toxic Risk Assessment*, 5 YALE J. ON REG. 89, 90 (1988).

*"In practice, [a] risk-assessment focus is likely to result in reduced public protection against potential toxic hazards, increased regulatory decisionmaking costs, and expanded opportunities for obstructive behavior by Agency bureaucrats or private parties hostile to toxics regulation."*

Jerry L. Mashaw, *Reinventing Government and Regulatory Reform: Studies in the Neglect and Abuse of Administrative Law*, 57 U. PITT. L. REV. 405, 419 (1996).

*"[T]ruth in packaging would require that [the omnibus regulatory reform bill considered in the 104th Congress] be titled 'The Administrative Gridlock, and Lawyers and Economists Relief Act of 1995.'"*

Sanford E. Gaines, *Science, Politics, and the Management of Toxic Risks Through Law*, 30 JURIMETRICS J. 271, 282.

*"Given the paucity, the softness, and the incompleteness of the scientific data in the context of public administrative decision making—in which the legal system demands, at a minimum, a 'rational basis' for an affirmative choice to regulate—it should be no surprise that administrators perpetually study, debate, and reanalyze their information, and then call for more study, and rarely propose concrete decisions."*

David M. Driesen, *The Societal Cost of Environmental Regulation: Beyond Administrative Cost-Benefit Analysis*, 24 ECOLOGY L.Q. 545, 601-05 (1997).

*Discusses the large "transaction costs" that agencies face in implementing a regulatory regime that employs a cost-benefit decision criterion.*

## Chapter 3 Endnotes

1. W. Kip Viscusi, *Regulating the Regulators*, 63 U. CHI. L. REV. 1423, 1441 (1996).

2. Committee on the Institutional Means for Assessment of Risks to Public Health, NRC/NAS (1983).

3. Other members of the committee included Dr. Morton Corn, the head of the Occupational Safety and Health Administration (OSHA) during the Ford Administration; Dr. Kenny S. Crump, an expert on risk assessment modeling; J. Clarence Davies, a political scientist who, at the time, worked for the Conservation Foundation; Richard Merrill, an administrative law expert from University of Virginia and a former chief counsel for the Food and Drug Administration; Richard E. Mirer from the United Auto Workers' Department of Health and Safety; and Gilbert S. Omenn, a physician who had at one time worked in the White House Office of Science and Technology Policy.

4. *See* Albert L. Nichols & Richard J. Zeckhauser, *The Perils of Prudence: How Conservative Risk Assessments Distort Regulation*, REGULATION, Nov./Dec. 1986, at 13; W. Kip Viscusi, *Equivalent Frames of Reference for Judging Risk Regulation Policies*, 3 N.Y.U. ENVTL. L.J. 431, 435 (1994).

5. *See* Richard B. Belzer, *Is Reducing Risk the Real Objective of Risk Management?*, in WORST THINGS FIRST? THE DEBATE OVER RISK-BASED NATIONAL ENVIRONMENTAL PRIORITIES 167, 178 (A. Finkel & D. Golding eds., 1994); John D. Graham, *The Risk Not Reduced*, 3 N.Y.U. ENVTL. L.J. 382, 393-95 (1994); Lester B. Lave, *Introduction, in* QUANTITATIVE RISK ASSESSMENT IN REGULATION 1 (Lester B. Lave ed., 1982).

6. *See* Mark Yellin, *High Technology and the Courts: Nuclear Power and the Need for Institutional Reform*, 94 HARV. L. REV. 498 (1981).

7. Milton Russell & M. Gruber, *Risk Assessment in Environmental Policy-Making*, 236 SCIENCE 286 (1987); Richard Wilson & L. Crouch, *Risk Assessment and Comparisons: An Introduction*, 236 SCIENCE 267 (1987).

8. *See* Robert W. Hahn, *Regulatory Reform: What Do the Government's Numbers Tell Us?, in* RISKS, COSTS, AND LIVES SAVED: GETTING BETTER RESULTS FROM REGULATION (1996); Richard H. Pildes & Cass R. Sunstein, *Reinventing the Regulatory State*, 62 U. CHI. L. REV. 1, 55 (1995).

9. Prof. Robert Kuehn is a Professor of Law at the University of Alabama. These excerpts are taken from *The Environmental Justice Implications of Quantitative Risk Assessment*, 1996 U. ILL. L. REV. 103.

10. The former president of the Society of Risk Analysis observed: "Risk assessment is not a science . . . . It is not only not a science. It is not anything like a science." *Environmental Issues: Hearings Before the Subcomm. on Transportation and Hazardous Materials of the House Comm. on Energy and Commerce*, 103d Cong. 104 (1993) [hereinafter Environmental Issues Hearings] (testimony of James D. Wilson, Monsanto Company).

11. SHEILA JASANOFF, RISK MANAGEMENT AND POLITICAL CULTURE 25 (1986) (citing Interagency Regulatory Group, Scientific Bases for Identification of Potential Carcinogens and Estimation of Risk, 44 Fed. Reg. 39,872 (1979)).

12. *Hearings Before the Subcomm. on Department Operations, Research, and Foreign Agriculture of the House Comm. on Agriculture* (Feb. 22, 1983) (testimony of Dr. Edward N. Brandt Jr.), *quoted in* J. Donald Millar, *Quantitative Risk Assessment: A Tool to Be Used Responsibly*, 13 J. PUB. HEALTH POL'Y 5, 11 (1992) (observing that Brandt's words "are as true today as they were in 1983").

13. 448 U.S. 607 (1980).

14. *Id.* at 644 (Stevens, J., plurality opinion).

15. Executive Order No. 12291, 3 C.F.R. §§127, 128 (1982) (§2(b)) (revoked by Executive Order No. 12866, 3 C.F.R. §638 (1994)).

16. *See* William D. Ruckelshaus, *Science, Risk, and Public Policy*, 221 SCIENCE 1028, 1029-30 (1983).

17. *See* Richard N.L. Andrews, *Risk-Based Decisionmaking, in* ENVIRONMENTAL POLICY IN THE 1990s, at 209, 211 (Norman J. Vig & Michael E. Kraft eds., 1994) (explaining that by increasing the burden of analytical requirements, business interests were able to slow the pace and number of regulations).

18. Professor Applegate teaches administrative and environmental law and environmental justice at Indiana University School of Law–Bloomington. This excerpt comes from *Comparative Risk Assessment and Environmental Priorities Projects: A Forum, Not a Formula*, published at 25 N. KY. L. REV. 71 (1997).

19. The Court's "benzene decision" exemplifies the difference. The Court required OSHA to demonstrate a definite and unacceptably high level of existing risk as the prerequisite to taking any regulatory action. Once restrictions were justified by a finding of the unacceptable risk, OSHA was permitted to require the lowering of the risk to the lowest "feasible" level. *See generally* 448 U.S. at 607.

20. Congress was, interestingly, the last to fall in line. Its initial foray into toxic substances regulation, the Delaney Clause, which banned any carcinogen at any level in food additives, required only a qualitative assessment that a substance was a carcinogen. By 1990, however, the Clean Air Act Amendments expressly regulated air toxics to a residual risk level of one in one million. 42 U.S.C. §7412(f)(2)(A) (1989).

21. *See, e.g.*, W. Kip Viscusi, *Equivalent Frames of Reference for Judging Risk Regulation Policies*, 3 N.Y.U. ENVTL. L.J. 431, 434 (1994); John F. Morrall III, *A Review of the Record*, REGULATION, Nov./Dec. 1986, at 25; Tammy O. Tengs et al., *Five Hundred Life-Saving Interventions and Their Cost-Effectiveness*, 15 RISK ANALYSIS 369 (1995).

22. *See* 448 U.S. at 607 (Marshall, J., dissenting) ("To require a quantitative showing of a "significant" risk * * * would either paralyze the Secretary into inaction or force him to deceive the public by acting on the basis of assumptions that must be considered too speculative to support any realistic assessment of the relevant risk.").

23. At the time that he wrote this article, Shere was Of Counsel to the Columbus, Ohio, law firm of Squire, Sanders & Dempsey. The passage quoted above is taken from *The Myth of Meaningful Environmental Risk Assessment*, 19 HARV. ENVTL. L. REV. 409 (1995).

24. *See* C. Richard Cothern et al., *Estimating Risk to Human Health*, 20 ENVTL. SCI. & TECH. 111, 115 (1986); Sidney A. Shapiro & Thomas O. McGarity, *Not So Paradoxical: The Rationale for Technology-Based Regulation*, 1991 DUKE L.J. 729, 732.

25. Alan Rosenthal et al., *Legislating Acceptable Cancer Risk From Exposure to Toxic Chemicals*, 19 ECOLOGY L.Q. 269, 295 (1992).

26. *Id.* at 360.

27. John S. Applegate, *Worst Things First: Risk, Information, and Regulatory Structure in Toxic Substances Control*, 9 YALE J. ON REG. 277, 280 (1992).

28. NRC, NAS, SCIENCE AND JUDGMENT IN RISK ASSESSMENT 165 (1995).

29. OSHA, Identification, Classification and Regulation of Potential Occupational Carcinogens, 45 Fed. Reg. 5002, 5198 (1980).

30. *Id.*

31. Donald A. Brown, *Superfund Cleanups, Ethics, and Environmental Risk Assessment*, 16 B.C. ENVTL. AFF. L. REV. 181, 191 (1988).

32. L. Daniel Maxim, *Problems Associated With the Use of Conservative Assumptions in Exposure and Risk Analysis, in* THE RISK ASSESSMENT OF ENVIRONMENTAL HAZARDS 526, 529-30 (Dennis J. Paustenbach ed., 1989).

33. *See* Mark Geistfeld, *Reconciling Cost-Benefit Analysis With the Principle That Safety Matters More Than Money*, 76 N.Y.U. L. REV. 114, 180-81 (2001); JOHN D. GRAHAM ET AL., IN SEARCH OF SAFETY: CHEMICALS AND CANCER RISK 177 (1988); Albert Nichols & Richard Zeckhauser, *The Perils of Prudence: How Conservative Risk Assessments Distort Regulation*, REGULATION, Nov./Dec. 1986, at 13; Alan Rosenthal et al., *Legislating Acceptable Cancer Risk From Exposure to Toxic Chemicals*, 19 ECOLOGY L.Q. 269, 360 (1992).

34. GRAHAM, *supra* note 33, at 203-05. *See also* Rosenthal et al., *supra* note 33, at 360.

35. At the time that Finkel wrote this article, he was a Fellow at Resources for the Future and a Senior Fellow at the Cecil and Ida Green Center for the Study of Science and Society at the University of Texas at Dallas. During the Clinton Administraton, Finkel served as the Director of OSHA's Health Standards Directorate. He now is a Regional Administrator for OSHA in its Denver regional office. This article, *A Second Opinion of an Environmental Misdiagnosis: The Risky Prescriptions of* Breaking the Vicious Circle, is excerpted from 3 N.Y.U. ENVTL. L.J. 295 (1995).

36. STEPHEN BREYER, BREAKING THE VICIOUS CIRCLE: TOWARD EFFECTIVE RISK REGULATION 47 n.75 (1993) (quoting Albert L. Nichols & Richard J. Zeckhauser, *The Perils of Prudence: How Conservative Risk Estimates Distort Regulation*, REGULATION, Nov./Dec. 1986, at 13, 13).

37. *Id.* at 50.

38. NRC, NAS, SCIENCE AND JUDGMENT IN RISK ASSESSMENT 206-10, 219-20 (1994).

39. BREYER, *supra* note 36, at 46 (citing John C. Bailar III et al., *One-Hit Models of Carcinogenesis: Conservative or Not?*, 8 RISK ANALYSIS 485 (1988)).

40. Bruce C. Allen et al., *Correlation Between Carcinogenic Potency of Chemicals in Animals and Humans*, 8 RISK ANALYSIS 531, 531 (1988).

41. Professor Kuehn is a Professor of Law at the University of Alabama. The article from which these excerpts are taken, *The Environmental Justice Implications of Quantitative Risk Assessment*, was published at 1996 U. Ill. L. Rev. 103.

42. K.S. Shrader-Frechette, *Scientific Method, Anti-Foundationalism, and Public Decisionmaking*, 1 RISK—ISSUES IN HEALTH & SAFETY 23, 28-29 (1990).

43. Frances M. Lynn, *The Interplay of Science and Values in Assessing and Regulating Environmental Risks*, 11 SCI., TECH. & HUMAN VALUES 40, 41 (1986). Government scientists were the most protective; university scientists fell between the government and industrial scientists.

44. George L. Carlo et al., *The Interplay of Science, Values, and Experiences Among Scientists Asked to Evaluate the Hazards of Dioxin, Radon, and Environmental Tobacco Smoke*, 12 RISK ANALYSIS 37, 41 (1992).

45. *Id.*

46. Peter Huber, *Safety and the Second Best: The Hazards of Public Risk Management in the Courts*, 85 COLUM. L. REV. 277, 333 (1985).

47. *See* Theodor D. Sterling & Anthony Arundel, *Are Regulations Needed to Hold Experts Accountable for Contributing "Biased" Briefs of Reports That Affect Public Policies?*, *in* RISK ANALYSIS IN THE PRIVATE SECTOR 243, 251 (Chris Wipple & Vincent T. Covello eds., 1985) (five policy specialists agreed that lack of neutrality among scientists acting as experts was at the core of the risk assessment problem).

48. Memorandum from Don R. Clay, Assistant Administrator, Office of Solid Waste and Emergency Response, U.S. EPA, to Regional Administrators, U.S. EPA, Performance of Risk Assessments in Remedial Investigation/Feasibility Studies (RI/FS) Conducted by Potentially Responsible Parties (PRPs) (OSWER Directive No. 9835.15) (Aug. 28, 1990). EPA was subsequently sued by the Chemical Manufacturers Association and amended the policy in 1993 to allow potentially responsible parties to conduct risk assessments "in appropriate cases." See Memorandum from Richard J. Guimond, Acting Assistant Administrator, Office of Solid Waste and Emergency Response, U.S. EPA, to Regional Administrators, U.S. EPA, New Policy on Performance of Risk Assessments During Remedial Investigation/Feasibility Studies (RI/FS) Conducted by Potentially Responsible Parties (PRPs) (OSWER Directive No. 9835.15b) (Sept. 1, 1993).

49. *See The Many Uses of Risk Assessment*, RACHEL'S ENV'T & HEALTH WKLY. (Envtl. Research Found., Annapolis, Md.), Dec. 15, 1994.

50. Barry Commoner, *The Hazards of Risk Assessment*, 14 COLUM. J. ENVTL. L. 365, 368-39 (1989).

51. SMOKING GUNS AND HIRED GUNS IN INCINERATOR RISK ASSESSMENTS, WASTE NOT (Work on Waste USA, Canton, N.Y., Dec. 1989).

52. *Id.*

53. Professor McGarity teaches environmental law and torts at the University of Texas School of Law. The excerpts come from an article, *Some Thoughts on "Deossifying" the Rulemaking Process*, published at 41 DUKE L.J. 1385 (1992).

54. KENNETH C. DAVIS, ADMINISTRATIVE LAW TREATISE §6.15, at 283 (1st ed. Supp. 1970).

55. E. Donald Elliott, Remarks at the Symposium on "Assessing the Environmental Protection Agency After Twenty Years: Law, Politics, and Economics," at Duke University School of Law (Nov. 15, 1990).

56. Industrial Union Dep't, AFL-CIO v. American Petroleum Inst., 448 U.S. 607 (1980).

57. *Evidence of "Grave Risk" Lacking for Emergency Formaldehyde Rule, DOL Says*, 13 O.S.H. Rep. (BNA) 663, 663 (Nov. 17, 1983).

58. 5 U.S.C. §611(a).

59. 42 U.S.C. §§4321-4370c (1988 & Supp. 1992).

60. [Ed.—Congress added additional regulatory analysis requirements for major rules in the Small Business Regulatory Enforcement Fairness Act of 1996. Pub. L. 104-121 §§212-13, 222-23, 231, 242, 244 104th Cong. (1996).]

61. 3 C.F.R. §127 (Comp. 1981).

62. Professor Watnick is currently an Assistant Professor in the Law Department, Baruch College, Zicklin School of Business, City University of New York. At the time she wrote the article from which these excerpts are drawn, Professor Zicklin taught law at City University of New York, Bronx Community College. The original article, *Risk Assessment: Obfuscation of Policy Decisions in Pesticide Regulation and the EPA's*

*Dismantling of the Food Quality Protection Act's Safeguards for Children* appeared at 31 ARIZ. ST. L.J. 1315, 1315-17, 1332-36, 1341-43, 1350-53 (1999).

63. Food Quality Protection Act of 1996, Pub. L. No. 104-170, 110 Stat. 1489 (codified as amended in various sections of 7 U.S.C. and 21 U.S.C.).

64. Frank B. Cross, *The Consequences of Consensus: Dangerous Compromises of the Food Quality Protection Act*, 75 WASH. U. L.Q. 1155, 1155 (1997) (quoting Letter from Charles Benbrook, former Director of the NAS' Agricultural Board, to Mike Thompson, California State Senator (July 31, 1996) (alteration in original)).

65. *See generally* DAN FAGIN & MARIANNE LAVELLE, TOXIC DECEPTION: HOW THE CHEMICAL INDUSTRY MANIPULATES SCIENCE, BENDS THE LAW, AND ENDANGERS YOUR HEALTH (1996) (asserting that the U.S. Environmental Protection Agency (EPA) does not strictly implement many of the FQPA's protections for children).

66. Junius C. McElveen Jr. & Chris Amantea, *Legislating Risk Assessment*, 63 U. CIN. L. REV. 1553, 1586 (1995).

67. Mark E. Shere is an attorney in Indianapolis, Indiana. The excerpt is drawn from the article, *The Myth of Meaningful Environmental Risk Assessment*, 19 HARV. ENVTL. L. REV. 409, 412 (1995).

68. OFFICE OF PREVENTION, U.S. EPA, 10X SAFETY FACTOR SHEET, PESTICIDES AND TOXIC SUBSTANCES 1 (1999).

# Chapter 4: The Use of Comparative Risk Assessment to Deny Complexity

Regulatory agencies obviously must set priorities for how to deploy their resources. But how? What strategies represent the most effective and rational uses of an agency's limited funding, research, staff, and time? Which hazards deserve greater attention than others, and why?

Answering such questions is difficult under any circumstances. There are always limits on the information available about risks to individuals and the environment. There may be difficult moral values and policy trade offs in choosing one regulatory priority over another. Should toxic waste sites be given greater attention than indoor air pollution, for example? And of course, there are usually conflicting political demands among the U.S. Congress, the White House, the affected industries, and the beneficiaries of regulation, about how to set regulatory priorities.

Over the past 20 years, two methodologies—comparative risk assessment and cost-effectiveness analysis—have emerged as the standard tools for setting regulatory priorities. Like quantitative risk assessment, these two methodologies put great stock in numbers. They presume that complex moral and social judgments, not to mention a daunting array of scientific findings and regulatory options, can be boiled down to a single numerical scale. With great confidence, the champions of these methods assert that comparative risk assessment and cost-effectiveness analysis are the most rational, scientific ways to regulate—and that critics are simply devotees of "junk science."

But as we will see in this chapter, the claims to scientific rigor amount to some willful self-deceptions and unsupported assumptions. Probe the methodologies and suppositions behind the numbers and the intellectual dishonesty and simple-mindedness are readily apparent.

## The False Precision of Comparative Risk Assessment

One of the recurrent claims made by industry and their academic allies is that regulatory agencies are focusing on the wrong priorities. Large hazards that pose enormous risks to the public and the environment are supposedly being ignored or not sufficiently regulated, while less significant hazards are aggressively regulated. Why is the U.S. Environmental Protection Agency (EPA) wasting its scarce resources on toxic waste sites, complain John Graham and Tammy Tengs (see excerpt below), when the radon gases of indoor air pollution pose a more serious threat?

The way to rectify such "irrational" priorities, according to academic critics like John Morrall and Graham, is to require agencies to use "comparative risk assessment." This methodology creates quantitative estimates of various risks to individuals that the government has authority to regulate, and then it ranks those risks according to which are the most dangerous, based on the specific risk assessment model employed.

To take a simplified example: if exposure to Chemical A is estimated to cause cancer in 1 out of 100,000 persons, and exposure to Chemical B causes cancer in 1 out of 500,000 persons—and if the entire population is exposed to both chemicals—then an agency should make it a higher priority to regulate Chemical A over Chemical B. On the other hand, if 10 times as many people are exposed to Chemical B as to Chemical A, then Chemical A should have priority.

The claim that government is setting poor regulatory priorities is based on a 1987 EPA study that performed a comparative risk assessment of 31 environmental problems.[1] The report concluded that EPA was paying greater attention to problems that, according to its risk estimates, posed less risk to the public than other problems. For example, the report concluded that the public was at greater risk from indoor air pollution than from hazardous waste sites. At the time, however, EPA had given little or no attention to the radon risk—an indoor air pollutant—but it had committed substantial agency and societal resources to addressing the risks of waste sites.

The report concluded that EPA should rank the risks posed by substances and activities that EPA had the authority to regulate, and then by focusing on the risks with the highest rankings. EPA's Science Advisory Board (SAB) endorsed these conclusions—although it also noted that the information that scientists use to measure environmental risks is often incomplete and that ranking of environmental risks also involves qualitative elements that the report had not taken into account.[2]

There is an obvious appeal to comparative risk assessment. It appears to offer a way to set regulatory priorities according to a uniform, quantitative scale that can rationalize regulatory agendas both within a single agency and governmentwide. Unfortunately, this aspiration is intellectually unsupportable.

There is a good reason why regulators struggle in setting priorities. Risk data are incomplete and difficult to compare. Converting such complex, fragmentary scientific knowledge into numbers denies the actual subtleties of risks in order to develop a numerical ranking. The use of comparative risk data in this circumstance simply creates a false sense of accuracy. A second problem is that a numerical ranking of quantified risk estimates fails to convey the reality that some risks have *multiple, interrelated* factors.

Despite such limitations, critics do not argue that regulators should ignore comparative risk data. Instead, they favor "soft" rather than "hard" risk comparisons. A "hard" assessment looks only at the quantitative estimates of risks employing models that do not consider the full range of relevant risk factors. A "soft" version, by contrast, frankly acknowledges the limited reliability of the data, uncertainties and other factors that cannot be quantified. Rather than relying upon a numerical ranking, the "soft" comparative risk assessments reports results in a narrative format.

In the following excerpt, Ellen Silbergeld describes a number of factors that make "hard" comparative risk analysis unreliable.[3] Hard risk comparisons fail to take into account that different types of risks are not formally comparable,

that risk estimates are often unreliable, and that risks that are ranked may interact in ways that confound a strict ranking. She notes that some risks are more
difficult to prevent than others and that cancer risks and noncancer risks are not
formally comparable. Finally, the lack of empirical data and appropriate analyses may make rankings unreliable. For example, scientists lack any methodology to quantify some significant types of risks, and there is little or no scientific
data concerning the risks posed by most chemicals.

---

Risk scales are often misleading and statistically inappropriate because the
"risk" numbers may not be formally comparable. For instance, comparing the risk of
death by airplane crash to the risk of death due to an etiologic-specific cancer cannot be done using the same population base: only persons who fly are at risk of
death from air crashes and only persons exposed to a carcinogenic chemical, such
as asbestos, are at risk of death from the cancer associated with the chemical.

Further, the risk of most diseases is age-stratified. Failure to note when the
risk should be age-adjusted or summed over lifetimes can result in inaccurate risk
calculations, which lead to faulty public policy. For example, the often quoted statistic that the risk of breast cancer in women is "one in nine" is frequently interpreted by the public to mean that at any age, women are at this level of risk; however, the "one in nine" statistic refers to overall lifetime risks of breast cancer in
women in the U.S.

*Uncertainties in Risk Estimates*
Risk comparisons assume that a great deal is known about the relationship between risk factors and human disease, and that risk assessment methods have a
high degree of quantitative validity and predictability. Unfortunately, neither assumption is well established. For example, as shown in Table 1, Doll and Peto determined that the entirety of occupational and environmental carcinogens contribute less than 10% to the overall incidence of cancer deaths in the world.

**Table 1: Contribution of Various Factors to
Cancer Deaths (Doll and Peto 1981)**

| Factor | Percent of Cancer Deaths | Range of Estimates |
|---|---|---|
| Tobacco | 30 | 25 - 40 |
| Alcohol | 3 | 2 - 4 |
| Diet | 35 | 10 - 70 |
| Food additives | < 1 | -5 - 2[a] |
| Reproduction and sexual behaviors | 7 | 1 - 13 |
| Occupation | 4 | 2 - 8 |
| Pollution | 2 | < 1 - 5 |
| Industrial products | < 1 | < 1 - 2 |
| medicines and medical procedures | 1 | 0.5 - 3 |
| geophysical factors[aa] | 3 | 2 - 4 |
| Infection | 10? | 1 - ? |
| Unknown | ? | ? |

a.   Some food additives may prevent cancer (antioxidants)
aa.  Such as exposure to UV radiation as a risk factor for skin cancer

However, less is actually known about the attributable risks of cancer than these estimates would imply. There is continuing scientific debate about the total burden of risk attributable to environmental and occupational exposures to carcinogenic chemicals. As noted by Baker and Landrigan, clinical and epidemiological detection of the associations between chemical exposures and occupational disease, where risks are admittedly higher than in nonoccupational settings, is highly incomplete. Thus, despite the assertions of some commentators, these uncertainties make it difficult to use epidemiological information as a "gold standard" for validating risk assessments.

*Multifactorial Nature of Risk*

Rank-order tables, such as Table 1, also introduce distortions and misconceptions into the policy debate because of their assumption that the factors on the list do not interact. In epidemiological studies it is usually not possible to ascribe simple cause-effect relationships—that is, to identify isolated factors causing disease in specific cases. Understanding the interactive significance of several contributing factors in multifactorial situations is much more difficult than publishing the simple tables offered by critics of regulation. Failure to acknowledge this difficulty implies that either it is assumed that chemical exposures (which figure in the categories "occupation," "pollution," and "industrial products") are not encountered by those who smoke, drink, have risky diets or reproductive histories contributory to cancer risk (such as pregnancy in women), or that these factors do not interact biologically. We know that this is untrue. * * * The likelihood that gene-environment and multiple environmental factors interact in cancer causation is now recognized by scientists at the molecular level, even if not in the circles of risk analysis.

*Is Lifestyle the Major Source of Preventable Risk?*

One frequent conclusion of comparative risk analyses is that voluntary "lifestyle" choices are the major causes of premature death. To the convenience of some, this places the responsibility for preventing risks to health and life upon individuals rather than on government or corporations. These assertions are based on data such as shown in Table 2.

**Table 2: Preventable Risks of Death in the U.S. (McGinnis and Foege, 1993)**

| Risk | Percent of Total Deaths | (Range) | Total Deaths/yr. |
|---|---|---|---|
| Tobacco | 19 | 14-19 | 400,000 |
| diet/activity | 14 | 14-27 | 300,000 |
| alcohol | 5 | 3-10 | 100,000 |
| microbial | 4 | — | 90,000 |
| Toxic agents | 3 | 3-6 | 60,000 |
| Firearms | 2 | — | 35,000 |
| sexual behavior | 1 | — | 30,000 |
| motor vehicles[a] | 1 | — | 25,000 |
| Illicit drugs | <1 | — | 20,000 |

a. motor vehicle-related deaths not involving alcohol or drugs

106

Although these data could be used to support substantial increases in efforts to prevent use of tobacco, alcohol, and other drugs, to improve diet, avoid risky sexual behaviors, and use firearms safely, its use in the risk prioritization debate is often disingenuous. As the current debate over tobacco illustrates, there are practical (and some would claim constitutional) limits to banning the use of highly addictive substances, and the prolonged national and local battle to set modest limits on the availability of firearms speaks for itself. Our ability to modify sexual behavior is modest * * * . In this context, controlling exposure to microbial and toxic agents may emerge as one of the more feasible options for preventing premature death.

## Differing Risk Metrics

Comparisons of carcinogens and noncarcinogens are inherent in comparative risk assessment. However, there are fundamental problems because the risk metrics are not the same. Since cancer is a dichotomous event (one either has or does not have cancer), increasing the dose of a carcinogen only increases the probability that an individual or the total number of persons in an exposed population are likely to have cancer. In contrast, the effects of exposure to noncarcinogens are continuous. In these cases, increasing dose increases the severity of likely effects. Sometimes noncancer effects are empirically dichotomized by defining toxicity at some level of dysfunction or damage. For example, the recent Centers for Disease Control (CDC) guidelines define a blood lead of 10 mcg/dL as a "level of concern." However, CDC was careful to state several times in its guidance document that levels below 10 mcg/dL were not devoid of toxic effect. While increasing the dose of a carcinogen does not change the nature of the disease, increasing the dose of a noncarcinogen such as lead induces substantially different clinical outcomes.

Because of the fact that most noncancer effects are distributed in the population, and often affect functions that are themselves distributed, the societal impact of low level exposures may be enormous. For instance, the effect of low level lead exposure is to increase blood pressure slightly but significantly. This must be considered in the context of the range of blood pressures in the population, including those already elevated from other causes. Because of this, the effects of noncarcinogenic toxins are most significant not at the median but at the tails of the distribution of function in the population absent exposure. The impact of increasing blood pressure by a few points as a consequence of lead exposure is most significant in that it increases the number of persons at risk for stroke. Moreover, because of the population distribution of blood pressures, this could place some people at very high risk for stroke even if the relatively small additional risk imposed by lead may be insufficient by itself to induce stroke. The concept of marginal risk analysis is needed in evaluating such outcomes.

## Limited Methods for Noncancer Endpoints

Aside from cancer risk assessment guidelines, regulatory agencies in the United States and elsewhere have not developed endpoint-specific methods for quantifying risks to human health. Despite several attempts with respect to neurotoxicity and reproductive toxicity, EPA has been unable to propose specific methods for quantifying these risks, although they are recognized as important in environmental health policy.

Methodological limits as well as gaps in data affect our ability to identify noncancer hazards. When data exists on carcinogenicity, it is usually more complete and comprehensive than data on, for instance, reproductive toxicity. The standard cancer bioassay involves testing a range of concentrations, over a lifetime, in both sexes of two species. Carcinogenicity is evaluated at several levels: appearance of frank tumors, benign or malignant; precancerous alterations in cell histology; biochemical signals of response; and effects detectable in genetic material. No other toxicity test guideline involves such comprehensive protocols that integrate cell, organ and organism information. The determination of other types of toxicity (hazard identification) generally relies upon evidence only at the level of the intact animal. * * * Thus our ability to detect more subtle, preclinical intoxication is limited for noncancer endpoints.

*Gaps in Available Data*
The gross lack of information on the risks of most chemicals, particularly for noncancer endpoints, has been frequently acknowledged, although its implications for comparative risk assessment have been ignored. Little has changed since the NRC noted 10 years ago that between seventy-three and eighty-nine percent of chemicals in commerce have almost no toxicity data upon which even a qualitative identification of hazard can be made. * * * The database for twenty-five of the 189 hazardous air pollutants (HAPs) listed by Congress in the 1990 Clean Air Act reveals enormous gaps in our knowledge of even those chemicals characterized as hazardous in legislation. For the total 189, EPA's Office of Pollution Prevention and Toxic Substances found that 40% had insufficient data even to be classified as carcinogenic or noncarcinogenic; of the sixty percent that could be classified, only seventy percent had sufficient data on which to base quantitative risk assessments. For noncancer endpoints, less than forty percent have sufficient data to quantify a critical effect, and for many of these, the data available is of poor quality in terms of sensitivity or specificity (e.g., often the available information indicates effects on weight or weight gain at high oral doses, with no systematic examination of tissues reported). * * * EPA's detailed analysis of the relevant biomedical databases for twenty-five selected hazardous air pollutants (HAPs) showed significant gaps with respect to respiratory effects and neurotoxicity.

---

## How Hidden Value Choices Mold "Hard" Numbers

The "hard" version of comparative risk assessment not only conveys a false sense of accuracy (due to data limitations, methodological difficulties and scientific complexities that it ignores). It tends to hide the value choices that go into the setting of regulatory priorities. This alone makes hard comparative risk assessment objectionable as a decisionmaking tool.

By comparison, the soft version starts from the premise that risk is multidimensional concept that reflects a variety of public values and attitudes. A soft ranking of risks, therefore, would tend to be more impressionistic than formulaic. It might use the number of fatalities as a rough starting point, but would modify the ranking by folding in various qualitative factors—the dread, mistrust, and uncertainty associated with each risk; the social equity (or lack thereof) in how each risk is borne by various sub-populations; and the perceived benefits that the risky substance or activity confers.

Comparative risk assessment fails to acknowledge that value judgments and intrinsic to our understanding of risk and public policy. As Profs. David Wirth and Silbergeld point out, there are at least three aspects of risk and six policy issues that embody value judgments, but which are not captured by hard comparative risk assessment.[4] The three aspects of risk are:

- the involuntary or voluntary character of exposure to the risk;
- the extent to which the risk is concentrated in particular populations; and
- the potential for catastrophic harm even if the long-term, chronic risk is low.

The six policy issues are:

- the availability of technological options to reduce or eliminate the risk;
- the necessity for collective or governmental action as opposed to individual responses;
- the kind and degree of collective action required, e.g., labeling as opposed to an outright ban;
- the extent to which the costs of regulation and the benefits may be unevenly distributed;
- the administrative resources likely to be required to reduce or eliminate risks; and
- the political acceptability of likely public policy responses.

The next excerpt describes how hard comparative risk analysis ignores these sorts of ethical and normative factors. Donald T. Hornstein explains how the use of quantified estimates of risk to set regulatory priorities ignores the ways in which risks are distributed in our society.[5] Yet the distribution of risks can clearly cause serious social inequities, and therefore is a compelling issue for regulatory policy to address. Why should regulations provide protections for the healthy and affluent individual, for example, while allowing the elderly, children, or residents of low-income neighborhoods to bear a disproportionate share of documented risks?

Comparative risk analysis is singularly unequipped to provide guidance on such issues. It is impossible for numbers to make moral choices about qualitatively different types of risk (chronic disease versus bodily trauma versus impaired mental functioning) or different types of vulnerable populations (asthmatics, chemically sensitive individuals, the elderly, children). Professor Hornstein writes:

---

Much of environmental law addresses public health risks carried through environmental media, such as the risks posed to human populations by air pollution and groundwater contamination. Typically, comparative risk analysts evaluate these risks according to their expected losses across populations (generally referred to as "population effects" or "population risk"). But in doing so, comparative risk analysts tend to emphasize aggregate effects and to downplay how public health risks are distributed. For example, if the widespread use of chlorine in public drinking water systems causes each year an estimated 400 excess cancers nationwide, an evaluation based on population effects would rank it as a worse cancer risk than that posed by active hazardous waste sites regulated under the Resource Conservation and Recovery Act (RCRA) if air and water pollution from such sites cause no more than 100 excess cancers annually. For the "hard" comparative risk analyst, the evaluation of these risks is simple arithmetic: 400 cancers are worse than 100. * * * [F]ull evaluation of these two risks is not so simple.

A system of environmental law must account for equities and inequities in risk-bearing if it is even to purport to incorporate one of the principal goals of any system of justice. Yet, after incorporating considerations of equity, a perfectly plausible case can be made that the risks posed by RCRA sites are "worse" than the risks posed by chlorine by-products in public drinking water: the ex ante chances of developing cancer from RCRA sites are concentrated on relatively few individuals rather than widely shared over the general population; the ex post distribution of actual cancers from RCRA sites is similarly concentrated, and unlike the case of low-level chlorine use, includes the heightened risk of destroying whole families or neighborhoods; and the cancer risks from RCRA sites are disproportionate in relation to the (indirect) benefits from hazardous chemical use enjoyed by the few risk-bearers.

That decisionmakers might plausibly reach different evaluations of environmental risks raises what I take to be an important attribute of environmental law: it must be able to reflect and define our values, and not simply count how many of us will suffer. * * *

To claim, as some comparative risk analysts do, that reducing risk should be the lodestar in environmental law, either says nothing at all or everything at once. Cancer risks, for example, can be measured in terms of aggregate population effects (such as the overall number of annual expected cancers in an exposed population), in terms of the average individual lifetime risk (the risk to an average member of the exposed population), or in terms of the maximum individual lifetime risk (the risk to the maximally exposed members of the population). Yet as Professors Frank Cross, Daniel Byrd, and Lester Lave have recently observed, the risk of one excess cancer case per year across the entire U.S. population poses the tiny individual lifetime risk of about three-in-ten-million, whereas a risk of only one-half case per year across a population of 50 would mean an individual lifetime risk level approaching 100%; the purely aggregate approach to risk "ignores the maximally exposed population, which surely merits some regulatory consideration."[6]

Comparative risk analysis gives no guidance on how to make moral judgments when confronted with such conflicting types of risk, except perhaps simply to ignore anything other than aggregate risk. Even this "guidance" is short lived. How exactly, for instance, is the comparison to be made between the aggregate non-cancer risk that 20,000 children exposed to small amounts of airborne lead will suffer a slight but discernible degree of mental sluggishness and the aggregate risk that 200 adults will develop leukemia due to low airborne concentrations of benzene? How is either of these risks to be compared to the risks to local shellfish populations posed by ocean dumping? Comparative risk analysis gives an undeserved assurance of scientific legitimacy to the inescapably collective (and political) process of establishing social policies and priorities on environmental problems. * * *

For all its ungainliness, the substance of modern environmental law is a composite of moral decisions—about the levels of protection to be accorded such noncommodity values as human health, aesthetics, and responsibility toward nonhuman species and ecosystems—and instrumental decisions about the best way to achieve these Morrally based goals.

---

## How Self-Appointed Experts Disenfranchise the Public

The hard version of comparative risk assessment differs from the soft one in another important respect. The hard version privileges the opinion of risk experts, whose elite and technical analyses are not likely to be understood or influenced by the public. The soft version, by comparison, is more accessible and open to public dialogue because it relies upon qualitative descriptions rather than quantitative estimates.

In a democracy, it seems an obvious principle that public input is an important source of legitimacy and evidence for regulatory actions, including priority setting. Yet professional risk assessors do not welcome public participation in the characterization of risks. Indeed, they often show contempt for the public's perceptions of risk, dismissing them as uninformed and overly influenced by sensationalist media portrayals. Regulatory agencies that heed the public will only misallocate regulatory resources, they argue, squandering the opportunity to prevent the more serious harms.

U.S. Supreme Court Justice Stephen Breyer, in his book, *The Vicious Circle*, is one of the chief proponents of this cult of expertise.[7] Written before Breyer was appointed to the Court, the book argues that regulatory agencies often address less significant risks than are warranted by comparative risk assessments. If regulatory agencies listened more closely to professional risk assessors—instead of a misinformed public—they would deploy their limited resources in a more rational, cost-effective manner. More lives could be saved and more injuries prevented. Unfortunately, regulatory agencies adopt misguided priorities, claims Breyer, because they respond to a public that misperceives the actual magnitude of the risks that they face. Congress reinforces these misguided pressures on agencies, he argues, by trying to be responsive to the public's (incorrect) perceptions of risk. Breyer ends *The Vicious Circle* by recommending the establishment of an expert cadre of risk assessors that could correct the current misallocation of agency resources.

In the following excerpt, Professor Hornstein rebuts the claim that public perceptions of risk are erroneous and that expert assessments of risk are more accurate.[8] Professional risk assessors argue that untrained individuals use rules of thumb (heuristics) to estimate risks instead of the rigorous mathematical approaches used by risk appraisers. They also argue that individuals are subject to mental biases (framing effects) that cause them to misperceive risks. While Hornstein acknowledges that the public may have distorted perceptions of risk, he argues that this is not a sufficient reason to turn priority setting over to risk experts, as Justice Breyer proposes. Any expert system of comparative risk assessment has its own set of cognitive limitations and distortions, Hornstein writes. Furthermore, public preferences reflect reasonable value judgments that are not taken into account by the experts.

---

* * * "Hard" comparative risk analysts scoff openly at the public's irrationality toward risk, noting with irony that the technologies which have propelled the country to such a high standard of living have also transformed it into a nation of worry-warts. Repeatedly, public rankings of risk are ridiculed when compared to those of experts. * * *

However widespread the use of heuristics and the occurrence of framing effects may be, there are several reasons why they do not compel the need for comparative risk analysis to displace the vicissitudes of public choices about environmental risk. The first reason, developed most recently by Gillette and Krier, is that any centralized, formal system of risk analysis will lack clear superiority in decisionmaking.[9] In part, this reflects the "cognitive" problems that will inexorably plague any system of comparative risk analysis that attempts to assess and compare *all* significant environmental risks. Not only will there be Herculean data gaps and processing costs, but there is considerable evidence that the experts will react to the inevitable uncertainties in the data by *themselves* using heuristics (which may, or may not, be that much better than the lay public's heuristics) when they calculate probabilities.

Indeed, seen in this light the enormous literature on various forms of agency capture may be viewed as documenting a particularly powerful set of influences that will prevent some (perhaps many) decisions from reflecting a fully unbiased, scientific assessment of probabilities. In addition, comparative risk analysts are hardly free of framing effects. By accepting some risks solely because there will be fewer fatalities if society attends to others (for example, tolerating the risks of cancer near RCRA sites so society can focus its efforts on the problem of chlorine by-products in drinking water), comparative risk analysts act much like long-shot bettors on the last race at a racetrack: they make bets that framed in other ways, would

112

be unacceptable to them. * * * It is not clear, even with heuristics and framing effects, that public decisionmaking about environmental risks is substantively poor.

As a starting point, it seems fair to insist that the case against public decisionmaking needs to be quite *clear* before a policy is adopted that rationalizes some human suffering and consciously suppresses public views. Yet even without this burden of proof, the proponents of comparative risk analysis put more weight on cognitive error theory than is justified. Without denigrating the insights that the theory may offer in some situations, when it is applied to public risk decisions there is a real possibility that decisions which exhibit some evidence of heuristics or artificial reference points may in fact also be explained by deeper public intuitions that are neither arbitrary nor irrational.

Consider, for example, that the availability heuristic may reflect a sensible way for the public to evaluate the *quality* of much statistical information about risk. Sociologist Charles Perrow notes that when a nuclear reactor suffers a major mishap, it is viewed by the risk analyst as "merely the occurrence of a rare event, that would be expected to occur, say, once in three hundred years for that reactor."[10] But the public, when it responds with concern to the available information about this single mishap, may not necessarily be committing the fallacy of extrapolating from a single datum point a higher risk curve for nuclear reactors. Instead, the public may legitimately be concerned that there was *no* reliable risk curve for reactors in the first place. Perrow continues:

> A significant event such as this is an indication to the public of what is possible; it is a signal that these plants can have serious troubles even though the experts say they will do so very rarely. Since some experts appeared to think it could almost *never* happen, expert predictions might reasonably be questioned by the public. If experts are wrong, then this may not have been the one time in three hundred years, but the first one of many, many times over three hundred years.[11]

To the extent the available heuristic reflects public concern that formal projections of risk may themselves be conjectural, it can hardly be characterized as irrational. Even those committed to the hardest of versions of comparative risk analysis will concede that formal risk assessments are often "speculative" and "elusive." * * * This conclusion is reinforced when one considers that environmental risks often involve irreversible and catastrophic possibilities that make the danger of false positives (such as those which may be produced by the public's use of heuristics) far less serious than the danger of false negatives (such as those which may be produced by the speculative assurances of formal risk analysis).

Even more importantly, public intuitions about risk can often be unpacked to reveal concern about a whole set of values that rational people may legitimately consider, values which are captured only dimly (if at all) in the technical risk estimates used by comparative risk analysts. Psychologist Paul Slovic, for example, has isolated "dread risk" as a decisionmaking factor (heuristic, if you like) that explains better than any other the difference between public and expert appraisals of risk.[12] Dread risk is associated with the public's concern with lack of control over an activity, high catastrophic potential for fatalities, inequitable distribution of risks and benefits (including the transfer of risks to future generations), and the way in which fatalities may occur (for example death by radiation, death by cancer). These are hardly inconsequential values that should clearly be ignored in any rational calculation of a risk's social utility. * * *

Nothing in this argument undercuts the potential usefulness of expected losses in the societal dialogue on risk. Certainly such information, especially when it discloses the strengths and limitations of the data, interjects a potentially valuable way to put the risk debate in perspective. But it adds only one perspective. A system of *comparative* risk analysis, in contrast, presumes that a comparison of expected losses is the only perspective that really matters. This presumption cannot be firmly, or even probably, established as a normative proposition.

---

Champions of comparative risk assessment make a critical error in failing to see regulatory agencies as democratically accountable. While many businesses rail against regulators as "unelected bureaucrats," they do not find fault with "unelected risk assessors" who wield an equal power. The point is that regulatory agencies are servants of the public and must be accountable to it. This means that the public must be able to understand and participate in risk assessment and risk management. A regime that is dominated by experts is likely to be lacking in public accountability.

Prof. Eileen Gay Jones, in the next excerpt, notes that public trust is essential to the success of any regulatory program.[13] If the public does not trust the risk assessments prepared by experts, who refuse to grapple with legitimate disagreements over values and social policy, then they will regard the outcomes with suspicion if not contempt. Professor Jones concludes that the public will not participate in agency prioritization decisions unless it believes that such input will make a difference. And this will happen only when people see that actual outcomes reflect their preferences and not those of the experts.

---

Risk assessment methodology seems scientific, and therefore beyond the pale of lay questioning. If the risk assessment were completely scientific, public input in the risk assessment process would be very limited and uncontroversial. That, however, is not the case. Individually, risk assessment and public participation are the subject of heated debates. Together, they may prove explosive. * * *

[C]itizen participation is endemic to American political culture. Although codification of public participation law is relatively recent, public involvement in governing can be traced to the birth of the nation. * * *

* * * In the absence of public participation, judgments about the distribution of environmental amenities or effects do not reside with those individuals and communities that will be affected most directly by the state of the environment. These putative decisionmakers are not elected representatives responsive or accountable to the public, but bureaucrats or agency employees. In turn, the public may feel the loss of its right to govern, either directly through deliberative means or in-

directly through elected representatives. At a minimum, the demands of American political culture require public confirmation of agency discretion. * * *

* * * [T]rust between citizen participants and agency employees is essential to productive public dialogue. * * * Trust is an indicia that an agency is, in fact, accountable to the public. Accountability to the public requires either that public voices are incorporated into environmental decisions in a manner acceptable to the public, or that the public otherwise accepts the agency's decision.

Value choices are made both while experts study environmental conditions and when conclusions about the use of that science are drawn. Yet scientists may not reflect the diversity of opinion in the population at large. Communities are composed of members of an infinite variety of backgrounds. Assurance that diverse concerns are vocalized requires direct public input. If an agency does not understand the local population, significant values or concerns may not be included or the substance of the risk assessment may not include sub-populations who may have unique or heightened risk concerns.

* * * Public participation may expose faulty underlying assumptions and value judgments made by scientists and other experts engaged in the risk assessment process. Each assumption or inference involves a choice among competing assumptions and inferences. Inevitably during the process, values influence the determinants. Values influence "the allocation of resources to studying specific risks or risks in general—and, thereby, produce the data needed to motivate action or quiet concerns. Values are also reflected in how risks are characterized."[14]

Since experts generally rank fears of certain hazards quite differently from the public there is a significant body of literature characterizing public perception of risk as "irrational." No one can seriously argue that, to some extent or in some instances, the public will act out of ignorance or make choices deemed undesirable by experts. That does not mean that the public's thoughts and preferences can be categorically dismissed, or the public is in error in some absolute sense. For these reasons, more critical thought needs to be directed toward the phenomenon of the expert/public knowledge and information gap. Simply dismissing the public as ignorant or irrational, or embracing the public as omnipotent, are two extreme ends, both of which would lead to undesirable consequences. Surely, we have experimented with the expertocracy model and found that wholly unsatisfactory.

The public will not participate in deliberative, consensus-building politics if they are not truly empowered in the process. The public's concerns, however, may find other alternatives for political expression. Americans simply reject authoritarian environmental decisionmaking. This has been repeatedly documented in literature noting how involuntariness, perceived arbitrariness, and exclusionary processes engender public skepticism and even outrage about environmental decisions.

* * * [A]gencies should have an affirmative duty to seek out public input. As an initial step, agencies should be required to understand the general demographics of the community that hosts the environmental facility or phenomenon at issue. Agencies should also be charged with creating public participation plans that are

tailored to all sectors of the community. These should extend beyond notice and include sponsorship of informational meetings. Interviews, questionnaires, focus groups, tours, small-group discussions, and educational seminars are among the variety of public participation mechanisms to be considered. Videotapes and written materials in appropriate languages should be considered as well as facilitators sensitive to local communities.

There are scholars advocating restrictions on public participation.[15] Public participation may be costly from an economist's viewpoint.[16] Regulators should ignore public sentiment, these scholars argue, which is grounded in "cognitive limitations, biased information sources, cognitive dissidence, control, or framing bias."[17] Some advocate rejecting public concern that a decision is morally repugnant because it involves the potential loss of life, even the low probability of loss of life.[18] This is risky. Depending on the salience of the public's sentiment and its ability to amass power and put this power into action, the viability of forcing an unacceptable decision is called into question. Because of this threat, mediatory and deliberative modes of political expression exist.

* * * The desire for open participatory politics, compensation in the face of injury, fair decisionmaking processes and outcomes acceptable to host communities, including concerns over Environmental Justice, are just part of our environmental challenge for the next century. Those who advocate restricted public participation in risk assessment should pause to consider the state of the environment in non-democratic or recently non-democratic countries. Authoritarian regimes where perhaps errant, rogue, or misguided "Philosopher-Kings" have held exclusive decisionmaking power, have lead their nations on a path to environmental Armageddon.

---

Our final selection about the role of self-appointed experts disenfranchising the public is from an article by Prof. John Applegate about successful state and local efforts to involve citizens in regulatory priority-setting.[19] The task of comparative risk assessment does not need to be left to the experts in order to establish rational priorities, argues Professor Applegate. Opening a deeper, ongoing dialogue with the public is an entirely feasible method for assessing the nature of risks and establishing reasonable regulatory goals.

---

As the title of this essay suggests, environmental priorities projects literally create a forum. They provide a place where a wide range of interested persons can come together to work through environmental issues. In this forum, the casually interested person can work with the regular advocate, government officials can work with private citizens, experts can work with non-experts (or experts in other fields), and elected officials can work with their constituents. Further, this can all take place outside the usual channels dominated by invested actors, adversarial proceedings, and crises. Existing institutions tend to be limited to technical or political insiders, so environmental priorities projects expand access to a wider group. It works in reverse, as well. Technical experts, regulators, and even elected officials often feel isolated from the general public by the nature of their jobs or by the need to render decisions. Environmental priorities projects can be an opportunity for them to work with the public toward a common purpose rather than in an adversarial setting.

Priorities projects encourage deliberation in several ways. Priority setting forces the recognition of choices, but avoids the adversarial nature of a particular dispute. A deliberative or dialogue process is easy to advocate in a contested situation, and it can be successful, but it is far easier when the consequences for any individual are less immediate. People can more easily step back and look at problems in new ways without fearing that they are weakening their positions in a particular dispute. The underlying question posed by comparative risk assessment—"What should we do to make our lives safer, given limited governmental resources to accomplish this?"—is a critical one for society, and environmental priorities projects can provide a framework and forum for answering it.

Most important, priority setting gives shape and structure to discussions. A brainstorming session on environmental problems may be a pleasant enough way to pass a few hours, but without a product it is unlikely either to garner much interest or to reach any useful conclusions. The requirement to produce a set of priorities imposes a structure on discussions—assessing information, ranking results, etc.—and it uniquely forces actual engagement with the issues. Without forcing choices, none will be made and all sides will resort either to disagreement or to agreement on platitudes. Priority setting "rubs our noses in the choices we must make to solve one problem or another,"[20] and thus forces us to confront our value choices. As this essay has suggested, a soft or modest version of comparative risk assessment does this better than the doctrinaire quantitative version, but the utility of priorities as a way to get to the hard questions is clear.

The existence of a common pool of information demands that participants make arguments based on that information instead of simply positioning themselves on an issue. Participants can explain why they take the position they do, and those reasons are subject to challenge. As Mark Sagoff has said, citizens are not simply collections of wants; they should act on principles, and principles (unlike mere preferences) are capable of being challenged and supported. The challenge and response is the essence of dialogue. One study of environmental priorities projects reported, "Virtually everyone we interviewed said that the effort of ranking risks (or risk management priorities) forced the participants to deal with the data and their values in a powerful and productive way."[21] * * *

The willingness to confront hard questions makes reaching consensus harder, of course. But, just as a priorities project challenges participants to work with the available information, seeking consensus challenges participants to look for common ground and areas of agreement. The search for agreement is a good way to test the limits of positions and the role of values. Even if consensus is not reached, areas of agreement and disagreement can be identified and reasons given. A project in which the participants simply "talk their way through the ranking[,] debating the reasons for calling a given problem a higher or lower risk"[22] improves the deliberative process and helps governmental decisionmakers to make more informed decisions. As with all of the elements of deliberative democracy, the process for reaching results can be of greater long-term importance than the particular outcome. * * *

Government officials and industry should know that their environmentalist critics are thoughtful and concerned with the good of the community as a whole, and environmentalists should know that government officials are genuinely trying to do their best under often difficult circumstances. When we only engage with people who already have our own perspective, we tend to demonize others, and that is only rarely fair. Building trust and a habit of cooperative environmental decisionmaking takes a long time and repeated interactions, but an environmental priorities project can be the first step down that road.

---

### Is Cost-Effectiveness Relevant to Regulatory Priority-Setting?

Cost-effectiveness analysis is the other methodology touted by industry critics of regulation as a more rational way to set regulatory priorities. These critics argue that current regulations vary widely in terms of their cost-effectiveness; it is a matter of common sense to devise a ranking of the cost-effectiveness of proposed regulations. Such a formula would save more lives than current regulations, or save the same number of lives at less cost.[23]

Like the other analytic models examined in this book, however, cost-effectiveness analysis is a morally stunted tool that ignores numerous complexities of science and social policy. Like comparative risk assessment, cost-effectiveness analysis aims at producing a single numerical scale for ranking vastly complicated problems. The goal in this instance is a ranking of "cost per death averted" for each regulation.

The analysis works like this: the estimated cost of a proposed regulation is divided by the number of premature deaths that the regulation is expected to prevent. The resulting "cost per death averted" permits analysts to rank regulations (or proposed regulations) according to the "best bargains," i.e., the most lives saved per dollar.

An alternative methodology divides the estimated cost of regulations by the number of years that the regulation is estimated to prolong the lives of protected individuals. This produces an estimate of the "cost per life-year saved," which, like the "cost per death averted" scale, seeks to establish a numerical ranking that compares the cost-effectiveness of regulations.

This section focuses on the intellectual flaws of using of cost-effectiveness measurements to set regulatory priorities. The following sections examine the claims that regulations vary widely in terms of their cost-effectiveness.

In the following excerpt, Prof. David M. Driesen points out the sly deceptions that inflect cost-effectiveness analysis.[24] The model assumes that if the government declines to promulgate an expensive regulation, it will enact a less expensive regulation or program that is simply more cost-effective. Driesen points out that this will not necessarily occur, however. For example, if EPA declines to promulgate regulation A in the prior example, it does not mean that the Occupational

Safety and Health Administration (OSHA) will then proceed to promulgate regulation B, the more cost-effective alternative. The economic modeling amounts to an abstract fantasy. In real life, the failure of EPA to promulgate regulation A may simply decrease the number of people who are protected from risks. Regulatory *expenditures* may decline, but this does not necessarily result in greater regulatory *efficiency.*

In short, an intellectual shell game is being run, and the public is being had. While we gaze at the shell marked "efficiency," the pea has been transferred to another shell marked "lower costs." We are supposed to think the two are identical, but of course they are not. The money saved because regulation A is not promulgated does not necessarily mean that other, more efficient regulations will be adopted to protect people's health or the environment. The failure to promulgate regulation A will merely increase the profit of the companies that would otherwise have been regulated. There will be no net gain for the public (even assuming such monetized calculations were the only values at stake).

Professor Driesen identifies a second problem with the use of cost-effectiveness in setting regulatory priorities: it sanctions the morally perverse ethic that corporations can create health, safety, and environmental harms with impunity so long as the costs of abating them are higher than the costs of abating other harms. Our regulatory system is currently based on the moral premise that people should take responsibility for the harms that they cause. Not surprisingly, some harms simply cost more to prevent than others. Driesen argues that this difference in cost is not a sufficient reason to let some companies continue to cause preventable damage to people or the environment. The fact that regulation A costs $5 million to save a life, while regulation B costs only $1 million, does not mean that the companies that would otherwise be subject to regulation A should therefore be free to harm their neighbors. Yet this is the net effect of cost-effectiveness analysis.

———————

This Article submits that regulatory reformers infer priority defects from evidence of allocative inefficiency. This helps explain (but not justify) some reformers' endorsement of CBA [cost-benefit analysis] as a priority-setting mechanism. Regulatory reformers' use of improved priority setting as a metaphor for improved allocative efficiency obscures the issues at stake in the regulatory reform debate. Priority-setting talk allows scholars and legislators to advocate a reform that addresses the stringency of regulation, while giving the impression that something as innocuous as an ordering of tasks is at stake. * * *

*Priority Setting: A Conceptual Framework*
The word "priority" comes from the Latin word "prior." "Prior" refers to the earlier or first of several items, although it has also referred to the most important of a number of things. Strictly speaking, priority setting involves establishing an ordering of some kind. Ordering implies that we plan to complete several tasks, but lack the resources to tackle them all at once; so we accomplish them in some rank order.

We commonly use the term "priority setting" a little less strictly to refer to decisions about performing some tasks while leaving others undone. This mode of priority setting, selection, involves a value judgment—in the context of limited resources—that some tasks are not worth doing.

We also make decisions to devote more of our time (or some other resource, like money) to one set of tasks rather than another. Some allocative decisions might function as secondary priority-setting decisions. We may unintentionally affect selection or ordering of tasks by decisions about resource allocation. Hence, for example, we may counsel a young father to spend less money on restaurant meals, because we fear that he will not save enough money to pay for his children's education. We may fear that a resource allocation decision may result in unintentional selection, a tacit decision not to educate his child after high school. I will refer to allocation decisions that affect ordering or selection as "allocative" priority setting.

Some allocation decisions, however, have little impact upon ordering or selection. We may have decided that one task is more important than another. We conclude from this that we must do a better job at a high-priority task than at a low-priority task. We therefore allocate more resources to the high-priority task. We might refer to this as a "performance allocation," since this type of allocation involves a decision to perform some tasks better than others. Perfectionists reject performance allocation altogether.

We might allocate more time to some tasks, however, precisely because we intend to perform all tasks equally well. Some tasks require more resources than others, because of the nature of the task. Hence, a lawyer may devote more time to an antitrust case than a simple divorce, because a competent trial of an antitrust issue may simply require more preparation than a competent trial of a divorce issue. We might refer to this as "difficulty allocation," trying to match resources to the difficulty of the task at hand. A difficulty allocation assumes an equal commitment to a set of tasks. This equal commitment bespeaks a decision not to set priorities among the tasks at hand. This means that some resource allocation decisions involve priority setting and others do not. * * *

*Stringency and Private Priority Setting*
    * * * [R]egulatory reformers link poor government priority setting, defined mostly by reference to overly stringent regulation, with a failure to seize opportunities for cost-effective life-saving measures, such as a more vigorous program of child vaccination. Yet they do not explain how relaxing even ridiculously stringent government regulation would increase the funding of childhood vaccination programs, or any of their other preferred public health programs.

[A] car company, if freed from [an] expensive regulation * * *, would realize greater profits or invest more in its own business in some fashion. This would not directly increase child vaccination. If the car company's reduced regulatory cost lowered the price of the car, [a consumer] might buy it as well as go on her vacation. It is a bit of a stretch, however, to assume that she would contribute to the funding of childhood vaccinations. * * *

The conceptual problem at the root of this involves conflating private and public resources. The concern about childhood vaccination might support an argument to divert public funds from EPA (or some EPA programs) to child vaccination
programs. But childhood vaccinations have relatively little relationship to decisions about regulatory stringency. Relaxing stringency would free up more private resources to pursue private ends.

Decisions to regulate weakly would not necessarily free up any agency resources to fund other government priorities. The stringency of a regulation has no
necessary relationship to the amount of government money devoted to its promulgation and enforcement.

While stringency does affect the allocation of private-sector monies, describing stringency decisions as a form of priority setting simply obscures what is at
stake. It leads to arguments that conflate the allocation of private monies with the
allocation of government revenues. This, in turn fuels very misleading arguments
for regulatory reform. * * *

*Variations in Dollars Per Life Saved*
* * * Regulatory reformers seem to view all private-sector resources as fungible
assets available for deployment to all conceivable health and safety projects.
Government through its stringency determinations allocates this money to various societal problems. Allocating too much money to trivial problems and not
enough to important ones could involve poor priority setting.

* * * Stringency determinations can only affect selection in the rarest of cases;
if the agency decides not to limit the activity it is regulating at all (an extreme version of a lax regulation), this may involve a secondary selection. But most decisions about stringency will not function as secondary selection decisions either.
Hence, inconsistent stringency determinations, while they affect allocation, do
not generally affect priority setting in its most commonly understood modes of ordering and selection.

Inconsistent stringency might involve what I have called a performance allocation, a decision to do some jobs well and others less well. I will let the reader decide whether performance allocations should be considered priority setting at all.
But clearly, it would be helpful to distinguish this from ordering and selection, the
most common forms of priority setting.

* * * Private-sector funds do not form a fungible pool of resources that a regulating agency can allocate to our most pressing regulatory priorities, so the first
assumption made in trying to link stringency to priority setting is suspect. While
government may require chemical plants to cleanup their own pollution, government cannot require the owners of chemical plants to improve automobile safety
through better designed passive restraints, even if this would save more lives
than control of toxic pollution from chemical plants.

Stringency determinations do not reallocate private compliance resources
among regulated industries. A decision to regulate toxics at a chemical plant
weakly allows the company to devote more money to chemical manufacturing,

but does not create more funding for auto safety. Similarly, a decision to regulate auto safety strictly does not reduce government opportunities to demand stringent reductions from chemical plants. Hence, stringency determinations have very little or no secondary impact on cross-program regulatory priority setting.

Finally, the view of stringency determination as a form of performance allocation seems odd, because it does not involve one actor performing some tasks well and others less well. Rather, it involves the government demanding a lot from some companies, while insisting upon less from others. It seems that characterizing inconsistent stringency as "priority setting" simply adds confusion, even if one accepts the concept of performance allocation as a kind of priority setting. Moreover, even if thinking of stringency determinations as a form of priority setting somehow aids analysis, it is not clear why variations in lives saved shows poor priority setting. Regulatory reformers think that dollars per lives saved should be somewhat even across regulatory programs. They do not explain why this should be so.

One would not expect regulatory programs to produce even approximately even dollars per lives saved costs. Our regulatory system, like the common law preceding it, is based on the assumption that people must take some responsibility for the harms they cause. Some harms simply cost more to remedy than others.

Furthermore, the regulatory system, again like the common-law system, sometimes takes equity into account in deciding how strict a compliance regime to impose on companies. Some companies can pay out large sums of money to take care of health and safety problems. Others would go bankrupt if subjected to strict regulation. Agencies often take this into account in writing regulation, with resulting unevenness in compliance cost. This helps avoid the kind of drastic consequences that could occur in theory under any regime imposing any cost. While one can criticize stringency adjustments based on equitable considerations, these adjustments hardly seem irrational.

---

## The Mythical Regulatory Costs Calculated by Morrall

Industry and academic critics of regulation contend that the wide variance in the cost-effectiveness of regulations proves that current regulatory priorities are misguided. If government were indeed rational and economic-minded in its priority-setting, goes the argument, it could save as many or more lives by concentrating on the least-cost regulations. According to this argument, a rational reallocation of regulatory resources would make it possible to increase health, safety, and environmental benefits at no extra cost!

The case for cost-effectiveness is essentially an efficiency argument. If regulation A has a cost of $5 million dollars per life saved and regulation B has a cost of $1 million dollars per life saved, then regulation B should have a higher priority because it would be more efficient. It would save five lives at a cost of $5 million, while regulation A would save only one life for the same cost. Regulation B is a "better deal."

But what is the evidence that current regulatory priorities are grievously irrational and "inefficient"? The prime source for this claim is a 1986 article by John Morrall, an economist at the Office of Management and Budget (OMB), who analyzed the cost-effectiveness of 44 proposed, final, or rejected regulations.[25] Morrall used data that agencies had submitted to OMB; he then made some adjustments in the data for purposes of his analysis.

Morrall found a wide variation in the regulatory cost of saving a life. The three least-cost regulations, for example, had a cost of $100,000 per life saved, while the most expensive regulation had a cost of $72 million per life saved. In addition, many of the regulations came with a high price tag. Twenty-four of the regulations cost more than $7 million per life saved, and 17 regulations cost more than $50 million per life saved. OMB twice updated Morrall's study during the Reagan and first Bush Administrations with similar results.[26]

Regulatory critics who have cited the Morrall study (or an update of it) have accepted the Morrall calculations at face value. After careful analysis, however, Prof. Lisa Heinzerling discovered that Morrall's calculations contain regulatory costs of "mythical proportions."[27] As the following excerpt explains, Morrall's numbers are suspect for a number of reasons. First, he makes many arbitrary adjustments to the economic valuation of regulatory benefits; the practical effect was to greatly reduce the dollar value of those benefits. Second, for the regulatory benefits that he studied, Morrall's results differ substantially from the estimates of regulatory benefits that agencies reported to OMB.

There are still other suspect elements in Morrall's calculations. Because his calculations examine only the potential of regulations to save lives—not other benefits such as a reduction in injuries or protection of the environment—Morrall *underestimated* the actual benefits of many regulations in his study. Finally, Morrall discounted the value of the benefits using a very high discount rate. As we will see in Chapter 7, the use of discounting is controversial, particularly when the user employs a rate as high as Morrall used.

Professor Heinzerling:

---

* * * What is the basis for these numbers? Morrall provides some explanation of the method he used to arrive at them. In estimating compliance costs, Morrall reports that he "generally" accepted agencies' estimates "without adjustment." He explains that although agencies have an incentive to underestimate costs, this underestimation may be offset by the fact that firms often come up with unexpected ways to reduce the costs of compliance.

In estimating the benefits of regulation, however, Morrall did not adopt the agencies' estimates. Instead, he made two significant adjustments to these estimates in developing his table. First, Morrall adjusted the agencies' estimates of future costs and benefits—including the number of lives saved by regulation—by applying a ten percent discount rate to them. This discount rate was in line with the guidelines then used by the OMB in performing cost-benefit analysis. * * *

Second, Morrall adjusted the agencies' estimates of the number of lives saved through regulation by relying on different—and lower—estimates of risk and regulatory effectiveness than those provided by the agencies. For safety regulations, Morrall "often" reduced agency assumptions about the efficacy of regulation "from 100-percent effectiveness to a more reasonable figure such as 50 percent." For health regulations, where the agency relied on the highest estimate in a range of risk estimates, Morrall sometimes picked an intermediate estimate supplied by the agency. In other cases, he selected what appeared to him to be "the most reliable" estimate of risk, provided in some cases by "published studies that appeared to reflect prevailing scientific views more accurately than the agency estimate." He specifically notes that he rejected OSHA's estimate of the risks of ethylene oxide and instead used the estimate of EPA because EPA purportedly had relied on epidemiological rather than animal studies. Beyond this example, Morrall does not elaborate on the specific adjustments he made to the agencies' estimates of cancer risk, nor does he elaborate on his specific reasons for making those adjustments. * * *

*Choosing the Rules for the List: Overinclusion and Underinclusion*
John Morrall and many others have used his table to argue that there is something systematically amiss in our system for regulating risk. That is, his table has not been used merely to point out the existence of some regulations that cost too much in relation to the benefits they confer or that cost too much in comparison to alternative ways of regulating risk. His table has been used instead to support wholesale regulatory reform. It is thus important to consider the legal status of the regulations appearing on Morrall's list. If it turns out that the current system for regulating risk managed to reject many of the costliest regulations on the list before they were ever implemented, that result would undermine the argument for wholesale reform; this is particularly true if the very reason for rejection was that the costs of the rules exceeded their benefits. It is also important to know whether the rules on Morrall's list comprise a representative sampling of the products of the current regulatory system. If they do not—and if they systematically err by, for example, excluding rules or rulemaking possibilities that imposed or would have imposed lower costs per life saved—this would also diminish the case for wholesale regulatory reform.

* * * As it turns out, Morrall's table is itself a crazy quilt. A substantial portion of the rules on the list were rejected by the relevant agencies on the very ground that their benefits did not exceed their costs. Although Morrall himself notes that cost-effectiveness was an important determinant of legal status, he only glancingly acknowledges that a substantial percentage of the rules at the bottom of his list were rejected for a reason he would presumably applaud. Still more troubling is the omission, in several updated versions of Morrall's list, of any mention of the legal status of the rules on the list; these versions of the lists imply, incorrectly, that all of the rules on the list are in force and generating current costs. Perhaps most perplexing, however, is that several of the rules on Morrall's list simply do not exist; two never existed, as far as I can tell, and two were proposed but not issued. Insofar as the list includes rules rejected for the very reason that their costs were deemed unjustified and rules that do not exist, the list is overinclusive.

124

In addition, although Morrall indicates that his criterion for inclusion of rules on the table was the availability of "reasonably complete information" on costs and benefits, there are many regulations, and failures to regulate, that fit this criterion but were nevertheless excluded from the list. These regulations imposed, or would have imposed, dramatically lower regulatory costs than many of the rules Morrall did include. In this sense, therefore, the list is underinclusive as well.

[E]ight out of the eleven rules at the very bottom of Morrall's list, and several others, do not belong on the list at all, either because they were rejected for the very reason that their costs exceeded their benefits or because they have, for other reasons, never taken effect. Excluding these rules dramatically narrows the range of cost-effectiveness reflected on Morrall's list. As I discuss in the next section, this range narrows still more when the agencies' estimates of risks and costs—rather than Morrall's—are used to derive the figures on cost-effectiveness.

## Competing Estimates of Costs per Life Saved

The selection of rules for Morrall's list is not the only shortcoming of the list. The costs per life saved reported by Morrall are also problematic. This section compares Morrall's estimates of the risks avoided by the regulations on his list and the costs they would impose with the agencies' estimates of those risks and costs. As we shall see, Morrall's estimates are strikingly different from—and inevitably higher than—the agencies' estimates. Indeed, as I explain below, there is as much as a 1000-fold variance between Morrall's estimates of costs per life saved and the agencies' (often implicit) estimates of these costs. These differences appear to stem from two sources: Morrall's discounting of the number of lives the regulations were expected to save in the future by ten percent per year and his adjustments to the agencies' quantitative risk assessments. * * *

* * * Morrall's figures on benefits and costs are starkly different from other reported estimates. As Table 3 shows, if one adopts either the agency's (often implicit) estimate of costs per life saved or the estimate offered by Morrall in other contexts, then in every case but two, one finds a cost per life saved of less than $5 million. Only OSHA's formaldehyde and arsenic regulations reflect a higher cost per life saved. This means that, as to virtually every rule, the costs per life saved as calculated by sources other than Morrall's 1986 table are below the range of current estimates of the monetary value of a human life based on studies of wage premiums for risky jobs. * * * [A] frequently cited range for the value of a human life is $3 million to $7 million. According to these estimates, therefore, all of these regulations save two pass even the test of cost-benefit analysis.

**Table 3. Competing Estimates of the Costs
of Various Risk-Reducing Regulations per Life Saved**

| Regulation | Morrall's 1986 Cost Estimate (Thousands) | Regulatory Agency's (Except as Noted) Cost Estimate (Thousands) |
|---|---|---|
| Asbestos (OSHA 1972) | $7,400 | $190 |
| Benzene (OSHA 1985) | $17,100 | $1,800 |
| Arsenic/Glass Plant (EPA 1986) | $19,200 | $4,800 |
| Ethylene Oxide (OSHA 1984) | $25,600 | $2,030–$3,880 |
| Uranium Mill Tailings/Inactive (EPA 1983) | $27,600 | $1,570 |
| Acrylonitrile (OSHA 1978) | $37,600 | $3,500 |
| Uranium Mill Tailings/Active (EPA 1983) | $53,000 | $2,500 |
| Coke Ovens (OSHA 1976) | $61,800 | $4,500 |
| Asbestos (OSHA 1986) | $89,300 | $2,800 |
| Arsenic (OSHA 1978) | $92,500 | $10,000 |
| Arsenic/Low-Arsenic Copper (EPA 1986) | $764,000 | $4,170 |
| Land Disposal (EPA 1986) | $3,500,000 | $2,380 |
| Formaldehyde (OSHA 1985) | $72,000,000 | $21,800 |

If one also considers the unquantified benefits of these rules, including avoidance of human illness other than cancer, prevention of ecological harm, and damage to values such as autonomy, community, and equity, the case in favor of these regulations becomes clearer still. And this is all without any adjustment for the well-documented tendency of agencies and industry to overestimate greatly the costs of compliance with proposed regulation. Such overestimation has, in fact, been confirmed in retrospective studies of the compliance costs of some of the rules on Morrall's list.

## The Dubious Number-Crunching of Graham

Another much-cited, widely publicized source on the value of regulation is John Graham, formerly of the Harvard Center for Risk Analysis. Graham now the head of the Office of Information and Regulatory Affairs at OMB.

At first glance, a 1995 study by Graham and his co-authors appears to confirm the results of Morrall article. Graham estimated the cost-effectiveness of 587 life-saving interventions, and divided them into three categories: fatal injury reduction, the control of toxins, and medical interventions. He measured cost-effectiveness according to the cost per life-year saved, which is the cost per year of preventing a premature death. His calculations revealed vast disparities in life-saving costs across interventions and across categories of interventions. The disparities were particularly large in the category of toxic control, where costs ranged from zero or less than zero (because the intervention saved more money than it cost) to $99 billion for each life-year saved.[28]

Like Morrall's study, the number-crunching by Graham is rife with serious methodological flaws. Georgetown University Professor Heinzerling outlined these deficiencies in congressional testimony in 2001.[29] Graham's calculations commit the same deception as Morrall's by including regulations (and other life-saving measures) that no agency ever implemented; some were never even proposed. Yet the costs of these measures are nonetheless cited as if they represented an actual or proposed regulatory intervention.

A second flaw in Graham's study is that many of the live-saving interventions cited can only be taken by individuals in their private capacities, such as quitting smoking or otherwise changing their behavior. Agencies can hardly be blamed for poor priority setting regarding activities that are not within their control.

The reader may wish to recall Driesen's point that reducing the stringency of environmental regulation will not save more lives if the additional life-saving requires actions by private individuals. Once again, a theoretical fantasy is invoked to spin a narrative that has little chance of actually occurring. Yet it is then presented as an entirely realistic scenario. Graham finds that reducing smoking is highly cost-effective (which is true enough), and therefore a better priority than EPA regulation. But he does not explain how a decision by EPA to regulate less stringently would somehow lead to a reduction in smoking. This illustrates how risk comparisons can be highly misleading. The government's decision to increase one type of life-saving activity (such as discouraging smoking) does not mean that it cannot or should not also aggressively protect the environment.

A third problem of Graham's study is its use of many duplicate estimates of regulatory costs. As a result, it overstates the degree of variation in life-saving measures. Like Morrall, Graham used discounted estimates in his calculations. Although he employed a lower discount rate (5% instead of Morrall's 10%), the use of discounting is still controversial, as we see in Chapter 7 below. Finally, Graham measured cost-effectiveness in terms of the number of years a regulation might prolong someone's life. As a result, his measurement of regulatory priorities assumes that saving the lives of the elderly is not as important as saving the lives of younger persons.

Professor Heinzerling writes:

---

\* \* \* In evaluating this study and in evaluating Dr. Graham's subsequent uses of it, it is important to understand several basic features of the study. These include the study's inclusion of many life-saving measures that have never been undertaken; the inclusion of both regulatory and non-regulatory life-saving measures; the duplication of measures on the list; the use of life-years saved as the sole metric by which to judge these measures; and the use of the technique of discounting future life-saving. \* \* \*

*The Inclusion of Unimplemented Life-Saving Measures.* The "Five-Hundred Life-Saving Interventions" study includes many life-saving measures that have never been undertaken by anyone. As Graham and his co-authors acknowledge, their study includes life-saving measures "that are fully implemented, those that are only partially implemented, and *those that are implemented not at all.*"

In fact, a very large number of the toxin controls studied by Graham and Tengs were never implemented by any agency, frequently for the very reason that their costs were thought to exceed their benefits. An equally large number of these controls were never even proposed by any agency. Indeed, although nine of the ten most expensive life-saving interventions in the entire study involved toxin control, *not one* of those nine interventions was ever implemented by a regulatory agency. The most expensive intervention on Graham and Tengs' list—the control of chloroform from paper mills, purportedly costing $99 billion per year of life saved—was never even proposed.

*The Inclusion of Both Regulatory and Non-Regulatory Life-Saving Measures.* This study also includes both regulatory and non-regulatory life-saving measures. Many of these measures would be undertaken, if at all, by individuals acting in their private capacities, such as doctors advising patients about quitting smoking or 35-year-old men undertaking an exercise regimen. Many other measures would entail government intervention. Indeed, the category of toxin control consists almost entirely of measures that might be (but in many cases have not been) undertaken by the government.

There is, of course, nothing inherently wrong with including both regulatory and non-regulatory life-saving programs in such a study. As will become clear, however, one must be careful to attribute life-saving costs to their appropriate source, and not to blame the regulatory system for any costs and misallocations found in the private sector.

*The Duplication of Life-Saving Measures on Graham and Tengs' List.* Graham and Tengs' study does not in fact look at 587 *different* interventions. In numerous cases, Graham and Tengs examined the very same life-saving measure, but from the perspective of different analysts. These analysts obviously had very different views about the costs and effectiveness of the very same life-saving measures. For example, Graham and Tengs report two estimates of the cost per life-year saved of a ban on urea-formaldehyde form insulation in homes; one estimate puts the cost at $11,000 per life-year saved, and another at $220,000 per life-year saved. To take another example, Graham and Tengs also offer two estimates of the costs of controlling arsenic emissions at glass plants; one estimate is $2.3 million per life-year saved, the other is $51 million per life-year saved. Graham and Tengs provide no guidance as to how one might choose between these strikingly different perspectives on the costs of the very same life-saving measures. They also do not face up to the strange consequence of their duplication of life-saving measures: one might conclude that we could save a large amount of money in arsenic control simply by adopting the views of the $2 million analyst rather than the $51 million analyst!

*Life-Years Saved as the Measure of Effectiveness.* In estimating the costs of these 587 life-saving measures, Graham and his research team used two significant and controversial analytical techniques. First, they defined the only relevant regulatory benefit to be the saving of *years* of life, or *life-years*. Put simply, this means that, in the view of Graham and his co-authors, a measure that saves the lives of the elderly is not as good as one saving the lives of the middle-aged, and likewise, a measure saving the lives of the middle-aged is not as good as one saving the lives of the young. It also means that benefits like the prevention of nonfatal illnesses and the protection of ecosystems are not taken into account in Graham and his co-authors' analysis.

*Discounting Future Life-Saving Benefits.* Second, in calculating the benefits of life-saving measures, Graham and his co-authors employed an analytical technique known as "discounting." Specifically, they reduced all future life-saving benefits by 5 percent per year. * * *

*Conclusions of the Study.* After applying these analytical techniques, Graham, Tengs, and their co-authors found that the costs per year of life saved varied widely across interventions and often reached very high levels. Graham and Tengs also found that toxin control was the most costly, in general, of the categories of life-saving interventions they considered. Specifically, they found that the costs of toxin control ranged from equal to or less than zero (meaning that some interventions saved more money than they cost) to as high as $99 billion for every year of life saved. As noted, however, many of the toxin controls considered by Graham and Tengs were never implemented, and many were never even proposed by a regulatory agency. * * *

## How Graham's Research Ignores Many Benefits of Health, Safety, and Environmental Protection

An important limitation of Graham's studies is that they assume that the only benefit of environmental protection is to prevent fatal illnesses in humans. Thus these studies ignore many significant benefits of environmental programs. Most obviously, their fixation on fatal illnesses ignores nonfatal harms to human health. Most lethal substances also cause nonfatal health effects. Toxic chemicals can, for example, cause respiratory, neurological, reproductive, hematological, and other health-impairing disorders. Not all of these disorders are fatal, yet they are nevertheless unpleasant and costly byproducts of toxic pollution. In addition, environmental toxins can cause harms to ecosystems, harms which simply do not show up in Graham's limited analysis.

Graham's analysis not only excludes the many benefits of health, safety, and environmental regulation that do not involve life-saving; it also excludes life-saving benefits themselves if these cannot be quantified. This often means that, in the context of toxin control, any life-saving benefits other than the prevention of cancer are ignored because cancer prevention is often the only life-saving benefit that can be quantified. * * *

## Whose Life Is Worth Saving?

The final problem with Graham's studies on regulatory costs involves the studies' assumptions about whose life is worth saving. Graham's studies do not assume that all human lives endangered by human action are equally valuable. On the contrary, these studies assume that it is better to save the lives of the young than the lives of the old, and they operationalize this assumption by focusing on the number of life-years, and not the number of lives, saved by an intervention. Graham also assumes that lives saved in the future are worth less than lives saved today, and he operationalizes this assumption by applying a 5 percent discount rate to future life-saving. Both of these analytical devices have a large negative effect on assessments of environmental programs in particular, and both are very controversial. * * *

It is not difficult to grasp the issues inherent in the question whether to evaluate life-saving programs according to the life-years, or according to the lives, they save. The question turns, essentially, on whether one views older people as equally worthy of protecting from the hazards of, say, air pollution as younger people. It seems to me that our society's norms of equality argue strongly against offering less protection to people based simply on age.

---

### Is the Government Committing "Statistical Murder"?

Critics are not content to say that current regulatory priorities are misguided or inefficient. In 1996, Graham published another study that claimed that the government's skew priorities were tantamount to "statistical murder."

Graham's study was based on the economic concept of "opportunity cost," which measures the gains that an entity might have achieved from an activity that it did not actually undertake. Graham argued that the government was supposedly squandering a huge opportunity cost by pursuing expensive life-saving interventions instead of less expensive alternatives. He calculated that the government could save an additional 60,200 lives a year if the life-saving interventions that cost $7.57 million or less per year were re-directed to more cost-effective interventions. This step would more than double the life-saving potential of current interventions, he asserted.[30]

To call attention to his findings, Graham testified before Congress that the current misguided allocation of life-saving regulatory resources constitutes "statistical murder" because it fails to save the lives of 60,200 unidentified persons. Naturally, Graham's startling claim received considerable attention in the media and in political circles.

But how rigorous are Graham's calculations? And how feasible would it be to reallocate government regulatory resources in the manner that Graham recommends? When Professor Heinzerling closely investigated the basis for his claim for her testimony to the U.S. Senate committee, excerpted below, she found numerous problems with Graham's inflammatory revelation.[31]

First, Graham's efforts to compare the cost-effectiveness of various livesaving opportunities included 90 environmental measures, but 79 of these regulations were never implemented. His study therefore offered little or no basis for concluding that the government adopted environmental regulations that were less cost-effective than other life-saving opportunities. Second, like Graham's first study, the second study contains numerous duplications.

Third, this study also uses discounted estimates, a controversial methodology discussed in Chapter 7.

Finally, Graham's conclusions simply do not follow from the results of his own study. Graham (and others who cite him) claim that government regulation results in the "statistical murder" of 60,000 persons each year. Yet, as noted in the last paragraph, the study includes only a handful of government regulations. Almost all of the potential for additional life-saving opportunities relate to health care expenditures and the reduction of fatal injuries. Thus, even if regulatory agencies adopted cost-effectiveness as the method of setting regulatory priorities, this change would not save 60,000 lives, as Graham and other critics claim.

Professor Heinzerling testified:

---

In a study building upon their "Five-Hundred Life-Saving Interventions" study, Graham and Tengs set out "to assess the opportunity costs of our present pattern of social investment in life-saving." In other words, what, they purported to ask, do we give up in addressing life-threatening risks the way we now do?

This second study considered a subset of the 587 interventions included in the "Five-Hundred Life-Saving Interventions" study. Because, this time around, Graham and Tengs required that data on costs and effectiveness be national in scope, the number of interventions included in the second study dropped from 587 to 185. Ninety of these interventions (almost half of all those included in the study) were toxin control measures that were under the jurisdiction of the Environmental Protection Agency (or would have been, if they had ever been proposed).

*Inclusion of Unimplemented Measures.* Of the 90 environmental measures included in the second study (representing almost half of all the measures considered), only 11 were ever implemented by the relevant agency, EPA. In other words, 79 of the environmental measures included in this study were never implemented. Most of these were rejected (or never even proposed) by EPA itself. * * *

*Inclusion of Regulatory and Non-regulatory Measures.* The "Opportunity Costs" study again included both regulatory and nonregulatory measures. This time around, however, the vast majority were (or would have been, if they had ever been undertaken) regulatory measures. * * * Again, although there is nothing wrong in principle with studying both regulatory and non-regulatory measures, one must be careful to avoid attributing the costs and misallocations of private decisions to governmental actors. * * * [T]his is precisely what has happened with respect to Graham's research.

*Duplication of Life-Saving Measures.* In this study, too, many life-saving measures appear more than once even though only one such measure would ever be undertaken or even proposed. * * *

*Limited Set of Life-Saving Measures.* * * * Although 90 of the 185 measures in the "Opportunity Costs" study were environmental measures—thus, superficially, suggesting a rather comprehensive look at environmental regulation—50 (over one-half) of these measures were (or would have been, if they had ever been adopted) implemented under just one provision of one environmental statute—section 112 of the Clean Air Act, dealing with hazardous air pollutants. Moreover, Graham and Tengs' analysis applies to measures undertaken (or, mostly, *not* undertaken) under an earlier version of section 112 *which no longer exists*. Fully 21 of the environmental measures were part of EPA's nationwide ban on asbestos, undertaken under section 6(a) of the Toxic Substances Control Act. That ban was overturned in court 10 years ago, and since then EPA has not banned a single substance under section 6. * * * [O]ut of 90 environmental measures considered by Graham and Tengs, 81 were undertaken (or not undertaken) under statutory provisions that are either formally or effectively defunct, and have been so for at least a decade. Therefore, to the extent one attempts to develop a critique of environmental protection based on this study, one's critique will be directed at the past rather than the present.

*Life-Years and Discounting.* In this second study, Graham and Tengs again used the analytical techniques they had used in the first study: they measured the effectiveness of interventions solely according to how many years of human life they saved, and they discounted future years of life by 5% per year.

*Conclusions of the Study.* Graham and Tengs' conclusions are now famous: they found that if resources were directed to the most cost-effective of the interventions they considered, we could save 60,200 more lives every year with the same amount of money, or, alternatively, we could save $31.1 billion and save the same number of lives.

Again, however, careful attention to the study's precise findings is necessary in order to understand the study's implications. The vast majority of lives saved through Graham and Tengs' proposed reallocation of life-saving resources occurred in the categories of fatal injury reduction and medicine; over half of the life-saving potential was found in the medical category alone. Only about 5% of the life-saving benefits found by Graham and Tengs came from the category of toxin control. Even more strikingly, less than 2% of the total life-saving benefits found by Graham and Tengs could be obtained by reallocating EPA's regulatory resources.

According to Graham's own logic, then, one would have expected him, after this study, to have concentrated his efforts on reforming, *first*, health-care expenditures (in particular, one would expect him to be in the vanguard of efforts to limit tobacco use), *second*, expenditures on fatal injury reduction, and, *only as a distant third*, toxin controls. Moreover, one would have expected EPA's operations to be of relatively little concern to Dr. Graham, given the quite small contribution even a major overhaul of this agency's priorities could make to overall life-saving results, according to his research. This is not, however, how Dr. Graham has allocated his own resources. Indeed, * * * he has used his research on life-saving costs in arguing for a major restructuring of our regulatory system. And he has reserved a special disfavor for environmentally protective programs.

### How Graham's Research Has Been Misused

Many observers have misinterpreted Graham's research. Most prominently, they have cited the "Opportunity Costs" study as if it shows that *government regulation* results in the "statistical murder" (to use Graham's phrase) of 60,000 Americans every year. This misinterpretation appears frequently in the academic, political, and popular literature on risk regulation. * * * The misrepresentations of Graham's data began, in fact, simultaneously with their initial publication: in the introduction to the book in which the "Opportunity Costs" study appears, Robert Hahn claims that the study by Graham and Tengs "compiles new data on hundreds of *regulatory interventions* and estimates their costs and life-saving benefits." This study, Hahn continues, "assesses the opportunity costs of the current activity and determines an 'optimal portfolio' of *regulatory activity* that could save more lives at less cost."[32] The ink was not even dry on Graham and Teng's study, in other words, before it was being misused as an indictment of government regulation. * * *

*Attributing Resource Misallocations to Regulation.* In congressional testimony, Dr. Graham has used the research just described as a basis for calling the present allocation of life-saving resources "statistical murder."[33] * * * In testifying in favor of "regulatory reform" bills several years ago, Dr. Graham stated:

> Based on a sample of 200 policies, [Professor Tammy Tengs] estimated that a reallocation of lifesaving resources to cost-effective programs could save 60,000 more lives per year than we are currently saving, at no increased cost to taxpayers or the private sector! In short, a *smarter regulatory system* can provide the public with more protection against hazards at less cost than we are achieving today.[34]

Similarly, * * * Dr. Graham joined a group of economists in signing onto a brief filed in the United States Supreme Court in a case challenging the constitutionality of the federal Clean Air Act. In that brief, Dr. Graham and his co-signatories urged the Court to interpret the Clean Air Act to require cost-benefit analysis of national air quality standards. They premised their argument on the perceived failings of current health, safety, and environmental regulation. As they put it:

> Both the *direct benefits and costs of environmental, health, and safety regulations* are substantial—estimated to be several hundred billion dollars annually. If *these resources* were better allocated with the objective of reducing human health risk, scholars have predicted that tens of thousands more lives could be saved each year.[35]

As it turns out, most of the toxin controls that Graham and Tengs found to be cost-effective have already been implemented. A handful of apparently cost-effective interventions regarding asbestos and benzene were not implemented, but these rules together would have saved a total of only 24 lives—nowhere close to the 60,000 lives cited in the Graham and Tengs study. The only large life-saving opportunity in the area of toxin control that is identified by Graham and Tengs is radon remediation in homes, as encouraged by government funding of low cost loans, tax write-offs, or other financial incentives.[36] In effect, then, what Graham is really arguing for is a wholesale shift of EPA's responsibilities from the regulation of pollution of the air, water, and land through mandatory controls on polluters to the encouragement of residential radon remediation—which typically involves simply caulking basements—through loans and tax incentives. Nowhere does

Graham face up to the shrinking, indeed trivialization, of environmental law that his proposals would entail.

---

## Conclusion

Setting regulatory priorities is not an easy task. The quality of information about risks to individuals and the environment is highly variable. There are complicated policy trade offs in choosing one priority over another. Many ethical and moral choices must be considered. And of course, there are conflicting political demands by regulatory beneficiaries, industry, Congress, OMB, and the White House.

To be sure, comparative risk assessment can offer useful information about regulatory priorities. But as currently practiced, comparative risk assessment sweeps aside many important issues: ethical concerns, qualitative complications, the moral legitimacy of agency action, and public participation.

Comparisons cannot be made solely on the basis of quantified estimates of risk. Such hard risk assessments are far less valid than soft assessments, which explicitly take account of differences in data quality and factors that cannot be quantified. The narrative form used in soft risk assessments is also more appropriate than hard, numerical rankings of risk, which disguise the actual complexities of risk and convey a false sense of accuracy.

No serious comparative risk assessment can avoid ethical and moral issues, such as how to choose among conflicting estimates of risk or how to compare different types of risks, such as risks to children, adults, and to the elderly. Yet such issues are essentially ignored by strictly quantitative risk assessments.

Comparative risk assessment should be popularly understandable and open to public scrutiny and dialogue; that is how regulatory actions achieve moral and democratic legitimacy. The soft versions of risk assessment seek to do this by honoring the qualitative and subtle dimensions of risks. By contrast, the hard version excludes the public by asserting that "experts know better" and by insisting that professional methodologies and jargon are the only legitimate discourse for understanding risk. If the layperson perceives risks in a different fashion than expert risk appraisers, it is because the average citizen is more likely to take into account ethical and moral judgments—and to recognize that experts are subject to their own types of cognitive errors and biases.

While some critics charge that government priority-setting is dismal—as evidenced by the wide variance in the "cost per life saved"—a close look at the evidence shows this to be untrue. The cost-effectiveness studies done by Morrall and Graham, for example, have serious methodological limitations and flaws.

More to the point, the enterprise of regulation is not *about* efficiency. It is about preventing harm for ethical, social, and environmental reasons, and it is about making businesses take responsibility for the harms that they cause. Judging the merit of regulations by an economic metric alone is simply inappropriate. To take such economic metrics and then concoct unrealistic, abstract

scenarios for changing regulatory priorities amounts to "nonsense on stilts."
The idea that smoking cessation should replace air quality regulation because
the former is more cost-effective is an intellectual sham because such re-
source-shifts are not politically or institutionally realistic.

The use of such intellectual shabby techniques suggests that hard comparative risk assessments are really meant to serve as a sophisticated shell game.
Plausible arguments for efficiency are used as a decoy to achieve the real
goal—reducing regulatory costs to industry.

### Suggestions for Further Reading

*The False Precision of Comparative Risk Assessment*

John S. Applegate, *Worst Things First: Risk Information and Regulatory Structure in Toxic Substances Control*, 9 YALE J. ON REG. 277,
349-52 (1992).
  *"The most important limitation, both theoretical and practical, on
inter-program priority setting is the difficulty in comparing health
risks in very different contexts."*

Lisa Heinzerling, *Reductionist Regulatory Reform*, 8 FORDHAM L.J.
459, 486-90 (1997).
  *"[T]he hope that comparative risk assessment will provide a
'common language' for comparing risks must prove forlorn if comparative risk assessment takes account, as it should, of risks to natural
resources."*

*How Hidden Value Choices Mold "Hard" Numbers*

Other authors stressing the moral and ethical dimensions of comparative risk
assessment include:

John S. Applegate, *Comparative Risk Assessment and Environmental
Problems: A Forum, Not a Formula*, 54 N. KY. L. REV 71 (1997).
  *"The problem is that risk per se does not constitute an all-inclusive
basis for comparison among environmental problems. Yet such comparisons are at the heart of the comparative risk assessment enterprise, which, by its own terms, treats all human health risks as inter-
changeable with each other and with effects on the natural environment and social welfare."*

Jonathan Lash, *Integrating Science, Values, and Democracy Through
Comparative Risk Assessment*, in WORST THINGS FIRST: THE DE-
BATE OVER RISK-BASED NATIONAL ENVIRONMENTAL PRIORITIES 69
(Adam M. Finkel & Dominic Golding eds., 1994).
  *"It is true that society must make decisions about priorities ... [b]ut
it essential to recognize that doing so involves values and judgments."*

Mary O'Brien, *A Proposal to Address, Rather Than Rank Environmental Problems*, in WORST THINGS FIRST: THE DEBATE OVER RISK-

BASED NATIONAL ENVIRONMENTAL PRIORITIES 87 (Adam M. Finkel & Dominic Golding eds., 1994).
*"There is no objective way to draw boundaries around a specific ecological or human health problem for the purposes of establishing relative risk."*
David A. Wirth & Ellen K. Silbergeld, *Risk Reform* (Book Review), 95 COLUM. L. REV. 1857, 1875-76 (1995).

*How Self-Appointed Experts Disenfranchise the Public*

The topic of public participation in administrative decisionmaking is vast and far beyond the scope of this anthology. The following articles contain treatments of public participation in the process of risk assessment:

John S. Applegate, *The Role of Risk Assessment in Environmental Decision-Making*, 63 U. CIN. L. REV. 1643 (1995).

Eileen Gauna, *The Environmental Justice Misfit: Public Participation and the Paradigm Paradox*, 17 STAN. ENVTL. L.J. 3, 9-10 (1998).

Robert R. Kuehn, *The Environmental Justice Implications of Quantitative Risk Assessment*, 1996 U. ILL. L. REV. 103, 129-32.

Thomas O. McGarity, *Public Participation in Risk Regulation*, 1 RISK: ISSUES IN HEALTH & SAFETY 103 (1990).

Robert V. Percival, *Responding to Environmental Risk: A Pluralistic Perspective*, 14 PACE ENVTL. L. REV. 513 (1997).

Ellen K. Silbergeld, *The Risk of Comparing Risks*, 3 N.Y.U. ENVTL. L.J. 405, 422-423 (1995).

*Is Cost-Effectiveness Relevant to Regulatory Priority-Setting?*

Many other scholars have questioned the suggestion of the regulatory critics that regulating on harmful activity will free up resources to protect against activities that might cause even greater harm.

Nicholas A. Ashford, *An Innovation-Based Strategy for the Environment, in* WORST THINGS FIRST?: THE DEBATE OVER RISK-BASED NATIONAL ENVIRONMENTAL PRIORITIES 275, 279 (Adam M. Finkel & Dominic Golding eds., 1994).
*Ashford argues that differences in cost per premature death averted are not irrational unless rationality is defined "tautologically" as minimizing costs per fatality.*

Adam M. Finkel, *A Second Opinion on an Environmental Misdiagnosis: The Risky Prescriptions of* Breaking the Vicious Circle, 3 N.Y.U. ENVTL. L.J. 295 (1995).

David A. Wirth & Ellen K. Silbergeld, *Risky Reform* (Book Review), 95 COLUM. L. REV. 1857, 1873-74 (1995).
*Wirth and Silbergeld note that cost-effectiveness aims to get the*

*most risk reduction per mitigation dollar spent, but other consider-ations, such as equity, individual controllability, and so forth may also matter.*

## Chapter 4 Endnotes

1. OFFICE OF POLICY ANALYSIS, U.S. EPA, UNFINISHED BUSINESS: A COMPARATIVE ASSESSMENT OF ENVIRONMENTAL PROBLEMS (1987).

2. SAB, U.S. EPA, RELATIVE RISK REDUCTION STRATEGIES COMM., REDUCING RISK: SETTING PRIORITIES AND STRATEGIES FOR ENVIRONMENTAL PROTECTION (1990).

3. Professor Silbergeld teaches epidemiolog and toxicology and environmental law at the University of Maryland at Baltimore. She has served as Senior Toxicologist with the Toxics Program of the Environmental Defense Fund. These excerpts are taken from *The Risk of Comparing Risks*, 3 N.Y.U. ENVTL. L.J. 415 (1995).

4. David A. Wirth & Ellen K. Silbergeld, *Risky Reform* (Book Review), 95 COLUM. L. REV. 1857, 1870-71 (1995).

5. Professor Hornstein teaches environmental and administrative law at the University of North Carolina School of Law. The excerpt here was drawn from the article, *Reclaiming Environmental Law: A Normative Critique of Comparative Risk Assessment*, published at 92 COLUM. L. REV. 562 (1992).

6. Frank B. Cross et al., *Discernible Risk—A Proposed Standard for Significant Risk in Carcinogen Regulation*, 43 ADMIN. L. REV. 61, 77 (1991).

7. STEPHEN BREYER, BREAKING THE VICIOUS CIRCLE: TOWARD EFFECTIVE RISK REGULATION (1993).

8. *See supra* note 5.

9. Clayton P. Gillette & James E. Krier, *Risk, Courts, and Agencies*, 138 U. PA. L. REV. 1027, 1088-99 (1990).

10. *See* CHARLES PERROW, NORMAL ACCIDENTS: LIVING WITH HIGH-RISK TECHNOLOGIES 320 (1984).

11. *Id.*

12. *See, e.g.*, Paul Slovic, *Perception of Risk*, 236 SCIENCE 280, 282 (1987); Paul Slovic, et al., *Facts Versus Fears: Perceived Risk*, in JUDGMENT UNDER UNCERTAINTY: HEURISTICS AND BIASES 483-89 (Daniel Kahneman et al. eds., 1982).

13. Professor Jones teaches environmental law at the Southern University Law Center. This excerpt is from *Risky Assessments: Uncertainties in Science and the Human Dimensions of Environmental Decisionmaking*, published at 22 WM. & MARY ENVTL. L. & POL'Y REV. 1 (1997).

14. Baruch Fischhoff, *Risk Perception and Communication Unplugged: Twenty Years of Process*, 15 RISK ANALYSIS 137, 139 (1995).

15. *See, e.g.*, BREYER, *supra* note 7, at 55-81 (arguing that a professional bureaucracy should make public environmental decisions); Paul J. Culhane, NEPA's *Impacts on Federal Agencies, Anticipated and Unanticipated*, 20 ENVTL. L. 681, 682-84 (1990); Peter Huber, *Safety and the Second Best: The Hazards of Public Risk Management in the Courts*, 85 COLUM. L. REV. 277, 278-79 (1985); David M. O'Brien, *The Courts and Science-Policy Disputes: A Review and Commentary on the Role of the Judiciary in Regulatory Politics*, 4 J. ENERGY L. & POL'Y 81, 104, 105 (1983) ("Expansion of public participation . . . frustrates rather than enhances administrative fact finding and decisionmaking."). *See generally* David Dickson, *Limiting Democracy: Technocrats and the Liberal State*, 1 DEMOCRACY 61, 66-69 (1981) (identifying critics of public participation).

16. Richard J. Zeckhauser & W. Kip Viscusi, *Risk Within Reason*, 248 SCIENCE 559 (1990).

17. Sarah Lichenstein et al., *When Lives Are in Your Hands: Dilemmas of a Societal Decision Maker, in* INSIGHTS IN DECISION MAKING: A TRIBUTE TO HILLEL J. EINHORN 91, 93 (Robin Hogarth ed., 1990). *See* Frank B. Cross, *The Public Role in Risk Control*, 24 ENVTL. L. 887, 950 (1994).

18. *See, e.g.*, Lichenstein et al., *supra* note 17, at 95-96.

19. Professor Applegate is the Walter W. Foskett Professor of Law and Associate Dean of the Indiana University School of Law-Bloomington. This excerpt comes from *Comparative Risk Assessment and Environmental Priorities Projects: A Forum, Not a Formula*, published at 25 N. KY. L. REV. 71 (1997).

20. Frederick R. Anderson, *CRA and Its Stakeholders: Advice to the Executive Office, in* COMPARING ENVIRONMENTAL RISKS: TOOLS FOR SETTING GOVERNMENT PRIORITIES 78 (J. Clarence Davies ed., 1996) [hereinafter COMPARING ENVIRONMENTAL RISKS].

21. RICHARD MINARD ET AL., STATE COMPARATIVE RISK PROJECTS: A FORCE FOR CHANGE (NORTHEAST CENTER FOR COMPARATIVE RISK, VERMONT LAW SCHOOL) 4 (1993).

22. Richard A. Minard Jr., *CRA and the States: History, Politics, and Results, in* COMPARING ENVIRONMENTAL RISKS, *supra* note 20, at 53.

23. *See, e.g.*, BREYER, *supra* note 7; Cass R. Sunstein, *Cognition and Cost-Benefit Analysis*, 29 J. LEGAL STUD. 1059, 1063 (2000); Cass R. Sunstein, *Legislative Foreword: Congress, Constitutional Moments, and the Cost-Benefit State*, 48 STAN. L. REV. 247, 257-60 (1996); W. Kip Viscusi, *Regulating the Regulators*, 63 U. CHI. L. REV. 1423, 1435 (1996).

24. Professor Driesen teaches environmental and constitutional law at Syracuse University School of Law. The article excerpted here, *Getting Our Regulatory Priorities Straight: One Strand of the Regulatory Reform Debate*, is published at 31 ELR 10003 (Jan. 2001).

25. John F. Morrall III, *A Review of the Record*, REGULATION, Nov./Dec. 1986, at 25.

26. *See* OMB, REGULATORY PROGRAM OF THE UNITED STATES, April 1, 1991-March 31, 1992 (1991); OMB, REGULATORY PROGRAM OF THE UNITED STATES, April 1, 1987-March 31, 1988 (1987).

27. Professor Heinzerling teaches environmental law and torts at Georgetown University School of Law. These excerpts are from an article, *Regulatory Costs of Mythical Proportions*, published at 107 YALE L.J. 1981 (1998).

28. Tammy O. Tengs et al., *Five-Hundred Life-Saving Interventions and Their Cost-Effectiveness*, 15 RISK ANALYSIS 369 (1995).

29. Professor Heinzerling presented the testimony excerpted here, *Testimony Concerning the Nomination of John D. Graham to Be Administrator of the Office of Information and Regulatory Affairs, Office of Management and Budget*, to the Senate Governmental Affairs Committee on May 10, 2001.

30. Tammy O. Tengs & John D. Graham, *The Opportunity Costs of Haphazard Social Investments in Life-Saving, in* RISKS, COSTS, AND LIVES SAVED: GETTING BETTER RESULTS FROM REGULATION 167 (Robert W. Hahn ed., 1996) [hereinafter *Opportunity Costs*].

31. *See supra* note 29.

32. Robert W. Hahn, *Introduction, in* RISKS, COSTS, AND LIVES SAVED, *supra* note 30, at 3 (emphasis added).

33. *Risk Assessment and Cost-Benefit Analysis: Hearings Before the Comm. on Science, U.S. House of Representatives*, 104th Cong. 1124 (1995) (written testimony of John D. Graham).

34. *Testimony of John D. Graham, Ph.D., Director, Center for Risk Analysis, Harvard School of Public Health, Before the Comm. on Governmental Affairs, U.S. Senate* (Apr. 21, 1999) (testimony on S. 746, the Regulatory Improvement Act of 1999); *see also Risk Assessment and Cost/Benefit Analysis for New Regulations: Joint Hearings Before the Subcomm. on Commerce, Trade, and Hazardous Materials and the Subcomm. on Health and Environment of the Comm. on Commerce*, 104th Cong. 307 (1995) (written testimony of John D. Graham) (identical quotation).

35. Brief Amici Curiae of AEI-Brookings Joint Center for Regulatory Studies et al., in American Trucking Ass'n v. Whitman, No. 99-1426, at 1-2 (U.S. 2000) (citing *Opportunity Costs, supra* note 30) (emphasis added).

36. *See* Kenneth L. Mossman & Marissa A. Sollitto, *Regulatory Control of Indoor Rn*, 60 HEALTH PHYS. 169 (1991).

# Chapter 5: The Fetish of Efficiency

The fundamental, if unstated, goal of sophisticated sabotage is to change the terms of regulatory discourse. Instead of defining the public good as the prevention of bodily harm and preservation of the environment, the public good is redefined in strictly *economic* terms. Agencies are told that their regulations are irrational unless they maximize societal wealth, a mandate that requires the monetization of various moral, social, and ecological values. Once all values have been expressed in dollar terms (through a variety of intellectual contrivances), the experts carry out theoretical transactions in an imaginary marketplace to determine which policies would "maximize societal wealth."

The drive to redefine regulation as an economic enterprise started with cost-benefit analysis, as we saw in Chapter 3, and expanded with comparative risk assessment and cost-effectiveness analysis, as we saw in Chapter 4. We turn now to still another quantitative tool that antiregulation advocates have promoted as a way to improve the regulatory process—the use of "revealed preferences" to maximize societal wealth, as measured by the so-called Kaldor-Hicks efficiency test. This tool, which is in reality a more elaborate application of the cost-benefit test for regulation, merely enhanced the sophistication of the sabotage.

Before introducing this new pinnacle of dubious economic modeling, it is worth recalling that economists see their job as explaining how regulatory policies affect the overall wealth of a society. They are concerned that regulations be "efficient." This, indeed, is the driving force behind cost-benefit analysis. Industrial groups and their academic partners argue that as long as the benefits of a regulation exceed its costs, a regulatory policy increases the total wealth of the society, as measured by money. (Of course, this assumes that both costs and benefits can be accurately measured, which, as Chapters 6 and 7 show, is not necessarily true.) When a regulatory policy increases the total wealth of a society, economists regard the policy as "efficient."

In pursuit of this imagined efficiency, regulatory critics have constantly sought to override the policy principles of health, safety, and environmental statutes by making the cost-benefit test the standard for setting appropriate levels of regulatory protection. One of the most ambitious attempts to redefine the goals of regulation was the Comprehensive Regulatory Reform Act of 1995, which contained a provision known as the "super-mandate" which would have superseded the standards for regulatory decisions contained in preexisting environmental statutes with a cost-benefit test. If this bill had been enacted, regulators would have been required to prove that the benefits of any major regulation exceeded its costs even if the governing statute mandated protection of the public health or environment regardless of the cost.[1]

Such a move would be highly objectionable for two reasons. First, existing laws embody a fundamental norm of justice that individuals must refrain from harming others. A cost-benefit test has a very different goal. It asserts that preventing death, injury, and illness are not "worth it" if the cost would exceed the profits that a corporation could otherwise earn from the activities that cause those harms. In this way, a cost-benefit test dramatically redefines the goal of regulation. Instead of serving ethical, social, and environmental goals, as mandated by existing laws, cost-benefit analysis would establish a new regulatory standard based on efficiency alone. Businesses would be entitled to harm individuals as long as their activities were efficient and increased the total wealth of society.

Second, existing laws embody a fundamental norm of justice that everyone is entitled to the same degree of protection from government. A cost-benefit test sweeps this standard aside. It makes a person's safety and health contingent upon his or her age, wealth, and other demographic circumstances. For example, because the lives of the elderly and the poor are "worth less"—because their life-expectancies are shorter and their earning power is less—they would receive less regulatory protection than younger persons and persons of greater wealth. To the extent that racial minorities are less affluent, they too would enjoy less regulatory protection under a cost-benefit test.

While the task of translating the value of a person's life into money is abhorrent on principle to most people, the sophisticated saboteurs have invented various methodologies that try to achieve a plausible approximation. In general, they try to look for evidence to determine how much individuals might pay to reduce their risks of death, injury, or disease from their workplaces or consumer products. Such evidence is known in economics as "revealed preferences" because they are surrogate market values that theoretically "reveal" a person's "preferences" for risk reduction.

Why go through all this complicated economic modeling? The use of revealed preferences as a measure of an individual's "social welfare" permits economic analysts to apply an economic model known as "Kaldor-Hicks" efficiency, named after the economists who proposed the methodology in 1939.[2] A regulatory policy is "efficient" according to the Kaldor-Hicks measurement if those who gain from the policy (the winners) can fully compensate those who lose out because of the policy (the losers). If, for example, the winners gain $10 million and the losers are harmed to the extent of $5 million, the policy is "Kaldor-Hicks-efficient" because it increases the wealth of the country by $5 million. This increase in wealth occurs because the "winners" could pay the "losers" $5 million and still gain $5 million from the policy.

The use of Kaldor-Hicks efficiency to analyze a proposed regulatory policy, however, *does not require that those who gain from a policy actually pay those who lose*. The only requirement is that *if* the payment were actually made, those who gained from it would still be better off. Thus, the group that benefits by $10 million in the previous example gets to keep the entire $10 million, and the group that loses $5 million must bear the entire loss. To economists, any actual compensation is irrelevant because a Kaldor-Hicks measurement of efficiency is concerned only with increases or decreases in total social wealth, not with the societal distribution of wealth.

The use of the Kaldor-Hicks efficiency measurement replaced an earlier efficiency criterion known as "Pareto superiority." A proposed policy is Pareto-superior if, and only if, at least one person benefits from a change in social policy and no person is made worse off by the policy. Using the previous example, the proposed policy would be a Pareto-superior policy only if the winners actually paid the losers. If the losers were paid, they would not be worse off because the winners would have compensated them for the costs that incurred from the policy change. Moreover, in this example more than one person is made better off because the winners still have a $5 million gain after they compensate the losers.

While the Pareto superiority model has the virtue of providing a modicum of distributional fairness (in economic terms only), the Kaldor-Hicks criterion is more realistic in its conception of modern government and its role in protecting its citizens and the environment. The problem with applying the Pareto-superior criterion to government policies is that *every* policy produces winners and losers. If the government could not act unless the winners actually paid the losers, it effectively would be prevented from adopting any regulatory programs, or doing much else besides. Furthermore, it is often not possible even to identify all of the winners and losers of a policy change, let alone effectuate a transfer of wealth between them (assuming the winners would not resist the transfer!).

The Kaldor-Hicks criterion is popular with economic analysts for another reason. The standard measure of a person's well-being, according to classical economics, is "individual utility," or the extent to which people felt that a market transaction makes them better off. The problem with "utility" as a standard for judging social policy is that interpersonal comparisons of utility are impossible. The Kaldor-Hicks approach, by comparison, is a more practical way to measure whether a policy is an improvement over the status quo. Prof. Herbert Hovenkamp explains how Kaldor-Hicks solved this problem:

> One can listen to A describe how much she enjoys the benefits of a publicly-financed job training program. One can also listen to B describe how much pain she feels at being taxed to pay for A's program. But there is no scientific way to compare A's pleasure with B's pain..... Measuring subjective utility presents a major problem of scientific verification. If we simply listened to the wealthy person and the poor person describe how much each would enjoy an expensive good, we could not decide who enjoyed it more, for that would require an impermissible interpersonal comparison of utility. On the other hand, we can observe that in the market the wealthy person will enjoy the expensive good and the poor person will not, for only the wealthy person will purchase it at its market price. Now we can say with some meaning that the wealthy person "values" the good more than the poor person does.[3]

The Kaldor-Hicks measurement of efficiency is a more easily employed public policy criterion than Pareto superiority or comparisons of individual utility. But it does not follow that regulatory policy should be based on the Kaldor-Hicks efficiency criterion. This chapter identifies a number of significant public policy problems with relying on the Kaldor-Hicks test to set regulatory policy.

## Should Kaldor-Hicks Efficiency Replace Common-Law Rights?

When economists espouse Kaldor-Hicks efficiency as the measure of social welfare, they are not just making a neutral economic statement; they are endorsing a dubious moral and policy principle as well.

Kaldor-Hicks assumes that a corporation (or person) is entitled to harm a person or the environment until the government can prove that the benefits of preventing the harm outweighs the costs. In other words, individuals (or the environment) are entitled to protection only if the costs are not too high. Moreover, the government will act to protect people only to the point where the regulatory costs begin to exceed the benefits. At that point, anyone else who might be protected by additional spending should be denied regulatory protection (because it would no longer be "efficient").

These assumptions replace the common-law approach in which a polluter, or anyone else who injures the public or the environment, is expected to pay compensation for the entire harm that it caused. The "common law" refers to the protection of persons and property that courts have adopted in property and tort law.

When the U.S. Congress enacted legislation to protect individuals and the environment, it generally maintained the common-law tradition of protection as the basis for the laws; it did not adopt the Kaldor-Hicks criterion. Almost all of the current safety, health, and environmental laws continue the common-law approach, that harm to individuals and the environment is a social harm that we should try to eliminate. The following excerpt by Jay Michaelson explains and defends Congress' decision to continue the normative approach embedded in the common law and to reject the normative approach of the Kaldor-Hicks criterion.[4]

---

Cost-benefit analysis has been, and will continue to be, an integral part of regulatory reform initiatives. * * * Yet this form of analysis is not a neutral tool of reform. * * * When it is used to decide the ends of environmental regulation (how much harm to have) as opposed to the means (how to attain the desired harm level), it is an ethical reorientation as well as a practical one, changing toxics regulation from a proxy liability rule where persons own the entitlement to their bodies to a proxy property rule where toxics producers own the entitlement to destroy it. * * *

It is clear that cost-benefit analysis reorders risk allocation. Remembering that environmental regulation evolved as a solution when tort remedies were unavailable,[5] cost-benefit analysis acts to shift regulation from a proxy liability rule in which persons receive the entitlement to their body to a proxy property rule in which toxics producers receive the entitlement to produce a profitable amount of poison. When health drives risk determination, regulation is triggered whenever a body is injured to a nonnegligible extent. When cost-benefit analysis drives risk determination, regulation is triggered not at the level of injury, but instead at the level of profitability, which may be higher or lower than that of injury, depending on the circumstances.

Thus cost-benefit risk determination gives toxics producers the right to kill until the entitlement price (that point at which it "pays" not to kill) is paid by the number of injured people. Cost-benefit risk determination, consequently, shifts toxics regulation from a proxy liability rule to a proxy property rule, and moves the entitlement from the owners of bodies to the producers of toxins. It is this shift in entitlements—apparent in point-specific environmental contexts such as most air and water cases but more obscure in diffuse contexts such as toxics—that brings about the ethical questions we ask here. * * *

A common misperception about risk regulation is that the state acts as every American's parentalistic nursemaid. People, clearly, engage in far riskier activities than breathing toxic fumes or ingesting pesticide residue; why is the state being so overcautious? The answer, simply, is that riding a bicycle is not like breathing the air; the former is voluntary, the latter involuntary. Any explicit or implicit "risk comparison" between such activities misses this distinction and assumes that what is chosen by some may be forced on all. At present, with the state "scientifically" measuring risk and ensuring that it does not exceed "safe" levels (whatever that may mean), no individual is compelled to accept nonnegligible risks because of another's activity. But if the state determines acceptability on the basis of a private actor's profit, individuals are compelled to accept nonnegligible risks because another actor bears the entitlement to produce harms.

This shift in entitlement is not justified by any communitarian concern. It is a simple private preference, in this case, an interest in profit. And, to keep clear the power relations of coercing cancer, it is worth noting that the preference is not typically one of private persons but of corporate entities, which in terms of power, rights, and responsibilities have been said to have more in common with the state than with individuals. While hardly revelatory, this reality check is worth juxtaposing with contemporary polemic; a *Wall Street Journal* editorial, for example, recently moaned that "runaway regulations remain as oppressive as ever." Government regulation is said to be burdensome and intrusive. Yet in toxics and in many other areas of life, the corporate sector is far more "intrusive" than the government.

This is so, once again, because of the dynamic of choice. No one compels a chemical manufacturer to make chemicals; the corporation does so because it seeks to make a profit. But we are all compelled to breathe, to walk on pesticide-laden lawns, and, to some extent, to use chemical-laden products. Thus, while the government restricts the preferences of the private sector, it does so to protect individuals from intrusions on their liberty. Not to do so would be, again, to compel individuals to suffer harms because of other actors' preferences. The libertarian position, then, ought to be the reverse of what it has historically been. Prohibiting nonnegligible risks protects individuals' entitlements to be free of bodily invasion by a proxy liability rule. Regulating toxics does not trample on liberty; regulation increases it.

To be sure, not every entity restricted by toxics regulations is a multinational corporation; some are individual farmers, small manufacturing interests, and the like. And individuals do ultimately shoulder some of the costs of regulation in the form of higher prices for goods and services. Yet this does not alter the fundamental interests protected by scientifically driven risk allocation: life and liberty. The only oppression toxics producers suffer is having the government restrict their ability to poison individuals.

In a purely utilitarian world, reversing the entitlement to bodily integrity may be justified if the costs of liberty are greater than its benefits. Yet in theory, our system believes that human beings are endowed with certain inalienable rights, and among these are life, liberty, and the pursuit of happiness, to borrow a phrase. All preferences are not created equal. Shifting the entitlement, coercing individuals to give up their right to live because another private actor wishes to make a profit, is not (yet) an ideologically available option. * * *

---

In the excerpt below, Prof. David Driesen expands on the ethical shift that occurs when efficiency criteria are used to set regulatory policies.[6] In effect, property owners are given the presumptive right to pollute or cause other harms and the burden of argument for stopping such harm is shifted to regulatory agencies. In the meantime, property owners enjoy a limited right to pollute without administrative interference, and a fundamental notion of justice—that we have no automatic right to harm others—is swept aside.

---

Suppose that a polluter causes $10,000 worth of harm and could remedy this harm by spending $15,000 to control this pollution. A strict cost-benefit criterion would forbid promulgation of an emission limitation fully remedying the $10,000 harm, because the "prevention" cost exceeds the "effects" cost. In other words, the cost exceeds the "benefit." A cost-benefit agency might still establish a more relaxed emission limitation that produces abatement costs that are less than $10,000. But this more relaxed emission limitation would not fully remedy the harm; the public would still suffer the harmful effects of the unabated pollution under the relaxed limitation. Even if the regulated company has ample resources to pay for a complete clean-up without significantly cutting back operations, cost-benefit criteria will prevent a full clean-up if the cost-benefit ratio is unfavorable to the citizen.

The very language of [cost-benefit analysis (CBA)] obscures the fact that CBA does not protect the public from environmental harm. The word "benefit" refers to harm averted in the future, not to benefits in the ordinary sense of the word. Specifically, an agency employing cost-benefit analysis assumes that but for the analyzed regulation, facilities would expand or continue polluting at current rates. However, this continuing pollution contributes to environmental degradation and damages people's health. If the regulatory agency demands reductions in pollution levels, then less harm will occur in the future than will occur if the facilities continue polluting as before. Regulators refer to this averted harm as a "benefit."

The use of the term "benefit" implies that in the absence of regulation, the polluter has the right to continue polluting in the future. The terminology implies that the agency, in its benevolence, confers a gratuitous benefit by limiting pollution.

"Averted harm" is a more precise term. It draws attention to the fact that property owners do not traditionally possess the right to use their property in a way that harms neighbors. Our law and customs recognize that we generally must refrain from harming other people. This ethic is fundamental, widely shared, and applies to harming others by fouling their water and air.

To be sure, the law has not always forbidden all pollution. While some common law courts have shut down polluting facilities that interfere with the enjoyment and use of neighboring properties upon proof of harm, others have declined to do so if the pollution only injured a small number of property owners and the shutdown seemed unjust. Yet even those courts that would not shut down facilities upon proof of harm are almost always willing to order installation of pollution controls or payment of damages as a matter of right. Thus, courts agree that polluters have no right to pollute, but differ as to when to shut down a facility to remedy harms.

Modern environmental law mirrors the remedial structure and conception of rights found in the common law. The "polluter pays" statutes reflect a right to a clean environment, but focus on pollution control, rather than shutdown of polluting facilities (or compensation for damages) as the predominant remedy. The "polluter pays" statutes contain provisions to minimize the necessity of shutdowns and usually require modification of production processes or installation of control devices. For the most part, modern environmental statutes have reserved cost-benefit balancing for product bans under FIFRA and TSCA; a situation somewhat analogous to the decision to shutdown plants that sometimes occasioned balancing at common law.

The very concept of treating actions ameliorating ongoing harms, not as harm amelioration, but as a benefit, something bestowed gratuitously, undermines a fundamental norm of justice: that we must refrain from harming others. Our government undermines that norm when it tells people suffering from pollution that allowing pollution to continue, but at a reduced rate, constitutes a benefit.

A cost-benefit criterion creates a limited right to pollute without administrative interference. Critics who have said that CBA does not take justice into account have understated the problem. Cost-benefit criteria do take justice into account by rejecting traditional justice norms.

* * * Economists who support CBA want to see that we have the optimal amount of pollution. While many people would think that means zero pollution, many economists mean something different by this phrase. Economists argue that clean air and water are amenities, just like other products we purchase on the market. In order to obtain these amenities, society must spend resources and forego other possible expenditures. In order to know whether one is spending the right amount on these amenities society must make sure that we are paying a cost equal in value to the "effects cost," sometimes called the social cost of pollution. * * *

CBA proponents claim that balancing costs and benefits is economically efficient using efficiency defined in the sense advanced by the economists Kaldor and Hicks. * * *

In order to treat pollution as something that has an economic cost, rather than just bad effects, one must imagine a free market where the right to pollute is bought and sold. One must imagine this because in the real world environmental and health effects have no price. If we assume that polluters have a right to pollute, then citizens, absent transaction costs,might pay polluters to reduce pollution. Economists assume that citizens would be willing to pay no more than the "effects" cost, which presumably reflects the value of the reduced pollution to them. Hence, charging a polluter a cost equal to the effects cost seems "efficient" because it duplicates a free market outcome.

---

The "polluter-pays" principle treats the cost of reducing pollution as a "production factor," something the polluter must pay for as part of the cost of manufacturing a product. The market for pollution control techniques determines the price, just as the market price of an essential piece of machinery must become part of the production price. CBA converts the control cost from a production factor into the price of a separate "consumer good" consisting of an environmental improvement.

## It's Only Statistical People

Under the Kaldor-Hicks efficiency criterion, a polluter (or any one else) is entitled to harm other persons as long as the costs of reducing that harm are greater than the benefits of reducing such harm to those people. As Michaelson noted in the previous excerpt, this approach "coerc[es] individuals to give up their right to live because another private actor wishes to make a profit." Almost all of the current safety, health, and environmental laws reject this position and embrace the common-law principle that individuals are not entitled to harm others.

Defenders of Kaldor-Hicks deny that this approach to public policy sacrifices some people in order that other people can make more money. They contend that regulatory policy is about the reduction of risks or the probability that someone will be harmed. Since regulatory policy is not about protecting any *identifiable* person from a preventable death, economists refer to "statistical deaths" in analyzing the benefits of regulation. By this reckoning, there is no inconsistency with common law, which only recognizes actual people who are harmed.

Prof. W. Kip Viscusi points out, for example, that the government will spend as much money as is necessary to rescue a child who falls down a well or a man who is trapped under a collapsed freeway after an earthquake. But when large numbers of anonymous people are exposed to small risks, argues Professor Viscusi, the government should follow a different ethical principle. Because they are not identifiable, the issue is simply how much people are willing to pay to reduce units of risk. This approach simply "reflect[s] attitudes toward small probabilities" of risk reduction, he argues. Analysts are merely asking "how much the individuals themselves value a particular risk reduction."[7]

In the following excerpt, Prof. Lisa Heinzerling takes issue with Professor Viscusi and his defense of the Kaldor-Hicks approach.[8] She argues that the concept of a "statistical death" permits economists to sidestep the uncomfortable fact that regulatory policy decisions determine the fate of actual people.

Heinzerling rejects Viscusi's defense for a second reason. To implement a Kaldor-Hicks efficiency test, analysts must explicitly put a price on the lives of people in advance of their deaths. This price will vary according to a person's age, health, disability status, and wealth. As a result, the extent to which people are entitled to regulatory protection depends on these factors. Thus, a Kaldor-Hicks approach denies a person the basic right to be protected from harm caused by polluters and others on equal terms with other people. If you are old, for example, you are not entitled to as much protection as younger people.

---

The use of cost-benefit analysis to evaluate the wisdom of lifesaving regulatory programs presents a puzzle. Deciding to allow one person to harm, even to kill, another person on the basis of how much it costs the person doing the harm to refrain from doing it denies the person harmed a right against harm. It makes a person's freedom from harm, indeed her life, contingent upon the financial profile of the life-threatening activity.

The puzzle is that we do not allow this kind of cost-benefit balancing in all life-threatening contexts. We do not, for example, believe that so long as it is worth $10 million to one person to see another person dead, and so long as current estimates of the value of human life are lower than $10 million, it is acceptable for the first person to shoot and kill the second. Indeed, in this setting we refrain entirely from placing a monetary value on life. Yet when it comes to regulatory programs that prevent deaths—deaths also due to the actions of other people—it has become commonplace to argue that the people doing the harm should be allowed to act so long as it would cost more for them to stop doing the harm than the harm is worth in monetary terms. Why are these two situations coming to be viewed so differently? * * *

* * * The analysts who have helped develop these monetary values readily explain that the values do not apply to "identified" lives, nor to the deaths of "named individuals," but only to "statistical" lives. They deny having any special knowledge of the value of identified lives, and they appear to tolerate, if not embrace, the widely held assumption that we will do more to avoid the death of an identified person than to avoid the death of a statistical person. As a result, identified lives remain unpriced while statistical lives wear price tags. * * *

The framing of life in statistical terms has generated, for statistical people, two disadvantages not suffered by those whose lives are not so framed. First, the people whose lives are framed in statistical terms are explicitly priced in advance of their deaths. Second, this pricing has come to vary depending on the age, health, disability status, and wealth of the people who might be harmed. Thus the most basic kind of right—the right to be protected from physical harm caused by other people, on equal terms with other people—is denied to those whose lives are framed in statistical terms.

[When the government relies on a cost-benefit standard to make regulatory decisions,] the government in essence decides that it is not worth more than a certain finite sum of money to prevent someone from dying, even when death will come about through the actions of another person, and even when the person being killed has done nothing wrong. This proposition is equivalent to saying that a person can kill another person if it would cost too much to avoid killing her. This is a striking proposition, and so far one that has been applied only to lives described in statistical terms. Indeed, as mentioned above, the major writers in the literature on the pricing of human lives take pains to emphasize that they are discussing only statistical lives. Government analysts have been equally fastidious about the distinction between the value of an identifiable life and the value of a statistical life.

The second disadvantage to being a statistical person is that statistical lives are valued differently from each other on the basis of characteristics not used to distinguish among nonstatistical lives. Some analysts lately have become dissatisfied with the practice of placing an equal monetary value on all statistical lives. Lives are never saved, they observe, but only prolonged, and thus, it only makes sense to ask by how much regulation prolongs the lives it protects. Thus, we now see a parade of normally equality-minded writers extolling the virtues of evaluating regulatory action on the basis of the number of "quality-adjusted life-years" saved by it. (Often the concept goes by the even more occlusive abbreviation "QALY.") This technical approach obscures its implications: that regulation saving the statistical lives of the elderly, the sick, and the disabled will be a lower priority than regulation saving the statistical lives of the young, the healthy, and the able-bodied. One's age, health, and disability status suddenly have become good grounds for distinguishing the value of one's life from another, for the explicit reason that the lives of those situated on the undesirable side of the statuses of age, health, and ability (the elderly, the sick, and the disabled) are worth less than the lives on the desirable side. And, although few analysts will admit it, the upshot of the prevailing method for valuing statistical lives—which asks how much individuals are willing to pay to reduce risk in their own lives—also favors the statistical lives of the rich over the statistical lives of the poor. * * *

One of the features thought to set the statistical life apart from the nonstatistical life is unidentifiability. We will spend a fortune, it is regularly remarked, to rescue miners trapped in a mine, or a little girl trapped in a well, or a downed balloonist, but we will not spend an equivalent amount to protect these people from getting in harm's way in the first place. Observers have asserted that the identifiedness of the miners, the little girl, and the balloonist makes us especially willing to help them. As an empirical matter, this assertion is unproved and probably mistaken. As a normative matter, it seems clear that the rights of people not to be harmed should not depend on the identifiedness of the people who will be harmed.

There is good reason to believe that our willingness to spend money, time, and other resources to save someone from harm does not turn on the identifiedness of the person who will be harmed unless we intervene. When Tylenol capsules were contaminated with cyanide and placed on the market in the fall of 1982, no one knew which capsules contained the cyanide. Accordingly, no one knew who would be poisoned if no preventive measures were taken. This unidentifiedness did not soften the response that followed the first poisonings. Indeed, it arguably magnified it, as unidentifiedness is a close cousin of the awful randomness—associated with terrorists and criminal maniacs—that many people uniquely fear.
* * *

* * * Making individual—or, worse, public—responsibility to aid another person turn on the extent to which the person who needs help is like the people who might help her is a covert, but effective, way of making characteristics like race, class, gender, age, and personal habits determinative of our obligations to others. This approach is, needless to say, the antithesis of a regime of rights. In this way, the issue of identifiability also bears a strong resemblance to the unequal treatment of statistical people. People whose lives are framed in statistical terms thus suffer twice: first, when their lives are labeled statistical simply because the people doing the labeling do not identify with them, and second, when their lives are devalued precisely because they are statistical. * * *

Returning, finally, to the paradigmatic cases of the identified victim—the trapped miner, the little girl in a well, the downed balloonist—it becomes obvious upon reflection that identifiedness—as in, what is the person's name? what does she look like?—probably has little to do with our willingness to help. Rescue workers traveled halfway across the world to try to locate survivors of the massive earthquake that hit Turkey in August 1999, yet most of those people found were not identifiable in advance of their rescues. They were known only by their cries for help. In that case, the important factor was that there was no doubt that the people buried in the rubble of the quake were in grave danger. The knowledge that might distinguish these victims from other people in need, therefore, is not knowledge of their personal identities, but knowledge of their need for help. Perhaps it is uncertainty, then, that distinguishes the statistical from the nonstatistical life.

This meaning of statistical life does not justify the monetization of, nor discrimination between, statistical lives. At most, the idea that statistical lives are different because the threat to them has been probabilistically identified, but not causally explained, suggests that we should proceed cautiously in our response to the hazard. If we believe that the probabilistic association we have identified is coincidental rather than causal, then we would be well advised to study the matter further before undertaking a major regulatory intervention. But if the statistical probabilities have been established over a large enough number of cases, in different settings, then the lack of a causal theory explaining the statistical association between the two events should not stop us from taking action. * * *

More fundamentally, cautiousness in the face of uncertainty is not the same as a distinction based on value. If scientific uncertainty is the issue, then the solution is not to declare that statistical lives are less important, less valuable, more expendable, than nonstatistical lives, or that the age or health or wealth of the people who might be harmed should inform our willingness to help them. Monetization of human life and distinctions among humans based on age, health, disability, and wealth, have nothing to do with the meaning of statistical life that I am here considering. If the uncertainty of probabilistic estimates distinguishes statistical from nonstatistical life, then this uncertainty should be inserted in the regulatory equation as an adjustment to the probabilities themselves, and not as an adjustment to the value being measured. Doing otherwise allows scientific disagreement over the existence and magnitude of risk to masquerade as a value choice about who in our society is worth saving and at what cost. * * *

In defending the monetization of, and discrimination among, human lives based on the statistical nature of those lives, economic analysts have dehumanized the suffering and death that scientific risk assessments tell us will occur due to particular hazards. It is hard to understand, much less empathize with, statistical pain and loss. It is easier to assume that statistical suffering and death are things that do not happen to us—real people—but only to others—statistical people—and then to assume that the other people—statistical people—do not exist. Describing pain and loss in statistical terms allows us to think coolly about them; it strips life-threatening risks of the moral and emotional texture they derive from their association with real humans with real bodies and real loved ones. Describing human lives in statistical terms thus creates the conditions under which human suffering and loss can be conceived of in economic terms, and under which this suffering and loss can be allowed to continue simply because the monetary value we have attached to them is lower than the costs of avoiding them. In inventing the statistical life, economic analysis has contrived the very entity it seeks to value.

---

### How Efficiency Criteria Hurt Children, the Poor, and the Elderly

As Professor Heinzerling indicated in the preceding excerpt, the pursuit of efficiency under Kaldor-Hicks means that the levels of regulatory protection will depend upon a person's age, wealth, and other attributes. After all, it isn't "efficient" to give an elderly poor person as much protection from harm as a young person with high earning power. The enshrinement of efficiency as the touchstone for regulation is a radical departure in our democratic polity, of course. Our nation rightfully prides itself on giving equal protection under the law to all citizens. This section considers these additional ethical and policy shortcoming of the Kaldor-Hicks efficiency criterion: the discriminatory impact on citizens.

As noted earlier, economic analysts like to find evidence of people's "revealed preferences" to avoid risk. This evidence can consist of empirical research into how much protection against risk people actually buy in markets where such options are available (safer products, higher insurance protection, etc.). Or it can consist of fictional markets that economists imagine to simulate people's willingness to "buy" greater safety.

But even if conducted with the utmost rigor, these exercises in market simulation dedicated to ferreting out "revealed preferences" have a more fundamental flaw. A person's market preferences depend critically upon that person's wealth. If a person cannot afford to buy a safer product—because he or she happens to have a low-paying job, say, or didn't inherit a fortune—an economic analysis concludes that the person simply does not "prefer" to be safer. An unalterable fact of life is redefined as a "choice." From this determination, the economist then concludes that the person does not *deserve* greater protection from harm.

Such is the inexorable moral logic of the Kaldor-Hicks efficiency test. People are entitled only to the levels of protection from harm that they "prefer," as revealed by their market behavior or plausible surrogates. And if it costs more to protect them than they would "prefer," i.e., *could afford*, then that is an inefficient result and should not be pursued. On the other hand, if these persons could "afford" more protection because they were wealthier, they should receive more protection from regulators under the Kaldor-Hicks approach because it would be more "efficient."

As one might imagine, a wide-scale adoption of the Kaldor-Hicks efficiency criterion as a guide to regulatory policy would result in many more people being injured, becoming ill, or even being killed than current regulatory approaches. But under the fanciful ethical norms of such economics, this would be a morally neutral result because people would simply be "choosing" the levels of protection they want. Fortunately, regulatory policy is not based on Kaldor-Hicks efficiency, and the economic status of potential victims is not an issue.

Kaldor-Hicks raises an important issue of equity: should some people receive less protection because they are less wealthy than others? Should the poor, elderly and children receive less protection because they are generally less well-off financially than others?

To the extent that persons of color tend to be poorer than the populace at large, the Kaldor-Hicks efficiency model has racial consequences as well. When governmental officials decide where to locate hazardous waste facilities, landfills, and other facilities that create environmental hazards, the Kaldor-Hicks approach often finds that it is more "efficient" to locate such facilities in poor neighborhoods. After all, people in wealthier neighborhoods pay more for their property than poorer persons, so their behavior indicates that they "value" their property more than poorer persons. The "neutral" economic logic of Kaldor-Hicks dictates that there are greater "benefits" to our society from locating a waste facility in neighborhoods with lower land values than in other neighborhoods.

While some economic analysts recognize the equity issues raised by Kaldor-Hicks, they are unwilling to abandon the cost-benefit decision criterion in order to address this problem. They argue society is better off if governmental policies increase the size of the economic pie (the net sum of all resources available to all members of society), and it is worse off if governmental policies waste resources and thereby reduce the size of the economic pie. In the words of Peter Asch: "Those who are 'done dirty' by the system are not likely to be helped by rendering the system more wasteful."[9] If equity is a social concern, these analysts argue, it should be addressed by government programs, like welfare, that redistribute income, rather than by adjusting regulatory policies to take equity into account.

The next reading explains why the equity concerns raised by Kaldor-Hicks efficiency cannot be resolved through income redistribution, such as welfare. Profs. Thomas O. McGarity and Sidney A. Shapiro also argue that use of a Kaldor-Hicks criterion in the context of occupational safety and health is inequitable because workers would not be compensated for the safety and health risks that remain unabated.[10] They contend that although this equity issue might be addressed outside of the context of occupational safety and health policy, it is highly unlikely.

---

Economists defend the use of cost-benefit standards in formulating social policy on risk reduction by arguing that, in some cases, it is less expensive for society when employers pay compensation for illnesses rather than spending money to prevent them. This argument, however, ignores the ethical distinction between preventing death and compensating the victim's family after death occurs. As the Supreme Court's *Cotton Dust*[11] reading of the OSHA Act's legislative history indicates, Congress apparently had this in mind when it rejected cost-benefit analysis for OSHA health standards. In addition, placing the entire burden of less stringent cost-benefit-based standards on workers is inequitable. Even if milder standards would ultimately make more resources available to society, there is no reason why workers should not be fully compensated for the losses they sustain that could have been prevented under more stringent standards. In other words, the resources saved by a switch to less stringent standards should go to the injured workers, rather than to the employers or their customers. Yet few economists advocate redistributing the efficiency gains of cost-benefit approaches to workers.

Indeed, economic analysts respond that the distributional consequences of their prescriptions are beyond their bailiwick. For example, [Professor John] Mendeloff recognizes that the winners of a policy prescription do not necessarily have to pay the losers for their losses under his cost-benefit approach:

Those who die because society rejects inefficient lifesaving programs will not be around to benefit from the bigger pie. Does this fact require condemnation of any policy that stops short of a maximum effort to prevent deaths? No. It is inevitable that public policy will create losers who are beyond the reach of compensation. But this fact should spur thinking about who the losers are and how we feel about their plight.[12]

Surviving family members of workers whose deaths could have been prevented at a cost somewhat greater than the economist's optimal expenditure will take no comfort in the assurance that the loss of their loved one will stimulate scholars to think more about how society should feel about their plight.

When the distributional consequences of a cost-benefit regulatory world are considered, it becomes obvious that cost-benefit approaches undercompensate workers in two ways. First, cost-benefit analysts underestimate the value of a life.

Second, compensation systems pay workers less than the full value of their lives, as defined by economists. Indeed, some workers are not compensated at all. Although public policy may inevitably create some losers beyond the reach of compensation, the cost-benefit approach creates too many uncompensated losers when compared with technology-based approaches.

---

In the next excerpt, Prof. Robert R. Kuehn explains that environmental justice requires the equal treatment of citizens concerning exposure to environmental risks.[13] He admits that it is difficult to find effective ways to address issues of environmental justice, but he insists that this does not make the claims of affected communities any less legitimate or the distributive inequities any less disturbing.

---

Distributive justice in an environmental justice context does not mean redistributing pollution or risk. Instead, environmental justice advocates argue that it means equal protection for all and the elimination of environmental hazards and the need to place hazardous activities in any community. In other words, distributive justice is achieved through a lowering of risks, not a shifting or equalizing of existing risks.

With such a strong focus on the inequitable distribution by race and income of environmental hazards, an often overlooked aspect of distributive justice is that it also involves the distribution of the benefits of environmental programs and policies, such as parks and beaches, public transportation, safe drinking water, and sewerage and drainage.

Allegations of Distributive Injustice

* * * Although the first national environmental justice protest occurred in 1982 over the planned disposal of polychlorinated biphenyl (PCB) wastes in Warren County, North Carolina, widespread allegations of inequality in the distribution of environmental risks emerged on the national scene in 1987 with the release of a study by the United Church of Christ. The study, "Toxic Wastes and Race in the United States," reviewed the demographic characteristics around commercial hazardous waste facilities and found that race was the most significant factor in predicting the likelihood of living near such a facility—communities with the greatest number of commercial hazardous waste facilities had the highest composition of racial and ethnic residents.[14] A 1994 update of the original study found that distributional inequities were increasing—the concentration of people of color living around commercial hazardous waste facilities had increased by almost 25% between 1980 and 1993.

A persistent national distributive justice problem involves pesticides and farmworkers. Ninety percent of the hired farmworkers in the United States are people of color, an occupation that exposes them to significant amounts of pesticides and leaves them unprotected by the Occupational Safety and Health Act, the National Labor Relations Act, and some provisions of the Fair Labor Standards Act. Besides the obvious issue that, as farmworkers, people of color receive less protection from the law and are disproportionately exposed to greater amounts of harmful pesticides, environmental justice advocates note that EPA has often taken quick action to address possible threats to the general public from consuming pesticide-tainted foods but has been painfully slow to regulate pesticides that pose threats to farmworkers.

Native American tribes have complained that their lands have been targeted for waste disposal facilities and disproportionately impacted by mining and nuclear weapons testing, resulting in harm to natural resources and public health with little direct benefit to tribal members.[15] * * *

The adverse impacts encompassed by complaints of distributive inequities need not involve only threats from pollution or the loss of natural resources. Noise, odors, blowing trash, aesthetic concerns, increased traffic, termites, decreased property values and uses, fires, accidents, psychological harm, and other nuisance or quality-of-life impacts also may support a claim of distributive injustice. * * *

Dramatic as these instances of disparity are, they do not provide a standard for determining when a disparate impact is inequitable. To date, there is no consensus as to what constitutes a "minority" or "low-income" community, the appropriate boundary of the "affected community," or the appropriate "reference community." Furthermore, there is no agreed methodology or standard for determining the degree of disparity that might be legally significant [* * *] and the issue of what would constitute an "adverse" impact * * * . Even were agreement reached on the methodological issues and a legally actionable disparate impact found, there is no consensus on what would be a fair way to address the inequities, with proposals ranging from doing nothing, to ensuring compensation for affected communities, to banning activities that will add to the disparity.

The inability to articulate standards for resolving allegations of distributive injustice does not make the claims of affected communities any less legitimate or the evidence of distributive inequities any less disturbing. It does mean, however, that until legislatures, agencies, or courts confront these political and legal issues, instances of distributive injustice are likely to go unresolved.

## Conclusion

Using a cost-benefit test as the standard for regulatory decisions adopts Kaldor-Hicks efficiency as the normative basis for regulatory policy. Such a choice dramatically changes the effective purposes of health, safety, and environmental laws. The only legitimate concern of government policy becomes whether a particular regulation is likely to increase the total economic wealth of the country.

In the cost-benefit literature, there are many normative objections to making economic efficiency the goal of regulatory policy. As a utilitarian standard, Kaldor-Hicks denies individuals any right to personal autonomy. They are entitled to protection from harm only so long as their economic status (earning power, high-value residence, etc.) might contribute to increasing the nation's economic wealth.

Almost all existing laws reject such a standard. They seek to preserve and strengthen the common-law principle that individuals must refrain from harming others. Health, safety, and environmental laws reject the principle implicit in Kaldor-Hicks that individuals should be coerced into giving up the right to live (or avoid harm) simply because another private actor could make more profit by continuing to inflict harm.

Economic analysts deny that Kaldor-Hicks efficiency results in such a shift in entitlements. They say that cost-benefit analysis merely makes small adjustments in the *probability* that someone will be injured or die. No identifiable people are injured or killed by the change in regulatory policy; the results are only "statistical deaths," in the words of Professor Viscusi. This argument does not alter the fact that real people are killed, maimed, and afflicted with disease because of weaker regulatory protections. The fact that harmed persons cannot be identified in advance offers no moral basis for treating them differently than identifiable persons at risk.

Finally, the Kaldor-Hicks efficiency ignores distributive justice. Through its reliance of revealed preferences, it allocates protection based on a person's financial circumstances and age, producing a discriminatory impact on children, the poor, the elderly, and many ethnic minorities. However important efficiency is within an economic context, it offends some of the most basic notions of justice in American law and public policy.

**Suggestions for Further Reading**

*Should Kaldor-Hicks Efficiency Replace Common-Law Rights?*

The literature on cost-benefit analysis is filled with books and articles on the tension between economic efficiency and other societal values not considered in cost-benefit analysis. Some of the more accessible works include:

RALPH D. ELLIS, JUST RESULTS: ETHICAL FOUNDATIONS FOR POLICY ANALYSIS 144 (1998).
 *EPA "must know how to avoid imposing an unjust burden of cancer risk on a certain population so that someone (either within that population or outside of that population) can buy cheaper plastic razors produced with a more hazardous technology."*

Steven Kelman, *Cost-Benefit Analysis and Environmental, Safety, and Health Regulation: Ethical and Philosophical Considerations, in* COST-BENEFIT ANALYSIS AND ENVIRONMENTAL REGULATIONS: POLITICS, ETHICS, AND METHODS 140 (Daniel Swartzman et al. eds., 1982).

MARK SAGOFF, THE ECONOMY OF THE EARTH, PHILOSOPHY, LAW, AND THE ENVIRONMENT chs. 2-3 (1988).

*Discusses why "political questions are not all economic" and the ethical implications of the allocation and distribution of resources.*

*It's Only Statistical People*

Other authors have also stressed the conflict between rights and the efficiency considerations that underlie the Kaldor-Hicks approach:

CARL F. CRANOR, REGULATING TOXIC SUBSTANCES: A PHILOSOPHY OF SCIENCE AND THE LAW 165 (1993).
*Cranor: "Preventative health protections have no special weight in most utilitarian schemes, and utilitarians have a difficult time defending a right to health protections."*

Steven Kelman, *Cost-Benefit Analysis: An Ethical Critique*, 10 REGULATION 33 (1981), *reprinted in* THE MORAL DIMENSIONS OF PUBLIC CHOICE THEORY 153 (John M. Gillroy & Maurice Wade eds., 1992).
*Kelman: "The notion of human rights involves the idea that people may make certain claims to be allowed to act in certain ways or to be treated in certain ways, even if the sum of benefits achieved does not outweigh the sum of costs."*

Mark Sagoff, *On Markets for Risk*, 41 MD. L. REV. 755 (1982).
*Sagnoff argues that environmental legislation reflects a desire to promote autonomy, not efficiency, in the sense it seeks to control the conditions under which we live.*

Thomas O. McGarity, *Media-Quality, Technology, and Cost-Benefit Balancing Strategies for Health and Environmental Regulation*, LAW & CONTEMP. PROBS., Summer 1983, at 159.
*McGarity makes the case that, when applied to "matters of intense personal interest," such as risk to life and highly valued environmental amenities, cost-benefit analysis ignore the "almost universal recognition that citizens of this country have a 'right' to a healthy environment and workplace, at least insofar as the societal pursuit of that right is not technologically impossible or prohibitively expensive."*

Most attempts to provide the human dimension to regulatory interventions (or the failure to do so) are by journalists, not legal and public policy scholars, who tend to focus on legal and policy theory. The following are representative examples:

COLIN CRAWFORD, UPROAR AT DANCING RABBIT CREEK: BATTLING OVER RACE, CLASS, AND THE ENVIRONMENT (1996).
*The book describes the human dimensions of a controversy over siting of a hazardous waste disposal facility in rural Mississippi.*

NICHOLS FOX, SPOILED: THE DANGEROUS TRUTH ABOUT A FOOD CHAIN GONE HAYWIRE ch. 1 (1997).
*Fox tells the story of a child who became infected with the bacterium E. coli O157:H7 after consuming a hamburger made of poorly regulated meat.*

JONATHAN HARR, A CIVIL ACTION (1995).
*Harr's famous story, later made into a major Hollywood movie, tells the legal and regulatory saga about groundwater contamination in Woburn, Massachusetts.*

ALICIA MUNDY, DISPENSING WITH THE TRUTH; THE VICTIMS, THE DRUG COMPANIES, AND THE DRAMATIC STORY BEHIND THE BATTLE OVER FEN-PHEN (2001).
*Mundy's book tells of the human consequences of the failure to regulate the diet drug fen-phen.*

*How Efficiency Criteria Hurt Children, the Poor, and the Elderly*

Among the many articles exploring the tension between a cost-benefit decision criterion and equity concerns are the following:

Robert D. Bullard, *Unequal Environmental Protection, Incorporating Environmental Justice Into Decision Making, in* WORST THINGS FIRST: THE DEBATE OVER RISK-BASED NATIONAL ENVIRONMENTAL PRIORITIES 237 (Adam M. Finkel & Dominic Golding eds., 1994).

Eileen Gauna, *The Environmental Justice Misfit: Public Participation and the Paradigm Paradox*, 17 STAN. ENVTL. L.J. 3, 9-10 (1998).

Thomas O. McGarity, *A Cost Benefit State*, 50 ADMIN. L. REV. 7 (1998).
*Considers whether equity concerns might be addressed after a cost-benefit analysis has been completed and concludes that this modest accommodation of equity considerations is likely to short-change those concerns.*

## Chapter 5 Endnotes

1. H.R. 1022, §202(b)(1), 104th Cong. (1995), *reprinted at* 141 Cong. Rec. H2634-35 (daily ed. Mar. 3, 1995).

2. *See* Nicholas Kaldor, *Welfare Propositions of Economics and Interpersonal Comparisons of Utility*, 49 Econ. J. 549 (1939); J. R. Hicks, *The Foundations of Welfare Economics*, 49 Econ. J. 696 (1939).

3. Herbert Hovenkamp, *Legislation, Well-Being, and Public Choice*, 57 U. Chi. L. Rev. 63 (1990).

4. At the time that this student note was written, Jay Michaelson was a student at Yale Law School. The note from which these excerpts are taken, *Rethinking Regulation Reform: Toxics, Politics, and Ethics*, appears at 105 Yale L.J. 1891 (1996).

5. Diffuse toxic harms, whose effects may not be known for years and that may be impossible to trace to a single actor, are a classic example of this situation.

6. Professor Driesen teaches environmental and constitutional law at Syracuse University School of Law. The article excerpted here, *The Societal Cost of Environmental Regulation: Beyond Administrative Cost-Benefit Analysis*, is published at 24 Ecology L. Rev. 545, 560-63 (1997).

7. W. Kip Viscusi, Risk By Choice: Regulating Health and Safety in the Workplace 20 (1983). *See also* Frank B. Cross, *The Public Role in Risk Control*, 24 Envtl. L. 888 (1994); Charles Fried, *The Value of Life*, 82 Harv. L. Rev. 1415 (1969).

8. Professor Heinzerling teaches environmental law and torts at Georgetown University School of Law. The article from which the above excerpts were taken, *The Rights of Statistical People*, appears at 24 Harv. Envtl. L. Rev. 189 (2000).

9. Peter Asch, Consumer Safety Regulation: Putting a Price on Life and Limb 59 (1988).

10. Professor Shapiro teaches administrative law at the University of Kansas School of Law and Professor McGarity teaches environmental law and torts at the University of Texas School of Law. The excerpted article, *Not So Paradoxical: The Rationale for Technology-Based Regulation*, appears at 1991 Duke L.J. 729.

11. American Textile Mfrs. Inst. v. Donovan, 452 U.S. 490, 11 ELR 20736 (1981).

12. J. Mendeloff, The Dilemma of Toxic Substances Regulation: How Overregulation Causes Underregulation at OSHA 9 (1988).

13. Professor Kuehn is a Professor of Law at the University of Alabama. The article from which these excerpts are taken, *A Taxonomy of Environmental Justice*, is published at 30 ELR 10681 (Sept. 2000).

14. Commission for Racial Justice, United Church of Christ, Toxic Wastes and Race in the United States 13-14 (1987). The United Church of Christ study confirmed an earlier study by the U.S. General Accounting Office (GAO) that found that African Americans comprised the majority of the population around three of the four hazardous waste landfills in the southeastern United States. U.S. GAO, Siting of Hazardous Waste Landfills and Their Correlation With the Racial and Socio-Economic Status of the Surrounding Communities (1983).

15. *See, e.g.*, Tom B.K. Goldtooth, *Indigenous Nations: Summary of Sovereignty and Its Implications for Environmental Protection*, *in* Environmental Justice: Issues, Policies, and Solutions 138, 143-45 (Bunyan Bryant ed., 1995) (summarizing dis-

parate environmental impacts on indigenous lands); Joe Sanchez, *The Western Sho-shone: Following Earth Mother's Instructions,* RACE, POVERTY & ENV'T, Fall 1992, at 10.

# Chapter 6: Pricing the Grand Canyon, Cashing Out a Life

To its proponents, cost-benefit analysis is the most "rational" way to go about managing health and environmental risks. The logic goes like this: cost-benefit analysis requires a monetary assessment of the costs and benefits of a proposed regulation as well as several alternative remedies (and not just the one preferred by the agency staff). The general goal is to require agencies to impose on the private sector only those regulatory restrictions that would increase overall allocative efficiency. [1] After all, no society can commit unlimited resources to protecting health and environmental quality. By helping to assure that each agency values the saving of a human life (or injury or disease averted) in roughly equivalent sums, cost-benefit analysis can reduce the alleged inconsistent burdens imposed by existing regulatory programs. [2]

This chapter explores the empirical difficulties and intellectual flaws of this line of thinking. Analysts are simply unable to measure what they claim to measure. The dollar values that analysts assign as the benefit of reducing premature deaths and avoiding injuries are often at best dubious and at worst specious. This chapter also considers how the "benefits" of regulation are often overlooked when regulatory analysis focuses exclusively on the costs of death and environmental calamities avoided. In its zeal to reduce both sides of the equation, costs and benefits, into monetary sums, cost-benefit analysis typically undervalues and distorts the considerable *non-monetizable* benefits resulting from regulation.

Finally, this chapter discusses the distortions that come into play when the "cash value" of future illnesses is subjected to economic "discounting"—a mathematical calculation that attempts to estimate the cost of an illness (or benefit of averting it) at some point in the future. Like so many other economic models, the methodologies used can be quite technical and obscure—yet highly influential on the policy outcomes. For example, the specific "discount rate" selected by the federal government can be used to make the benefits of preventing cancer and other latent diseases seem modest relative to the costs of implementing a regulatory program.

## Wage Premiums as a Measure of Life's Value

Faced with the difficulty of assigning a dollar value to statistical people under the traditionally employed "willingness-to-pay" measure, some regulatory economists very early on hit upon the idea of looking to the workplace for real-world data. The most frequently cited estimates of the value of human life are those compiled and continuously updated by Prof. W. Kip Viscusi. Professor Viscusi reasons that if a worker is facing an average annual job risk of 1:10,000, such a worker will demand a wage premium of $500 to incur the risk. A group of ten thousand such workers, one of whom is expected to die, consequently will receive $5 million in return for this additional risk. This kind of value-of-life calculation goes well beyond the monetary loss associated with the risk of mortality and is generally accepted in the economics literature as the appropriate measure of society's willingness to pay for risk reduction.[3]

Over the years, economists have conducted numerous "wage premium" studies to gather empirical information on the willingness of workers to pay for safer workplaces. Many federal agencies have employed these numbers in their cost-benefit analyses of life-saving regulations.

Other serious students of the realities of workplace conditions and power arrangements, however, have challenged Professor Viscusi's reasoning process. They argue that his metric fundamentally depends upon the ability of workers to in fact extract additional wages from employers, in amounts that reflect the valuation that they place upon the added risks that they face in dangerous workplaces. Careful analyses of real-world workplace relationships, however, cast serious doubt upon the validity of wage premium studies. In fact, there are serious questions about whether a wage premium exists at all in situations in which workers have few realistic choices.

The following passage, written from a fairly technical perspective, suggests that it may not be wise to place too much stock in measures of human life drawn from wage premium studies. Profs. Peter Dorman and Paul Hagstrom suggest that there may, in fact, be no wage premium for hazardous work.[4] They argue that if the so-called wage premium is real, its size is very much in dispute.

The basic problem is that Viscusi's studies depend upon a large number of assumptions, some of which are highly questionable. Viscusi assumes, for example, that the employer-employee relationship is characterized by full information on both sides and perfect competition—patently absurd premises to anyone familiar with dangerous workplaces. In those workplaces in which there is apparently a wage premium for dangerous work (as inferred from wage statistics), it is not surprising to learn that such work is heavily unionized; workers therefore have greater bargaining power to represent their interests, including greater pay for more dangerous work.

Wage premium studies are probably doing little more than identifying workplaces in which worker's possess bargaining power. And even these statistics can be deceptive when the so-called premiums are averaged across all workplaces, including those in which workers have little power and premiums are nonexistent.

---

The theoretical case for wage compensation for risk is plausible but hardly certain. If workers have utility functions in which the expected likelihood and cost of occupational hazards enter as arguments, if they are fully informed of risks, if firms possess sufficient information on worker expectations and preferences (directly or through revealed preferences), if safety is costly to provide and not a public good, and if risk is fully transacted in anonymous, perfectly competitive labor markets, then workers will receive wage premia that exactly offset the disutility of assuming greater risk of injury or death. Of course, none of these assumptions applies in full, and if one or more of them is sufficiently at variance with the real world, actual compensation may be less than utility-offsetting, nonexistent, or even negative—a combination of low pay and poor working conditions. Therefore, the empirical researcher should not assume equalizing differences, but should attempt to identify the relationship between risk and wages in models employing the most defensible specifications and reliable data, whatever they may prove to be. That is, studies succeed if their results are reliable and robust, not necessarily if they generate large, statistically significant coefficients on risk. It is from this perspective that we turn to a consideration of previous work.

[After an extensive analysis of existing wage premium studies and the 1982 raw data, the authors reach the following conclusions:]

Estimations of wage compensation for risk are highly sensitive to model specification and choice of risk variable; indeed, in only a few specifications does statistically significantly positive compensation appear at all. Moreover, incorporation of industry-level controls appropriate to a world of less-than-perfect competition results in the near disappearance of evidence for offsetting wage differentials for risk of fatal and nonfatal injury, and the sole risk of fatality measure that generates positive compensation estimates in this specification * * * is the one that possesses the least plausibility. These results cast doubt on the very existence of compensating differentials for all workers, union and nonunion alike.

The different results for union and non-union workers pose an additional question, however. The presence of estimated wage compensation for risk does not * * * imply that this compensation is fully offsetting in worker utility, and that the estimates can therefore be extrapolated to provide a value of human life or health. Additional evidence is required for this second step. Yet the large differences in the wage-risk relationship between union and nonunion workers suggest the opposite, that the interpretation of risk coefficients as market willingness-to-pay is unwarranted. In general, only among those workers most insulated from labor market competition are these coefficients ever statistically significant and positive, and it is reasonable to suppose that the increased tendency of these workers to display wage compensation has more to do with bargaining power than with systematically different utility schedules. This interpretation, in turn, implies that even those workers receiving compensation may receive less-than-equalizing premia.

If coefficients on risk are not interpreted as workers' revealed preference for safety, however, how should they be interpreted? One possibility is that they represent the degree to which worker preferences, whatever they may be, are given weight in market outcomes. On this view, for example, unionized workers might receive a measure of wage compensation for risk while the nonunionized do not, not because of a difference in utility maps, but because they have a greater opportunity to influence the provision of wages and working conditions under circumstances in which market-based options alone do not provide sufficient leverage. One might say that workers who belong to a union are rewarded by their employers "as if" they had higher values of life and health.

Alternatively, we can say that life appears to be of little value for disadvantaged workers not because they attach less value to life, or even because their desired tradeoff between income and safety is sensitive to low wages * * * but because they face a restricted set of options in which their preferences for safety are not given much weight. In plain terms, nonunion workers in dangerous jobs are, in many cases, simply unlucky: they have found their way into situations of high risk and low pay and would presumably move to a better job it they could. If such workers are numerous enough, their lives will appear disposable, as indicated by negative coefficients on risk. This would suggest a meaning to the phrase "value of life" different from the one that characterizes most of the literature, but it is hardly devoid of significance. From the perspective of public policy, dropping the assumption that risk coefficients fully reflect workers' desired tradeoffs strengthens the case for regulatory policies to promote safe working conditions, but differences in wage compensation across the work force provide a basis for assigning a higher priority to policies that target the conditions of the less-compensated.

In summary, the evidence adduced in this paper supports the view that one or more of the assumptions underlying the conventional theoretical model of equalizing differences is strongly inapplicable. * * * Unionized workers may or may not receive hazard pay, but nonunionized workers in dangerous jobs are likely to be paid less than their counterparts in less dangerous jobs—a result far more consistent with limited mobility or segmented labor markets than with the frictionless competitive model that is typically the basis for deducing compensating wage differentials.

---

### The Subtle Deceits of the "Willingness-to-Pay" Standard

For most items that are traded in markets, the generally accepted value of a particular item is the price it can fetch on the open market. That price reflects the amount that willing purchasers will pay to willing sellers of the item. At this market-determined price, the amount that the purchaser is willing to pay matches the amount for which the seller is willing to sell.

When the only resources placed at risk by a polluter are commonly traded in the marketplace, the change in value caused by governmental intervention, e.g., to reduce the level of the pollution, can be easily calculated. Each unit of the resource can be monetized by referring to its market price. Thus, the U.S. Environmental Protection Agency's (EPA's) "Section 812 report" to the U.S. Congress—which estimated the costs and benefits of the Clean Air Act from 1990 to 2010—noted that the "willingness to trade-off between goods is measured as willingness-to-pay (WTP) or willingness to accept compensation (WTA)." These sums are "essentially dollar equivalents to the changes in the level of consumption of a good or service so that the individual maintains the same level of well-being," according to the report. [5]

For very highly valued things that are not traded in markets, however, it is not obvious that the willingness-to-pay (WTP) measure of value is equivalent to the willingness to accept (WTA) measure. The EPA report continues:

While WTP and WTA represent an individual's own assessment of the dollar value of better health, they are not necessarily equivalent measures. WTP, in the case of health, is the largest amount of money a person would pay to obtain an improvement (or avoid a decline) in health. When faced with two options, to either (1) pay a certain dollar amount to enjoy the health improvement or (2) abstain from paying the dollar amount and not experience the health improvement, the individual feels either choice provides the same degree of well-being. Alternatively, willingness to accept compensation (WTA) is the smallest amount of money a person would voluntarily accept as compensation to forego an improvement, or endure a decline, in health. The individual feels that to accept the payment and not experience the health improvement or refuse the compensation and experience improved health will provide the same degree of well-being. [6]

In a footnote, the report notes that the appropriateness of either WTP or WTA also depends on property rights:

In the case of a policy aimed at reducing existing pollution levels, a WTP measure implicitly assumes that the property rights rest with the polluting firm. Alternatively, WTA measures implicitly assume that the property rights rest with the public. [7]

Interestingly, EPA acknowledges that the two tests may render cost-benefit analysis "incoherent" or "schizophrenic" because the value as determined by WTP may differ (perhaps dramatically) from the value as determined by WTA. Still, the report, like nearly all other attempts to monetize mortality risks, relies exclusively upon the WTP measure, which generally yields a lower dollar value and assumes that the polluting firms have a presumptive "right" to pollute.

In the next reading, Prof. Douglas R. Williams critiques this fairly universal tendency to use WTP measures in monetizing the value of things (like mortality risks) not traded in markets. [8] He focuses on a phenomenon in the psychological literature known as the "endowment effect." The term refers to situations in which people are willing to pay much less to retain an entitlement than they are willing to accept in order to forfeit the same entitlement. Depending upon the context (an existing entitlement vs. a new, purchased entitlement), the same entitlement may be valued differently. The same individual may assign different "prices" for the same good depending on whether she currently believes that she possesses an entitlement to that good.

This phenomenon may be inconsistent with the economist's "axiom of rational choice," but it is nevertheless real, and it seems especially real in the context of health, safety, and environmental risks. Thus, by focusing exclusively upon willingness to pay as the default test of value that government should protect, economists systematically *underestimate* how people in the real world value those protections.

---

The regulative ideal * * * rests ultimately on the idea that political choices should be a perfect reflection, or mirror, of the aggregated preferences of citizens. Importantly, then, pricing rhetoric's appeal to this legitimating criteria presupposes that the methods of economic theory are sufficient or suitable for implementing its regulative ideal. This claim, I now shall argue, is wildly implausible.

167

To understand the implausibility of the claims pricing rhetoric makes, it is important to get a fix on precisely what pricing rhetoric means when it speaks of "preferences" and of rational choice. To that end, I begin this inquiry in what might be considered an odd place—call it the middle—by examining a phenomenon known as the "endowment effect." This is a useful starting place because it sharply particularizes the inquiry. Furthermore, from this examination a more generalizable problem becomes more readily apparent, a problem that is intimately connected with the idea of corrective justice as the means to preserve institutional integrity.

The endowment effect is an anomaly in economic theory. It "arises because the price many people are willing to pay for a particular entitlement may be significantly less than the price they are willing to accept in order to give up the same entitlement." [9] Stated more simply, the same individual may assign different "prices" for the same good depending on whether she currently believes that she possesses an entitlement to that good.

Explanations for the endowment effect often attribute its influence to what is perceived by the valuing individuals to be the status quo. The status quo serves as an "anchor" or reference point for these individuals, providing a frame from which the expected consequences of various choices are evaluated. The most prominent explanation of this view has become known as "prospect theory." [10] Changes from this anchoring point are experienced and will affect individual choices very differently, depending on the direction of those changes. Individuals demand more money, sometimes much more, to accept losses from that anchoring point than they are willing to pay to obtain what appears from an external perspective to be equivalent gains. A useful hypothesis might be stated in the following form: Status quo endowments come to be regarded "naturally" or "by right" as the property of their respective holders; loss of these "rights" are consequently not experienced merely as losses of wealth. Instead, "downward" changes from the status quo are assigned quite different meanings, and are experienced as a loss of or affront to something more integral to personality, social solidarity, or even the natural order.

The disparities between individual willingness to pay (WTP) to avoid losses and individual willingness to accept (WTA) payment in return for those losses are particularly prominent with respect to environmental degradation. They cannot convincingly be explained on the basis of income or wealth effects alone—i.e., the differences in one's budget associated with pre-choice ownership of a particular entitlement (and thus the value it represents), on the one hand, and nonownership of that entitlement, on the other. For this reason, the endowment effect is inconsistent with economic theory's axioms of rational choice, because it implies that the same individual can assign different value to the same good, depending on the context for evaluation—in short, the endowment effect yields intransitive preference orderings. For example, if I currently own good A, and I am faced with the choice between retaining it or exchanging it for good B, I may prefer to retain A. By contrast, if I currently own good B, and am faced with the choice of retaining it or exchanging it for good A, the endowment effect may support a "preference reversal": I may prefer to retain B. Observed endowment effects thus appear to many economists as paradigmatic examples of "irrational" behavior.

Against this background, assume for the moment that the means of eliciting individual WTP and WTA, respectively, reflect in tolerably accurate ways the choices individuals would actually make concerning the fate of natural environments in the circumstances described in the elicitation method. If these measures diverge frequently and significantly, policy analysts face an important choice regarding how the "bargaining game" is to be initiated and played.

In the context of [the Comprehensive Environmental Response, Compensation, and Liability Act and the Oil Pollution Act], selecting the appropriate bargaining procedure ought to be relatively uncontroversial. The statutes themselves establish the relevant endowments by demanding that responsible parties compensate the public—the citizens collectively considered—for the losses they have sustained. A properly constructed market would therefore seek to elicit how much, in the aggregate, individuals would demand as compensation (WTA) for the harm they have experienced. The alternative measure—willingness to pay—represents the choice as a "bribe"; it implicitly assigns extortion rights to the polluter, requiring the public to pay these individuals and entities not to engage in socially offensive behavior.

* * * Both DOI and NOAA acknowledged that, in theory, WTA (or compensation demanded) is the appropriate elicitation procedure in the natural resource damages context, at least to the extent that this measure diverges from the WTP measure. Nonetheless, both agencies, when confronted with the very large dollar figures this elicitation procedure has generated with CV, abandoned theory and refused to require that markets and their associated bargaining relations be constructed on this basis.

The basis for this requirement seems hard to justify. A willingness-to-pay measure will, if the endowment effect obtains, systematically understate the "market price" of natural resource degradation. Moreover, employing WTP effectively misleads valuing individuals about what the legal status quo assigns to them, and thus exactly what it is they are being asked to value (i.e., the protection of their endowments or a commodity to be purchased); it thus "mis-frames" the choices individuals are asked to make.

---

### The Ultimate Turnaround: *Regulation* Kills People

Some observers are convinced that risk regulation that is not sufficiently sensitive to costs will have the perverse effect of killing more people than it saves. According to attorney Mark Shere:

> Economic studies suggest that regulatory costs may impair public health, a point that has been picked up by some judges.[11] Under this view, every dollar that goes to regulatory costs is unavailable for things that tend to promote health, such as extra medical exams, better neighborhoods, safer cars, shorter work hours, or basic nutrition. Moreover, investigators report that mortality data show a correlation between health and wealth. They suggest from this data that

each $3 million to $7 million spent on regulatory costs may lead to one additional premature death. [12]

Justice Stephen Breyer approvingly cites a study by Prof. Ralph L. Keeney purporting to demonstrate that "every $7.25 million spent on a cleanup regulation will, under certain assumptions, induce one additional fatality." [13] By such evidence, argues Breyer, regulations that cost more to implement than the value of a statistical life saved are counterproductive. More recently, Robert Hahn, Randall Lutter, and Viscusi used a similar calculation to argue that one-half of the health, safety, and environmental regulations that they examined killed more people than they saved. [14] They based their conclusion on arithmetic showing that "a decline in income of $15 million, if shared among a large population, leads to an increase in the expected mortality of one."

In the following passage, Jonathan Bender, who was on the staff of the Carnegie Commission on Science, Technology, and Government, joins many others who have challenged this sort of logic as extremely simplistic in concept and probably wrong in practice. [15] First of all, there is no assurance whatsoever that the money that companies save by not having to comply with stringent health, safety, and environmental protections, will indeed be spent on cheaper alternative remedies (such as preventive health care, better nutrition and less stressful lifestyles).

Second, the Hahn/Lutter/Viscusi assertion badly confuses correlation with causation. Correlations between expenditures on regulation and lives saved do not establish a cause-and-effect relationship. (Paradoxically, while companies approvingly cite these sorts of correlations as proving their ideological point, they frequently criticize epidemiological studies of diseases as mere correlations.)

Even assuming that regulatory spending might directly affect health outcomes, this effect is likely to be felt only among low-income families, who have very little discretionary income. While most other Americans might spend a few additional dollars on healthier food or safer cars (as a result of reduced spending on federal regulations), it is just as likely that we will spend it on sporting events or more french fries. In any case, there is no assurance that the reduced spending will find its way into consumers' pockets; it may simply offset other line items in the federal budget.

Finally, to the extent that increased unemployment is the source of mortality risks, as Justice Breyer and others suggest, then health, safety, and environmental regulation is not an especially good target. A more powerful tool for addressing this problem is the Federal Reserve Board, whose role in setting interest rates is far more influential than regulation in affecting unemployment rates and the mortality risks that may correlate with them.

---

*"Richer is Safer" and SRR*

Even if there are problems in trying to reallocate savings from environmental deregulation to better uses, some proponents contend that the very costs that regulation imposes on society result in deaths. Accordingly, it makes sense to

170

regulate only where the number of deaths caused by a regulation is less than the number of deaths the regulation prevents. Many environmental regulations, proponents believe, do not meet this test.

One of this thesis' earliest exponents, Professor Aaron Wildavsky, described it as "richer is safer." [16] According to the "richer is safer" theory, as an individual or nation's wealth increases, her or its health increases because the newfound income is spent on salubrious practices such as preventive health care, better nutrition, or increased leisure. When income falls, less is spent on such practices, and morbidity and mortality increase. Regulatory compliance costs decrease income since businesses pass them on to consumers and workers. Many costly regulations purportedly save only a small number of lives. Given these premises, Wildavsky argues, it appears that some regulations actually increase rather than decrease deaths. [17]

In 1990, Professor Ralph Keeney published an article in which he attempted to quantify the "richer is safer" effect. Professor Keeney estimated that, under certain conditions, each $7.25 million spent on regulation will cause one death. He based this calculation on three factors: the annual risk of dying as a function of income; the distribution of annual income prior to imposition of the cost of the regulation; and the relative one-time cost of the regulation to an individual. [18]

*Application of "Richer is Safer" to Individual Regulations*

In 1991, in *International Union, UAW v. OSHA,* [19] Judge Stephen Williams cited the "richer is safer" theory with approval. In *UAW,* the D.C. Circuit Court of Appeals invalidated an OSHA safety rule on the grounds, *inter alia,* that the agency had insufficiently cabined its discretion under the Occupational Safety and Health Act. The agency had taken the position that, once it identified a significant safety risk, it could impose any regulation that was "feasible." The court held that this interpretation would result in an unconstitutionally broad delegation. The court remanded the rule with instructions to OSHA to select a reading of the statute permissible under the delegation doctrine. A requirement that OSHA safety rules meet a cost-benefit standard, the court noted, would constitute such a permissible interpretation.

In a separate concurring opinion, Judge Williams wrote that, while cost-benefit analysis might sometimes result in less stringent regulations, reduced stringency would not necessarily decrease health or safety:

> More regulation means some combination of reduced value of firms, higher product prices, fewer jobs in the regulated industry, and lower cash wages. All the latter three stretch workers' budgets tighter (as does the first to the extent that the firms' stock is held in workers' pension trusts). And larger incomes enable people to lead safer lives. [20]

Judge Williams went on to cite Professor Keeney's assertion that under certain assumptions one death will result for every $7.25 million in regulatory costs. Citing Professor Wildavsky's work, Judge Williams explained that "[l]arger incomes can produce health by enlarging a person's access to better diet, preventive medical care, safer cars, greater leisure, etc. " [21]

In 1992, the Office of Management and Budget's Office of Information and Regulatory Affairs (OIRA), citing Judge Williams's concurrence in *UAW*, used the Keeney estimate to "determine" that a proposed OSHA health rule, the "Air Contaminants Standard," would cause a net loss of life. [22] OIRA reached this result by dividing the estimated cost of the rule by the cost expected to result in one additional death, and subtracting the number of expected deaths from the number of deaths OSHA estimated its rule would prevent. Based on this finding, OIRA suspended its review of the rule and remanded it to OSHA for further "risk-risk" analysis.

*Critique of "Richer is Safer" as a Basis for Risk Reduction*

Such views are not shared throughout the federal government, however. In a 1992 report, the General Accounting Office (GAO) lambasted the Air Contaminants Standard suspension and the "richer is safer" assertions on which it was based. [23] The report first took OIRA to task for confusing correlation with causality, noting (as had Judge Williams in *UAW*) that many confounding factors could explain the observed association between wealth and health. Moreover, the report noted, Professor Keeney's own graph of the health/wealth relationship showed no significant differences in health for annual family income levels ranging between $85,000 and $20,000, and only marginal differences between $20,000 and $15,000. Hence, even if all other "richer is safer" assumptions hold true, the effect would only be material for those families whose incomes were reduced to levels below $15,000 per year.

The report also observed that Professor Keeney's model relies on macro-level income data that may not illuminate the effects of a rule on segmented populations. For instance, OSHA calculated the cost of the Air Contaminants Standard at $145 million. The report found that "[e]ven in the unlikely event that the entire cost of the rule were absorbed by the workers in that industry (rather than dispersed widely to the general public through increased prices), workers would lose an average of only $29 annually." [24] It concluded that such a loss would be "highly unlikely" to seriously diminish workers' health. [25]

GAO noted as well that neither the Keeney model nor OIRA's interpretation of it took account of possible indirect benefits. Compliance costs do not necessarily equal economic loss; indeed, a regulation's offsetting economic benefits could lead to an economic gain. Among the factors that could produce such benefits, said the GAO report, are the availability of substitute products, education, efficiency gains from technological innovations, changes in consumption level, and growth of new industries.

One can go beyond GAO's criticisms of "richer is safer" by reference to simple common experience. For instance, Judge Williams cites access to safer cars, greater leisure, and better diet as three avenues through which wealth can produce health. [26] Yet increased income could just as well be used to decrease health with these things. An individual with newfound income might trade in her big, sturdy sedan for a small, flimsy sports car; splurge on red meat instead of purchasing more healthful, less expensive alternatives such as chicken and vegetables; and devote increased leisure time to risky hobbies such as skiing, motorcycle riding, etc. Professor Mitchell says newfound income from deregulation could be used for items such as bicycle helmets and fitness programs. Yet both of these items are relatively inexpensive, at least for ordinary varieties. [T]here is no reason to believe that families who do not already purchase these items would buy them rather than, say, more movie tickets, if their incomes rose by a small amount.

---

### The Economic Value of an Ecosystem

The valuation issues raised by cost-benefit analysis of regulatory action becomes especially difficult when the benefits are nonhuman environmental interests. Does the value of wildlife, wetlands, endangered species, and the atmosphere hinge on the ability of human beings to perceive that value? Most cost-benefit analyses adopt a decidedly anthropocentric view when it comes to the monetization of value. In assessing whether a decision may advance human needs or desires, analysts make no effort to take account of the perspectives of other species or the larger ecosystem's needs.

The essay that follows identifies some of the difficulties that arise in placing a monetary value on the "services" that ecosystems provide to human beings. Prof. James Salzman's essay is both a commentary on the process of valuing ecosystems and a review of an important anthology on the services that ecosystems provide to human beings. [27]

Salzman dismisses the idea that just because ecosystems provide their services for free, they cannot be valued. The services they provide are implicitly valued in the decisions we make about whether to destroy ecosystems or protect them. His point is that if we do not explicitly value them, they will wind up grossly underestimated in the implicit decisionmaking that goes on in the unimpeded marketplace. For example, the nitrogen that nature provides free of charge would cost hundreds of billions of dollars if purchased from fertilizer companies. Other services that ecosystems provide, like decomposing waste matter are more difficult to value, because we do not have markets for such services.

Salzman concludes that the value of ecosystems cannot be treated as an "additional consideration" in cost-benefit analyses of regulations aimed at protecting ecosystems. Putting dollar values on such services in a credible way, however, is a difficult analytical effort. Ultimately we need more information on the benefits that ecosystems directly and indirectly provide to human beings. In particular, we need to study how particular actions aimed at protecting ecosystems create value for society. In the final analysis, it is unlikely that regulators will be able to calculate the dollar value of ecosystem services for most protective actions. As a substitute, Salzman suggests that a system of economic indicators, much like those employed by stock market analysts, could at least inform decisionmakers.

---

Perhaps the most fundamental policy challenge facing ecosystem protection is that of valuation—how to translate an ecosystem's value into common units for

173

assessment of development alternatives. The tough decisions revolve not around whether protecting ecosystems is a good thing but, rather, how much we should protect and at what cost. For example, how would the flood control and water purification services of a particular forest be diminished by the clearcutting or selective logging of 10%, 20% or 30% of its area? At what point does the ecosystem's net value to humans diminish, and by how much? Can the degradation of these services (in addition to ecosystem goods) be accurately measured? And, if so, how can partial loss of these service be balanced against benefits provided by development or pollution?

One might argue that ecosystem services cannot be evaluated, but this is clearly incorrect. We implicitly assess the value of these services every time we choose to protect or degrade the environment. The fundamental question is whether our implicit valuation of ecosystem services is accurate, and if not, what should be done about it. Indeed, studies such as Nature's Services indicate that our valuations are grossly and systematically understated. This essay explores the importance—and the challenges—of integrating ecosystem services research with the law. The potential is exciting, for a focus on ecosystem services would significantly change the way we understand and apply environmental law.

Take, for example, soil's service of providing nitrogen to plants. Nitrogen is supplied to plants through both nitrogen-fixing organisms and recycling of nutrients in the soil. As mentioned above, the authors rely primarily on replacement costs to estimate the value of ecosystem services. If nitrogen were provided by commercial fertilizer rather than natural processes, the lowest-cost estimate for its use on crops in the U.S. would be $45 billion, the figure for all land plants $320 billion. Most of the services identified in the book, however, such as breaking down dead organic material, are not valued in dollars because no technical substitutes are available.

Overall, Nature's Services reaches four conclusions. First, the services that ecosystems provide are both wide-ranging and critical. The question, "where would we be without ecosystem services?" is nonsensical, for we simply would not exist without them. Second, as Biosphere II's failure showed, the substitute technologies for most ecosystem services are either prohibitively expensive or non-existent. Massive hydroponic gardening in the absence of soil is at least conceivable, if unfeasible. Substitutes for climate regulation are neither conceivable nor feasible. Third, our overall understanding of ecosystem services—the contributions of individual species, threshold effects, synergies, etc.—is poor. Finally, even taking into account the inevitable imprecision of such valuation exercises, ecosystem services have extraordinarily high values. A recent study in the journal *Nature* estimated their aggregate value at between $16-54 trillion per year. The global GNP is $18 trillion.

Whether such a total estimate is precisely accurate is beside the point. The sheer magnitude of their dollar figures dictates that ecosystem services cannot be treated as merely add-on considerations. Nor can they be shunted aside as soft numbers (as often occurs with scenic beauty or existence value) when assessing the impacts of development or pollution. Tastes may differ over beauty, but they are in universal accord over fertile soil. If the goal of ecologists is to wake people up with big numbers, Nature's Services delivers. But are these numbers a convertible currency?

The ideal method to assess development alternatives would be to give local ecosystem services an accurate monetary value. As a complement to the more subjective and controversial non-use measures such as existence and option values, dollar figures for ecosystem services would reflect practical benefits delivered to society. More important, this method would also permit direct comparisons between investments in physical capital and investments in natural capital as well as projections of future costs and benefits. Beyond ensuring wiser development, this method would respond to the regulatory mandates of wetlands mitigation banking, environmental impact statements, and natural resource damages that specifically request such figures.

How does one measure dollar figures for indirect non-market resources—ecosystem services—which may have the greatest value of all the economic categories? A recent investment choice made by the city of New York provides one elegant example. The watershed of the Catskills mountains provides New York City's primary source for drinking water. Water is purified as it percolates through the watershed's soil and vegetation. Recently, however, this water failed EPA standards for drinking water, due both to habitat degradation in the Catskills from development, and to increased sewage, pesticides, and fertilizers. New York faced two starkly different choices as to how to obtain large quantities of clean water. It could invest in physical capital, building a water purification plant with a capital cost of $4 billion plus operating expenses. Or, it could invest in natural capital at a much lower cost, restoring the integrity of the Catskills watershed through land acquisition and restoration. Choosing the latter option, last year New York floated an "environmental bond issue" to raise just over $660 million. The cost of restoring the ecosystem service of water purification provided a payback period of five to seven years as well as increased flood protection at no extra charge. The lesson: investments in natural capital can be more financially profitable than those in physical capital.

Currently, there are three challenges to incorporating benefits of ecosystem services more directly into decisionmaking: identifying services on a local scale, measuring the value of these services, and projecting their future value. First, ecologists must understand the services provided by a specific ecosystem. * * * But in most cases, our scientific knowledge is inadequate to predict with any certainty how specific local actions affecting these factors will impact the local ecosystem services themselves.

This lack of knowledge is due both to the lack of relevant data and to the multivariate complexity of the task. Analysis of how ecosystems provide services has proceeded slowly because ecosystem level experiments are difficult, costly, and lengthy. More important, research to date has focused much more on understanding ecosystem processes than determining ecosystem services, and how an ecosystem works is not the same as the services it provides. * * *

[E]cosystem services rarely are exchanged in functioning markets or have readily determined replacement costs. As a result, ecologists face a second challenge in deducing the monetary value of these services from non-market valuation techniques. Contingent valuation (CV), also known as willingness-to-pay, is an important valuation method in the regulations that implement the Oil Pollution Act's provisions for natural resource damages. In the context of ecosystem services, CV suffers from a number of serious shortcomings. Most important, polling people's willingness to pay to preserve specific ecosystems assumes a knowledge of the services provided. Given the difficulties ecologists face in quantifying services provided by discrete ecosystems, it is specious to assume John and Mary Doe have an informed idea of ecosystem services, much less in a site-specific context. * * *

Valuing an ecosystem service becomes even more difficult because that value is contextual. [A]n ecosystem's benefit to humans is not a straightforward biophysical measure, for identical ecosystems in different locations will have very different values. In valuing each ecosystem service, and indirectly the "cost" of its diminution, substitutes become important. * * * Will the threatened service be replaced by other natural processes? Is it redundant or scarce? To what extent can technology overcome or mitigate these harms? If the loss of a service is important and non-linear, when will it become asymptotically more valuable approaching the point of collapse? None of these questions can be answered without intricate, localized knowledge of the ecosystem service itself.

The combination of methodological difficulty, inherent complexity, and lack of data makes placing absolute dollar figures on local ecosystem services unfeasible in many cases. At the same time, the current research and regulatory focus on ecosystems' biophysical measures is too removed from valuation of services. Is there a middle ground to inform decisionmakers? Wall Street and IBM's stock price may provide some guidance. * * * [M]any of the sources on which analysts rely to value stocks are not, in fact, monetary. They are composite indicators such as market strength, consumer confidence, and housing starts. Similarly, some of the most advanced work in wetlands valuation is now focusing on non-monetary indicators. This research area combines traditional biophysical measures (i.e., the capacity to provide ecosystem services and goods) with landscape context to determine the opportunity and impact of providing these services to people. Such indicators do not provide dollar figures for ecosystem services, but they do provide more accurate bases for assessing relative qualities of different ecosystems (which is particularly important in the context of wetlands mitigation banking and natural resource damages).

---

Prof. Robert R.M. Verchick observes that the proponents of free market capitalism see the world as a giant marketplace in which the free trade of goods and resources begets efficiency. Economic efficiency, in turn, makes more resources available to everyone (as described in the discussion of Kaldor-Hicks in Chapter 5). This, in turn, is said to represent an increase in overall happiness.

176

# CHAPTER 6: PRICING THE GRAND CANYON, CASHING OUT A LIFE

According to this economic view, nature is to be exploited so long as the benefits of that exploitation no longer exceed the costs. The problem is that the exploiters who reap the benefits, e.g., mining companies, timber companies, are not necessarily in the best position to measure the costs, which are typically borne by others.

Thus, when government intervenes to protect natural resources from overexploitation, the cash value of the benefits of the intervention [the reduced costs to the victims] is very difficult to assess. After all, the benefits of an intact ecosystem are not typically traded in markets. We all enjoy the "services" provided by wetlands and jungles free of charge; there is no readily apparent market value to preventing overexploitation of the resource.

In this excerpt, Professor Verchick critiques the intellectual assumptions of resource economics and offers a "pragmatic" approach to resolving the "unproductive tension between moral advocates and market advocates." He dubs these contending philosophies "Feathers and Gold," [28] and introduces three prominent techniques for valuing natural resources: restoration and replacement cost, behavorial use, and contingent valuation. Especially when measured by the last technique, the values assigned to natural resources are often so large that regulatory agencies, under strong industry pressure, tend to disregard them.

---

History teaches that wherever there is Gold, there is economics. In a capitalist system, economics attempts to allocate scarce resources in an efficient way so as to free people from undue governmental constraint and enrich the spirit through choice and personal satisfaction. When applied to environmental protection policies, economics helps define how society will tend its gardens, always assuming that nature's bounty exists to be consumed in some manner for human benefit. A society's economic structure will influence its notion of good governance, its ethical responsibilities toward nature, and its ethical responsibilities toward citizens. Economic thinking also produces powerful methodologies for explaining problems and encouraging people or institutions to solve them.

Our society's faith in Adam Smith's hidden hand and its tendency toward resource exploitation remains strong in the twenty-first century. Liberal economics—along with its jurisprudential spin-off, law and economics—has influenced environmental policy in significant ways. Beginning with the idea that resource consumption begets self-realization, the liberal economist believes that the goal of environmental policy is to allocate natural resources efficiently, so as to optimize the aggregate benefits of resource use as measured against the aggregate cost of resource degradation. In this view, resource use should be allocated to the user who is willing to pay the most for the resource (here employing willingness to pay as a proxy for expected utility). In an ideal market, the purchase price of resource use reflects at least the total cost of making the resource available for such use, and therefore a user will purchase resources as long as her resulting benefits outweigh the aggregate costs associated with use. The liberal economist's dream is a world where users can squeeze the utility from nature's fruit, up to the very point where aggregate costs begin to overtake aggregate benefits.

In practice, of course, many costs of exploitation (pollution, erosion, and loss of wildlife) are often externalized to third parties and, thus, excluded from the manufacturer's costs. For the liberal economist, the role of government is to shore up market failure and to contain externalities. Government may pursue this goal through various interventionist means, including tort liability, command-and-control regulations, tax incentives, and nontraditional markets in pollution and use credits. Under the common law, doctrines such as nuisance or unjust enrichment are invoked to compensate plaintiffs for being forced to absorb a defendant industry's externalized pollution. Under the federal Clean Water Act (CWA), fines for permit violations are based in part on the amount a polluter is estimated to have saved by ignoring regulations. When permitted or required, agencies employ cost-benefit comparisons in setting standards to allow resource consumption up to the limit of undue (that is, "inefficient") societal harm. * * *

The efficacy of such market proposals depends on economists' ability not only to measure the benefits of resource consumption, but also the costs of losing a sometimes irreplaceable natural resource. The study of such assessments, called "resource economics," is taken up [next].

Resource economics attempts to assign economic value to naturally produced goods and services, from a ton of coal mined in West Virginia to a day's worth of air filtration in the Amazonian jungles. As the second example suggests, resource economics is increasingly recognizing natural services that lie outside the market. These services include "actual lifesupport functions, such as cleansing, recycling, and renewal," and "many intangible aesthetic and cultural benefits as well. " [29] The journal *Nature* published a study in 1997, estimating the aggregate value of ecosystem services to total $16-54 trillion per year. [30] In contrast, the global Gross National Product is $18 trillion per year. [31] Figures like these, even allowing for inaccuracies, are sobering and will likely serve general environmental goals by raising public awareness. The numbers are too big and their subject too broad, however, to inform any particular decision about the exploitation of any particular forest, marsh, or prairie.

Thus, over the last quarter-century we have seen a trend in economics that seeks to measure the utilitarian value of specific "non-market" resources, such as regional biodiversity, wilderness areas, or unique geological features. The valuation methods fall into three main categories: (1) valuation based on restoration and replacement costs, (2) behavioral use valuation, and (3) contingent valuation. Before reviewing these, a word on terminology is in order. By "non-market," I mean having benefits that are not measurable through a direct market transaction. Non-market values can be divided into two categories: use value—benefits that while not directly traded are actively used by human beings (such as a public beach)—and "non use" values—passive benefits based on a human being's mere knowledge of the resource's existence, or on the supposed intrinsic value that a resource possesses. Use values and existence values presuppose a human perspective and are, therefore, termed "anthropocentric." Intrinsic values exist independent of human beings and are often termed "biocentric."

## Valuation Based on Restoration and Replacement Costs

Tort law has long recognized restoration and replacement costs as a means of valuing resources lost to environmental degradation. Under this method an evaluator sets the value of a resource at what it would cost in dollar terms to restore the damaged resource or to replace it with a similar one somewhere else. * * *

The method has limits. Where the costs of restoration or replacement would exceed the value of the resource as measured in dollar terms, courts and policymakers almost always defer to the lesser value. By negating any recognition of non-market values greater than market values, this practice defeats the whole purpose for environmentalists * * * . In addition, the restoration or replacement of many resources is, sadly, beyond our capability, rendering the method meaningless in such situations.

## Behavioral Use Valuation

Behavioral use valuation includes a wide spectrum of techniques designed to measure non-market use value through observation of behavioral patterns. One model in this category, known as the "hedonic model," considers the ways in which environmental benefits or burdens affect the value of marketed goods. [32] Suppose your house is just a short walk from the beach. Because people generally enjoy using this beach for recreation or other purposes, we might assume the market value of your house is higher than it would be were your home located in a more neutral environment. This increase in value reflects part of the behavioral use benefit of the beach resource. In contrast, were your house located near a Superfund site, we would expect the market value of your house to be lower than if it were located in a more mundane environment.

## Contingent Valuation

Valuation becomes more complicated when we seek to put a price on resources we cannot replace and do not consume. One strategy to deal with such a situation is offered by contingent valuation, where economists attempt to assign surrogate or "shadow" prices to nonuse, ecological values such as aesthetics, moral obligation, and philosophic engagement. This pricing method depends upon carefully administered surveys designed to find out what people would be willing to pay or give up to keep a given natural resource. [33] In some cases subjects are asked about resources they may someday have the option to visit (called "option value"); in other cases they are asked about resources they may never visit, but still have an interest in (called "existence value").

Contingent valuation has sparked significant controversy. For supporters, contingent valuation offers the best way to put intangible environmental benefits on the balance sheet. * * * To some opponents, contingent valuation is both practically and logically impossible—as hopeless as quantifying the benefits of beauty or truth.

Despite its flaws, economics offers two powerful advantages to the environmental cause. First, currency provides probably the best universal translator of human preferences across time, space, ideology, and culture. * * * Reliance on "tradable property entitlements" may prove especially helpful in negotiations among nations based on different cultural attitudes.

Second, money is a source of great social power in the United States and in the rest of the world. A citizen able to use environmental laws to threaten polluting companies with exorbitant fines or damage awards can get the attention of multi-national corporations and perhaps influence their conduct in ways that a purely political or value-based strategy could not. In addition, money negotiated or won from polluters can empower victims whom the government or the market previously ignored. Money can provide the means of moving to a less polluted area, securing better medical care, improving a family's diet, or accessing better schools. Money can never substitute for healthy surroundings and a clean environment, [34] but there remains a place for economic compensation to polluted communities, particularly in the courts.

---

### Whose Values?

Many professionals who advocate risk assessment and cost/benefit analysis have very definite opinions about what goals agencies should pursue and the relative priorities of those goals. John Graham, the head of the Office of Management and Budget's (OMB's) Office of Information and Regulatory Affairs, recognizes that "scientists, like other citizens, may hold strong policy views that can influence their evaluations of particular studies. "[35] When they attempt to hide their own policy preferences behind the veneer of scientific objectivity, they are making political, not scientific, decisions. Cost-benefit analysis can exacerbate any elitist tendencies of its practitioners by allowing them covertly to substitute their personal or professional valuation criteria for the ethical and political judgments embodied in health and environmental legislation.

For example, Professor Viscusi, perhaps the most prominent advocate of cost-benefit-driven health and environmental decisionmaking, complains that a precautionary bias in risk assessment tends to "institutionalize[] an irrational form of economic behavior." Noting that "when faced with the prospect of losses, individuals would rather face a known probability of incurring a loss rather than an imprecise probability," he concludes that this tendency "contradicts usual models of expected utility theory." Since this conflict with the economists' theory is, in Viscusi's view, plainly irrational, he urges governmental decisionmakers not to "mimic these shortcomings in individual behavior, but rather make the kinds of rational and balanced decisions that people would make if they could understand risk sensibly." [36]

Prof. Victor B. Flatt, in the passage quoted below, is willing to entertain the possibility that the cost-benefit paradigm advocated by Professor Viscusi may present an incomplete picture of health and environmental decisionmaking and that the government is not necessarily manifesting the "irrationality" of individual decisionmakers when its regulatory programs contradict expected utility theory. [37] He demonstrates that the "hollow and one-sided" cost-benefit paradigm that Viscusi employs does not yield decisions that are more rational, but merely decisions that can be more easily explained through the economic paradigm. The problem, however, is that the paradigm ignores many benefits of regulation that are not easily quantified and monetized. In Professor Flatt's view, agencies like EPA should reject the paradigm altogether and work to develop a new paradigm that considers all relevant values:

---

Although it is anathema to some decision choice theorists, I am convinced that the implementation of environmental laws cannot be done correctly without a recognition of certain "squishy" values that have not been historically quantifiable by the traditional benefit-cost analysis. Although this does make the process susceptible to a certain subjectivity, it does so no more than ignoring these values altogether in an attempt to claim rational decisionmaking. And, by this method decisionmakers can at least be aware of, and acknowledge limitations caused by, this subjectivity. Ultimately, this will force those who are required to choose among subjective policy choices (our Congress and state legislatures) to make choices in an open manner with full input and not escape the hard choice by claiming that an environmental agency need only apply a technical formula to determine the right answer.

Many a struggling environmentalist has had to try to justify why recycling certain goods is an appropriate personal decision in the face of "objective" studies showing that recycling certain kinds of materials is not cost-effective. Imagine how much more difficult it is to explain why, in order to protect wildlife diversity, an isolated wetland should not be filled in one case but can be filled in another. It is no wonder that EPA moves in the direction of justifying decisions based on rational, reproducible values. Unfortunately, this is not the benefit-cost paradigm that could dictate the perfect decision, but one that is hollow and one-sided (biased toward the more easily "explainable" decision). For that reason, it may lead to a decision that is as or more arbitrary than a decision that is not explicitly justified by "rational" calculations.

The major problem with the use of benefit-cost analysis to make decisions in the environmental context is that we do not have a common way to express or discuss all the "goods" and the "bads" or reduce them to numeric values. Thus, many types of "goods" and "bads" that would influence our individual environmental decisions are simply ignored. This leaves benefit-cost analysis a poor vehicle for selecting our preferences. * * *

In the environmental context, this problem is particularly acute. The degree of benefits and risks from controlling pollution is uncertain, due to uncertainties in scientific understanding of the impacts of pollution on human health and the environment. Most environmental testing is done through animal studies at extremely high doses and questionable extrapolation and through uncontrolled past history epidemiological studies. This leaves the level of harm for amounts of a pollutant uncertain and makes it difficult to compare harm to benefits. Thus, benefit-cost analysis tends to focus on costs and benefits that can be more easily quantified in dollar terms. Harm to ecosystems is often calculated by using market value for natural resources, even though most environmental amenities are not sold on the open market and are not completely valued if they are. Quantification of harms in benefit-cost analysis is usually attempted in the area of human health, but although this can put the decision in sharper focus, it still requires an answer to the question: "How valuable is a human life?"—a value that many would say is philosophically unquantifiable.

EPA, along with other regulatory agencies, has shown some willingness to delve into these issues when it is trying to quantify human health values, but that is only part of the picture. EPA still routinely underrates other environmental values that Congress has specifically indicated are to be given weight in environmental decisionmaking. This focus on human health or market goods alone, to the exclusion of other important environmental values, undermines the legitimacy of environmental values that are specified by Congress and are important to the public. How does one calculate the value of an endangered snail darter and compare it to the value of a major dam on a major river system? What about the value of a beautiful view? Even more difficult is how to give voice to the philosophical values of environmental law that plainly inform our society and even our laws.

Because of these problems, criticism of EPA's use of the traditional benefit-cost paradigm to make environmental decisions has been legion. The use of this paradigm also contributes to much uncertainty about policy direction, as it is unclear just which values EPA can shoehorn into its old paradigm for decisionmaking. The very failure to speak in a common language about which values we are considering or should consider may explain much of the current conflict over environmental policy in our country. * * *

However, despite the failings of this paradigm, the uncertainty over its use, and its illegality when used in a way that ignores legislatively-mandated requirements, the push to continue such analysis and eliminate any non-quantifiable value judgments that remain in the process is inexorable in our modern society. In the United States there is a growing chorus of regulatory reformists who want to push EPA and other federal agencies into utilizing a more stringent form of benefit-cost analysis, particularly one that only looks at these so-called objective, reproducible values. The further we go down the "broad and wide" path, the wider it becomes and the harder it is to turn back. In the name of science and good public policy, we have already moved far from the aspirational goals of environmental protection that began the environmental movement. If we do not stop soon, "redemption" may be too late.

What is clear is that traditional benefit-cost analysis as the sole basis for agency decisionmaking does not work in the environmental context because it ignores important environmental values that Congress has indicated must be considered in environmental decisionmaking. By focusing entirely on this paradigm, EPA strives for more and more technical certainty, causing its vision of the problems and issues to narrow. It also plays into the hands of those who stress that EPA decisionmaking must fit into benefit-cost analysis. It seems there is a belief that if there were better air quality modeling or if the causal pathways of cancer were better understood, the regulatory decisions of EPA would be better. Of

course more information is desirable, but this will only go so far in the environmental arena because of the great diversity of values and issues at play there. No
amount of fine tuning of benefit-cost analysis and no amount of externality pricing
is going to make EPA regulation better unless EPA and Congress can again understand, appreciate, and address the totality of environmental values and concerns that underlie our federal environmental laws. This calls for the rejection of
the benefit-cost paradigm. A new paradigm for EPA decisionmaking must consider all values, environmental and otherwise, and point out policy questions and
deficiencies so that Congress and the democratic process can address them and
they are not simply buried for the benefit of one interest group or the other.

---

### Bias Against the Future?

One of the most frequently visited battlefields in the ideological war over
cost-benefit analysis is the debate over the role that discounting should play in
monetizing future health and environmental benefits. Most economists maintain that both future benefits and future costs should be "discounted to present
value" to permit the decisionmaker to compare apples with apples instead of or-
anges when she measures costs against benefits. [38] According to Professor
Viscusi:

> The [OMB] has long specified a 10% rate of discount as the main reference
> point for [discounting]—an approach that will drastically reduce the attrac-
> tiveness of policies such as those that reduce cancer risks or have long-term
> implications for our ecological well-being.
> * * * [I]f the appropriate rate of discount is in fact 10%, then the rate of expected
> productivity growth in the economy also must be quite substantial to justify
> such a high rate. This growth will boost the income of future generations,
> which in turn will raise the value that they attach to the risk-reduction bene-
> fits. * * * Valuing health risks through use of high discount rates should not
> drastically affect the attractiveness of policies with long-term implications
> provided that the benefit values are adjusted appropriately. [39]

Critics of cost-benefit analysis argue that discounting future benefits with high
discount rates undervalues life-saving interventions that do not yield results for
many years. Discounting also discriminates against future generations, because costs are almost always incurred in the short term and benefits can extend
for many years.

In the following reading, Prof. Lisa Heinzerling lays out the case against discounting evironmental values. [40] Noting that environmental law is primarily
about protecting present and future generations against harm, Heinzerling
questions the economist's propensity to discount the value of such protections
solely because they occur in the future. After explaining how discounting
works in the context of financial investments, she demonstrates how the monetary value of extremely valuable future protections can become diminished
through discounting to such a degree that they do not compare favorably with
even modest present-day costs.

Professor Heinzerling disputes the notion that discounting is appropriate because people ordinarily discount future risks in their daily lives. There is no empirical verification for this claim, she argues. Many people make present-day sacrifices on the assumption that the future is just as important as the present; such frugality and sacrifice is generally regarded as a virtue. More importantly, even assuming that individuals did systematically prefer to shift present-day risks to future generations, it begs the difficult moral question of whether the regulatory process should honor the moral proposition that our preferences for self-preservation (or indulgence) should come at the expense of our grandchildren. Finally, there is the question of law. When EPA and other agencies discount future benefits, their actions frequently conflict with statutes designed to protect present and future generations from myopic decisionmaking.

---

[I]t is often thought that, above all, environmental law prevents future harm and preserves future opportunities. To some extent this follows from environmental law's largely preventive, rather than compensatory, focus; it is impossible to prevent a harm that has already happened. But the future orientation of environmental law goes beyond this. What seems to set environmental law apart from other preventive measures is the sheer vastness of the temporal period that appears to separate regulatory action now, such as the removal of a toxic substance from the ambient air, from its full range of beneficial consequences. These consequences include the prevention of long-latency human diseases such as cancer and the prevention of long-term ecological harm. Some of these good consequences may come to the present generation, but perhaps only in later life, many years from now. Others appear to accrue only for the benefit of future generations, decades or even centuries from now. In this way, environmental regulation is often contrasted with safety regulation, which, in theory, can begin to save lives as soon as the regulation is in place. A regulation requiring motorcyclists to wear helmets, for example, may save lives the first day it takes effect.

Thus an important question in environmental policy today is how we should value the future when the present, too, cries out for help. * * * [T]he federal government has embraced an assumption that we value future harms less than present harms, and that, even when it comes to human life, the appropriate tradeoff between present and future life-saving can usually be struck by consulting prevailing rates of return on financial investments.

Discounting is the calculation of the present value of a future sum of money. It is typically used in comparing sums of money paid or received over different time periods. By computing the present value of future sums of money, discounting helps an investor choose between investment opportunities. If, for example, one wants to know whether one should pay $10 today for bonds that will pay $20 five years from now, or should instead spend the $10 to buy bonds that will pay $30 ten years from now, one cannot conclude that the latter investment is better just because thirty is a larger number than twenty. Quite apart from the effect of inflation, the time value of money means that money received later is worth less than the same amount of money received earlier; while one waits for the later money to arrive, one could have been investing the earlier money in some other venture. In addition, one may simply prefer to receive money sooner rather than later because one is anxious to consume the goods money can buy. For both of these reasons (money is productive over time, and people are impatient), in order to compare two investments that pay benefits over different periods of time, one needs not only a common currency (here it is dollars), but one also needs to state that currency in common temporal terms. This leads to the idea of computing present value through discounting.

In order to calculate the present value of a future sum of money, one must apply a discount rate to the sum of money one expects to receive, over the period of time one must wait before one receives the money. Thus, the present value of a future sum of money may be described as a function of three variables: the sum of money one expects to receive in the future; the discount rate; and the number of years that will pass before one receives the money. The discount rate depends in large part on which of the rationales for discounting (the productive value of money over time, or simple consumer impatience) applies in a given situation. In evaluating private financial projects, economists appear to agree that the appropriate discount rate is the opportunity cost of capital for the investor. In the usual case, this would be the prevailing interest rate.

The larger the discount rate, the smaller future benefits and costs will appear. For instance, the present value of a benefit of $1 million to be received in ten years from now is $900,000 if one uses a 1% discount rate, but only $390,000 if one applies a 10% discount rate. Discounted at 10%, one dollar received fifty years from now is worth slightly less than a penny today-a difference of two orders of magnitude. Even more dramatic, "if one discounts present world GNP over two hundred years at 5% per annum, it is worth only a few hundred thousand dollars, the price of a good apartment. Discounted at 10%, it is equivalent to a used car." High discount rates thus significantly reduce the apparent attractiveness of projects, which produce future benefits; low discount rates reduce their attractiveness to a much lesser extent.

* * * OMB currently directs federal agencies conducting cost-benefit analyses of their regulations to discount future costs and benefits at 7% per year, even if these costs or benefits take the form of goods that are difficult to monetize because they are not directly traded in markets or, indeed, have not been monetized at all. This means that agencies following OMB's advice will either discount what they take to be the monetary value of a human life, or discount each life saved directly, when they are evaluating regulatory activities that save lives in the future. In emphasizing latency periods, OMB also effectively directs agencies to discount the life-saving benefits of their rules from the date on which the illness being prevented (such as cancer) would, absent the regulation, have become clinically evident, since this is the date that marks the end of latency as medical science currently defines it.

One of the primary justifications for discounting in the life-saving context is that it reflects people's preferences about risk. This argument rests on premises which are flawed from both empirical and normative perspectives.

The argument from preferences assumes that when people make decisions about risk, they prefer, predictably and systematically, to avoid a hazard that will materialize in harm today to avoiding one that will materialize in harm at a later date. The empirical evidence of people's actual preferences is, however, considerably more mixed than this argument suggests.

The empirical evidence used to support the preference-based argument for discounting is riddled with problems. Careful analysis of the limited data available on individuals' risk-related discount rates reveals that a substantial percentage of citizens do not discount future health-related harms; that those who do, do so at wildly different rates, and at rates that decline with time; that much of the evidence purporting to find that individuals prefer remote harms to immediate ones in fact only shows that individuals prefer that others be hurt instead of themselves; and that individuals' risk-related preferences depend in part on the nature of the risk in question. For all of these reasons, the preference-based argument for discounting is, empirically speaking, very weak. This argument also rests on dubious normative foundations.

The preference-based argument for discounting holds that individuals' risk-related temporal preferences, as revealed or expressed in their roles as consumers, should control the government's treatment of the temporal dimension in risk regulation. The normative premise of this kind of argument is that "the government ought not, at least as a general rule, to be in the business of evaluating whether a person's choice will serve his or her interests, or even whether the choice is objectionable, except when the choice causes harm to others." [41]

By its own terms, this justification does not embrace one person's preference for another person's harm. Thus, it cannot support discounting in the intergenerational context, in which people's preferences for current life-saving over future life-saving merely reflect a preference for self-protection over protection of others. Nor can it support discounting even in the intragenerational context, if the preferences invoked in support of discounting are based on the implicit assumption that the people doing the preferring are not themselves going to be the ones affected by their preferences. Although both OMB and EPA have acknowledged that the intergenerational setting may pose special challenges for discounting, both also ultimately embrace a default discount rate, even in this setting, based on an estimate of the preferences of the people living today for the present over the future. Moreover, both have defended their assumption that discounting comports with individual preferences, in the intragenerational context, by reference to empirical studies that * * * appear also to reveal people's preferences for their own health over others' health as much as they reveal people's temporal preferences with respect to health outcomes affecting themselves.

In any event, saying that a particular government decision reflects private preferences cannot conclude the debate over regulatory policy. A vast portion of our regulatory state interferes with private preferences, and a correspondingly vast literature has emerged to defend it. It now seems incontestable that private preferences, revealed in people's capacity as consumers, may not reflect public preferences, revealed in people's capacity as citizens. The divergence between the preferences expressed in these different contexts may, indeed, be most pronounced in the case of temporal preferences.

Discounting seems inconsistent with rational behavior in another way as well, at least if the term "rational" can be applied to behavior which, though it violates standard tenets of economic theory, would be regarded by most people as sound and sensible. In the view of many, one of the hallmarks of maturity is the capacity to form habits that, in the short run, are difficult to maintain but that, over the long run, help a person to grow and to flourish. Habits of diet and exercise, of learning and hard work, of frugality in spending and generosity in love—all of these take discipline and dedication to form. Yet most people, I think, would agree that these are the kinds of habits they admire, even the kind they wish to pass on to their children. It is difficult, maybe impossible, to form such habits—which must depend on a kind of presumption that the future is as important as the present—while simultaneously believing that the future should be discounted, or depreciated, relative to the present. Thus the discounting embraced by the federal government ultimately fails to promote a compelling conception of human rationality.

* * * There is, indeed, a jarring asymmetry between EPA's coolly confident claim that "effects that occur farther in the future are worth less in today's terms than those that occur earlier in time" [42] and the widespread impression that environmental law was developed, and the EPA created, precisely in order to protect ourselves and future generations from this kind of myopia.

---

**Conclusion**

The history of assigning cash values to intangibles—nature, human lives, speculative risks—is not an edifying chapter in the history of public policy. It is fraught with highly artificial attempts to redefine vast swaths of human life as market activities and then to build theoretical constructs to mimic the behavior of markets. Despite the intellectual contortions that ensue, the outcomes are said to be rational, morally legitimate, and a reliable basis for public policy. This chapter suggests that the determined attempt to monetize regulatory benefits is largely a benighted exercise.

Philosophers would call this process a "category mistake." Trying to monetize benefits that are not ordinarily the subject of market transactions—mortality risks and the value of endangered species—is necessarily an artificial process. Worse, it seriously distorts the reality of why they are important in the first place—because they *aren't* bought and sold in the marketplace. They are inalienable values.

One response to the difficulties encountered in monetizing the benefits of health, safety, and environmental regulation is to ignore those benefits that cannot be monetized. Thus, EPA's cost-benefits analyses frequently ignore risks to ecosystems and other objects of statutory protections that are more difficult to quantify and monetize. Yet to the extent that policymaking has become a balancing of economic costs versus economic benefits, the equation purports to measure something meaningful while ignoring enormous potential regulatory benefits because the variables are too "soft." How, indeed, can one begin to place a serious cash value on properly functioning ecosystems? They are priceless and beyond monetization.

Many economists make a similar sort of error when they claim that the so-called wage premium is the best measure of the value of a human life. To preserve the assumptions of his theoretical model, the economist presumes that employers pay employees who engage in hazardous work higher wages. Of course, the realities of most workplaces and local job markets refute this idea. Most workers do not have the economic power to extract wage premiums from employers for more hazardous work; they feel lucky to have a job.

The triumph of theory over empirical realities is also seen in the use of "willingness-to-pay" models for valuing risks to human life. Unlike the economic models that claim humans act rationally in their own self-interest, the so-called endowment effect shows that people tend to view the loss of status quo entitlements differently than the gain of additional wealth. The so-called offer-asking conundrum—in which people are willing to pay less to reduce a life-threatening risk imposed by another than they would demand to accept that risk voluntarily—punctures some of the core assumptions of the economic model.

Still another theoretical contrivance designed to understate regulatory benefits is the use of economic discounting of future health, safety, and environmental benefits. High discount rates mean that any government interventions that do not produce immediate benefits have less value. Since there is great opportunity to jigger the outcomes of discounting models by choosing a high discount rate, and few opportunities for the non-specialist to question such choices, the technique can easily be abused. Its very obscurity provides an effective cloak for policymakers to insert their own elitest values without public scrutiny. Use of the discount rate is especially objectionable when there is little empirical evidence to suggest that people actually prefer to avoid short-term risk to long-term risk. Certainly the idea of displacing known risks onto future generations has little moral force.

Sometimes the harshness of placing a dollar value on human life flares into a public controversy, threatening to discredit the legitimacy of the theoretical models. The typical response of policy analysts is that governmental regulation is not designed to protect identifiable individuals from certain death but rather to protect large populations from collective mortality risks. Of course, this response ignores the fact that statistical risks manifest themselves in real harm to real people. That is precisely why laws were enacted to authorize regulation. Reducing policymaking to mere statistical analysis dehumanizes the real human suffering that is the core purpose of regulation.

As if to defend against such charges, some extreme proponents of cost-benefit analysis have tried to turn the tables by arguing that regulation itself can itself kill people by diverting resources from other activities that could make people richer or save greater lives—the "richer is safer" theory. There is no empirical support for this proposition, however, and there are very good reasons to believe that it is specious.

## CHAPTER 6: PRICING THE GRAND CANYON, CASHING OUT A LIFE

The pricing of the Grand Canyon and the valuation of a human life are ultimately matters of moral and social value. Whether through personal conviction or professional training, economic-minded policymakers believe that the most important values can be expressed in dollar sums. They have little time for the "squishy" qualitative values expressed in agency statutes or other public values. Any reclamation of the regulatory process, however, must begin by challenging the growing stranglehold of economic models for dictating regulatory outcomes. Economic effects cannot be ignored, but there are some larger values at stake.

**Suggestions for Further Reading**

*Wage Premiums as a Measure of Life's Value*

For additional challenges to the conventional wisdom that wage premiums serve as a reasonable surrogate for individual willingness to pay for risk reducing interventions, see the following.

Martha T. McCluskey, *The Illusion of Efficiency in Workers' Compensation "Reform,"* 50 RUTGERS L. REV. 657, 751-77 (1998).
*"In the real world neither workers nor employers are likely to be perfectly informed and perfectly free in their efforts to bargain over work-accident costs."*

Peter Railton, *Benefit-Cost Analysis as a Source of Information About Welfare, in* VALUING HEALTH RISKS, COSTS, AND BENEFITS FOR ENVIRONMENTAL DECISION MAKING 55, 70 (P. Hammond & R. Coppock eds., 1990).

JAMES C. ROBINSON, TOIL AND TOXICS: WORKPLACE STRUGGLES AND POLITICAL STRATEGIES FOR OCCUPATIONAL HEALTH 75-76 (1991).
*Suggests that the riskier jobs tend to go to poorly paid workers with few real choices.*

Sidney A. Shapiro & Thomas O. McGarity, *Not So Paradoxical: The Rationale for Technology-Based Regulation*, 1991 DUKE L.J. 729.
*Provides several reasons to believe that wage premiums, such as they exist, are not an accurate measure for the value of human life.*

*The Subtle Deceits of the "Willingness-to-Pay" Standard*

The "offer-asking" conundrum has by now become a familiar component of the debates over cost-benefit analysis. The following articles are illustrative.

Herbert Hovenkamp, *Legal Policy and the Endowment Effect*, 20 J. LEGAL STUD. 225, 247 (1991).

Duncan Kennedy, *Cost-Benefit Analysis of Entitlement Problems: A Critique*, 33 STAN. L. REV. 387 (1981).

Russell Korobkin, *Policymaking and the Offer/Asking Price Gap: Toward a Theory of Efficient Entitlement Allocation*, 46 STAN. L. REV. 663 (1994).

Thomas McGarity, *Media Quality, Technology, and Cost-Benefit Balancing Strategies for Health and Environmental Regulation*, 46 LAW & CONTEMP. PROB. 159, 172 (1983).

Christopher H. Schroeder, *Clear Consensus, Ambiguous Commitment*, 98 MICH. L. REV. 1876, 1888-89 (2000).
  *"Before CBA can even be applied, the analyst must first decide whether to price various factors according to what a person is willing to pay (WTP) to acquire them or avoid having them imposed on him, or according to what a person is willing to accept (WTA) to have a benefit taken away or a cost imposed."*

*The Ultimate Turnaround: Regulation Kills People*

Scholarly commentators have not been kind to the suggestion that governmental interventions aimed at reducing health and safety risks kill more people than they save. For some representative examples, see the following articles.

Adam N. Finkel, *A Second Opinion of an Environmental Misdiagnosis: The Risky Prescriptions of* Breaking the Vicious Circle, 3 N.Y.U. ENVTL. L.J. 295, 324-27 (1995).

Thomas O. McGarity, *A Cost-Benefit State*, 50 ADMIN. L. REV. 7, 40-49 (1998).
  *"If there is any truth at all to the "wealth makes health" thesis, then its advocates should take aim at the Federal Reserve Board, whose conscious efforts to maintain high unemployment rates have been far more effective in keeping people out of work than all the regulations of EPA and OSHA combined."*

Jay Michaelson, *Rethinking Regulation Reform: Toxics, Politics, and Ethics*, 105 YALE L.J. 1891, 1915-16 (1996).
  *Argues that "some arguments in this vein seem like tortured attempts to spread the cost of obeying the law."*

*The Economic Value of an Ecosystem*

There is a growing body of literature on the difficulties of monetizing the value of precious natural resources. The entirety of issue number 2 of volume 20 of the *Stanford Environmental Law Journal* is devoted to the topic of ecosystem services. 20 STAN. ENVTL. L.J. 309-536 (2001). Other interesting articles include the following:

Brian R. Binger et al., *The Use of Contingent Valuation Methodology in Natural Resource Damage Assessments*, 89 NW. U. L. REV. 1029 (1995).

Frank B. Cross, *Natural Resource Damage Valuation*, 42 VAND. L. REV. 269 (1989).

Douglas E. MacLean, *Comparing Values in Environmental Policies: Moral Issues and Moral Arguments, in* VALUING HEALTH RISKS, COSTS, AND BENEFITS FOR ENVIRONMENTAL DECISION MAKING 83 (P. Hammond & R. Coppock eds., 1990).
   *"To assign . . . exchange value to such benefits is to treat them as commodities when they really have a different kind of value—a sacred value perhaps—and should be regarded as such."*

Douglas R. Williams, *Valuing Natural Environments: Compensation, Market Norms, and the Idea of Public Goods*, 27 CONN. L. REV. 365, 370 (1995).
   *Argues against the use of contingent valuation measures of the value of nature and noting that "it is doubtful that the very idea of 'aggregated preferences' is useful in evaluating" decisions on whether to protect natural entities.*

VALUING ENVIRONMENTAL PREFERENCES (Ian J. Bateman & Kenneth G. Willis eds., 1999).

*Whose Values?*

For further assessments of the tendency of proponents of cost-benefit analysis to advance their own value judgments through the technique, see the following articles.

Thomas O. McGarity, *A Cost-Benefit State*, 50 ADMIN. L. REV. 7, 33-36 (1998) (relating substitution of policy preferences by analyst Robert W. Hahn).

SOCIAL THEORIES OF RISK (Sheldon Krimsky & Dominic Golding eds., 1992).
   *Anthology contrasting the "expected utility theory" approach to risk assessment with the broader "psychometric" paradigm.*

Douglas J. Amy, *Why Policy Analysis and Ethics Are Incompatible*, 3 J. POLICY ANALYSIS & MGMT. 573, 577-78 (1984).
   *Highlights the tendency for analysts to incorporate personal and professional values into their analyses.*

*Bias Against the Future*

For a more detailed statement of Professor Heinzerling's posiitions, see Lisa M. Henizerling, *Environmental Law and the Present Future*, 87 GEO. L.J. 2025 (1999).
   For provocative philosophical inquiries into the moral basis for discounting, see the following expositions.

Jeffrey M. Gaba, *Environmental Ethics and Our Moral Relationship to Future Generations: Future Rights and Present Virtue*, 24 COLUM.

J. ENVTL. L. 249 (1999).
*Rejects the argument that the current generation has an obligation to future generations, but maintaining that "[t]hrough virtue theory, the morality of our actions are to be evaluated, not from the perspective of demands or claims that the future might be said to make on us, but rather from the recognition that our concern for the future is an expression of our best virtue."*

Richard L. Revesz, *Environmental Regulation, Cost-Benefit Analysis, and the Discounting of Human Lives*, 99 COLUM. L. REV. 941 (1999).
*Argues that discounting future benefits to existing individuals or regulatory interventions aimed at reducing latent risks is entirely appropriate if done correctly, but discounting regulatory interventions aimed at protecting future generations is "ethically unjustifiable."*

## Chapter 6 Endnotes

1. *See* A. FREEMAN ET AL., THE ECONOMICS OF ENVIRONMENTAL POLICY (1973); A. KNEESE & C. SCHULTZ, POLLUTION, PRICES, AND PUBLIC POLICY (1975); LESTER LAVE, THE STRATEGY OF SOCIAL REGULATION 23-25 (1981); E.J. MISHAN, ECONOMICS FOR SOCIAL DECISIONS 11-13 (1973).

2. *See* STEPHEN BREYER, BREAKING THE VICIOUS CIRCLE: TOWARD EFFECTIVE RISK REGULATION 21-22 (1993) (pointing to great inconsistencies in cost per life saved across regulatory programs).

3. W. Kip Viscusi, *Regulating the Regulators*, 63 U. CHI. L. REV. 1423, 1430-31 (1996). *See also* Richard Thaler & Sherwin Rosen, *The Value of Saving a Life: Evidence From the Labor Market, in Household Production and Consumption* 265-66 (Nestor E. Terleckyj ed., 1976).

4. Professors Dorman and Hagstrom teach economics at Evergreen College and Hamilton College, respectively. This excerpt is drawn from an article, *Wage Compensation for Dangerous Work Revisisted*, published at 52 IND. & LAB. REL. REV. 116 (1998).

5. U.S. EPA, THE BENEFITS AND COSTS OF THE CLEAN AIR ACT 1990 TO 2010: EPA REPORT TO CONGRESS H-1 (1999).

6. *Id.* at H-2.

7. *Id.* at H-2 n.2.

8. Professor Williams teaches environmental and constitutional law at Saint Louis University School of Law. The excerpts are drawn from an article, *Valuing Natural Environments: Compensation, Market Norms and the Idea of Public Goods*, published at 27 CONN. L. REV. 365 (1995).

9. Herbert Hovenkamp, *Legal Policy and the Endowment Effect*, 20 J. LEGAL STUD. 225, 225 (1991) [hereinafter Hovenkamp, Endowment Effect].

10. Daniel Kahneman & Amos Tversky, *Prospect Theory: An Analysis of Decision Under Risk*, 47 ECONOMETRICA 263 (1979).

11. *See, e.g.*, International Union, UAW v. Occupational Safety & Health Admin., 938 F.2d 1310, 1326 (D.C. Cir. 1991) (Williams, J., concurring) (explaining that recent studies predict that "each $ 7.5 million of costs generated by regulation may . . . induce one [premature] fatality" in the public through reduced availability of resources for medical care and safety). *See also* Ralph L. Keeney, *Mortality Risks Induced by Economic Expenditures*, 10 RISK ANALYSIS 147, 155 (1990).

12. Mark E. Shere is an attorney in Indianapolis, Indiana. The excerpt is drawn from the article, *The Myth of Meaningful Environmental Risk Assessment*, 19 HARV. ENVTL. L. REV. 409 (1995).

13. BREYER, *supra* note 2, at 23. *See* Ralph L. Keeney, *Mortality Risks Induced by the Costs of Regulation*, 8 J. RISK & UNCERTAINTY 95 (1994); Ralph L. Keeney, *Mortality Risks Induced by Economic Expenditures*, 10 RISK ANALYSIS 147 (1990).

14. ROBERT W. HAHN ET AL., DO FEDERAL REGULATIONS REDUCE MORTALITY? 12 (2000). *See also* Randall Lutter & John F. Morrall III, *Health-Health Analysis: A New Way to Evaluate Health and Safety Regulation*, 8 J. RISK & UNCERTAINTY 43 (1994).

15. At the time that he wrote this article, Jonathan Bender was on the staff of the Carnegie Commission for Science, Technology, and Society. The article *Societal Risk Reduction: Promise and Pitfalls*, was published at 3 N.Y.U. ENVTL. L.J. 255 (1994).

16. Aaron Wildavsky, *Richer Is Safer*, 60 PUB. INTEREST 23, 25 (1980). The thesis has also been referred to as the "risk-risk" principle.

17. *Id.* at 24–25. Prof. Aaron Wildavsky uses limited data from only two countries to support the "richer is safer" theory. He does not discuss whether environmental safety is one of the salubrious practices in which wealthier societies invest, or whether environmental hazards are confounded with income in poor countries.

18. Ralph L. Keeney, *Mortality Risks Induced by Economic Expenditures*, 10 RISK ANALYSIS 147, 155 (1990).

19. 938 F.2d 1310 (D.C. Cir. 1991).

20. *Id.*

21. *Id.* at 1326.

22. Robert D. Hershey Jr., *Citing Cost, Budget Office Blocks Workplace Health Proposal*, N.Y. TIMES, Mar. 16, 1992, at A13.

23. U.S. GENERAL ACCOUNTING OFFICE, RISK-RISK ANALYSIS: OMB'S REVIEW OF A PROPOSED OSHA RULE (1992).

24. *Id.* at 8.

25. *Id.*

26. 938 F.2d at 1326.

27. Prof. James Salzman teaches environmental law at the Duke Law School. The full article, *Valuing Ecosystem Services*, appears at 24 ECOLOGY L. REV. 887 (1997).

28. Professor Verchick teaches environmental and property law at the University of Missouri-Kansas City School of Law. The reading is taken from a longer article, *Feathers or Gold? A Civic Economics for Environmental Law*, at 25 HARV. ENVTL. L. REV. 95 (2001).

29. Gretchen C. Daily, *Introduction: What Are Ecosystem Services?*, in NATURE'S SERVICES: SOCIETAL DEPENDENCE ON NATURAL ECOSYSTEMS 3 (Gretchen C. Daily ed., 1997).

30. *See* R. Costanza et al., *The Value of the World's Ecosystem Services and Natural Capital*, 387 NATURE 253 (1997).

31. *See* Salzman, *supra* note 27, at 891.

32. *See* Kenneth E. McConnell, *Indirect Methods for Assessing Natural Resource Damages Under CERCLA*, in VALUING NATURAL ASSETS, THE ECONOMICS OF NATURAL RESOURCE ASSESSMENT 153, 163 (Raymond J. Kopp & V. Kerry Smith eds., 1993).

33. The term "contingent valuation" derives from the fact that subjects' responses are contingent on a set of hypothetical events. *See* David S. Brookshire & Michael McKee, *Is the Glass Half Empty, Is the Glass Half Full? Compensable Damages and the Contingent Valuation Method*, 34 NAT. RESOURCES J. 51, 67 (1994).

34. *See* Eileen Gauna, *Federal Environmental Citizen Provisions: Obstacles and Incentives on the Road to Environmental Justice*, 22 ECOLOGY L.Q. 1, 38 (1995) (criticizing such efforts as "environmental blackmail").

35. JOHN D. GRAHAM ET AL., IN SEARCH OF SAFETY: CHEMICALS AND CANCER RISK 189 (1988).

36. W. Kip Viscusi, *Regulating the Regulators*, 63 U. CHI. L. REV. 1423, 1447 (1996).

37. Professor Flatt teaches environmental law at the University of Houston Law Center. The reading is from an article, *Saving the Lost Sheep: Bringing Environmental Values*

*Back Into the Fold With a New EPA Decisionmaking Paradigm*, published at 74
WASH. L. REV. 1 (1999).

38. *See* U.S. EPA, Guidelines for Preparing Economic Analyses, Review Draft, at E-15
(July 17, 1998) [hereinafter Review Draft]; Clayton P. Gillette & Thomas D. Hopkins,
*Federal Agency Valuations of Human Life*, *in* ADMINISTRATIVE CONFERENCE OF THE
U.S., REPORT FOR RECOMMENDATION 88, 368, 406 (1988); Daniel A. Farber & Paul
A. Hemmersbaugh, *The Shadow of the Future: Discount Rates, Later Generations,
and the Environment*, 46 VAND. L. REV. 267, 277-79 (1993); Michael J. Moore & W.
Kip Viscusi, *Discounting Environmental Health Risks: New Evidence and Policy Im-
plications*, 18 J. ENVTL. ECON. & MGMT. S-51, S-59 (1990).

39. W. KIP VISCUSI, FATAL TRADEOFFS: PUBLIC AND PRIVATE RESPONSIBILITIES FOR
RISK 145 (1992).

40. Professor Heinzerling teaches environmental law and torts at Georgetown University
School of Law. These excerpts are from an article, *Discounting Our Future*, published
at 34 LAND & WATER L. REV. 39 (1999).

41. *See* Cass R. Sunstein, *Legal Interference With Private Preferences*, 53 U. CHI. L.
REV. 1129, 1131-32 (1986); *see also* U.S. EPA, Review Draft, *supra* note 38, at E-9
(emphasizing "consumer sovereignty").

42. U.S. EPA, Review Draft, *supra* note 38, at 25.

# Chapter 7: Slipshod Methods for Estimating Regulatory Costs

An estimate of the costs of complying with a regulation is the foundation of a cost-benefit analysis. But how shall those costs be estimated? And are they even required?

Some provisions, like the Clean Air Act's (CAA's) requirement for establishing national ambient air quality standards, do not allow cost considerations to enter the picture. Many environmental statutes, however, explicitly require the agency to consider costs in enacting protective regulations. For example, in establishing technology-based standards, the U.S. Environmental Protection Agency (EPA) must consider the cost of compliance along with the availability of pollution reduction technologies. The Occupational Safety and Health Act (OSH Act) implicitly includes cost as part of the "feasibility" determination for occupational health standards and as part of the "reasonableness" determination for occupational safety standards.

Since the mid-1970s, under a variety of Executive Orders promulgated by every president since President Richard Nixon, federal regulatory agencies have routinely developed estimates of the cost of complying with proposed regulations (even those for which costs are irrelevant). During this period, a number of grand assessments of the costs imposed on society by health, safety, and environmental regulation have appeared. A 1980 report by National Economic Research Associates, Inc., prepared for the Business Roundtable, concluded that the direct costs on the private sector attributable to air quality regulations promulgated under the 1970 CAA Amendments would exceed $400 billion over the years 1970 to 1987—without even considering the impact of considerably more stringent regulations required by the 1977 Amendments. [1]

Prof. Thomas Hopkins, formerly an Associate Director of the Office of Management and Budget's (OMB's) Office of Information and Regulatory Affairs, estimated in 1996 that federal regulations impose annual costs of $668 billion on regulatees, with about one-third of those costs attributable to environmental protection and risk reduction. [2] In 2001, the Mercatus Center estimated that OSHA regulations imposed a total of $41 billion in regulatory costs on employers. [3]

Estimating costs seems straightforward. Most policymakers believe that all a regulator must do to develop a cost estimate is to ask affected industries for estimates of the incremental cost of complying with a proposed regulation, and then extrapolate those costs to all affected by the rule. The uncertainties that plague risk assessments are assumed to be absent when estimating costs. That assumption is wrong.

The academic literature on cost estimates is sparse. Agency guidelines for preparing costs estimates are limited. Agencies generally ask the industries affected by regulations what they estimate compliance will cost; in developing overall estimates, agencies generally take industry self-reporting at face value. The regulatees obviously have incentives to exaggerate the expected costs of compliance they report, since the higher the predicted cost, the less likely that stringent regulations will be adopted.

It would seem logical for agencies to prepare retrospective comparisons of the predicted costs of compliance with the actual costs of promulgated rules. Yet this is rarely done. When such ex ante and ex post costs have been compared, researchers have found that the predicted costs of regulation are often dramatically higher than the actual costs.

This chapter explores the uncertainties that arise in cost estimates and the notable fact that agency cost estimates often wildly inflate the estimated costs of compliance. Because estimates of the cost of entire regulatory programs are usually based in large part on such (inflated) program-specific estimates, the "grand totals" of the sort made by the Business Roundtable, the OMB, and others are also likely to be unrealistically high. Moreover, the costs of regulatory programs, even if very high, are not the appropriate measure of their worth, according to the economic theory espoused by the regulatory reform proponents. Even if the costs are quite large, the issue, from an economic perspective, is whether the benefits exceed the costs. Those analysts who criticize regulation for imposing large aggregate costs ignore the even larger aggregate benefits that such programs generate.

## Uncertainties in Measuring Costs

The burdens allegedly imposed by health, safety, and environmental regulation on business was a top priority of the Republican "revolutionaries" who gained control of both houses of the U.S. Congress in 1994. To advance their antiregulatory agenda, a U.S. House of Representatives committee asked the U.S. General Accounting Office (GAO) to conduct an empirical, retrospective survey of the costs that federal regulations imposed on 15 representative companies.

The GAO's conclusions are striking: few businesses were willing to participate in the GAO's study; of those that participated, few understood which regulations applied to them. [4] The participating businesses could not provide comprehensive information on the direct costs of regulation and could not isolate the incremental cost of complying with new regulations. In other words, the GAO found that regulated companies generally have no method of measuring the cost of federal regulations, and federal agencies have no means of verifying the estimates they provide. The regulatory cost estimates that were bandied about were largely based on crude *guesses*:

---

*Measures of Regulatory Costs Vary*

Cost studies * * * vary in terms of the types of costs considered attributable to regulatory requirements. Studies could include all expenditures by the regulated entity that are in any way related to the regulatory requirements at issue. In such studies, for example, if a company spent a total of $1 million during the course of a year on worker safety training and equipment, the full $1 million would be counted toward the company's regulatory costs. However, because the cost study includes all of the company's expenditures in this area, such an approach implicitly assumes that the company would have spent nothing on worker safety training and equipment during that year in the absence of regulatory requirements. Because many companies probably spend some money to protect their workers in the normal course of business, attributing those expenditures to regulatory requirements is erroneous and overstates the burden of regulations. [5] Another approach does not include all expenditures in the measurement of regulatory costs, focusing only on the incremental costs directly attributable to the regulations in question. If, in the above example, the company had spent $600,000 on worker safety training and equipment, regardless of any regulatory requirements, the incremental cost attributable to regulations in that year would be $400,000 ($1 million minus $600,000).

The scope of the cost studies we reviewed also varied widely. Some studies, such as the work of Thomas Hopkins, attempted to estimate the cost of regulations to the economy as a whole. [6] * * * Hopkins estimated in 1993 that the cumulative cost of federal regulations to the economy would be $607 billion in 1995. However, some economists believe that one of the elements of Hopkins' study—transfer costs—should not be considered part of the cost of regulations to the economy because transfers represent a loss to one group and a corresponding benefit to another. [7] There are also concerns about the accuracy of some of the data included in Hopkins' analysis. [8]

*Companies Generally Could Not Provide Comprehensive, Incremental Cost Data*

To assess the burden of federal regulations on the 15 companies participating in our review, we used an approach that was similar in some respects to the approach used in the Arthur Andersen study. Like the Arthur Andersen study, we asked each of the companies to provide information on their direct incremental costs. However, unlike the Arthur Andersen study, we focused on costs associated with complying with all federal regulations during 1994, not just selected agencies and programs. Also, we did not require the companies to estimate the costs associated with regulatory compliance. Instead, we left it to the companies to provide what information they believed was appropriate.

Because we wanted to be sure that the companies described their regulatory costs consistently, we provided extensive instructions to the companies regarding what should and should not be included in their tabulations. For example, because our focus was on incremental costs, we told the companies that any costs that would have been incurred in the normal course of business during that period should not be included in their cost measures. Because indirect costs are more difficult to measure, we told the companies to provide cost data on direct costs and asked for examples of indirect costs. We also delineated other types of costs that should be excluded from their tabulations, including lobbying costs; costs associated with nonfederal rules; and payments to the federal government, such as taxes and fines for noncompliance.

\* \* \* We told the companies that their accounting and financial records should be their primary source of the cost data, and that we would like to collect, or at least review, any documentation of these costs.

Although all of the 15 companies participating in our review provided at least some data on their compliance costs, none of the companies provided cost data that were both comprehensive and incremental. Some of the officials with whom we met recognized that the data provided were not what we had asked them to provide. Our interviews with these company officials and our review of the information they provided revealed various reasons why the companies' cost data were neither comprehensive nor incremental.

*Companies' Cost Data Were Not Comprehensive*
Although we asked each of the companies to provide cost data for all the regulations they faced, none of the companies provided comprehensive cost data. The uncomprehensive nature of the cost data provided was sometimes a function of the difficulty company officials had in citing all applicable regulations. Because we asked each company to provide cost information for all applicable federal regulations, and because company officials generally said they could not identify all applicable regulations, they, therefore, could not provide a measurement of their regulatory costs that they believed reflected all of their responsibilities.

Another reason company officials said they had difficulty providing data on their companies' federal regulatory compliance costs was because they found it difficult to distinguish between federal requirements and those of other governmental jurisdictions. \* \* \* Making this distinction was particularly difficult for the companies in regulatory areas where state governments enforced federal standards and could also attach additional requirements. Officials from a company operating in California said that California enforces all of OSHA's regulations and some of EPA's regulations—often adding stricter state requirements.

In other cases, company officials recognized federal regulatory requirements in certain functional areas but still did not provide any cost data for those functional areas. \* \* \* The cost data the companies provided were also incomplete in other ways. For example, one company provided data on its incremental regulatory costs, but only for a portion of its labor expenses. [9] The company did not provide comprehensive data on capital or other types of costs, and the labor cost data did not include the company's hourly workers.

*Companies' Cost Data Were Not Incremental*
Although we requested that companies provide incremental compliance costs because we believe they are more accurate measures of regulatory burden than total expenditures in areas covered by regulations, most companies did not provide incremental cost data. As previously noted, calculation of incremental costs requires company officials to decide what actions their company would have taken in the absence of the identified regulations—a determination that can be difficult, if not impossible, to make in retrospect.

Reflecting the difficulty in separating regulatory and business-related costs, the officials also said their companies' accounting and financial records did not capture the information necessary to determine incremental compliance costs. For example, officials from the petrochemical company told us their company's accounting systems were not designed to uniquely categorize the costs of new and ongoing regulatory requirements. These officials said that there is little incentive to isolate and monitor these costs because such information has little business value.

Company officials also said they could not provide incremental regulatory cost data because the companies' regulatory responsibilities were sometimes difficult to distinguish from their regular processes and functions. For example, officials from the glass company said regulatory responsibilities were woven into individuals' jobs, and it was difficult to separate what was being done strictly for regulatory reasons. * * * Officials from the petrochemical company said there is little incentive to isolate and uniquely monitor the explicit costs associated with new and ongoing regulatory requirements because they generally view regulations as nonrevenue-producing mandates.

———————

Surprisingly little research has been done comparing the predicted costs of health and safety regulation with the actual costs that eventually were borne by businesses. In 1995, the Office of Technology Assessment (OTA), a now-defunct congressional research agency, conducted a comprehensive analysis of the predicted and actual costs of compliance with the Occupational Safety and Health Administration's (OSHA's) regulations. [10] It found OSHA's cost estimates often exceeded the actual costs of compliance.

One of the OTA's more significant findings was that compliance cost estimates fail to take into account technological innovation following adoption of a health and safety rule. Such innovation often has the effect of lowering regulatory costs:

———————

In brief, [OTA's] effort encompassed four main areas. First, more than a dozen of OSHA's major health and safety standards were examined—a few of the major rules issued in the 1970s, but most from the early 1980s up through the early 1990s. This effort was intended to appraise the characteristic methods, data foundations, and uses of the feasibility and regulatory impact analyses prepared for the agency's rulemakings. Second, for eight of the standards, OTA assembled data on the nature of affected industries' actual adjustment to the compliance provisions and examined the accuracy of the rulemaking estimates (vis-à-vis predominant control measures adopted, compliance costs, and other economic impacts) against these post-promulgation outcomes. Third, to gain a better appreciation of the agency's internal procedures and capabilities for conducting technology and regulatory impact analyses, the operation and budgetary resources of the parts of the agency principally involved in these efforts were reviewed. Finally, to judge how OSHA's practices compared with those of other government organizations, the health and safety decisionmaking approaches of other federal agencies and those of some of the major trading partners of the United States were examined.

*Major Conclusions*
\* \* \* The overall conclusions that OTA draws from these are as follows:

1. The 1970 OSH Act, particularly as the courts have subsequently interpreted its procedural requirements, executive orders (mandating the conduct of "regulatory analyses"), and other legislation (in particular, the 1980 Regulatory Flexibility Act) combine to impose an extensive set of analysis and evidentiary stipulations concerning hazard control options and regulatory impacts that OSHA must satisfy in promulgating its health and safety standards. By and large, the agency has developed a coherent and credible set of procedures and methods that are responsive to these various requirements—and which generally provide a reasonable channel for engagement of the views of direct stakeholders and other interested parties.

2. The agency's findings and estimates on hazard control options and regulatory impacts are often the subject of vigorous review and challenge by stakeholders and various experts on all sides of rulemaking issues. But this reaction does not generally indicate underlying agency analytical neglect. The agency's rulemakings are often lightning rods for controversy and are conducted in a politically polarized setting. The stakeholders, industrial health and safety professionals, and various government bodies involved in rulemakings often diverge widely when it comes to such basic issues as the intrinsic need for enhanced protection, the likely efficacy of new compliance measures, and the benefits and costs to arise. Furthermore, the analytical questions with greatest bearing on these matters are often not amenable to fully conclusive determination for various reasons: the complexity of the technical considerations involved (e.g., to what extent will risk be reduced as a result of the installation of particular control measures on an existing production process); the inevitable shortages of data on important parameters (which arise because, as a practical matter, the agency often does not have the budget, work calendar, or access to industry needed to collect all relevant data on the many technical factors involved); and attendant imponderables (such as what pertinent operating conditions will prevail over time in affected or otherwise involved industries).

3. OSHA's examinations of prospective control measures and the possible economic effects of their adoption occur principally in the course of procedurally obliged demonstrations that the compliance provisions of an intended standard are generally feasible in technical and economic terms for affected industries. It appears from the sample of existing standards OTA examined for this report, that the agency has generally performed this task with workable accuracy—that is, standards determined by OSHA to be "feasible" in the course of its analytical deliberations have usually proved to be so when industries took the necessary steps to comply. (However, a few failures in this respect were evident in the cases, and point to some analytical deficiencies the agency should consider in future work.)

Nonetheless, the agency's demonstrations of feasibility are often based on conservative assumptions about what compliance responses will predominate across affected industries. As a result, there are often sizable disparities between OSHA's rulemaking projections of control technology adoption patterns, compliance spending, and other economic impacts, and what actually happens when affected industries respond to an enacted standard. In a good number of the cases that OTA examined, the actual compliance response that was observed included advanced or innovative control measures that had not been emphasized in the rulemaking analyses, and the actual cost burden proved to be considerably less than what OSHA had estimated.

4. Benefit-cost comparisons are not at present a formal basis on which OSHA sets its standards—the result of Congress's original crafting of the 1970 OSH Act and the various interpretations and guidelines provided by the courts in the years since.

5. The rulemaking cases OTA examined largely confirmed one of the stronger criticisms of OSHA's analytical priorities and practice: that the agency devotes relatively little attention to examining the potential of advanced technologies or the prospect of regulation-induced innovation to provide technologically and economically superior options for hazard control. Most attention does appear to be placed on "conventional" control measures (e.g., increased ventilation and production equipment enclosure), rather than on "new technology" (ranging from sophisticated emissions control devices to technologies capable of supporting basic shifts in production processes, including process redesigns, product reformulations, and material substitutions). Such a bias is not surprising, given the "feasibility demonstration" orientation of the agency's rulemaking logic and the need for control technology assumptions capable of standing up well under "substantial evidence" scrutiny by the courts later. But this narrowed focus leaves a significant gap in the vision of the potentially available control options that OSHA can bring to the policymaking debate. Furthermore, in a few of the rulemakings OTA examined, it appears that greater attention to the potential of new technology during the rulemaking might have supported more stringent hazard reduction provisions than were actually promulgated.

6. Finally, it is surprising, given the long-standing and contentious public debate about the benefits and costs of OSHA's regulatory interventions, how little systematic knowledge exists about the actual effects of the agency's standards. OSHA would, no doubt, significantly benefit from a more routine effort to collect and interpret information pertaining to actual regulatory outcomes and impacts—to aid the agency in identifying possible needs for mid-course policy adjustments, to better inform the public on the balance between new costs and new benefits being realized, and to provide insights that might help OSHA shape the content of future rulemakings.

To be sure, complete answers to these questions imply data collection and analysis efforts that are probably beyond practical reach (and beyond beneficial return for the agency's primary responsibilities). But the experience of the few existing evaluative studies on past rulemakings suggest that informative and useful findings (on industry compliance responses, incurred costs, and extent of hazard reductions) can be derived from something less than exhaustive studies. What is needed is a more systematic effort on the agency's part to develop this kind of information.

---

## Are Costs Systematically Overestimated?

The preceding readings suggest that agency cost estimates may often overstate the economic burden of federal regulation. The disparities between predicted costs and actual costs can be quite dramatic.

In the following excerpt, Prof. Thomas McGarity of the University of Texas School and Prof. Ruth Ruttenberg of the George Meany Center-National Labor College survey the literature about regulatory cost estimates. [11] They identify several areas of cost inflation, including reliance on regulatees for empirical data; conservative cost assumptions; starting with zero baselines; overinclusiveness; and static analysis.

Professors McGarity and Ruttenberg examined several retrospective studies comparing the cost estimates made by agencies at the time regulations were promulgated with actual compliance costs. The former were generally much larger than the latter, often by very large amounts.

Professors McGarity and Ruttenberg suggest several explanations for this fact. First, agencies rely very heavily upon the regulated industries themselves for the data used in agency cost estimates, and regulatees have a strong incentive to err on the high side. Second, agencies typically employ conservative assumptions out of fear that the OMB or the courts will disallow their regulations.

One key source of inflated cost estimates is the assumption that companies would do nothing to protect health, safety, and the environment in the absence of federal regulation. Tort law and public image considerations are obvious influences on companies to address workplace safety, product safety, and the environment. Yet business expenditures on these purposes are often blamed on regulation. In the same vein, agency cost assessors often conflate regulatory costs with normal corporate expenditures on renovation and modernization that may have nothing to do with regulation. Finally, agencies make no allowance for how their regulations may stimulate the evolution of new technologies, which may result in myriad savings in compliance costs, production efficiencies, and even spinoff products.

---

Despite predictions by the Council of Economic Advisors that compliance with EPA's stringent 1997 revisions to the national ambient air quality standards for ozone and particulate matter would cost regulated industries $60 billion and somewhat less dire predictions by EPA's own economists that the regulation would cost $6-8 billion, then-EPA Administrator Carol Browner predicted that the costs would not approach even the lower estimate, because the industry would find ways to implement the requirements more cheaply. [12] Although it is certainly possible that the Administrator's rosy prediction was unduly optimistic, there are many reasons to believe that she was not far off base. Given the nature of the empirical basis for direct regulatory cost assessments and the uncertainties in predicting how companies will react to performance-based standards, it seems likely that both prospective, and even retrospective, cost assessments are biased in an upward direction.

*Evidence That Prospective Studies are Biased Upward*

Goodstein and Hodges found that in 11 out of 12 regulatory initiatives that they examined, "the initial estimates were at least double the actual costs." [13] * * * In many of the cases they examined, the initial estimates were made by regulated entities or industry consultants. Thus, these estimates could be seen as more in the nature of debating points than objective cost assessments. In most of the other cases, the initial estimates were made by the agency or (more frequently) agency consultants and were therefore not as easily dismissed.

Numerous other studies support the general conclusion that ex ante cost estimates tend to be much higher than real-world compliance costs. In a review of compliance costs associated with OSHA's 1974 vinyl chloride standard, Ruth Ruttenberg reported that an industry contractor predicted compliance costs of $65-95 billion based on the assumption that the vinyl chloride production was likely to cease. Relying upon the same assumption, an OSHA contractor predicted compliance costs of only $1.95 billion, because consumers could easily shift to plastics other than polyvinyl chloride. After OSHA's vinyl chloride standard went into effect, two marginal plants did in fact shut down, but several others either began to produce vinyl chloride or expanded existing capacity. An industry trade association later calculated that the industry invested $200 million in capital and an additional $100 million in research and development to meet the standard. A 1978 Wharton School study estimated the combined capital costs of the OSHA standard to all affected companies was no more than $182 million, and the Congressional Research Service of the Library of Congress determined that the cost to users was about $300 million. [14]

A review of more than two dozen environmental and occupational safety regulations undertaken by Winston Harrington, Richard Morgenstern, and Peter Nelson concluded that "ex ante estimates of total cost have tended to exceed actuals." [15] Another study by Timothy Bresnahan and Dennis Yao of auto industry compliance with the first round of air pollution control requirements concluded that experience and improved technology "have allowed increases in automobile quality so that incremental costs of recent [air pollution] standards are much lower than previously believed." [16] An EPA retrospective study of the cost of reducing emissions under the agency's acid rain program indicated that the actual costs were much lower than initially estimated. [17]

*Reliance on Regulatees for Empirical Data*

One clear message of the existing studies of cost assessment in regulatory agencies is that solid empirical data on regulatory costs is hard to come by. Professor Hopkins noted in his original 1992 paper that "in many cases it was not possible to get the data," and he concluded generally that "data support is thin indeed." [18] In its first annual report to Congress on the costs and benefits of federal regulation, the

Office of Management and Budget conceded that "there are still enormous data gaps in the information available on regulatory benefits and costs" and "accurate data is still sparse." [19] In the final analysis, agencies must rely on regulatees for much of the empirical information used in cost assessments.

To the extent the agencies depend upon regulatee-supplied data without attempting to validate them, the accuracy of the input data is suspect and the resulting estimates are likely to be high. Knowing that the agency is less likely to impose requirements that cost a great deal of money or that threaten to drive a substantial number of regulatees out of business, regulatees have a clear incentive to inflate cost estimates in the hope of securing a less stringent regulation. At the outset of their study of agency-prepared regulatory impact analyses, Harrington, Morgenstern, and Nelson cautioned that "finding bias in the cost estimates from industry . . . sources is perhaps to be expected." [20] Well aware of the importance that cost assessments play in many rulemaking initiatives, sophisticated trade associations frequently hire consultants to provide "independent" cost assessments for agency use. Harrington, Morgenstern, and Nelson note that "the mere existence of such studies may exert upward pressure on regulators' cost estimates."[21]

*Conservative Assumptions*

Agencies are well aware of the high probability that regulations that have a significant impact on regulated industries will be challenged in court. Even under the not especially deferential "hard look" doctrine that has evolved over the last two decades, agencies know that litigants face an uphill battle in challenging the empirical basis for agency fact-finding in rulemaking. The reviewing judges are likely to be much more receptive to challenges to the assumptions that go into the economic models that cost assessors employ when they venture beyond the existing empirical data. Knowing this, agencies are likely to adopt conservative assumptions that will survive predictable industry challenges to their regulations. Thus, the OTA study of OSHA cost assessments concluded that a frequent cause of poor ex ante cost estimates was "'conservatism' in OSHA's assumptions." [22]

*Zero Baselines*

* * * OMB guidelines provide that the proper measure of the cost of complying with a regulation is the incremental cost above the "baseline" state of the world that would have existed in the absence of the regulation, including any other federal regulation, any state and local regulation, and any applicable tort liability rules. [23] Yet, the baseline scenario is often difficult to define and measure. Perhaps for this reason, many cost assessments * * * start with a zero baseline that reflects the broad assumption that regulatees would have taken no action whatsoever to protect health, safety and the environment without the stimulus of a federal regulation. To the extent that this assumption is erroneous, ignoring the baseline scenario necessarily results in an overestimation of compliance costs.

*Overinclusiveness*

In his doctoral dissertation, economist Peter J. Wilcoxen examined investment in environmental controls in several plants and concluded that "when firms shut down their plants to install environmental capital, they take account of the adjustment costs and often concurrently replace other older capital equipment." [24]

Economist James C. Robinson has likewise noted that companies that are forced to meet health, safety, or environmental regulatory requirements may elect to purchase new equipment that reduces risks but also increases output efficiency, and he concludes that it would therefore be inappropriate to assign the full capital costs of the equipment to the regulatory requirement. [25] It is, however, often difficult for the cost assessor to distinguish the proportion of a regulation-induced capital expenditure that is properly attributed to the regulatory requirement. * * * When the cost assessor abandons the effort to segregate capital costs attributable exclusively to the regulation from capital expenditures on plant and equipment that the company would have made in any event, the resulting cost assessment will be biased upwards.

*Static Analysis*

Most regulatory analysis fails to capture the dynamic and innovative ways in which regulatees often comply with performance-based regulations. When an agency is attempting to identify potential control technologies at the outset of the rulemaking process, companies have no incentive to devote resources to identifying innovative solutions to the problem that the agency is trying to solve. If anything, they are likely to point to expensive, existing "off-the-shelf" technologies in the hope that the agency will promulgate a lax standard. On the other hand, company scientists and engineers can respond to the incentives that a regulatory requirement provides by designing new controls, fashioning prevention techniques, or identifying substitutes for hazardous substances, all with a view toward achieving compliance with performance-based standards at a lower cost than installing the model technologies that agency cost assessors factored into the ex ante cost assessment.

* * * Cost assessors too often ignore the "learning curve"—industry's capacity over time to learn, innovate, and thereby reduce the cost of meeting regulatory requirements. Companies frequently adapt control technologies from other industries to meet new regulatory requirements. Sometimes, companies come up with innovative new control technologies to meet regulatory requirements. Finally, the stimulus of a regulatory requirement can induce industry scientists and engineers to create new processes and products to meet past needs. [26]

---

## Can Regulation Enhance Economic Performance?

Prof. Nicholas Ashford, a long-time observer of industry attempts to implement regulatory requirements, argues that regulation can actually induce technological innovations that benefit the industry as well as consumers and the environment. Professor Ashford surveyed environmental, health, and safety regulations of product and manufacturing process adopted between 1970-1985. He concluded that the stricter the regulation, the more likely it is to induce technological innovation and, eventually, lead to lower compliance costs. Although it may appear counterintuitive, less stringent regulations can be more costly to business in the long run than more stringent rules that stimulate or induce product and process innovations. Regulatory uncertainty, on the other hand, is likely to deter innovation. [27]

---

The review [undertaken here, of ten regulatory cases] was restricted to regulation between 1970 and 1985 under the U.S. Clean Air and Water Acts, the Toxic Substances Control Act, the Occupational Safety and Health Act, and the Consumer Product Safety Act.

The history demonstrates that standard setting can be used to encourage all the varieties of technological innovation as well as diffusion for both product and process change. The period from 1970 to 1985 reveals significant innovation and essential compliance with very stringent regulation. Product-focused regulation primarily elicits a product response (substitution by existing products or a new product). Sometimes the new product (e.g., lead-free gasoline) is accompanied by significant process innovation as well. Process-focused regulation can elicit either a process or a product change. If a process restriction is stringent enough, product substitution may be the only practical response.

Stringency of regulation can be evaluated in terms of both the extent to which it reduced risks and the extent to which it forces development of new technology. Stringent regulations that do not require new technological solutions may appear sufficient but fall far short of their potential to achieve maximum protection. For example, the failure to adopt a 0.1 fiber/cc [OSHA] standard, the lowest level detectable, for worker asbestos exposure inhibited development of substitute products by the asbestos industry. The industry was able to comply with the 2 fiber/cc standard simply by installing existing pollution control equipment. By failing to adopt the more stringent standard, OSHA effectively inhibited new product development and product substitution. Thus, contrary to the widely held belief that too stringent a regulation inhibits innovation, in some cases a standard that is not stringent enough may inhibit innovation. A more recent example, lax regulation of formaldehyde levels for occupationally exposed garment workers, similarly failed to stimulate new product development.

Stringency may be affected, in practice, by legislative directive of the agency issuing the regulation. For example, EPA, OSHA, and the Consumer Product Safety Commission (CPSC) have different legislative mandates. The OMB directed the EPA Office of Toxic Substances to construe the scope of its regulatory authority narrowly and to refer appropriate regulation to other agencies. In particular, the OMB directed EPA not to ban three uses of asbestos, but to pass on the regulatory responsibility to OSHA. Since it has questionable authority to ban dangerous substances, OSHA could probably only regulate worker exposure in the manufacturing process or user industries. Thus, the directives would provide for regulation of ambient levels, rather than a ban, encouraging the diffusion of ventilation technology rather than the substitution of new industrial products.

Uncertainty in regulatory signals or agency position can also deter innovation. Faced with uncertainties that create risks that the technology developed will not ultimately be needed or will be unnecessarily costly, potentially innovative industries will simply adopt low-risk existing technology. Thus, only diffusion will occur. Both standard setting designed to encourage innovation and innovation waivers have encountered problems with regulatory uncertainty in the past.

The preceding discussion focuses on the regulation of existing chemicals, though some new chemicals are developed as part of the technological response. If EPA desires to encourage the development of new chemicals to replace toxic chemicals currently in use, it must take more definitive actions. First, it must be clear about its premanufacturing notification process by providing definite guidelines regarding the specific safety evaluations that should be undertaken on different classes of chemicals. Second, it must increase the likelihood of market penetration by appropriate regulation of existing toxic chemicals. This consolidation of new and old chemical regulation is essential to effect the desired product transition.

Innovation waivers apply mostly to process change, are expressly innovation forcing, and do not promote diffusion. The regulatory designer seldom uses a waiver mechanism for promoting radical process innovation because of the long time generally necessary to develop the innovation. The waiver mechanism, however, might well encourage both incremental process innovation and acceleration of radical innovation already underway. Success requires EPA to give early, clear, and certain signals to the developer of the technology to minimize the risk of that technology being found unacceptable. Furthermore, good faith efforts resulting in significant though incomplete achievement of the pollution reduction goal should be rewarded by fail-safe strategies, using appropriate and adjustable economic sanctions.

Thus, the model of the effects of regulation on innovation applied to the history of standard setting and innovation waivers can contribute to more rational deliberate design of regulation. The design should combine an assessment of the innovative capacity of the possible responding industrial section with levels and forms of regulation tailored to that capacity. The entire process should reflect a realistic evaluation of the best possible achievable technological goal. In that way, regulation can be used both to stimulate technological change for health, safety, and environmental purposes and to bring about a desirable restructuring of the industrial process.

---

Prof. Michael E. Porter, of the Harvard Business School, makes a point similar to Professor Ashford, that regulation spurs technological innovation and lowers compliance costs. [28] In his view, pollution is evidence of bad resource management in the manufacturing process. Environmental regulation, by forcing business to focus on better allocating resources, provides economic benefits not taken into account when regulatory costs are estimated. The excerpt below describes why environmental regulation improves economic efficiency.

An important side effect of stringent regulation is that the United States may become more competitive in the international marketplace. The converse is also true: countries that experience regulation-induced innovations often out-compete U.S. companies in world markets. At the very least, Professor Porter sees little evidence to support the proposition that stringent regulation hampers international competitiveness.

---

Do strict environmental standards make American industry less competitive in international markets? Many observers answer yes. Richard Darman, [former] director of the OMB, has quipped that "Americans did not fight and win the wars of the 20th century to make the world safe for green vegetables."

The conflict between environmental protection and economic competitiveness is a false dichotomy. It stems from a narrow view of the sources of prosperity and a static view of competition.

Strict environmental regulations do not inevitably hinder competitive advantage against foreign rivals: indeed, they often enhance it. Tough standards trigger innovation and upgrading. In my book *The Competitive Advantage of Nations*, I found that the nations with the most rigorous requirements often lead in exports of affected products.

Although the U.S. once clearly led in setting standards, that position has been slipping away. Until the passage of the Clean Air Act in 1990, itself the result of 12 years of foot-dragging, Congress had passed little environmental legislation since the mid-1970s. Today the U.S. remains the only industrialized country without a policy on carbon dioxide, and our leadership in setting environmental standards has been lost in many areas. Even Japan, a nation many think of as relatively unconcerned about the environment, has moved ahead of the U.S. in important fields. Japan's $NO_x$ emission standards for vehicles are significantly more stringent than those in the U.S. and Europe: its stationary $SO_x$ and $NO_x$ standards are set in terms of rigorous daily (versus yearly) average hourly emissions.

As other nations have pushed ahead, U.S. trade has suffered. Germany has had perhaps the world's tightest regulations in stationary air-pollution control, and German companies appear to hold a wide lead in patenting—and exporting—air-pollution and other environmental technologies. As much as 70% of the air pollution-control equipment is produced by foreign companies. Britain is another case in point. As its environmental standards have lagged, Britain's ratio of exports to imports in environmental technology has fallen from 8:1 to 1:1 over the past decade.

In contrast, the U.S. leads in those areas in which its regulations have been the strictest, such as pesticides and the remediation of environmental damage. Such leads should be treasured and extended. Environmental protection is a universal need, an area of growing expenditure in all the major national economies ($50 billion a year in Europe alone) and a major export industry. Without competitive technology, America will not only forsake a growth industry, but more and more of our own environmental spending will go to imports.

Even in the broader economy, strict environmental codes may actually foster competitiveness. Exacting standards seem at first blush to raise costs and make firms less competitive, particularly if competitors are from nations with fewer regulations. This may be true if everything stays the same except that expensive pollution-control equipment is added.

But everything will not stay the same. Properly constructed regulatory standards, which aim at outcomes and not methods, will encourage companies to re-engineer their technology. The result in many cases is a process that not only pollutes less but lowers costs or improves quality. Processes will be modified to decrease use of scarce or toxic resources and to recycle wasted by-products. The 3M Company, for example, estimates that its "Pollution Prevention Pays" program has saved $482 million since 1975, while eliminating more than 500,000 tons of waste and pollutants, and has saved another $650 million by conserving energy.

Strict product regulations can also prod companies into innovating to produce less polluting or more resource-efficient products that will be highly valued internationally. As a result of the U.S. proposed phaseout of chlorofluorocarbons (CFCs), for example, Du Pont and other American firms are pioneers in finding substitutes.

This is not to say that all companies will be happy about tough regulations: increased short-term costs and the need to redesign products and processes are unsettling at the least. The aversion to tough standards will be particularly strong in industries that feel threatened by international competition, as is too often the case in America today. The auto industry, for example, has been fighting mandates to improve fuel efficiency, even though meeting them could stimulate innovations that made products more competitive.

The strongest proof that environmental protection does not hamper competitiveness is the economic performance of nations with the strictest laws. Both Germany and Japan have tough regulations, and both countries continue to surpass the U.S. in GNP growth rates and rates of productivity growth. Japan has become a world leader in developing pollution-control equipment and cleaner, more efficient processes. It is noteworthy that in America many of the sectors subject to the greatest environmental costs have improved their international trade performance, among them chemicals, plastics, synthetics, fabrics and paints.

Turning environmental concern into competitive advantage demands that we establish the right kind of regulations. They must stress pollution prevention rather than merely abatement or cleanup. They must not constrain the technology used to achieve them, or else innovation will be stifled. And standards must be sensitive to the costs involved and use market incentives to contain them.

Because U.S. environmental regulations have traditionally violated these principles, the substantial amount we spend on protecting the environment has not yielded the benefits it could have. In the 1970s, for example, ambient air-quality standards encouraged tall smokestacks, some as high as 800 feet, which exported pollution somewhere else instead of reducing it. Even today most standards are met with end-of-pipe technology, where equipment is simply added to the end of a process.

211

The resurgence of concern for the environment, then, should be viewed not with alarm but as an important step in regaining America's preeminence in environmental technology. EPA must see its mandate as stimulating investment and innovation, not just setting limits.

In companies, the "Chicken Little" mind-set that regulation inevitably leads to costs and an adversarial posture toward regulators must be discarded. Environmental protection can benefit America's competitiveness if we simply approach it properly.

## Conclusion

Given the huge difficulties encountered in monetizing the benefits of health, safety, and environmental regulations, it should be much easier to estimate the costs of complying with those regulations. Moreover, since those costs are generally fairly short term in nature, the calculations ought to be more accurate.

In fact, economists attempting to estimate the costs of regulation encounter many uncertainties. They stem primarily from the fact that companies do not generally compile data on the direct regulatory costs of compliance with specific regulations. The numbers that they do provide tend to be self-servingly inflated. Uncertainties also arise in attempting to determine the "baseline" situation that would have existed if no regulations had been promulgated. In the absence of federal regulation, companies are still incurring costs to protect health, safety, and the environment (chiefly as a result of tort actions and public relations concerns). This fact is not always recognized, and when it is, it remains difficult to determine the actual magnitude of expenditures.

The few retrospective cost assessments that have been undertaken have generally concluded that the ex ante agency estimates of regulatory costs overestimate costs, often by very large margins. This is not a surprise. Most cost information comes from the regulated industry, a not unbiased source, and much of that is subject to trade secrecy claims. Agency surveys of industry seldom elicit sufficient data to support accurate costs extrapolations. Fearing the rebuke of the courts and the OMB, agencies tend to rely upon "conservative" cost assumptions and fail to consider how innovative companies may end up complying with performance standards at low cost in response to federal requirements. Finally, cost estimates are exaggerated because agencies rarely implement regulations with the stringency that is originally proposed or even mandated; deadlines get extended, variances get granted, and enforcement discretion tacitly allows violations.

Few agencies, let alone industry, consider the possibility that regulations in some contexts may actually enhance economic performance. Instead of implementing patch-and-repair solutions, companies that embrace broad-scale innovation in processes and product substitution may become dramatically more efficient. The case of asbestos is a good example. In international markets, countries that adopted the most stringent regulations to control asbestos exposure generally outperform countries with lax regulations. At the least, this suggests that strong health, safety, and environmental regulation is not an impediment to economic growth. Businesses that substituted a less dangerous insulated product years ago would probably be in a far more competitive position today.

Government agencies and business-supported think tanks are fond of generating studies on the cost of regulatory compliance. Unfortunately, they are rarely grounded in solid empirical data. Retrospective assessments of the actual costs of individual regulations frequently show the estimates to be wildly inflated. They should be taken with a large grain of salt.

## Suggestions for Further Reading

*Uncertainties in Measuring Costs*

Surprisingly, there are very few retrospective studies of the costs imposed by federal agencies on the private sector. Those studies that do exist tend to draw heavily upon prospective predictions of what regulations are likely to cost, rather than on retrospective evaluations of what the regulations did in fact cost. A good example is the following EPA report:

> U.S. EPA, ENVIRONMENTAL INVESTMENTS: THE COST OF A CLEAN ENVIRONMENT (1990).
> *Estimates the costs of environmental programs administered by EPA.*

In 1999, the GAO conducted a follow-up study to its 1995 report, focusing exclusively upon EPA's cost assessments. Its conclusions were much the same.

> U.S. GAO, ENVIRONMENTAL PROTECTION: ASSESSING THE IMPACTS OF EPA'S REGULATIONS THROUGH RETROSPECTIVE STUDIES (1999).
> *Notes that the only source of national industry-level pollution abatement cost data for EPA regulatory impact analyses has been sporadic surveys of companies conducted by the Bureau of Economic Affairs of the U.S. Department of Commerce.*

*Are Costs Systematically Overestimated?*

As Professors McGarity and Ruttenberg suggest, numerous studies have documented instances in which contemporaneous cost estimates made by agencies were considerably higher than the actual costs incurred by the regulated industries. See, for example:

> JOSEPH L. BADARACCO JR., LOADING THE DICE: A FIVE-COUNTRY STUDY OF VINYL CHLORIDE REGULATION 52 (1985).
> *Examines overestimates in the cost of complying with OSHA's vinyl chloride standard.*

> WINSTON HARRINGTON ET AL., ON THE ACCURACY OF REGULATORY COST ESTIMATES ii (Resources for the Future, Discussion Paper No. 99-18, 1999).

Concludes that "ex ante estimates of total (direct) costs have tended to exceed actuals."

U.S. EPA, THE BENEFITS AND COSTS OF THE CLEAN AIR ACT, 1970-1990, at A-5 (1997).

Observes that "when firms shut down their plants to install environmental capital, they take account of the adjustment costs and often concurrently replace other older capital equipment."

James C. Robinson, The Impact of Environmental and Occupational Regulation on Productivity of U.S. Manufacturing, 12 YALE J. ON REG. 405 (1995).

Companies that are forced to meet health, safety, or environmental regulatory requirements may elect to purchase new equipment that reduces risks but also increases output efficiency. It would therefore be inappropriate to assign the full capital costs of the equipment to the regulatory requirement.

Can Regulation Enhance Economic Performance?

Few empirical studies exist of the extent to which environmental regulations inspire innovations that improve economic efficiency and/or international competitiveness. The following sources offer additional analyses.

OMB, REPORT TO CONGRESS ON THE COSTS AND BENEFITS OF REGULATIONS 13 (2000).

Reports that "[t]echnological improvements are often cited as the reason that predicted costs of compliance often turn out to be less than actual costs."

Michael E. Porter & Class van der Linde, Toward a New Conception of the Environment-Competitiveness Relationship, 9 J. ECON. PERSP. 97 (1995).

U.S. CONGRESS, OTA, GAUGING CONTROL TECHNOLOGY AND REGULATORY IMPACTS IN OCCUPATIONAL SAFETY AND HEALTH 98 (1995).

Concludes that OSHA's standard for powered platforms for building maintenance resulted in overall cost savings of about $1.7 million a year.

214

## Chapter 7 Endnotes

1. NATIONAL ECONOMIC RESEARCH ASSOCIATES, INC., COST-EFFECTIVENESS AND COST-BENEFIT ANALYSIS OF AIR QUALITY REGULATION 1-15 (1980).

2. THOMAS D. HOPKINS, REGULATORY COSTS IN PROFILE 1, 11 (Center for the Study of American Business Policy Study No. 132, 1996).

3. JOSEPH M. JOHNSON, A REVIEW AND SYNTHESIS OF THE COST OF WORKPLACE REGULATIONS 20, tbl. 10 (Mercatus Center Working Paper, 2001).

4. The GAO is an investigatory arm of Congress. The report, REGULATORY BURDEN: MEASUREMENT CHALLENGES AND CONCERNS RAISED BY SELECTED COMPANIES, was prepared for Congress by the GAO in November 1996.

5. GAO/GGD-94-28.

6. THOMAS D. HOPKINS, COST OF REGULATION (Regulatory Information Serv. Ctr., 1991); FEDERAL REGULATORY BURDENS (RIT Public Policy Working Paper, Rochester, N.Y.: Rochester Institute of Technology, 1993); REGULATORY COSTS IN PROFILE (Policy Study No. 132, St. Louis: Center for the Study of American Business, 1996).

7. GAO/PEMD-95-18BR.

8. GAO/PEMD-94-3. In his 1996 study, Hopkins said that "[t]he regulatory cost estimates that appear in this paper lay no claim to precision; both conceptual and empirical challenges make precision unattainable.

9. To obtain these data, the company surveyed its salaried employees and asked them to: (1) develop a list of the federal regulations that they encountered in doing their jobs; and (2) estimate the amount of time they or their subordinates spent each month complying with those regulations. Using the results of this survey and its knowledge of the employees' salaries, the company estimated its direct incremental labor costs for salaried employees to be $145,000 in 1994—about 5% of its total payroll of $2.5 million.

   Thirteen company officials provided cost data for certain problematic regulations, but did not provide any other data on the company's comprehensive, incremental costs. For example, the officials said that the company spent $200,000 for capital improvements to its wastewater treatment facility and spent $1,000 per month for water testing to comply with specific EPA water quality requirements.

10. The OTA was established by Congress to provide advices to Congress and its committees on matters involving technology and society. It was one of two agencies abolished during the 104th Congress that assembled after the 1994 elections. Published in 1995, this report, GAUGING CONTROL TECHNOLOGY AND REGULATORY IMPACTS IN OCCUPATIONAL SAFETY AND HEALTH, AN APPRAISAL OF OSHA'S ANALYTIC APPROACH, was one of the office's last.

11. Professor McGarity teaches environmental law and torts at the University of Texas School of Law. Professor Ruttenberg is a Senior Staff Associate, George Meany Center for Labor Studies, National Labor College. This article, Counting the Cost of Health, Safety, and Environmental Regulation, was supported by the Deer Creek Foundation and published at 80 TEX. L. REV. 1997, 1998-2000 (2002).

12. Eban Goodstein & Hart Hodges, Polluted Data: Overestimating Environmental Costs, AM. PROSPECT, Nov./Dec. 1997, at 64.

13. Id.

14. Ruth Ruttenberg, The Incorporation of Prospective Technological Changes Into Regulatory Analysis Which Is Used in the Planning of Occupational Safety and Health Reg-

ulations 32-33 (1981) (unpublished Ph. D. dissertation, University of Pennsylvania) (on file with authors).

15. WINSTON HARRINGTON ET AL., ON THE ACCURACY OF REGULATORY COST ESTIMATES 23 (Resources for the Future, Discussion Paper No. 99-18, 1999), *available at* http://www. rff. org/disc<uscore>papers/PDF<uscore>files/9918. pdf.

16. Timothy F. Bresnahan & Dennis A. Yao, *The Nonpecuniary Costs of Automobile Emissions Standards*, 16 RAND J. ECON. 437, 437 (1985).

17. U.S. GAO, ENVIRONMENTAL PROTECTION: ASSESSING THE IMPACTS OF EPA'S REGULATIONS THROUGH RETROSPECTIVE STUDIES 5 (1999).

18. Thomas D. Hopkins, *Costs of Federal Regulation*, J. REG. & SOC. COSTS, Mar. 1992, at 9, 19.

19. OMB, 1998 REPORT OF OMB TO CONGRESS ON THE COSTS AND BENEFITS OF FEDERAL REGULATIONS 2 (1998).

20. HARRINGTON ET AL., *supra* note 15, at 2.

21. *Id.* at 21.

22. U.S. CONGRESS, OTA, AN APPRAISAL OF OSHA'S ANALYTICAL APPROACH, GAUGING CONTROL TECHNOLOGY AND REGULATORY IMPACTS IN OCCUPATIONAL SAFETY AND HEALTH 64 (1995).

23. OMB, ECONOMIC ANALYSIS OF FEDERAL REGULATIONS UNDER EXECUTIVE ORDER 12866 (1996), *available at* http://www. whitehouse.gov/omb/inforeg/riaguide.html [hereinafter 1996 OMB Guidelines].

24. U.S. EPA, THE BENEFITS AND COSTS OF THE CLEAN AIR ACT, 1970-1990, at A-5 & n. 5 (1997) (citing Peter J. Wilcoxen, The Effects of Environmental Regulation and Energy Prices on U.S. Economic Performance (1988) (unpublished Ph.D. thesis, Harvard University)).

25. James C. Robinson, *The Impact of Environmental and Occupational Regulation on Productivity of U.S. Manufacturing*, 12 YALE J. ON REG. 387, 405 (1995).

26. Michael Porter & Claas van der Linde, *Toward a New Conception of the Environment-Competitiveness Relationship*, 9 J. ECON. PERSP. 107 (1995) (citing several examples of compliance with regulatory requirements through process changes).

27. Professor Ashford teaches courses in law and technology at the Massachusetts Institute of Technology. The material upon which this reading is based, *Understanding Technological Responses of Industrial Firms to Environmental Problems: Implications for Government Policy*, was published in ENVIRONMENTAL STRATEGIES FOR INDUSTRY (K. Fisher and J. Schot eds., 1993).

28. Professor Porter is a leading expert on competitiveness and economic development at the Harvard Business School. This excerpt, *America's Green Strategy*, is drawn from an article published in the April 1991, issue of SCIENTIFIC AMERICAN.

# Chapter 8: Better Ways to Regulate

If one thing has become apparent in our review of the sophisticated sabotage of regulation, it is that the self-styled "reformers" do not truly believe in regulation. In practice if not in theory, tools such as quantitative risk assessment, comparative risk assessment, and cost-benefit analysis serve chiefly to obstruct responsible regulation. *Reform* is a misnomer. The sophisticated saboteurs have succeeded in "reforming" the regulatory process into a voracious consumer of expensive information and analysis that is almost incapable of providing health, safety, and environmental protections beyond what the regulated industries are grudgingly willing to provide.

At the same time, progressive defenders of regulation have been slow to provide forceful defenses of regulatory approaches that have worked exceedingly well in the past. This is an extremely difficult and perhaps insuperable task, given the complicated welter of political, scientific, technological, legal, cultural forces that converge on the regulatory process. The groups that seek to advance the public interest through health, safety, and environmental regulation are usually too busy warding off deregulation to focus on what an effective regulatory regime should look like. Still, it is clear that a road to "reform" paved with cost-benefit analyses and other reductive, quantitative tools is a highway to nowhere. It will not help our nation meet the statutory targets declared by the U.S. Congress years ago, nor will it help us craft effective new protective strategies for the future.

Although the sophisticated saboteurs largely control the regulatory apparatus at present, the undeniable indicia of environmental degradation, workplace deaths and injuries, and highway carnage continue to mount. This is the most searing indictment of the so-called regulatory reforms. *They do not work.* The regulatory process is collapsing under the weight of diversionary data-gathering and regulatory procedures. Of course, this is precisely the outcome sought by regulated industries.

As the preventable human suffering and environmental degradation get worse, the time will come when the public will demand accountability from the corporations responsible. It may take a domestic tragedy like a Bhopal or a Chernobyl to turn the tide, or an outbreak of mad cow disease may alter the political climate for safety regulation.

In any case, it is time to begin framing a new agenda for health, safety, and environmental regulation. If the preceding chapters document the intellectual poverty of the sophisticated saboteurs, this chapter begins the process of building a new intellectual foundation for regulation. A forthcoming book, entitled *The New Progressive Agenda*, from the Center for Progressive Regulation will expand upon and add to the suggestions that follow.

The first step in this exercise is to rediscover the vital principles that motivated the environmental, safety, and consumer movements in the first place and which continue to command public support. We therefore enumerate the broad, fundamental principles that should animate the implementation of existing legislation and the search for new statutory solutions. Many of the regulatory principles and operational models are already well-developed in the existing literature.[1] The "precautionary principle" and the "polluter-pays principle," for example, are two well-known and compelling approaches. Other innovative ideas are ripening on the vine while still others are rapidly germinating.

Drawing from a rich body of scholarship, this chapter showcases some of the most promising alternative decisionmaking frameworks for regulation. Unlike the cost-benefit decisionmaking model, which begin with the assumption that government's only legitimate function is to fix broken markets, these alternative models seek to make serious progress in protecting health, safety, and environment while taking account of other societal concerns, including economic costs.

## Safety First

Societal decisions concerning the appropriate level of health, safety, and environmental protections must necessarily reflect a number of sometimes-conflicting considerations. Indeed, as we have seen, one of the reasons that quantitative cost-benefit analysis cannot serve as the exclusive decisionmaking determinant is its inability to capture many considerations that are critical to wise decisions. Not all considerations deserve equal weight; some are more important than others.

A "precautionary" view of regulation holds that government has a paramount obligation to prevent harm to human health and the environment, and not simply to deal with harm after it has occurred. Although scholars and policymakers understand the "precautionary principle" in different ways, it is perhaps best understood as an attempt to apply the age-old injunctions: "Look before you leap" and "it is better to be safe than sorry." Prof. John S. Applegate traces how this common-sense proposition has in recent years found its way into many important international treaties and into the domestic practice of many countries.

This section explains why it is rational and desirable to "err on the side of safety" in governmental decisionmaking about health, safety, and the environment. Professor Applegate describes the four primary elements of the precautionary approach—trigger, timing, response, and iteration—and defends that approach as applied in Europe, against claims made by some cost-benefit proponents, that it represents a Luddite rejection of modern technology.[2]

---

The precautionary principle has its origins in a German environmental concept, Vorsorgeprinzip or "foresightedness principle," which can be freely translated as the obligation to "foresee and forestall" environmental harms.[3] Foresight in this context implies looking over the horizon for unexpected dangers ***. While there is no single statement of the precautionary principle, and the various formulations differ in several respects, it has been adopted by industrialized countries, *** by developing countries *** and globally in the Convention on Biological Diversity, the United Nations Framework Convention on Climate Change, and of course the Rio Declaration. Most recently, the precautionary principle was adopted by the Stockholm Convention on Persistent Organic Pollutants, which was signed by the US, EU, and a host of industrialized and developing states.

While the precautionary principle has become something of a fixture in international environmental treaties, the main response in American academia has been dismissive. Unfortunately, much of this criticism is based on a caricature which depicts a draconian, unreasoning, inflexible command that rejects all technologies that have emerged since the Industrial Revolution. * * * Some zealous advocates of the precautionary principle have taken positions something like this, but the reality of the text, scholarship, and real-world implementation is a flexible, pragmatic, and cautious approach to the uncertainty that characterizes new technologies like genetic modification. In short, it is the foresight principle, not the Luddite Principle. It seeks to anticipate the risks of new and existing technologies so as to avoid or minimize them. As implemented, it is neither rigid, nor the enemy of serious scientific inquiry.

The precautionary principle can be broken down into four distinct elements that cut across all of its versions: trigger, timing, response, and iteration. Together, they provide a framework for identifying, evaluating, learning more about, and avoiding or minimizing the risks of technology and for providing the time ("breathing space," as Levidow and Carr put it) [4] for doing so.

The trigger incorporates two prerequisites: an anticipated serious or irreversible harm, and a minimum amount of scientific information on the basis of which harm is foreseen. * * * The precautionary principle is frequently criticized in the United States for allowing any imagined harm * * * to trigger regulatory action. * * * [M]ost commentators are in agreement that anticipated harms must have some scientific basis. * * *

The core purpose of the precautionary principle is the management of uncertainty, and so timing—the relationship between taking regulatory action and the degree of scientific knowledge concerning the risks of concern—is its distinctive feature. The precautionary principle goes beyond preventive regulation, which addresses known risks with a goal of avoiding familiar harms. The timing element permits regulatory action before the causal relationship between the activity and the potential harm has been fully proven; that is, it holds the activity of concern in abeyance in the period between the scientifically credible identification of risks and their characterization sufficient to make a comprehensive regulatory determination. The term that best describes this timing is anticipatory, the "forestall" part of the "foresee and forestall" interpretation of the Vorsorgeprinzip.

The existence of uncertainty is also, in some views, a prerequisite to the application of the precautionary principle. If examination of the existing science reveals a well characterized risk, the precautionary principle is no longer "relevant," * * * and a final, reasoned regulatory decision should be reached on traditional grounds. This is not total uncertainty, of course, in the sense of pure speculation or the fevered imaginations of Greenpeace activists. Consistent with the informational prerequisite in the trigger, uncertainty means the lack of a definitive cause-and-effect relationship or a quantifiable dose-response relationship. * * * This is hardly a radical position. Indeed, it has been criticized as merely restating the obvious point that true certainty never exists. In fact, however, the precautionary principle would shift the practice, established in the United States in the *Benzene* decision, of demanding a high degree of proof of the existence and magnitude of a risk in advance of regulatory action.

The most misrepresented aspect of the precautionary principle is the nature of the regulatory response it mandates. [I]ts critics are fond of charging or assuming that there is but one response: to ban or forgo an activity or technology altogether. This is transparently untrue. None of the texts of the principle says this. Some speak of avoiding or minimizing the anticipated harms, and of course precautionary timing may result in delays in adopting technology, but both are a far cry from entirely abjuring a new, potentially beneficial technology. Moreover, while "minimizing" harm may not satisfy the preference of some critics for an economically optimal level of harm, it is not the same as an expectation of zero risk. The commentary makes it clear that an absolutist view of the precautionary principle is untenable, and instead that it embraces a range of regulatory responses. Bans may be appropriate in some cases, but in others it may mean (in the case of [Genetically Modified Organisms]) process controls, isolation of field tests, limited periods of approval, pre-release testing, investigation of alternatives, or further research. The precautionary principle, in other words, can be a roadblock or simply a speed bump.

The common feature of all of these variations is that the precautionary principle anticipates revisiting the judgments that are based on it. Uncertainty may be unavoidable, but it is not desirable, and efforts to reduce uncertainty are worthwhile (up to a point). Science policymakers are increasingly recognizing that toxic substances cannot be evaluated or regulated once and for all. Two recent American studies of risk assessment and management have recommended an iterative or cycling process of investigation, regulation, and learning, that is the kind of feed-back loop that is standard in science.

----

In the next excerpt, Prof. Mark Geistfeld, a proponent of cost-benefit analysis in many contexts, explains why it is altogether appropriate for society to insist that those who expose others to risks to advance their own economic interests should have the burden of demonstrating why those risks are acceptable. Recall Professor Applegate's observation that the U.S. Supreme Court's notorious *Benzene* decision helped reverse that burden, forcing agencies to demonstrate why restraints on those risk-producing activities are justified. [5] By contrast, a precautionary approach justifies governmental constraints on risk-producing conduct and rejects the "willingness-to-pay" test. [6]

----

[N]o one really wants to spend everything on safety. But the widespread resistance to tradeoffs between safety and money is plausibly linked to the principle that "safety matters more than money," what I refer to as the safety principle. The principle has been embraced by many moral philosophers and is reflected in important legal practices.

Laws regulating health and safety often have distributive impacts that implicate difficult normative issues. These laws protect the interest that potential victims have in their physical security, while burdening the economic and liberty interests of those engaged in the risky activity. * * * According to some moral theories, the interest potential victims have in their physical security is more important than the burdens imposed on risk-creating actors who must expend money on safety precautions or pay damages or fines. The underlying rationale is that physical injury is more disruptive for potential victims than is the expenditure of money for potential injurers, justifying a legal rule that gives safety interests greater weight than economic interests.

The safety principle influences the procedures regulators use to evaluate risk. When a risk is unknown, most agencies rely on risk estimates likely to exceed the actual risk. The Environmental Protection Agency, for example, overestimates the risk that a substance might be carcinogenic by at least a factor of seven, and quite likely more. Procedures designed to overestimate risk are justified on the ground that safety concerns (the possibility that the substance might be hazardous) are more important than economic considerations (the possibility that the substance will be subject to costly regulation even though it is not hazardous).

This precautionary approach to risk regulation is embodied in the "precautionary principle" in the field of international environmental law. According to the precautionary principle, any uncertainty regarding the hazardous properties of a substance or activity ought to be resolved in a manner that favors regulation (and the associated possibility of risk reduction), with cost considerations of secondary importance.

Regulators expend great effort on determining the hazardous properties of substances. They look for plausible biological or chemical interactions that might produce injury, and study how the substance affects human cells and the health of laboratory animals. This risk assessment, though helpful, does not eliminate scientific uncertainty. The fact that mice have a higher incidence of cancer after being exposed to high doses of the substance does not mean that humans exposed to low doses will develop cancer. Often we will not know whether a substance is hazardous, or the level of risk it poses, until it is introduced into the environment.

The need to make regulatory decisions in the face of scientific uncertainty is endemic. To deal with this pervasive problem, regulators in a wide variety of circumstances have adhered to the precautionary principle, the notion of "better safe than sorry." The precautionary principle, like the safety principle, emphasizes safety concerns (the possibility that the substance might be hazardous) over economic considerations (the possibility that the substance will be subject to costly regulation even though it is not hazardous). By relying on the precautionary principle, regulators can control stringently or ban a substance on the ground that it is potentially hazardous, even if the underlying scientific data are inconclusive. * * * The reach of the precautionary principle is enormous given the widespread scientific uncertainty about how substances interact with humans and the environment. * * *

To be sure, this regulatory approach can be criticized on the ground that the potential victim's preferred assessment of the risk—the worst case scenario * * *—will often mischaracterize the risk. At times, the best case scenario will characterize the risk correctly. Most of the time, the scenario supported by the weight of scientific evidence presumably will be correct. But no approach will provide the correct characterization always. Estimates of uncertain outcomes will not be correct each and every time. Mistakes will be made. Mistakes create error costs, which will be borne by potential injurers, potential victims, or both parties. The distribution of these error costs is a normative matter. The regulatory approach based on the precautionary principle places the error costs on potential injurers, a resolution of the distributive problem that is defensible.

Consider a regulation based on the potential victim's reasonable assessment that [an injurer's] activity poses a substantial risk. Suppose the risk in fact is moderate. Regulations based on the assumption of substantial risk will produce error costs—potential injurers will be forced to take more costly precautions than would be required in a world of complete scientific knowledge—but what is unfair about this outcome? Potential victims face a lower level of nonconsensual risk than they otherwise would face in a world of no scientific uncertainty, as regulations for substantial risks impose more demanding safety requirements than do regulations for moderate risks. Any amount of nonconsensual risk, however, makes potential victims worse off than in a world without the risk. In what way, then, does this regulatory approach unfairly advantage potential victims? The approach is "advantageous" to potential victims only insofar as it makes potential injurers bear the error costs. However, potential injurers directly benefit from the potentially hazardous activity and do not face the prospect of physical injury. Moreover, potential injurers can avoid the more burdensome regulatory requirements by financing the research needed to reduce the uncertainty.

Cases of scientific uncertainty therefore pose a particular type of distributive problem. In such cases, regulatory errors are inevitable, and someone must bear the associated costs. A regulatory approach based on the precautionary principle places the burden of factual uncertainty on those who directly benefit from an activity that is the source of the uncertainty and concern. * * *

---

## Address the Source, Not the Victim

Regulatory approaches that focus initially on the source and seek maximum pollution reductions are likely to be more effective and fair than "victim-oriented" strategies. This truth has been obscured by proponents of cost-benefit analysis, who frequently advocate strategies that require changes in individual behavior rather than systemic changes in technology or industrial practices.

The argument goes like this: Since the technology-based strategies used in the past have plucked all of the "low-hanging fruit"—the cheaper, easier solutions—regulators must now turn their attention from sources of harm to the "recipients." In this view, the most cost-beneficial strategies for abating remaining pollution are to move people away from polluting industries, require workers to wear respirators, and screen "susceptible" individuals out of chemical-laden environments.

This section will examine why the legal system considers the pollution source as the first problem to address. Contrary to the claims of cost-benefit proponents, there is still a great deal of "low-hanging fruit" for source-oriented strategies to address. For example, sources that continue to receive "grandfather" exemptions from existing requirements should be phased out, and new programs should be implemented to reduce pollution from "non-point" sources such as agriculture and construction sites. Regulation should require or encourage sources to reduce absolute levels of pollution rather than focusing on the rate of pollution. [7]

Profs. Frank Ackerman and Lisa Heinzerling note that a source-oriented approach that focuses on available technology has worked very well in the past. This cannot be said about cost-benefit-based regulatory strategies. [8]

---

For the most part, environmental programs rely on a form of "technology-based" regulation, the essence of which is to require the best available methods for controlling pollution. This avoids the massive research effort needed to quantify and monetize the precise harms caused by specific amounts of pollution, which is required by cost-benefit analysis. In contrast, the technology-based approach allows regulators to proceed directly to controlling emissions. Simply put, the idea is that we should do the best we can to mitigate pollution we believe to be harmful.

Over the years, EPA has learned that flexibility is a good idea when it comes to technology-based regulation and thus has tended to avoid specifying particular technologies or processes for use by regulated firms; instead, the agency increasingly has relied on "performance-based" regulation, which tells firms to clean up to a certain, specified extent, but does not tell them precisely how to do it. Technology-based regulation generally takes costs into account in determining the required level of pollution control but does not demand the kind of precisely quantified and monetized balancing process that is needed for cost-benefit analysis.

---

When asked to identify the most important innovation in environmental law during the past 30 years, Prof. Wendy Wagner concluded that the clear winner was source-oriented, technology-based standard-setting. If one were to believe the economics literature, this approach to protecting health, safety, and the environment is an abysmal failure. In the real world, however, it has been a spectacular success. While the technology-based approach is sometimes discounted as tried-and-true, Professor Wagner believes that it remains an innovative alternative to cost-benefit balancing approaches that have been in place for just as long but have not been as successful. [9]

---

In my review of the last three decades of mind-numbing legal activity, the innovation I find to be the most important, and one that likely will continue to guide us well into the future, is one of the earliest innovations—technology-based standards. Technology-based standards are not a particularly admired approach to pollution control. [10] With the exception of a few environmental law scholars, [11] nobody has exactly thrown bouquets to these old-fashioned standards. Ironically, in fact, as technology-based standards have gradually been incorporated into an increasing number of environmental statutes, their popularity among academics seems to have diminished proportionately.

Nonetheless, when one considers the important role technology-based standards have played in reducing pollution levels over the past thirty years, it becomes immediately apparent that their weed-like invasion into almost every facet of environmental law is no accident. Due to the considerable scientific uncertainty that surrounds policy discussions of man's impact on nature and public health, the standards' finger-in-the-dike approach continues to provide one of the most reliable methods for controlling pollution. * * *

Technology-based standards (sometimes referred to as "design standards") are predominantly employed to control pollution entering surface waters, outside air, public drinking water supplies, and, to a lesser extent, workplaces and the land. In most instances, Congress requires EPA to survey currently available (or soon-to-be-available) pollution control technologies for classes and categories of industry and to select the technology in each industrial category that best fulfills congressional goals under the circumstances. EPA then converts the pollution reduction capabilities of the selected technology to numerical effluent or emission limits for each pollutant of concern. This step, which requires making assumptions about "average" industry pollution loads and how well the selected technology reduces pollution, can be quite controversial. EPA must become familiar with the capabilities of the nation's industries, the variety of pollution control equipment available, and how this equipment actually works when employed in the field.

### 1. The Moral Imperative

The moral message of technology-based standards is that regulated entities must do their best, or nearly their best, when public health and the environment are at stake. Although this command is a kindred spirit with the precautionary principle, which calls for caution and some form of regulatory intervention in the face of uncertainty, it is more focused. Rather than placing the burden on the proponent of precaution to both identify circumstances under which uncertainty is so great that regulation is justified and detail the form of regulation that is appropriate, technology-based standards skip over this nonsense by assuming that there is pollution, that it is undesirable, and that a strong effort to reduce the pollution is needed. These standards can also be designed to place the burden on the polluter to demonstrate that the technology selected is inappropriate.

### 2. The Results

With regard to the results achieved, technology-based standards excel in four important respects that, when taken together, cause these standards to reign supreme over their base innovation competitors in most, but not all, pollution circumstances. First, they are relatively easy to promulgate and thus accomplish pollution reductions expeditiously. In addition, they tend to be superior with regard to their enforceability and predictability, even-handed in their application to various regulated entities, and adaptable to additional refinements using other, very different types of regulatory tools. * * *

### a. Expeditious

[T]echnology-based standards * * * significantly outpace—generally by a factor ranging from three to ten times—the promulgation rate of most alternatives, such as standards based on environmental needs, health-related needs, or a cost/benefit analysis of what level of protection is appropriate. The reason technology-based standards are promulgated more quickly than other approaches to pollution control is straightforward—the work associated with promulgating such standards is several times simpler than the alternatives. In contrast to the tremendous information demands posed by science-or cost/benefit-based standards, technology-based standards have information demands that are significant but still attainable. * * * Indeed, over half of the major federal statutory provisions that utilize technology-based standards adopted them specifically because alternative approaches resulted in so few standards being promulgated. * * *

### b. Enforceable and Predictable

Technology-based standards are also more enforceable and predictable than most alternative approaches to pollution control. From the standpoint of the regulated entities, technology-based standards provide unparalleled predictability with respect to compliance obligations. * * * This predictability and ease of compliance stands in stark contrast to most and perhaps all other approaches to pollution control. * * * These factors may explain why industry seems to have embraced technology-based standards as the preferred base innovation, even though these standards may require more pollution abatement from some individual sources than is economically justified.

Moreover, it follows that the clearer the permit requirements, the more streamlined the regulatory oversight. Regulators can compare a source's emissions or discharges against a set of national numerical requirements. * * * Criminal sanctions also work smoothly and effectively, with little need for the rule of lenity in determining whether the limitations applied to a particular source are clearly within reach of the statute. Finally, unambiguous pollution limits allow self-monitoring programs to operate more effectively. * * *

### c. Even-handed

Regulatory interventions that change how companies operate have the potential to create inequities in competition or barriers to entry. When implemented properly, however, technology-based standards are quite equitable in how they affect industry. Generally, all members of the same class of an existing industry are treated in the same way, although distinctions can be built into the selection of technology-based standards to ensure that smaller businesses are not put at a competitive disadvantage. * * * Other common regulatory problems, such as agency capture, the benefits of sophisticated counsel, or the unwillingness of competitive industries to sell their rights to pollute, are also avoided when standardized national standards are set in advance. * * *

d. Adaptable

A final virtue of technology-based standards is that they can easily be supplemented or even supplanted as improved approaches to controlling pollution become available. Unlike pollution markets, voluntary compliance obligations, or other types of command-and-control standards, technology-based standards are not incompatible with most secondary innovations and thus serve as quintessentially hospitable and adaptable base innovations. * * * Since technology-based standards are uniformly and expeditiously applied across all industries and geographic locations, they can be used to ensure that at least some environmental protection is in place if pollution markets do not work or are slow to become operational. Likewise, environment-based controls, which are theoretically compelling, work best when complemented by "environment-blind" technology-based standards. Because toxicity data or other critical information needed to set ambient standards or perform cost/benefit analyses is often incomplete, technology-based standards can be used to protect the environment until the needed information has been assembled and the requisite analysis performed.

Conditions continue to be ripe for using technology-based standards, and they are unlikely to change soon. Even if they do, technology-based standards can be fine-tuned with a variety of secondary regulatory strategies such as ambient-based controls, markets, or other incentive-based approaches. Although it may be tempting and is certainly human to ignore these realities in the excitement over new ways of doing things, it is unwise to forget the advances in pollution control that technology-based standards have made possible. They have succeeded where others have failed. Since we have not yet outgrown or exhausted the benefits that can be achieved by using this most simple and trustworthy of our environmental tools, I am hopeful that we will not forget them in our rush to be innovative.

---

**Radical Technology-Forcing**

Some of the most successful governmental interventions in the past have consisted of "radical technology-forcing" through banning and phasing out risky activities. [12] When the U.S. Environmental Protection Agency (EPA) forced a phaseout of tetra-ethyl lead in gasoline, the petroleum industry criticized it. Now, in retrospect, that action is cited by observers across the political spectrum as an environmental success story. Even John Graham, the regulatory czar of the George W. Bush Administration, has concluded that the lead phasedown represented an appropriate exercise of governmental power [13]—this, despite the fact that it caused great disruption in the petroleum marketing industry and put many small companies out of business. [14]

Below, Prof. Thomas McGarity notes that banning environmentally disruptive activities and products is not a universal solution. Radical technology-

226

forcing will probably not work when there are multiple sources of multiple pollutants and no reasonable prospect of available alternatives. Nor will bans work if an agency's authority to ban or phaseout a product or activity is unclear. Nevertheless, there are many situations in which radical technology-forcing is a viable alternative that policymakers should be more willing to consider.

---

In the opening scene of *Putney Swope*, an off-beat, low-budget movie of the late 1960s, the chairman of the board of a large advertising agency, in the midst of delivering some bad financial news to the board of directors, suffered a fatal heart attack and fell face down on the large conference table. With the chairman spread out on the table, the board proceeded immediately to the next order of business—electing a new chairman. The bylaws, however, prevented any board members from voting for themselves. Nearly all of the board members voted for the token African-American director, a musician named Putney Swope, because each concluded that none of the other directors would vote for him. Having been duly elected, Swope moved to the head of the table to address the nervous group of aging white gentlemen. Swope then launched into his speech: "The changes I'm going to make will be minimal. I'm not going to rock the boat. Rocking the boat's a drag. What you do is sink the boat. And there's no sense sinkin' nothin' unless you can salvage with productive alternatives." [15] The scene suddenly shifted to the same boardroom a short time later. Swope was still the chairman, but a garish assembly of social outcasts replaced the old board and proceeded to take the company in a hazily conceived, but radically different direction.

Although the remainder of the movie is entirely forgettable, the opening scene left such a strong impression on me that the title is now a verb in my lexicon. For me, to "Putney Swope" something is to replace it with something radically different, even in the face of substantial doubts that the replacement will work or that such a substitute even exists. An author Putney Swopes an early draft of a manuscript when he or she throws it in the trash, rather than attempting to revise the existing work product. The United States government has Putney Swoped the federally sponsored projects such as the breeder reactor, the Super Sonic Transport, and the superconducting supercollider, and it may one day Putney Swope nuclear warheads. The federal government can also Putney Swope private activities that pose unacceptable health and environmental risks in the hope that private entrepreneurs will produce better alternatives within reasonable time frames. This Essay will briefly examine radical technology-forcing through banning, or phasing out items or activities a la Putney Swope. * * *

EPA adopted a * * * radical approach with respect to the pesticide mirex. After initiating and partially completing a lengthy formal information-gathering hearing regarding mirex, a potent killer of the notoriously aggressive imported fire ant, EPA initiated settlement negotiations. Initially the primary parties involved in these negotiations included the Environmental Defense Fund (EDF), an environmental group that wanted mirex canceled; Allied Chemical Company, the sole registrant of technical grade mirex; the United States Department of Agriculture, which sprayed mirex out of B-26 bombers over hundreds of southern counties as part of the federally sponsored fire ant eradication program; the Southern Plant Board, composed of the agriculture commissioners of the states to which the eradication program's federal dollars were directed; and EPA, which maintained an official position of strict neutrality with respect to the question of whether mirex should be canceled.

Allied Chemical Company decided to cease production of pesticides in the wake of a disaster in Hopewell, Virginia, in which a fly-by-night company operating from an abandoned gas station polluted the James River and the lower half of Chesapeake Bay with a related pesticide, kepone, which Allied provided to the company. Although Allied sold the mirex manufacturing plant to the State of Mississippi for one dollar, some state legislators were uncomfortable about the state's entry in the pesticide manufacturing business. Pressure also grew on the USDA to abandon the costly eradication program. As a result of the considerable leverage that these events provided to the EDF in the settlement negotiations, it refused to settle for anything short of a complete ban of mirex.

The problem with a complete ban was the absence of any registered substitute for killing fire ants except for chlordane, which itself was subject to cancellation proceedings. While USDA and EPA program officials fretted that with no pesticidal weapons on the horizon the fire ants would march unimpeded across the South and Midwest, EDF and EPA attorneys confidently predicted that if fire ants were enough of a problem to inspire a market for fire ant killers, innovative American companies would come up with suitable alternatives. Conversely, so long as the USDA was willing to provide mirex free of charge, it would be overused and a market for substitutes would never develop. Ultimately, the parties agreed to produce and use mirex in diminishing quantities during a two-year phase-out period. As predicted, four companies asked the EPA to register substitutes for mirex well within the phase-out period.

Fifteen years later, fire ants remain a nuisance in all of the states that were part of the fire ant eradication program, but their range has not extended appreciably. When an infestation becomes unmanageable, a landowner can choose from among several formulations of direct-action insecticides or baits, and can even apply a slower acting but more effective biological ant killer. Most importantly, the natural environment of the nine southern states is no longer exposed to an exceedingly persistent, potentially carcinogenic organochlorine pesticide.

The primary advantage of radical technology-forcing is its ease of implementation. The media quality inquiry is simply whether the risks at existing levels of exposure are acceptable. If not, then a ban may be appropriate. The economic and technological feasibility inquiry extends only to whether feasible substitutes are likely to be available at the time that the ban or phase out takes effect. Although an agency adopting that approach will have to evaluate the risks posed by the relevant substance or activity and the availability of substitutes, it will not necessarily have to engage in a finely tuned analysis of what risks are associated with particular ambient concentrations—as it must under the media quality approach. Nor will it be required to estimate pollution reduction loads and allocate them among existing sources. * * *

A second significant advantage of radical technology-forcing is its potential to induce genuine technological innovation. The technology-based approach can bring the laggards up to speed, but it rarely brings about actual technological change. The media quality approach is capable of forcing technology indirectly into areas in which it will be difficult to meet the standards by the relevant deadlines. If sources in such areas are confident that they will not be grandfathered and that the deadlines will not be extended, then they may be induced to invest in innovative controls. The record in that regard, however, is not encouraging. * * *

Radical technology-forcing enables the agency to "take a leap of faith" in cases in which substitutes are not presently available. As in the case of mirex, the agency is able to place its faith in the ingenuity of American industry to develop substitutes for the banned substance or activity by the specified deadlines. If, however, no substitutes appear on the immediate horizon, then the agency will be able to adopt a phase-out approach. A phase-out period significantly reduces the economic impact of banning a substance or activity; it provides time for substitutes to be developed, and it allows companies to shift production away from the banned product. The agency must be aware, however, that scientific and political circumstances may change in a manner requiring an extension of the phase-out period. It is always easier to extend a phase-out period than it is to shorten one. * * *

However, radical technology-forcing is not appropriate in all environmental contexts. It will not work when an environmental problem has complex causes—for example, dissolved oxygen in heavily used rivers—that cannot be addressed by banning a single substance or activity. It is best adapted to situations in which a single substance or activity is causing particular environmental problems.

The approach is also risky when the consequences of the failure to inspire technological innovation are very high. For example, despite efforts by environmentalists in the early 1970s to ban the internal combustion engine, Congress and EPA were unwilling to risk the turmoil that would have resulted if automobile manufacturers had failed to come up with a suitable engine for passenger vehicles. The approach is best suited for the opposite situation in which the consequences of not taking any action are relatively severe.

Finally, * * * an agency should be reluctant to rely upon radical technology-forcing when there is a serious question about whether its statutes authorize it to adopt that approach. Not only are American courts reluctant to Putney Swope activities in common-law nuisance cases, they are also reluctant to allow federal agencies to Putney Swope things without congressional blessing. Courts will probably carefully examine the agency's legal authority to adopt that approach, and will certainly take a "hard look" at the scientific and technical basis for the agency's action.

Although the Putney Swope approach is not a universal solution to the problem of regulating activities that pose a threat to the human environment, it should be a more often used weapon in the regulatory arsenal. The Putney Swope approach is responsible for some of the clearest environmental success stories. The agency that would adopt a radical technology-forcing approach must have courage and imagination. It must have the flexibility to extend the deadlines when the facts prove that it is being overly optimistic, but it must sternly resist attempts by the regulated industry to avoid change through artful brinkmanship. In short, the agency must carefully seek out situations in which a major disruption of an unacceptable status quo will lead to a better future.

---

## Costs Should Be a Consideration, Not an Obsession

Cost-benefit proponents frequently criticize environmentalists for not caring about the economic costs of environmental protections. This is simply untrue. Proponents of strong health, safety, and environmental protections are not cost-oblivious; they are merely concerned that costs not dominate the decision-making outcomes. The cost-benefit paradigm is not the only process for assessing costs in a serious way.

As we saw in Chapter 7, cost-benefit analysis tends to exaggerate costs because the regulated industries normally control the relevant information and can provide self-serving estimates. Likewise, as we saw in Chapter 6, benefits tend to be understated because they are not as easily quantified and monetized as costs.

In the following excerpt, Prof. Alyson C. Flournoy suggests that one way to cure the unidimensional focus of cost-benefit analysis is to use a more realistic form of decisionmaking analysis known as "multiple alternative-multiple attribute analysis." [16] One must understand that what is really going on in risk management decisionmaking is a selection among many options, each of which has advantages and disadvantages ranging along many dimensions.

---

Traditional quantitative cost-benefit analysis has provided and can continue to provide helpful information for assessing the trade offs involved in environmental disputes. But we know that not all benefits can be quantified adequately, and that economic valuation can provide little guidance on the value of resources over a long period of time. So important normative judgments must be made in resolving controversies over resource use that quantitative cost-benefit analysis cannot cover. We must at least question, in light of our richer understanding of the complexities involved, whether existing statutes and the current applications of quantitative techniques—such as cost-benefit analysis—under these laws provide a sufficient framework for addressing the more complex array of facts and values.

When fundamental value choices must be made among preservation of unique ecosystems—for the services they perform as well as their inherent value—and short- and long-term economic impact on individuals and a region with due regard for the role in the conflict played by international trade policies, industry management decisions, and historic government practices in public land management, traditional applications of cost-benefit analysis may be inadequate. To integrate the multiplicity of variables and systematically evaluate the impact of various policy options may demand more sophisticated applications of cost-benefit analysis that can coherently integrate both quantifiable and nonquantifiable values. The analysis must be able to accommodate a certain degree of what we might call vagueness or fuzziness. The best analytic tool may not be one that produces a single, neat answer in quantitative form—which may mask important value choices—but a method that informs decision makers and the public about what policy options are available in light of what science and economics can tell us. Such a method will permit us to make the best-informed choices in light of the complexity we confront, neither reducing it to an artificial simplicity nor allowing it to paralyze us.

A methodology of this type was used in a controversial regulatory decision involving wetlands in the Green Swamp in central Florida. Resource economists, building on the principle of multiple alternative-multiple attribute evaluation, developed information on existing uses of the area and the impact of proposed alterations on these uses. The analysts developed a series of arrays or charts that showed graphically how six alternative uses of the relevant wetlands correlated to a variety of values, some of which were difficult to measure quantitatively. When quantification was not appropriate, the arrays indicated whether the correlation was positive, negative, uncertain, or nonexistent. This provided a systematic framework within which all interested parties were able to assess the impact of the alternatives on various values. The process went beyond commonly employed forms of cost-benefit analysis in accommodating the complexity of the natural systems and human values involved. The analysis avoided the illusory precision of a strained quantification, and presented the qualitative information that was available in a systematic format, providing a clearer view of the policy choices to be made. Multiple alternative-multiple attribute evaluation provided decisionmakers and members of the public an accessible summary of the net impact of various alternative uses of the wetland parcel.

Multiple alternative-multiple attribute analysis is not a radical departure from the methods commonly employed in wetlands decisions. Indeed it is a form of cost-benefit analysis. The question is whether it moves us in the direction of better or more efficient decision making. Several features of the analysis are significant in this regard. First, the analysis encourages and facilitates consideration of more than two options—thus moving beyond the limiting permit-no permit framework and presenting decisionmakers and the public with information on a variety of uses, providing a broader frame of reference. Second, multiple alternative-multiple attribute analysis facilitates systematic comparison of the impact of two or more options on nonquantifiables, such as aesthetic and cultural values—something not as easily accomplished by an unstructured narrative discussion of such values. Third, consideration of the cumulative impact of the options on a variety of nonquantified values is facilitated by the systematic nature of the analysis of these values.

These attributes of multiple alternative-multiple attribute analysis facilitate comparison and more rational selection among options, notwithstanding the complexity and uncertainty associated with the decision. This is not to suggest that multiple alternative-multiple attribute analysis or any other particular technique is a panacea for the problems associated with resource use decisions. Serious challenges face decisionmakers under this methodology as well. The more basic point is not that we should adopt this analytic technique, but that opportunities exist to improve our decision making. Lawmakers and regulators must maintain a broad focus and pay attention to opportunities to cope with uncertainty and complexity.

-----

## The Pragmatic Perspective

The signal deficiency of quantitative regulatory approach is its reliance on static numbers of dubious significance. Profs. Sidney Shapiro and Robert Glicksman argue that an adaptable, pragmatic approach that constantly adjusts regulatory requirements in light of ongoing real-world feedback is a better method to address regulatory imperfections. [17] In the following passage, they recommend that agencies rely on a "back-end" strategy of adjusting a regulation once its actual impacts are known, rather than trying to perfect regulation on the "front-end" by use of cost-benefit analysis and similar techniques.

In a newly published book, *Risk Regulation At Risk: Restoring a Pragmatic Approach*, we argue that "pragmatism" [offers] a set of philosophical principles that rationalize the environmental laws. Our claim is that the application of these principles—which, put briefly, look at the real world effects of policy choices and make adjustments accordingly—is a better way of deciding issues of environmental policy than the cost-benefit and other mechanistic methods employed by the critics, even if Congress did not consciously rely on pragmatism in drafting these laws.

The critics have attempted to perfect regulation on the "front end" by subjecting proposed policies to careful scrutiny using cost-benefit analysis and other similar techniques, but pragmatism rejects the idea that policy can be optimized by the application of such methodologies. Instead, pragmatism seeks to improve policy on the "back end" by engaging in incremental adjustments of policy as new information is obtained about how the policy affects the real world. Although the supporters of environmental policy are suspicious of such back end adjustments because it affects the certitude of implementation and enforcement, we believe such adjustments can mitigate the occasional but unavoidable difficulties of current environmental legislation in an accountable manner and without sacrificing the goals that the legislation is intended to promote.

In pragmatism, an idea is rational and worthy of implementation when it solves better than existing beliefs and understandings. The pragmatist makes this determination on the basis of practical experience. Determining the worth of an idea—its capacity to improve society—may be a complicated task in light of the inescapable role of contingency and chance in the universe. This is one reason that the pragmatist deems it essential to consider a plurality of traditions, perspectives, and academic orientations in devising solutions to society's problems. As a result, pragmatic beliefs are often composed of disparate ideas in the sense that they arise from different sources. Despite this messiness, pragmatic understandings can be more persuasive than an idea derived solely from one set of precepts, such as economics.

A pragmatic perspective agrees that the regulatory process has been overwhelmed with analytical obligations of questionable value. Pragmatism also suggests, however, that there is a better method of addressing regulatory problems, such as an imbalance between regulatory costs and benefits or the creation of regulatory inequities, than trying to avoid them at the front end of the regulatory process before a regulation is adopted. We recommend that EPA and other environmental agencies make greater use of incremental regulation in which regulators adjust general regulatory commitments in light of the specific circumstances of some regulated entities or the availability of new information. In other words, a pragmatic approach would focus on the back end of the process and make regulatory adjustments in light of actual experience.

What all of these mechanisms have in common is that they acknowledge bounded rationality and seek to make regulatory adjustments on the basis of actual experience rather than trying to anticipate regulatory consequences before a regulation is actually enacted. These approaches are pragmatic because they seek to solve problems on the basis of experience. Because they operate on a case-by-case basis, they focus agency activity on problems that actually exist and do not hold up the implementation of a regulation in areas where such problems do not exist. Moreover, because all of the exception and variance mechanisms place the burden of persuasion on the applicant rather than EPA, they tend to be more protective of health and the environment than front end efforts to estimate the consequences of regulation before they occur. Finally, experience with backend adjustments shows their potential as the system of choice for evaluating regulatory effectiveness and making appropriate changes.

---

## Make the Polluter Pay

To most citizens, the costs that polluters impose on society are more visible than the products and services that they sell. Economists regard such costs as "externalities"—costs that companies attempt to avoid by shifting them to their workers, communities, and the environment. The "polluter-pays" principle, which has its origins in international law, attempts to force polluters to bear these costs themselves, or internalize them. In theory, if the polluter is faced with the option of paying to install safety devices or pollution controls now—or paying even larger fines and damages later—it will have an incentive to internalize costs it might otherwise displace onto others.

Prof. David Driesen elaborates on how the "polluter-pays" principle has considerable advantages over "static" cost-benefit-based decisionmaking. He also notes how cost-benefit analysis mischaracterizes anti-pollution programs as "benefits" rather than as "averted harms." Cost-benefit analysis inverts our ethical expectation that people should refrain from harming another by making "averted harm" seem like a discretionary choice, not a moral imperative. The polluter-pays principle, by contrast, characterizes governmental efforts to ameliorate health, safety, and environmental risks as the price the polluter must pay for public toleration of harm-producing conduct.

Health-based and technology-based standards imposed under the polluter-pays principle have many valuable economic effects. They encourage investment in more efficient pollution-reduction technologies. They encourage a shift away from nonrenewable resources to renewable resources. Finally, the monies spent by polluters to comply with regulations do not simply go down a drain or even into the public treasury (to reduce the deficit); they pay for the installation of pollution control technologies, thereby providing additional jobs to workers in the control technology industry. [18]

---

Most public health and environmental statutes have the goal of protecting public health and the environment, rather than balancing that protection against economic interests. This reflects a "polluter pays" principle that assumes that the prices of goods should reflect the "prevention" costs. It treats these costs as part of the cost of doing business, i.e., as production costs.

Generally, the "polluter pays" statutes require EPA to use one of two criteria to determine the stringency of pollution control regulations. Some provisions use "health-based" (or "effects-based") criteria, requiring a level of reduction sufficient to protect public health and/or the environment. Others use "technology-based" criteria, requiring the agency to demand reductions achievable through available technology.

Congress usually requires or allows federal agencies and States to take cost into account in determining polluters' precise pollution control obligations. Generally, the statutes make cost considerations relevant in order to meet equitable goals, such as appropriately distributing pollution control obligations among polluters. The authority to consider costs enables agencies to mandate reductions from polluters that have reasonable control options. At the same time it allows agencies to avoid extraordinarily expensive controls, lower productions, or shut downs. The statutory provisions requiring promulgation of health and technology-based standards do not make the ratio of costs to benefits a relevant factor in agency decisionmaking, even when they authorize an agency to take costs into account. While statutes using technology or health-based standards have not met their overall goal of fully protecting public health and the environment, they have generated significant environmental improvement during a time of growing population, increased mobility and economic growth.

The very language of cost-benefit analysis (CBA) obscures the fact that CBA does not protect the public from environmental harm. The word "benefit" refers to harm averted in the future, not to benefits in the ordinary sense of the word. Specifically, an agency employing cost-benefit analysis assumes that but for the analyzed regulation, facilities would expand or continue polluting at current rates. However, this continuing pollution contributes to environmental degradation and damages people's health. If the regulatory agency demands reductions in pollu-tion levels, then less harm will occur in the future than will occur if the facilities continue polluting as before. Regulators refer to this averted harm as a "benefit."

The very concept of treating actions ameliorating ongoing harms, not as harm amelioration, but as a benefit, something bestowed gratuitously, undermines a fundamental norm of justice: that we must refrain from harming others. Our gov-ernment undermines that norm when it tells people suffering from pollution that al-lowing pollution to continue, but at a reduced rate, constitutes a benefit.

The traditional "polluter pays" paradigm offers an economic advantage over a system based on cost-benefit balancing. This advantage becomes apparent once the economics are considered dynamically. The "polluter pays" principle de-mands that the producer clean-up to at least the minimum level necessary to pro-tect human health and the environment, and then allows consumers to "vote," through purchase decisions, for productivity improvements and greater eco-nomic efficiency if the costs are too high. It assigns the task of fine-tuning the costs of regulation to the free market, rather than to regulators.

Furthermore, the "polluter pays" principle will tend to encourage investment in pollution-reducing technologies and in products that meet our needs with less pollution over time. Since the world's population is growing and industrialization is spreading, world demand for products and services that meet human needs with a minimum of pollution may increase in the future. Hence, increased investment in less polluting (or nonpolluting) approaches may enhance the export potential for American products and services that pollute less or reduce pollution.

CBA assumes that polluters should not have to pay the full costs of preventing harmful pollution if the "prevention" cost exceeds the "effects" cost to today's con-sumer. However, economically, it may be better to have resource users pay more than the "effects" cost to provide incentives to conserve resources, especially when pollution or resource use may cause long-term degradation of the environ-ment. This approach may encourage a shift from using nonrenewable resources to renewable resources, slow down the rate of harvesting a renewable resource to a pace that nature can keep up with, and encourage the use of materials that degrade into harmless compounds rather than accumulate in the tissue of plants and animals.

Regulatory requirements produce economic benefits whenever they force polluters to pay people, either their own employees or contractors, to carry out pollution control. Furthermore, these expenditures often generate blue collar em-ployment, which has been in short supply in recent years. Ironically, Congressio-nal CBA supporters usually cite the need to avoid job destroying excesses in en-vironmental regulations as a justification for the use of CBA. Instead, empirical lit-erature shows that environmental regulations, mostly the product of "polluter pays" statutes, have caused a small net increase, not a decrease, in jobs. [19]

CBA does not separate job-creating from job-destroying regulations because a regulation's capacity to destroy or create jobs has nothing to do with the ratio be-tween costs and benefits. Rather, a regulation is likely to destroy jobs only if the expenditures are so high as compared with the overall capacity of a company to spend money that it forces the company to cut costs by firing workers or closing down. Even then, a rival company may expand production and hire more workers because its competitor has shut down or decreased production. Until expenditures reach a level that produces these effects, higher costs will tend to generate more jobs rather than lower costs by forcing regulated companies to pay people to clean-up. While the ratio of cost to the firm's ability to pay has some effect on employment, the ratio of costs to benefits has nothing to do with employment.

---

## Distribute Health, Safety, and Environmental Risks and Benefits Fairly

The proponents of cost-benefit decisionmaking acknowledge that cost-benefit analysis does not take distributional effects of costs and benefits into account. Health and safety risks, however, are not distributed equally across the population. Workers in hazardous industries, like the construction and petrochemical industries, face much higher risks of disease and injury than persons employed as business executives. There is little empirical evidence for the assumption routinely used in the cost-benefit paradigm that workers in high-risk jobs are actually compensated for the greater risks that they face. Similarly, low-income and minority populations are generally at greater risk of contracting pollution-related diseases than wealthier people who are able to move to cleaner neighborhoods.

Public decisions, however, must make a socially equitable reckoning. If private markets driven by individual cost-benefit analyses cannot yield a fair distribution of health, safety, and environmental risks and benefits, then government must intervene to do so.

Cost-benefit-based decisionmaking is perfectly willing to tolerate social inequities. Its champions even argue that such disparities are healthy signs of efficiency-enhancing competition at work. Most citizens, however, are not convinced that gross disparities in health, safety, and environmental risks are either fair or socially benign. If the best measure of the degree to which a society has become civilized is the way it treats its least powerful and most vulnerable citizens, then other approaches to regulation are in order.

At the most basic level, companies should not be allowed to treat workers and their families as guinea pigs by exposing them to toxic substances and safety risks.[20] They should be required to reduce those risks to the greatest extent technologically possible, and cost considerations should be influential only at the point at which mandatory protections will result in a serious loss of jobs.

Professors McGarity and Shapiro suggest that the aging Occupational Safety and Health Act (OSH Act) has proved ineffective in achieving its announced goal of providing workers safe employment and safe places of employment. Although many "patch and repair" solutions are available, workers are likely to remain at risk until Congress amends the act to eliminate the "significant risk" threshold for health regulation that the Court erected in the famous *Benzene* case.[21] Although the Court declined to read the statute to require the Occupational Safety and Health Administration (OSHA) to balance costs against monetized health benefits, it did implicitly require OSHA to engage in quantitative risk assessment and prove that workplace contamination posed a "significant risk of material impairment" to workers before it could require employers to implement "feasible" safety technologies. [22]

Below, Professors McGarity and Shapiro suggest a "tiered" approach to OSHA health-based standard-setting that borrows from the successful "prevention of significant deterioration" program of the Clean Air Act. Under this approach, industry would be required to achieve more stringent controls depending upon the category of the risk. Since most workplace hazards would initially fall in the residual category in which the "best available technology" would be required, OSHA could rapidly force the laggards to come up to speed by installing state-of-the-art technology without having to make a difficult-to-establish threshold finding of "significant risk." For those workplaces in which that threshold was crossed, the agency would be required to push the industry even farther. If the industry could demonstrate the absence of significant risk with less stringent controls, OSHA would require only that the laggards come up to the industry "consensus" standards. This change should bring about a general improvement in occupational health across many industries with a minimum of economic disruptions. Yet in cases where serious risks remained after the installation of the best available technology, the agency would still have the option of pushing a particular industry to explore the limits of feasibility. [23]

---

Congress should act not only because the potential for internal reform is limited, but also because the current statute is the cause of many of OSHA's problems. Congress has given OSHA less flexibility than most other health and safety agencies, has failed to hold OSHA as accountable as other agencies, and has created unique organizational impediments to effective action by OSHA. Without legislative change, it is highly likely that OSHA will continue to regulate at its current slow pace, imposing extensive requirements on a few industries while leaving most workers without adequate protections.

OSHA's most ambitious effort to increase its regulatory productivity—its generic cancer policy—came to a grinding halt in 1980 when the Supreme Court handed down its remarkable plurality opinion in the *Benzene* case. The immediate effect of the decision was to end OSHA's generic cancer policy. Over the long term, the Court's significant risk test has been a significant impediment to effective implementation of OSHA's statutory mandate. Having imposed the test on an unsuspecting OSHA, the Court failed to give coherent guidance as to the meaning of the term. As a result, OSHA may not act to protect workers until it has accumulated substantial evidence that a chemical is dangerous; moreover, it often hesitates to act out of fear of judicial reversal even when it may have sufficient evidence to do so.

Congress could incorporate its experience in the environmental area into a regulatory mandate for OSHA by adopting a regulatory scheme that requires OSHA to establish a list of chemicals and other substances that "could reasonably be anticipated to cause a material impairment of health or functional capacity." The scheme would presume that any chemical substance on the list was a Class II hazard unless OSHA redesignated it as Class I or III. For all Class II hazards, OSHA would promulgate standards requiring the installation of the "best available technology" (BAT).

OSHA would redesignate a chemical or substance if it would be inappropriate to treat it as a Class II hazard. The proposal would require OSHA to redesignate the hazard to a more stringently regulated category (Class I) if regulation under Class II would leave workers exposed to a "significant risk of material impairment to health or functional capacity." For Class I hazards, OSHA would reduce exposure to the extent "feasible." This would mean applying the stringent technology-based test that OSHA currently uses to require exposure reductions in workplaces posing a significant risk. OSHA would redesignate a hazard to a less stringently regulated category (Class III) if regulation under Class II was unnecessary to avoid a "reasonable anticipation of material impairment of health or functional capacity." For Class III hazards, OSHA would reduce exposure to the extent permitted by any applicable nongovernmental standard, which would connote the consensus test that OSHA used to adopt its original health standards.

Although the proposed classification scheme should increase the protection available to workers, workers may object that the proposal weakens the substantive principle, established by the existing statute, that workers are entitled to be protected to the extent "feasible." This asserted right, however, was substantially diluted by the *Benzene* decision, which held that workers are entitled to maximum protection only if OSHA can first prove that a hazard presents a "significant risk." The reality is that in many cases either OSHA cannot meet that burden of proof or it takes so long to do so that it cannot regulate more than one or two hazards a year. Internal reforms are unlikely to accelerate greatly OSHA's productivity. Any given worker might be protected by standards somewhat less stringent under the proposed regime than under the existing regime, but the new approach should protect many more workers than the current scheme.

Employers are likely to object that the proposed scheme gives OSHA too much discretion to promulgate regulations whose costs exceed their benefits. There are at least three responses to this objection. First, unless OSHA's burden of proof is adjusted, it cannot protect workers in the manner Congress intended. Second, in cases where OSHA has a lower burden of proof, it has regulatory authority only to impose regulatory requirements that are likely to be less costly. Finally, when OSHA proposes an inappropriate regulation, employers can reduce compliance costs by proving that a lower classification is appropriate.

When Congress created OSHA, it adopted the worthy goal of protecting every American worker from dangerous and disabling workplace conditions. This noble aspiration, however, can be attained only if the lessons of the [past] become the impetus for OSHA to reform itself and for Congress to reform OSHA. These reforms will not, of course, instantly transform OSHA from an overworked agency struggling with a nearly impossible task to a paragon of administrative efficiency, but they should send OSHA on its way toward effective implementation of its statutory responsibilities.

---

At another level, low-income communities should not be placed at greater risk from industrial siting decisions; rich and poor alike should benefit equally from government health and environmental protections and amenities. Although this concern for unfair environmental impacts on low-income and minority communities is easy to articulate in theory, it is exceedingly difficult to achieve in the real world. As Prof. Eileen Gauna relates in the following excerpt, if fairness in the allocation of health, safety, and environmental risks is to be attained in the real world, the decisionmaking process itself will have to be modified substantially.

As we saw in Chapter 2, the kind of expertise that typically informs environmental decisionmaking often does not incorporate information and values that are relevant to the concerns of poor and minority groups, especially Native American populations. The poor, minority and Native American groups are not just another set of claimants for a seat at the negotiating table. They represent affected citizens whose perspectives are fundamentally different in nature than the economic claims made by industry and other interest groups.

Professor Gauna suggests that regulatory agencies must abandon the studied "neutrality" that has long characterized their approach to health, safety, and environmental disputes, and instead adopt an explicitly non-neutral posture with respect to the participation of disadvantaged groups. [24] An agency cannot fulfill its regulatory responsibilities if it assumes the role of umpire who passively responds to the inputs of others. Poor and minority communities, almost by definition, lack economic and political power. Ordinarily they cannot afford to hire experts to weigh in with reports and economic analyses to influence agency decisionmaking. Nor can they afford to hire the lawyers and lobbyists necessary to represent their interests when regulatory controls are negotiated.

If regulatory agencies simply respond to the loudest voices, groups that are economically and culturally disadvantaged will suffer corresponding disadvantages in regulatory decisionmaking. Rather than sitting back and letting the interest groups and experts slug it out, the agency must affirmatively empower low-income and minority groups by preferentially making resources available to them.

---

Agency expertise should be recognized, but unrelenting insistence upon scientific proof and a myopic technological focus should be curbed to make way for alternative forms of knowledge which can inform environmental regulation. Agencies should discard the pretense of objectivity in quantifying, comparing, and managing risk and instead consider normative concerns to inform regulation. Self-interested preferences and private economic interests should be considered to a degree, but agencies should recognize that health and healthy ecosystems have an ethical dimension that cannot be addressed adequately within a benefit-cost approach.

Additionally, agencies should view environmental justice advocates not as merely members of another special interest group but as representatives who present a claim that is fundamentally different. A deliberative approach which pursues civic virtue and elevates the public good could be a potent means to addressing environmental justice issues, but agencies should ensure that deliberation is not perverted into pretextual expressions of public good. The belief that the product of the deliberative process is necessarily a transcendental, universal public good should be tempered, but agencies should also recognize that non-economic and ethical values are easily overshadowed by utilitarian interests.

This environmental justice perspective of public participation would involve public participation in private decision-making as well. Site-specific advisory boards and good neighbor agreements with industry transcend the public/private distinction and the traditional sphere of landowner autonomy. It is not only agencies that must change in order to respond to distributional inequities; private entities must abdicate autonomy in favor of other private citizens. In this sense, community oversight and participation arrangements begin to resemble private land use controls, like servitudes or homeowners' associations. Industry consent to these controls could reflect, to a limited degree, an emerging recognition that more than utilitarian preferences are at stake.

In each participation context * * * a better agency response would be to adopt an introspective critical approach and non-neutral intervention as regulatory ideals. * * * A critical approach would require an extension of this trajectory. It would require agency officials to deliberately contemplate the limitations inherent in formal expertise and in the utility-oriented "stakeholder" approaches to participation when addressing environmental justice issues. The realization of the limitations could in turn enable the agency to utilize alternative forms of knowledge. For example, once community residents and activists are perceived to be on par with representatives who have formal expertise, agency officials can become educated by community experience and hopefully will begin to grasp the full implications of what it means to be exposed to multiple contaminants where people live, work and play.

Perspectives rooted in the affected communities also can serve to challenge predominant misperceptions about the poor, racial minorities, and ethnic minorities, such as the perception that these groups are more interested in jobs than in environmental amenities, and at the other end of the spectrum, that these groups tend to overreact to risk. Community perspective can potentially challenge misinformation about a particular proposal, such as an overstatement of project benefits to the community (economic revitalization, tax revenue or increased availability of jobs), or an understatement of risk. Essentially, the regulatory ideal of self-critique is an implicit recognition of the agency's limited position within a larger cultural, social, and economic context.

The agency as decisionmaker is undoubtedly important, but it is not the pinnacle of environmental protection or environmental justice. The engine that drives environmental justice is empowered communities, not enlightened officials. However, by recognizing that the inaccessible discourse of experts and the shortsighted vision of pluralism serve to disempower and exclude, the agency official can help the environmental justice vision by promoting the equal status of community participants.

Similarly, the regulatory ideal of non-neutrality and its implicit corollary, responsibility, is necessary because equitable protection is a collective value that is non-utilitarian and therefore does not fit within traditional benefit-cost calculations. Non-neutrality does not mean that the agency will accept uncritically what it perceives to be the environmental justice perspective on all issues and disputes. Non-neutrality is not bias toward environmental justice advocates. Non-neutrality is a working tool, albeit a crude one, within a larger framework that stubbornly perpetuates environmental injustice.

Recognizing that there are structural impediments to environmental justice goals, but also recognizing the agency of community groups, environmental agencies must first concede their complicity in the status quo and proceed to redefine their responsibilities. Their complicity occurs largely when agency officials uncritically lapse into familiar decision-making approaches during regulatory activities * * * . Redefinition of responsibility could be as straightforward as making sure that environmental justice advocates are included in all major deliberative fora. However, non-neutrality does not end at increasing participation avenues; it requires a commitment to equalize resources by outreach efforts to educate community residents about applicable legal requirements and technical issues, and in the promotion of partnerships between industry and communities.

Non-neutrality and responsibility could take more subtle forms as well, such as rigorous probing of cost-benefit or technical analysis to expose the underlying socio-economic factors and cultural assumptions that perpetuate environmental inequities. Non-neutrality would entail careful consideration of community accounts of environmental problems to attempt to determine how the relevant scientific and technical analysis might have missed important areas of inquiry. Although non-neutrality means sensitivity to distributional and process issues, it means more than that. In essence, non-neutrality means that, at the level of implementation as well as at the policy level, the agency is a promoter of environmental justice. In short, environmental justice would become a higher agency priority than short-term efficiency or the compromised trade-off.

---

Finally, states should not be allowed to engage in a "race-to-the-bottom" as they implement federal programs. This pathology can result as states seek to attract new investment, industry relocations, or campaign contributions for the party in power. [25] Prof. Rena I. Steinzor, in the passage below, notes that states play a major role in implementing federal environmental laws. There are many very good reasons for this arrangement, including the fact that the states are typically closer to the problems and are more sensitive to local political and economic needs. Conceding that it is far too late in the day to federalize all of environmental law, Professor Steinzor nevertheless counsels against greater "devolution" of regulatory responsibility to the states, especially those that have proven they are willing to subordinate national environmental goals to the economic interests of powerful local political constituencies.

Professor Steinzor shows how the push by polluting industries and their allies in Congress toward greater "devolution" of authority to the states has the effect of unevenly distributing environmental protections throughout the country. The negative impact of federalism on the distribution of environmental protections has two aspects. First, it is not clear why the health of citizens in some states is any less important than the health of the citizens in neighboring states. In this regard, health and environmental protections should trump "states rights" in the same sense that civil rights protections do.

Second, some states, in order to attract new industry or to keep existing industries happy, will let it be known that they do not require as much in the way of environmental protection as other states. They are willing to become "pollution havens" at the expense of the health of the some of their citizens to advance the economic interests of other citizens. Proponents of cost-benefit-based decisionmaking argue that this is an altogether efficient outcome. Those states that value economic growth over environmental protection will attract industry, and those that place a higher value on health and the environment will be happy to have less economic growth. Professor Steinzor, however, argues that this allows companies to manipulate states into unhealthy "races-to-the-bottom" at the end of which the citizens of all states are worse off.

A better way to regulate, says Professor Steinzor, is for the federal government to play a strong "differential oversight" role. First, state regulatory programs must develop transparent criteria for determining their effectiveness in attaining stringent federal goals. Those states that adequately meet federal goals should be rewarded with reduced federal oversight. Conversely, when states are not devoting sufficient efforts toward attaining the threshold federal goals, EPA should be aggressive in withdrawing state authority and taking over regulatory responsibility. Differential oversight should reduce state-federal tensions while at the same time ensuring that citizens of some states are not unfairly deprived of minimum federal health and environmental protections.

------

All of the major federal environmental laws divide the authority to implement programs between the federal and state governments. These provisions give the states an opportunity to apply for a federal delegation of authority; EPA administers the program in states that do not volunteer for this responsibility. Delegated states must promise to maintain a program at least as strong as the program defined by EPA, but they retain the authority to adopt more stringent requirements, making federal programs the floor for state efforts to tailor protection of the local environment. * * *

our justifications for centralized regulation are relevant to the overarching mission of protecting public health: (1) mastery of the complex technical and scientific challenges of effective pollution control; (2) mitigation of the damage caused by transboundary pollution; (3) achievement of "distributive justice" [26] in the maintenance of public health among citizens of the United States; and (4) the likelihood that the states will engage in a "race-to-the-bottom" that weakens environmental protection. While it is possible to debate the validity of each of these principles, cumulatively they make a compelling theoretical case against [greater] devolution.

It is difficult to imagine any rational participant in the debate over devolution who would deny that giving the states more authority will result in disparate levels of protection for their citizens. However, people may well disagree on the importance of those differences. Some would argue that so long as the citizens of the fifty states receive a minimal level of protection from the most egregious environmental threats, they should remain free to determine at the state level what degree of public health protection they are willing to support.

While this point may be valid, it is also true that when the states fail to provide a minimal level of protection, their citizens have a legitimate grievance with the national government. As the Federal government has recognized in a variety of other arenas, Americans, as citizens of a unified nation, have rights and expectations that transcend the capacity and limitations of their state and local jurisdictions. Aside from a few extreme examples, it may well prove very difficult to achieve broad agreement on the precise level of protection that defines an essential federal floor. However, * * * there is ample evidence that in many states the level of protection has fallen well below the norm provided in the more competent jurisdictions.

Studies have shown that the states with environmentally progressive reputations also enjoy the strongest economies, suggesting that companies' threats to relocate when a state adopts such policies are rarely carried out. Nevertheless, the states are sufficiently overwrought about their ability to attract employers and create jobs that even idle threats by industry probably have an effect on governors and legislators. Recent empirical research by Professor Kirsten H. Engel supports the speculation that races-to-the-bottom are real phenomena that occur in a significant number of key states. This research is confirmed by the passage of laws in more than half the states ceding the authority to go beyond federal environmental standards. Significantly, close to half the states have enacted laws ceding their authority to go beyond minimum federal requirements, largely in response to the demands of regulated industries. [27]

If states are willing to sacrifice their authority to develop more stringent local laws, they are also more likely to weaken state regulation when federal standards are devolved. Unless the Federal government responds to such backtracking by withdrawing delegated authority, levels of protection could reach a bottom that is unacceptably low. Moreover, as mentioned earlier, EPA has never carried out a threat to withdraw a delegation, undermining its credibility as a referee of such races-to-the-bottom.

Differential oversight serves the equally important roles of offering incentives to capable states and providing a safety net for their less competent colleagues. Basing differential oversight on state environmental conditions rewards states that adequately protect public health and assists those that do not.

* * * The indispensable foundation for a system of differential oversight is the development of transparent, public criteria for gauging state performance, with the recognition that it may take many years for such criteria to evolve into true assessments of environmental conditions and their effect on public health.

The most significant impediments to adoption of a performance-based system are technical and political. Technical issues include the dearth of data on the condition of the environment and the high costs of filling that gap. Political problems include the resistance by overextended state bureaucrats to the imposition of checks that would allow their federal overseers to gauge whether their work is doing any good. Too often, these distinct issues become intertwined, as federal and state negotiators confuse technical and political concerns and ultimately resolve disputes by sacrificing important performance standards.

Admittedly, criteria to evaluate state institutional capacity per se must return initially to the much-denigrated counting of beans, beginning with indicia that describe the strength of a state's programs. What levels of resources, in terms of both money and personnel, are devoted to various aspects of a state's mission? How does the state deploy those resources? How many inspections does it conduct? How many enforcement actions has it brought? How many permits does it write? And, on a more negative note, how many major source permits are expired? How many more abandoned hazardous waste sites remain to be cleaned up?

The next phase of the effort to evaluate state capacity is to place these measures of institutional adequacy in the context of indicia that gauge the environmental challenges the state must face. What is the nature and scope of industrialization in the state? How severe is the existing burden of air, water, and soil pollution? What role do entities outside the regulatory system play in causing such pollution?

To these statistics, some measurement of ideal effort must be added. How many times should state inspectors visit facilities categorized as major holders of permits under the Clean Water Act? What level of enforcement will create the perception that regulated entities causing the worst environmental degradation run a real risk of discovery if their compliance falters? Which categories of permits are subject to new requirements and therefore cannot be allowed to expire for more than short periods?

On the basis of such factors, EPA must adopt some method for categorizing the states' institutional capacity. Such judgments must reflect subjective evaluation of the discrepancy between a state's resource commitment and the challenges it faces, as well as the prospects for improving that ratio in the foreseeable future. Categories must be applied on a program-specific basis; a state may be doing a decent job of implementing one major program but falling far short with respect to others. EPA should collaborate with the states in developing these criteria, but must retain the authority to categorize state capacity on its own.

Finally, it is extremely important that EPA staff reduce their oversight of states that are judged capable of doing as good a job as federal regulators. Only by relinquishing control to capable states will the Agency demonstrate its commitment to sensible devolution and conserve enough resources to improve its own performance.

In the end, EPA must be prepared to exercise the authority to withdraw delegated authority from the weakest states. * * * EPA must stand ready to take over programs that are deemed insufficient, on an interim or permanent basis. To work effectively, incentives must be both positive and negative, with fear of the latter enhancing the value of the former.

_____

## Repay Our Debt to the Future

We did not inherit the earth from our parents; we are borrowing it from our children. We therefore have an obligation to leave the world in a better condition than we found it. Chapter 6 related how cost-benefit analysis ignores this wisdom by discounting future benefits to present value. Instead of discounting the value of current protective actions to future generations, we should be doing what we can to live within the physical limits imposed by "Spaceship Earth." Drawing on the budding discipline of "ecological economics," Prof. Douglas R. Kysar highlights new ways of conceptualizing regulatory costs by acknowledging the "absolute limits" that nature imposes on the capacity of human beings to appropriate and utilize natural resources.

Government action is warranted when present-day activities pose a risk of irreversible harm. [28] Thus, the habitat of endangered species has value beyond its current market appraisal. Similarly, special precautions should be taken before allowing genetically modified organisms to enter environments where they could out-compete natural organisms. Governments should acknowledge that the release of greenhouse gases today will imperil our grandchildren.

In such situations, attempts to value the benefits of protective regulation might be "negatively discounted" to recognize the *enhanced value* of government action to future generations. At the very least, the interests of future generations should be a major consideration in how we consume the earth's limited resources.

Ultimately, we need to cultivate a culture that encourages sensible consumption. We should explore ways for government to educate consumers and encourage them to avoid activities that pose unacceptable risks to themselves, others and future generations. What, for example, can we learn from tobacco-free kids campaigns about the potential for culture-shaping advertising? Professor Kysar believes that the economic approaches to environmental regulation have failed to acknowledge the reality of resource limits, and have therefore begged the larger question of how much is too much. He suggests that a clear acknowledgment of limits should be invigorating, because it invites us to come up with ways to use limited resources more efficiently and to think about how our lives can be enriched other than through consumption. [29]

_____

[T]he failure of existing environmental trading programs to inspire serious democratic deliberation about environmental goals is caused in no small part by a fundamental conceptual flaw in our background assumptions about the natural world and its relation to our economic activity. Specifically, because mainstream economic accounts generally fail to recognize absolute limits imposed by nature on the ability of humans to appropriate and utilize natural resources, they also fail to provide an adequate conceptual basis on which to make the political judgments required by tradable permit schemes. Just as cost-benefit analysis seems incoherent under the moral absolutism of 1970s-era environmental statutes, setting aggregate limits to annual sulfur dioxide emissions appears nonsensical, or at least not urgent, within a theoretical model that recognizes no ultimate constraints to economic growth.

Fortunately, an alternative vision exists: ecological economics. During the shift to efficiency-oriented environmental regulation, legal scholars have paid little attention to this emerging academic field that seeks to bring multidisciplinary rigor to the study of nature's role within human economic production. By fusing insights from ecology, population biology, and physics with the theoretical framework of economics, ecological economists attempt to provide a more nuanced understanding of human-ecosystem interactions than those offered independently by either economists or conservationists. Significantly, ecological economists rely on a preanalytic vision of human activity that is presumed to be bounded by natural constraints. This vision, or worldview, provides a simple yet surprisingly radical departure from mainstream economic thought. It also provides the basis for an alternative conception of the goals of collective governance, one that brings much-needed coherence to environmental decisionmaking within the paradigm of market-based regulation.

In early 2001, Daimler Chrysler A.G. began marketing a four-wheel drive vehicle so massive in dimension and weight that it must comply with federal regulations applicable to eighteen-wheel trucks. The vehicle, called The Unimog by Daimler, is three feet taller than the tallest sport-utility vehicle, nearly two feet wider than a typical car, and one foot longer than the Ford Excursion, the longest sport utility previously available on the consumer market. It weighs 12,500 pounds, a heft equal to "more than two Chevrolet Suburban sport utility vehicles or four Toyota Camry sedans." [30] The Unimog averages only ten miles per gallon of diesel fuel and is restricted from traveling on some roads and bridges because it exceeds local weight and height limits. Nevertheless, Daimler offers the vehicle to affluent suburbanites, whether they are off-road enthusiasts or simply "moms [who] want to take it to the grocery store." [31]

The Unimog provides an apt symbol of the debate between ecological economists and their more conventional counterparts. Most economists today would recognize that the Unimog produces a variety of negative externality problems. Its poor fuel efficiency, to give just one example, highlights the contribution of petroleum-powered vehicles to global climate change through the emission of greenhouse gases. Thus, in order to ensure that the Unimog represents a welfare-enhancing use of society's resources, prevailing economic theory would require that it (and all other vehicles) bear a tax representing the uncounted costs of pollution caused by the vehicle's production and use.

Beyond using Pigouvian taxes to address pollution externalities, however, most conventional economists would not be concerned whether petroleum-based plastics, metals, and other nonrenewable resources required to produce the six-and-a-half ton behemoth should be preserved by society for future applications. Nor would they be particularly concerned that the Unimog's marketing materials reflect a culture of competitive consumption that may waste scarce resources in a sort of S.U.V. "arms race." Such considerations would not figure prominently in the conventional economist's analysis of the Unimog because, so long as the price of the vehicle internalizes tangible external costs, one would have little reason to believe that its natural capital components could be allocated to other, more beneficial uses, either currently or in the future.

Ecological economists, on the other hand, believe that those excluded considerations raise vital issues of intra-and intergenerational resource distribution. A pollution tax on the Unimog would be a good start, according to the ecological economists, but it hardly would answer the more fundamental question of how to ensure that humanity equitably distributes its finite endowment of natural capital within and across generations. Indeed, ecological economists might well view the Unimog as emblematic of a wasteful society that forsakes its obligations to the future in exchange for a present, but ephemeral natural resource binge. Although the makers of the Unimog assure customers that "wanting to conquer the great outdoors is simply not a good reason to give up . . . air conditioning," ecological economists would argue that there are other, more theoretically sound reasons to forego both.

Conventional economists often state that growth of human economic production is not checked by restrictions imposed by nature. In other words, they treat the human economic process as an open system that draws resources and emits wastes through a relatively undefined and unexamined relationship with nature. In contrast, ecological economists view the means of production and nature as components of the same closed system. On this account, the human economic process faces hard constraints imposed by the absolute or temporal scarcity of nonrenewable resources and renewable resources, as well as by the limited capacity of ecological mechanisms to absorb the pollution produced by exploitation of those resources. As a consequence of such constraints, society must remain cognizant of the extent and quality of existing resource stocks, as well as the capacity for natural systems to absorb waste outputs created during the transformation of those stocks into human goods.

In a 1966 article entitled *The Economics of the Coming Spaceship Earth*, [32] economist Kenneth Boulding first identified the competing preanalytic visions that form the heart of the present schism between conventional and ecological economists. In Boulding's view, mainstream economics reflected the notion of the "cowboy economy," [33] in which natural frontiers are seen as limitless, resources inexhaustible, and wastes innocuous. Under such a conception, increases in the sheer volume of economic activity, as measured by gross domestic product

(GDP), would appear to be a logical and defensible goal for society to adopt. In other words, if there are no significant environmental or social repercussions to economic growth, then society should rather uncontroversially pursue growth as a means of increasing the total amount of wealth available for distribution among its members.

Boulding contrasted the cowboy economy with a "spaceman economy," [34] in which the earth is seen as a closed system necessitating careful focus on the consequences of human economic activity. Once humanity nears the maximum sustainable biological limit or carrying capacity of the "Spaceship Earth," it must value resource flows qualitatively, with specific reference to their ability to become enduring, efficient, and useful capital stocks, rather than simply value them quantitatively as an assumed proxy for increasing human welfare. As Boulding put it, "the essential measure of the success of the economy is not production and consumption at all, but the nature, extent, quality, and complexity of the total capital stock, including in this the state of the human bodies and minds included in the system." [35] Focusing on the sheer magnitude of income flows jeopardizes the environment on which humanity ultimately depends and, in any event, provides only an indirect indicator of social welfare by equating material progress with human progress.

Building on these early contributions, economist Herman Daly has devoted his career to providing a more formal theoretical framework for analyzing the intersection of ecological and anthropic spheres. Most fundamentally, he recognized the concept of "scale," which refers roughly to "the physical scale or size of the human presence in the ecosystem, as measured by population times per capita resource use." [36] Theoretically, society may pursue an entire range of scales, including ones so minimalist in their resource use as to inappropriately deprive humans of present utility, and ones so profligate in their consumption as to jeopardize the very future of the species. Daly holds the position that the optimal scale of the human economy is a sustainable one. That is, as a normative matter, governments should regulate the scale of the economy so that it requires no more resources or produces no more wastes than can be regenerated or absorbed, respectively, by the environment. In this manner, governments can provide future generations with an ecological context that, at least theoretically, will continue to support present standards of living.

The distinction between ecological and conventional economics is startlingly simple: ecological economists view the human economy as a subsystem of the environment, while conventional economists view the environment as a subsystem of the economy. The former vision emphasizes natural constraints on the expansion of human production, including both the scarcity of resource inputs to the economic process and the scarcity of pollution sinks to absorb waste outputs of the process. The latter vision admits of no such limits on human economic growth, given that no conceptual superstructure, such as the environment, exists "around" the economy to constrain it. Economic growth is limited only by the availability of human-made capital and labor, not by natural resources.

This elementary shift in preanalytic vision leads to surprisingly dramatic changes in policy recommendations. As leading ecological economist Herman

Daly puts it, "when we draw a containing boundary of the environment around the economy, we move from "empty-world' economics to "full world' economics. Economic logic stays the same, but the perceived pattern of scarcity changes radically and policies must be changed radically." [37] Particularly, the goal of market regulation becomes more complicated than merely seeking to maximize allocative efficiency. In addition to establishing market conditions that allow resources to be devoted to their most valued use, governments also must moderate the absolute scale of the human macroeconomy in light of the carrying capacity of the relevant ecosystem.

Until the nation adopts a language that avoids both the absolute prohibitivism of 1970s-era ethical environmentalism and the absolute permissivism of the most bullish forms of growth economics, it will continue to struggle in its efforts to mount a democratic discussion regarding environmental quality. [E]cological economics provides the necessary language. Just as efficiency has become a meta-principle informing all areas of law and regulation, so too can the ecological economist's conception of scale. Indeed, if the ecological economists are correct in their assessment that scale is a vital, though neglected, concept in economics, then efficiency analysis by itself is nothing more than a one-bladed scissors. An economy that puts an ever-increasing strain on its natural environment may still allocate productive resources efficiently, but in doing so it simply will be making the best of an increasingly desperate situation.

----

## Conclusion

Fortunately, cost-benefit-based decisionmaking is not the only game in town. To the great consternation of business-oriented economists, public health and environmental statutes typically adopt a "precautionary" approach in the face of scientific uncertainty. Economists frequently scoff at the precautionary approach as being unconstrained and incoherent because it does not balance rough estimates of costs against even rougher estimates of benefits.

The analysis presented in Chapter 5 makes it clear, however, that cost-benefit analysis is no paragon of coherence. Rather than gamble on the black art of risk assessment and allow cost considerations to dominate the conversation, the precautionary approach stresses statutory goals, safety and protection. It should not be surprising that the precautionary approach is very attractive to the vast majority of citizens who do not directly profit from risk-producing activities.

We saw in Chapters 3-5 that cost-benefit-based decisionmaking, if done properly, is an exceedingly resource-intensive, time-consuming process that, at the end of the day, does not even yield effective regulatory results. For many environmental problems, a far more attractive alternative is to insist that the sources of the risk-producing activities "do the best they can" to protect others from those risks. Rather than blaming the victim, the technology-based approach to regulation forces the sources to take protective action in a predictable and enforceable way. Because the same performance-oriented requirements apply to all companies, the technology-based approach prevents one company from securing a competitive advantage by externalizing risks onto others.

In many cases, a balancing of many relevant factors will be warranted. It need not, however, be the sort of narrow cost-dominated balancing made by many advocates of quantitative cost-benefit analysis. As we saw in Chapter 3, quantitative cost-benefit analysis belittles or effectively excludes many important factors simply because they are not easily susceptible to quantification. Multiple alternative-multiple attribute analysis offers a more nuanced, qualitative approach. Rather than reducing all of the complexities of health, safety, and environmental regulation to a single matrix of quantified and monetized costs and benefits, a multiple alternative-multiple attribute analysis can provide a clearer picture of the trade offs involved and the alternatives available.

Moreover, by relying on back-end adjustments, an agency can address cost considerations, among other issues, without using a cost-benefit test to determine the extent of regulation. For example, an agency might issue performance-oriented standards based upon the capabilities of a very stringent technology so long as it is prepared to adjust its requirements at the "back-end" of the regulatory process (through variances and other ameliorative techniques) once the "front-end" controls are in place for most of the sources in the category. This approach is pragmatic and flexible enough to incorporate even "radical technology-forcing," in which the regulator phases out a particular risk-producing product or technology based upon a "leap of faith" that better alternatives will be developed by the end of the phaseout period. If subsequent developments prove that the leap of faith was unwarranted, the technology-forcing effort can be adjusted at the back-end.

The application of the pragmatic approach to radical technology-forcing, however, suggests a caveat. The sources of the risk-producing activity must be convinced that unwarranted adjustments will not be made at the back-end. In the hands of an industry-friendly regulator a back-end approach can serve as a charade in which the agency looks very tough at the front end, but, with a wink and a smile, lets sources of risk know that adjustments will be made later on. This attitude can completely undermine radical technology-forcing. If the sources suspect that the phaseout period will be extended indefinitely, they will have little incentive to invest in more protective alternatives or comply with front-end approaches.

One widely accepted risk management principle that does not depend upon quantitative risk assessment and cost-benefit analysis is the "polluter-pays" principle. The simple idea is that the costs of environmental degradation must be borne by those who cause it. Once the prices of goods reflect the actual costs of producing and distributing those goods—including any pollution, companies will strive harder to find alternative techniques and technologies to reduce those costs. Rather than forcing the government to conduct a complicated, finely tuned cost-benefit balancing analysis before it may regulate, the polluter-pays principle places that burden on the companies. The sources of risk-producing activities, after all, are the ones who should properly bear the costs of coming up with cost-effective solutions. Among other things, this alternative enlists market forces to encourage companies to shift their output away from activities resulting in high-risk activities to those with lower risks.

No regulatory approach should be deemed acceptable in a modern society if it unfairly discriminates against minority and economically disadvantaged communities. Most would agree that workers and low-income populations should not serve as guinea pigs for those of us who can afford to live and work in less risky environments. And all but the most committed free-market economists would agree that workers and the poor do not live and work in riskier environments because they choose to do so. If labor and environmental justice considerations are to be given more than passing consideration, Congress and regulators must mandate both procedural and substantive regulatory programs to advance those goals.

Finally, while government can do only so much to change culture, regulatory programs should be designed to discourage overconsumption of our limited natural resources. The newly emerging discipline of "ecological economics" can help regulators take account of finite resources and help protect future generations as well as current populations. A more holistic understanding of "efficiency" would begin to recognize the appropriate scale of human activities. The government in a democracy cannot, and should not, force people to place a higher value on the living conditions of their grandchildren than they place on the excitement of driving an armored military vehicle, but the government need not denigrate the former and subsidize the latter. Government should craft the rules of the game so that those who prefer lavish lifestyles pay the full costs that their extravagance imposes on present and future inhabitants of "Spaceship Earth." Such leadership can even have a multiplier effect, inspiring all of us to follow our natural inclination to be good stewards of our shared environment and to repay our debt to the future.

**Suggestions for Further Reading**

*Safety First*

The primary sourcebook for understanding the precautionary principle is the compilation edited by Carolyn Raffensperger & Joel Tickner, PROTECTING PUBLIC HEALTH AND THE ENVIRONMENT: IMPLEMENTING THE PRECAUTIONARY PRINCIPLE (1999). For a more recent update, focusing especially on the scientists' perspective, see PRECAUTION, ENVIRONMENTAL SCIENCE, AND PREVENTIVE PUBLIC POLICY (Joel Tickner ed., 2003).

Much of the discussion of the precautionary principle may be found in the literature on international law.

Barbara Stark, *Sustainable Development and Postmodern International Law: Greener Globalization?*, 27 WM. & MARY ENVTL. L. & POL'Y REV. 137 (2002).
*Noting that the United States has consistently rejected the precautionary principle in the international context, Prof. Barbara Stark argues that this position "gives important leverage to those who can pay*

*for as many studies as it takes to generate 'uncertainty' regarding claims of serious or irreversible damage. "*

David A. Wirth, *The Rio Declaration on Environment and Development: Two Steps Forward and One Back, or Vice Versa?*, 29 GA. L. REV. 599 (1995).

    *Prof. David Wirth explains the historical origins of the precautionary approach as stated in Principle 15 of the Rio Delcaration.*

However, the approach to regulation that "errs on the side of safety" has been around much longer than the precautionary principle has been in fashion.

John S. Applegate, *The Precautionary Preference: An American Perspective on the Precautionary Principle*, 6 HUM. & ECOLOGICAL RISK ASSESSMENT 413 (2000).

    *Professor Applegate examines the precautionary principle from the U.S. perspective.*

Wendy E. Wagner, *The Precautionary Principle and Chemical Regulation in the United States*, 6 HUM. & ECOLOGICAL RISK ASSESSMENT 459 (2000).

    *Professor Wagner demonstrates how the basic elements of the precautionary principle are present in the statutory approaches to chemical regulation in the United States.*

Thomas O. McGarity, *Politics by Other Means: Law, Science, and Policy in EPA's Implementation of the Food Quality Protection Act*, 53 ADMIN. L. REV. 103 (2001).

    *Professor McGarity explains the precautionary "margin of safety" concept as it applies to the 1996 Food Quality Protection Act.*

*Address the Source, Not the Victim*

Many scholars join Professor Wagner in advocating source-oriented technology-based standards.

David M. Driesen, *Is Emissions Trading an Economic Incentive Program?: Replacing the Command and Control/Economic Incentive Dichotomy*, 55 WASH. & LEE L. REV. 289 (1998).

    *Prof. David Driesen finds technology-based standards generally preferable to market-based programs.*

Howard Latin, *Ideal Versus Real Regulatory Efficiency: Implementation of Uniform Standards and "Fine-Tuning" Regulatory Reforms*, 37 STAN. L. REV. 1267 (1985).

    *Prof. Howard Latin elaborates on the relative ease of administering technology-based standards, and he defends them against the argument that they are economically inefficient.*

Sidney A. Shapiro & Thomas O. McGarity, *Not So Paradoxical: The Rationale for Technology-Based Regulation*, 1991 DUKE L.J. 729.

    *Professors Shapiro and McGarity advocate technology-based standard-setting in the context of workplace safety.*

*Radical Technology-Forcing*

Professor McGarity may be the only observer to reference *Putney Swope* in referring to radical technology-forcing, but others have advanced the idea.

> NICHOLAS A. ASHFORD & CHARLES G. CALDART, TECHNOLOGY, LAW, AND THE WORKING ENVIRONMENT (1996); Nicholas A. Ashford et al., *Using Regulation to Change the Market for Innovation*, 9 HARV. ENVTL. L. REV. 419 (1985).
>
> *Prof. Nicholas Ashford advocates radical technology-forcing in the context of regulating workplace risks.*

> ROBERT GOTTLIEB, ENVIRONMENTALISM UNBOUND: EXPLORING NEW PATHWAYS FOR CHANGE 56-57 (2001).
>
> *Professor Gottlieb explores the potential for local community groups to achieve a degree of radical technology-forcing by "plugging the outfalls" that pollute local environments, thereby forcing upstream changes in the manufacturing process.*

One of the more successful international efforts to address global environmental problems is the Vienna Convention for the Protection of the Ozone Layer, which was ratified by the U.S. Senate in 1986, and the associated Montreal Protocol on Substances That Deplete the Ozone Layer, which was ratified by the Senate in 1988. Senate Treaty Doc. 100-10, *reprinted at* 26 I.L.M. 1541 (1987). Although the hole in the ozone layer appeared to be shrinking for a time, the treaty has not been a complete success, and it is likely that some countries are cheating. Among the many articles on the Montreal Protocol are the following:

> Laura Thomas, *A Comparative Analysis of International Regimes on Ozone and Climate Change With Implications for Regime Design*, 41 COLUM. J. TRANSNAT'L L. 795, 796 (2003).
>
> *Laura Thomas reports that the Montreal Protocol is "now recognized as a landmark accord in the most effective international environmental regime to date."*

> Joel A. Mintz, *Keeping Pandora's Box Shut: A Critical Assessment of the Montreal Protocol on Substances That Deplete the Ozone Layer*, 20 U. MIAMI INTER-AMERICAN L. REV. 565 (1989).
>
> *Prof. Joel Mintz praises the sentiment underlying the Montreal Protocol, but criticizes its weak enforcement provisions.*

More recently, the Stockholm Convention on Persistent Organic Pollutants (POPs Convention) was made available for signing in May, 2001. Stockholm Convention on Persistent Organic Pollutants, pmbl., May 22, 2001, app.II, 40 I.L.M. 532. This international convention, which the United States has signed, is to some extent built upon the proposition that the best way to address the health and environmental risks posed by chemicals that are toxic, persistent and mobile is to phase them out and rely upon the ingenuity of industry to come up with appropriate substitutes. Some recent articles on the POPs Convention include the following:

Joel A. Mintz, *Two Cheers for Global Pops: A Summary and Assessment of the Stockholm Convention on Persistent Organic Pollutants*, 14 GEO. INT'L ENVTL. L. REV. 319 (2001).
*Recognizing that the Stockholm Convention represents "a major step forward in the world community's collective efforts to combat pollution, Professor Mintz concludes that "the inclusion of an express reference to costs . . . creates a troubling possibility that environmentally needed approaches to reducing the release of listed POPs will be set aside and that less costly and less effective technical solutions may be employed instead."*

Pep Fuller & Thomas O. McGarity, *Beyond the Dirty Dozen: The Bush Administration's Cautious Approach to Listing New Persistent Organic Pollutants and the Future of the POPs Convention*, 28 WM. & MARY J. ENVTL. L. & POL'Y 1 (2004).
*Pep Fuller and McGarity applaud the Bush Administration for seeking Senate ratification of the POPs convention, but criticize the Bush Administration's OMB for insisting that the United States undertake a separate evaluation of the costs and benefits of a chemical before acquiescing in the decisions of the international body empowered by the convention to make additions to the POPs list.*

*The Pragmatic Perspective*

Other advocates of pragmatic approaches to regulation include the following:

DANIEL A. FARBER, ECO-PRAGMATISM (1999).
*Prof. Daniel Farber suggests a rule of thumb for risk regulation: "When a reasonably ascertainable risk reaches a significant level, take all feasible steps to abate it except when costs would clearly overwhelm any potential benefits. Meanwhile, take prudent precautions against uncharted, but potentially serious, risks."*

Bradley C. Karkkainen, *Adaptive Ecosystem Management and Regulatory Penalty Defaults: Toward a Bounded Pragmatism*, in THE JURISDYNAMICS OF ENVIRONMENTAL PROTECTION: CHANGE AND THE PRAGMATIC VOICE IN ENVIRONMENTAL LAW (Jim Chen ed., Envtl. L. Inst. 2003).
*Prof. Bradley Karkkainen argues that a "regulatory penalty default" can help meet the concern of environmentalists that the adaptive management at the center of environmental pragmatism stands in tension with the fundamental rule of law precepts. A "regulatory penalty default" is "a harsh or quasi-punitive regulatory requirement that applies as the default rule if parties fail to reach a satisfactory alternative arrangement."*

*Costs Should Be a Consideration, Not an Obsession*

Multiple alternative-multiple attribute analysis has not been the subject of much commentary in the legal literature. The following article is one of the few.

Jamie A. Grodsky, *Certified Green: The Law and Future of Environmental Labeling*, 10 YALE J. ON REG. 147, 224-26 (1993).
*Jamie Grodsky suggests multiple attribute analysis for determining which products warrant "green" labels.*

Multi-attribute analysis has a stronger pedigree in the decision sciences literature. The following are good examples.

RALPH L. KEENEY & HOWARD RAIFFA, DECISIONS WITH MULTIPLE OBJECTIVES: PREFERENCES AND VALUE TRADEOFFS 282-353 (1976).
*Profs. Ralph Keeney and Howard Raiffa explain, among many other things, the essential elements of "multi-attribute utility analysis."*

DIANA B. PETITTI, META-ANALYSIS, DECISION ANALYSIS, AND COST-EFFECTIVENESS ANALYSIS: METHODS FOR QUANTITATIVE SYNTHESIS IN MEDICINE (1994).
*Prof. Diana Petitti provides a comprehensive and complex treatise on various methods of decision analysis.*

Less structured "alternatives assessment" approaches are also available. Indeed, alternatives assessment, accompanied by a general, non-quantitative consideration of the costs and benefits of proposed major federal actions is the hallmark of the analysis required in an environmental impact statement prepared pursuant to the National Environmental Policy Act.

MARY O'BRIEN, MAKING BETTER ENVIRONMENTAL DECISIONS: AN ALTERNATIVE TO RISK ASSESSMENT (2000).
*Mary O'Brien critiques quantitative risk assessment and suggests forms of qualitative decisionmaking that are, in her view, much more legitimate.*

*Make the Polluter Pay*

The "polluter-pays" principle, in one form or another, has many academic advocates both in international and domestic law. The following are representative:

Sanford E. Gaines, *The Polluter-Pays Principle: From Economic Equity to Environmental Ethos*, 26 TEX. INT'L L.J. 463 (1991).
*Prof. Sanford Gaines argues that the polluter-pays principle "expresses a fundamental moral judgment about the allocation of responsibility for environmental protection in complex societies."*

Jonathan Remy Nash, *Too Much Market? Conflict Between Tradable Pollution Allowances and the "Polluter-Pays" Principle*, 24 HARV. ENVTL. L. REV. 465 (2000).
*Observing that the core of the polluter-pays principle "stems from the fundamental, logical, and fair proposition that those who generate pollution, not the government, should bear pollution costs," Jonathan Nash explains how cap-and-trade marketable permit regimes are inconsistent with that principle.*

*Distribute Health, Safety, and Environmental Risks and Benefits Fairly*

Workplace Safety and Health

There is not a vast literature on the statutes protecting occupational safety and health, and much of the existing literature consists of theoretical analyses of whether government should intervene to protect workplace safety. There are, however, a few books and articles on worker safety and health regulation after the enactment of the OSH Act. The classic treatments are NICHOLAS ASHFORD, CRISIS IN THE WORKPLACE (1976) and BENJAMIN W. MINTZ, OSHA: HISTORY, LAW, AND POLICY (1984). More recent publications include:

THOMAS O. MCGARITY & SIDNEY A. SHAPIRO, WORKERS AT RISK: THE FAILED PROMISE OF THE OCCUPATIONAL SAFETY AND REVIEW ADMINISTRATION (1992).
    *Profs. McGarity and Shapiro provide a comprehensive description of the history of OSHA and set out numerous suggestions for reform.*

Marc Linder, *Fatal Subtraction: Statistical MIAs on the Industrial Battlefield*, 20 J. LEGIS. 99 (1994).
    *Prof. Marc Linder describes "profit-maximizing and injury-inducing entrepreneurial strategies" that result in workplace fatalities, and he observes that the enactment of the OSH Act "failed to dissolve employers' resistance to systemic change."*

Environmental Justice

The literature on environmental justice is extensive and growing. For a good sampling of the literature, see ENVIRONMENTAL JUSTICE: LAW, POLICY, AND REGULATION (Clifford Rechtschaffen & Eileen Gauna eds., 2002). Excellent treatments of the subject can be found in the following articles:

Robert R. Kuehn, *A Taxonomy of Environmental Justice*, 30 ELR 10681 (Sept. 2000).
    *Noting that "environmental justice" has been broadly defined in many different contexts, Prof. Robert Kuehn suggests a nuanced approach to understanding environmental justice that views environmental justice as distributive justice, procedural justice, corrective justice, and social justice.*

Catherine O'Neill, *Variable Justice: Environmental Standards, Contaminated Fish, and "Acceptable" Risk to Native Peoples*, 19 STAN. ENVTL. L.J. 3 (2000).
    *Prof. Catherine O'Neill critiques EPA's use of risk assessment techniques in establishing water quality standards for toxics, like dioxin, that can cause disproportionate harm to Native American populations because of their patterns of high consumption of fish.*

CHAPTER 8: BETTER WAYS TO REGULATE

Devolution

The legal literature is filled with arguments for and against devolving authority to administer health, safety, and environmental regulatory programs from the federal government to the states. The most prominent proponent of greater devolution is Dean Richard L. Revesz:

> Richard L. Revesz, *Rehabilitating Interstate Competition: Rethinking the "Race-to-the-Bottom" Rationale for Federal Environmental Regulation*, 67 N.Y.U. L. REV. 1210 (1992); Richard L. Revesz, *The Race-to-the-Bottom and Federal Environmental Regulation: A Response to Critics*, 82 MINN. L. REV. 535 (1997).
> *Dean Revesz argues forcefully that competition for industry among the states produces more economically efficient and democratic health, safety, and environmental decisionmaking.*

Many other authors join Professor Steinzor in their skepticism of this view.

> Kirsten H. Engel, *State Environmental Standard-Setting: Is There a "Race" and Is It "to the Bottom"?*, 48 HASTINGS L.J. 271 (1997).
> *Prof. Kirsten Engel assembles an impressive array of empirical evidence to demonstrate that competitive races between states for industry results in lax environmental regulation.*

> Daniel C. Esty, *Revitalizing Environmental Federalism*, 95 MICH. L. REV. 570 (1996).
> *Prof. Daniel Esty takes issue with those who argue that devolving greater authority over health, safety, and environmental regulation will produce more economically efficient regulation.*

> Arnold W. Reitze Jr., *Federalism and the Inspection and Maintenance Program Under the Clean Air Act*, 27 PAC. L.J. 1461 (1996).
> *Prof. Arnold Reitze examines the failure of the Clean Air Act's automobile inspection and maintenance program in the mid-1990s once other states realized that the federal EPA was not going to impose sanctions on California for failure to implement the unpopular program.*

> Lori M. Wallach, *Accountable Governance in the Era of Globalization: The WTO, NAFTA, and International Harmonization of Standards*, 50 KAN. L. REV. 823 (2002).
> *Wallach explores the race-to-the-bottom theme in the international context.*

*Repay Our Debt to the Future*

The science of ecological economics was first fully developed by Prof. Herman E. Daly. *See* HERMAN E. DALY, ECOLOGICAL ECONOMICS AND THE ECOLOGY OF ECONOMICS 50 (1999). Ecological economics is having an increasingly influential impact on legal thinkers and policy analysts. Recent attempts to employ ecological economics concepts to environmental law include the following:

David W. Case, *The EPA's Environmental Stewardship Initiative: Attempting to Revitalize a Floundering Regulatory Reform Agenda*, 50 EMORY L.J. 1 (2001).

*Prof. David Case explores how product stewardship programs, already in place in Europe, make manufacturers responsible for the costs of their products from the time of creation until their ultimate disposal and thereby encourage recycling and reuse.*

Barton H. Thompson Jr., *Markets for Nature*, 25 WM. & MARY ENVTL. L. & POL'Y REV. 261 (2000).

*Prof. Barton Thompson explores the possibility of establishing "ecosystem service markets" as an adjunct to traditional regulation to achieve environmental goals.*

## Chapter 8 Endnotes

1. The New Progressive Agenda Project of the Center for Progressive Regulation (CPR) is an effort by CPR scholars to present just a framework for a new regulatory regime for health, safety, and the environment. This chapter draws on the already published work of several of the scholars who are currently engaged in that project, the results of which will be published in late 2004. More information on CPR and the New Progressive Agenda Project is available at http//www.progressiveregulation.org.

2. Professor Applegate is the Walter W. Foskett Professor of Law and Associate Dean of the Indiana University School of Law–Bloomington. The excerpt is taken from John S. Applegate, *The Prometheus Principle: Using the Precautionary Principle to Harmonize the Regulation of Genetically Modified Organisms*, 9 IND. J. GLOBAL LEG. STUD. 207, 246-55 (2001).

3. Carolyn Raffensperger & Joel Tickner, *Introduction: To Foresee and to Forestall, in* PROTECTING PUBLIC HEALTH AND THE ENVIRONMENT: IMPLEMENTING THE PRECAUTIONARY PRINCIPLE 1, 4 (1999).

4. Les Levidow et al., *Genetically Modified Crops in the European Union: Regulatory Conflicts as Precautionary Opportunities*, 3 J. RISK RES. 189, 191 (2000).

5. *See also* Wendy E. Wagner, *Choosing Ignorance in the Manufacture of Toxic Products*, 82 CORNELL L. REV. 773 (1997).

6. Professor Geistfeld is a Professor of Law at the New York University School of Law. This excerpt is taken from Mark Geistfeld, *Reconciling Cost-Benefit Analysis With the Principle That Safety Matters More Than Money*, 76 N.Y.U. L. REV. 114, 116-19, 173-76, 181-83 (2001). Professor Geistfeld's analysis turns on his conclusion that in the context of risks that actors involuntarily impose upon others, the appropriate valuation measure is "willingness-to-accept" risk, rather than "willingness-to-pay" to avoid risk. *See also* the analysis of the distinction between willingness-to-pay and willingness-to-accept in Chapter 6, *supra*.

7. *See* ROBERT GOTTLIEB, ENVIRONMENTALISM UNBOUND: EXPLORING NEW PATHWAYS FOR CHANGE viii (2001) (advocating "linking environmental justice and pollution prevention through a more radical, community- and workplace-centered, or production-focused and place-based approach).

8. The excerpt is taken from Frank Ackerman & Lisa Heinzerling, *Pricing the Priceless: Cost-Benefit Analysis of Environmental Protection*, 150 U. PA. L. REV. 1553, 1581-82 (2002).

9. Professor Wagner is the Joe A. Worsham Professor of Law at the University of Texas School of Law. The excerpt is taken from Wendy E. Wagner, *Innovations in Environmental Policy: The Triumph of Technology-Based Standards*, 2000 U. ILL. L. REV. 83, 84, 88-89, 112-13.

10. *See* BRUCE A. ACKERMAN ET AL., THE UNCERTAIN SEARCH FOR ENVIRONMENTAL QUALITY 328-30 (1974) [hereinafter THE UNCERTAIN SEARCH]; ALLEN V. KNEESE & CHARLES L. SHULTZE, POLLUTION, PRICES, AND PUBLIC POLICY 58-63, 72-73, 82-83 (1975); Bruce A. Ackerman & Richard B. Stewart, *Reforming Environmental Law*, 37 STAN. L. REV. 1333, 1335-40 (1985); A. Myrick Freeman III, *Air and Water Pollution Policy, in* CURRENT ISSUES IN U.S. ENVIRONMENTAL POLICY 49-58 (Paul R. Portney ed., 1978); Cass Sunstein, *Administrative Substance*, 1991 DUKE L.J. 607, 627-42; *Technology-Based Emission and Effluent Standards and the Achievement of Ambient Environmental Objectives*, 91 YALE L.J. 792, 795-800 (1982).

11. Law scholars who have publicly applauded the use of technology-based standards can be counted on one hand. *See generally* David M. Driesen, *Is Emissions Trading an Economic Incentive Program?: Replacing the Command-and-Control/Economic Incentive Dichotomy*, 55 Wash. & Lee L. Rev. 289 (1998); Howard Latin, *Ideal Versus Real Regulatory Efficiency: Implementation of Uniform Standards and "Fine-Tuning" Regulatory Reforms*, 37 Stan. L. Rev. 1267 (1985); Sidney A. Shapiro & Thomas O. McGarity, *Not So Paradoxical: The Rationale for Technology-Based Regulation*, 1991 Duke L.J. 729.

12. *See* Clifford Rechtschaffen, *How to Reduce Lead Exposures With One Simple Statute: The Experience of Proposition 65*, 29 ELR 10581 (Dec. 1999); Thomas O. McGarity, *Radical Technology-Forcing in Environmental Regulation*, 27 Loy. L.A. L. Rev. 943 (1994).

13. George M. Gray et al., *The Demise of Lead in Gasoline, in* The Greening of Industry: A Risk Management Approach (J.D. Graham & J.K. Hartwell eds., 1997).

14. Professor McGarity holds the W. James Kronzer Chair at the University of Texas School of Law. The excerpt is taken from Thomas O. McGarity, *Radical Technology-Forcing in Environmental Regulation*, 27 Loy. L.A. L. Rev. 943, 943-44, 945-47, 955-58 (1994).

15. Putney Swope (RCA/Columbia 1969).

16. Prof. Alyson Flournoy teaches environmental law at the University of Florida School of Law. The reading comes from Alyson C. Flournoy, *Coping With Complexity*, 27 Loy. L.A. L. Rev. 809 (1994).

17. Professor Shapiro is the John M. Rounds Professor of Law at the University of Kansas School of Law. Prof. Robert L. Glicksman is Professor of Law at the University of Kansas. The excerpt is taken from Sidney A. Shapiro & Robert L. Glicksman, *The Missing Perspective*, Envtl. F., Mar./Apr. 2003, at 41.

18. Professor Driesen teaches environmental and constitutional law at Syracuse University School of Law. The article excerpted here is published at David M. Driesen, *The Societal Cost of Environmental Regulation: Beyond Administrative Cost-Benefit Analysis*, 24 Ecology L. Rev. 545, 560-63 (1997).

19. E.B. Goodstein, Jobs and The Environment: The Myth of a National Trade-off 41 (1994).

20. *See* Thomas O. McGarity & Sidney A. Shapiro, Workers at Risk: The Failed Promise of the Occupational Safety and Health Administration (1992).

21. Industrial Union Dep't, AFL-CIO v. American Petroleum Inst., 448 U.S. 607, 10 ELR 20489 (1980).

22. American Textile Mfrs. Inst. v. Donovan, 452 U.S. 490 (1981).

23. Professor Shapiro is the John M. Rounds Professor of Law at the University of Kansas School of Law. Professor McGarity holds the W. James Kronzer Chair at the University of Texas School of Law. The excerpt is taken from Sidney A. Shapiro & Thomas O. McGarity, *Reorienting OSHA: Regulatory Alternatives and Legislative Reform*, 6 Yale J. on Reg. 1, 45-50, (1989).

24. Professor Gauna is a Professor at Southwestern University School of Law. The excerpt is taken from Eileen Gauna, *The Environmental Justice Misfit: Public Participation and the Paradigm Paradox*, 17 Stan. Envtl. L.J. 3, 52-57, 69-71 (1998).

25. Professor Steinzor is a Professor of Law and Director of the Environmental Law Clinic at the University of Maryland School of Law. The excerpt comes from Rena I. Steinzor,

*Devolution and the Public Health*, 24 HARV. ENVTL. L. REV. 351, 357-59, 366-420, 448-63 (2000).

26. This term is borrowed from John Rawls, and is intended to signify the principle that "each person is to have an equal right to the most extensive basic liberty compatible with a similar liberty for others . . . ." JOHN RAWLS, A THEORY OF JUSTICE 60 (1971). In other words, everyone in America should be afforded a level of environmental protection necessary to prevent the damage pollution causes to their health.

27. Jerome M. Organ, *Limitations on State Agency Authority to Adopt Environmental Standards More Stringent Than Federal Standards: Policy Considerations and Interpretive Problems*, 54 MD. L. REV. 1373, 1432-34 (1995).

28. *See* Frank Ackerman & Lisa Heinzerling, *Pricing the Priceless: Cost-Benefit Analysis of Environmental Protection*, 150 U. PA. L. REV. 1553 (2002).

29. Professor Kysar is an Assistant Professor of Law at Cornell Law School. The excerpt is taken from Douglas A. Kysar, *Law, Environment, and Vision*, 97 Nw. U. L. REV. 675, 676-83, 728-29 (2003).

30. Keith Bradsher, *Daimler to Offer a Monster SUV*, N.Y. TIMES, Feb. 21, 2001, at C1.

31. *Id.* at C4.

32. Kenneth E. Boulding, *The Economics of the Coming Spaceship Earth, reprinted in* VALUING THE EARTH: ECONOMICS, ECOLOGY, ETHICS 297 (Herman E. Daly & Kenneth N. Townsend eds., 1993).

33. *Id.* at 303.

34. *Id.*

35. *Id.* at 304.

36. HERMAN E. DALY, BEYOND GROWTH 50 (1996).

37. *Id.* at 50.

# Index

263